JAPANESE LA

D0562493

Contract Clauses

1) merger/intergration clause
   - this is the agreement, no oral agreements

2) Choice of Law

3) choice of forum

4) arbitration/mediation

5) execution by counterparts
   ↳ need to have the same document signed
      this allows different agreements to be signed

6) Acts of God what happens?

7) Definition Section
   How to amend
   who are the parties
   timeframe

What is the problem addressed
by the law.

Studies in Law and Economics
A series edited by William M. Landes and J. Mark Ramseyer

JAPANESE LAW

AN ECONOMIC APPROACH

J. Mark Ramseyer

Minoru Nakazato

THE UNIVERSITY OF
CHICAGO PRESS
Chicago and London

THE UNIVERSITY OF CHICAGO PRESS, CHICAGO 60637
THE UNIVERSITY OF CHICAGO PRESS, LTD., LONDON

© 1999 by The University of Chicago
All rights reserved. Published 1998
Paperback edition 2000

07 06 05 04 03 02 01 00   2 3 4 5

ISBN: 0-226-70384-3 (cloth)
ISBN: 0-226-70385-1 (paperback)

Library of Congress Cataloging-in-Publication Data

Ramseyer, J. Mark, 1954–
    Japanese law : an economic approach / J. Mark Ramseyer,
Minoru Nakazato.
      p. cm.—(Studies in law and economics)
    Includes bibliographical references and index.
    ISBN 0-226-70384-3 (alk. paper)
    1. Law—Japan. 2. Law and economics. I. Nakazato, Minoru.
II. Title. III. Series: Studies in law and economics (Chicago, Ill.)
KNX68.R36   1999
349.52—dc21   98-23875
                                     CIP

For Norma Wyse and Emi Nakazato
For Jennifer and Geoffrey Ramseyer, Mari and Mao Nakazato

CONTENTS

CONTENTS

TABLES AND FIGURES

Tables

Figures

PREFACE

If you can't annoy somebody, Kingsley Amis once said, there's not much point in writing. In this book, we explain the basics of Japanese law in a way that we hope you—whether lawyer, law student, or legal scholar—will find clear, amusing, and maybe even annoying. If you read it through, we shall consider it a success. If you turn to the index to solve the legal problem you face, we shall think it a failure.

Make no mistake. If you want to use the index in this book to find the answer to your problem, do not bother. You will not find it. If you insist on trying, you commit malpractice. Inside every fat book is a thin book struggling to get out, and here it has gotten out. This is an anorexic book despite its three hundred pages, and as befits an anorexic essay, we have slashed all the detail. In fact, we have slashed whole areas of important law, whether antitrust, intellectual property, securities regulation, or any one of a dozen other fields. Instead, we have covered only the basic subjects that most U.S. lawyers and law students will have studied.

One cannot understand the details without the larger picture, and in this book, we offer that overview. This is not a book to read through the index. It is a book to read from front to back. Find a comfortable chair. Put on a CD. Get something to drink. And read. Worry about your legal problem later.

We offer no "essence" of Japanese law in this book. We capture no "core" of the Japanese legal system. We propose no generalization about the gist of Japanese law that distinguishes it from other advanced capitalist legal systems. We offer no essence, no core, no gist—because there is none. Law is not a coherent system that follows central organizing principles—not here, not in Japan, not even in those classic code countries like Germany and France. Anyone who claims otherwise is either wrong or lying. Law is an unruly, disjointed corpus. It reflects nothing more than the accumulated exigencies of lawmaking by legislatures, courts, and administrative agencies over time.

In Japan, the extant legal system reflects more than a century of lawmaking. During the earliest decades, Japan was an oligarchy. During the latest decades, it has been a fully functioning democracy. During the decades between, it was sometimes a democracy, sometimes a police state, and sometimes an occupied colony. The law in place today reflects law-making during that entire period.[1]

Hypothetically political change could let a government start the law over. Hypothetically it could—but governments rarely do. For reasons explained at length in the new "positive political economy" literature, legal change in functioning democracies is seldom cheap to reverse.[2] As a result, legislators will seldom devote many resources to wiping the legal slate clean. Instead, the legal system will reflect the long-term accumulated detritus of political promises made and broken by shifting and reshifting coalitions over time. Although this process of lawmaking will follow coherent social scientific principles, the resulting body of law will be anything but coherent. Lawmaking depends on democratic politics, democratic politics reflects what voters want and interest groups will buy—and few voters or interest groups will care much about coherence. The resulting body of law—whether statutory or common law—will be internally chaotic. And that chaos is what this book is all about.

Mind you, legal chaos need not generate analytical incoherence. That the law lacks an internal logic does not mean our analysis need lack it, too. Instead, social scientific logic takes us a long way toward predicting both the effect that the law will have on what people do and the way that people will try to manipulate and use the law.

In discussing that interplay between law and human behavior, we take an economic approach. Some conclusions the economic model generates straightforwardly. One of the more basic involves the impact that a legal system can have on economic development, a theme we follow throughout the book. But the economic model also leads to a series of more detailed and perhaps counterintuitive observations that we scatter throughout the book.

Although we begin each chapter with a summary of the law, we follow each with a—very distinct—series of applications. There we use an economic intuition to explore some of these (often empirical) ramifications of the law in more detail. When we use that intuition, rest assured we keep it simple. We realize the world is composed of three types of people—those who can count and those who can't—and have written this book with the last group in mind.

We do not use economics because we think everyone (or anyone) always rationally maximizes. We all know no one does. We use economics because we think classic Chicago-school economic intuition (taken alone and simply, without much elaboration) goes far toward explaining much (not all) law-related behavior in Japan. Surely, many readers will protest, Japan is a complex place, a multifaceted universe where every phenomenon results from the subtle interplay of myriad disparate and interconnected causes. Surely, they will claim, describing Japan as a world of rational maximizers is about as helpful as soprano Jane Eaglen's description of Norma as an opera where the druid princess is "pissed off with her husband because he's having it off with one of her virgins." We agree (how could we not?). But unless our critics tell us which of the myriad causes has what relative impact (they rarely do), the complexity is not much of an improvement.

The same readers will probably insist that we could explain more if we added culture to our spare model. What we would gain in explanatory breadth, however, we believe we would lose in theoretical parsimony. Consider this book an exercise in parsimony in comparative law. Consider it, in other words, an attempt to show just how far extremely spare economic models go toward explaining the world of law-related behavior.

'Nough said. The test of theory is in the application. White cat, black cat, who cares so long as it catches mice, Deng Xiaoping once remarked. Consider this an attempt to show how well the economic cat catches legal mice. We do not think the model explains all of Japanese law-related behavior. We do not think it is the only way to explain that behavior. We do think it explains many of the more basic contours of that behavior—and leave it to you the reader to judge.

Readers who know Japanese law already will recognize that we ditch much of the intellectual baggage Japanese legal scholars use to explain their law to each other. In explaining the law, we do not explain it as Japanese law professors explain it. Rather, we use the categories, terms, and concepts that American professors use to explain U.S. law. Each chapter we self-consciously and straightforwardly organize according to the questions that U.S. scholars and lawyers ask of their own law.

We do this deliberately—but not out of any lack of respect for our Japanese colleagues. We do it for pedagogy—to enable readers readily to compare how U.S. and Japanese courts solve common problems. Most of the apparent differences between U.S. and Japanese law, we believe, are not differences in the ways courts decide cases. Instead, they capture differences in the ways academics explain the law to their audience. On most of the issues that matter, in most of the ways the law "hits the road," U.S. law and Japanese law give very similar results. To make that point, we use our self-consciously parochial approach.

Maybe an analogy would help. On the one hand, if one asked a software engineer to contrast Macintosh OS with the latest Windows release, he would describe two radically different programs. After all, the two operating systems (at least so we are told) have radically different internal configurations. On the other hand, if one asked your average lawyer to contrast the two systems, he would describe two very similar programs. After all, the two systems (and this we know from experience) produce quite similar results. At least as the operating systems "hit the screen," they are for most purposes nearly identical.

Neither way of comparing the two systems is better than the other. It all depends on what one wants to do. One way contrasts the internal logic, and one contrasts the end result. For most lawyers, it is the end result that counts. For that simple reason, in this book we opt for the latter approach and give you the end result.[3]

ACKNOWLEDGMENTS

Many people tirelessly read parts or all of this manuscript: Albert Alschuler, Frank Bennett, Stephen Choi, Richard Craswell, Kenneth Dam, John Donohue, Richard Epstein, Eric Feldman, Harry First, Daniel Fischel, Keigo Fuchi, Elizabeth Garrett, Tom Ginsburg, Andrew Gordon, John Haley, Christopher Hanna, Yoshiko Hiwano, Norichika Ikeda, Temple Jorden, Dennis Karjala, William Klein, Dan Klerman, Robert Leflar, John Lott, Jonathan Macey, Toshiki Magome, Yuri Matsubara, Curtis Milhaupt, Geoffrey Miller, Hisayuki Ohyanagi, Kenneth Porte, Richard Posner, Dan Rosen, Arthur Rosett, Richard Samuels, Tomoko Sasho, Stephen Schulhofer, Gary Schwartz, Zen'ichi Shishido, Joe Sommer, Hiroshi Uchima, Frank Upham, David Weinstein, Mark West, Stephen Yeazell, Eric Zolt, several anonymous referees, and students in seminars at the University of Tokyo. For their wonderfully thoughtful help, we gladly thank them.

To produce this book, Ramseyer received generous financial assistance from the Sarah Scaife Foundation, the Lynde and Harry Bradley Foundation, The University of Chicago Law School, and The University of Chicago Committee on Japanese Studies. To produce parts of chapters 2, 6, and 9, Ramseyer and Nakazato enjoyed the hospitality of the Second Section of the Institute for Monetary and Economic Studies of the Bank of Japan. For this generous assistance, we are extremely grateful.

Throughout this project, we were fortunate to receive the always stimulating, helpful, and kind encouragement of Professor Hiroshi Kaneko, emeritus professor of the University of Tokyo and professor of law at Gakushüin University.

Several portions of this book have appeared as separate essays. We include them here in modified form with the permission of the publishers. Portions of chapter 4 originally appeared in J. Mark Ramseyer and Minoru Nakazato, "The Rational Litigant: Settlement Amounts and Verdict Rates in Japan," 18 *Journal of Legal Studies* 263 (1989), reprinted by permission of the Journal of Legal Studies; and in J. Mark Ramseyer, "Products Liability through Private Ordering: Notes on a Japanese Experiment," 144 *University of Pennsylvania Law Review* 1823 (1996), reprinted by permission of the University of Pennsylvania Law Review. Part of chapter 5 originally appeared in Steven N. Kaplan and J. Mark Ramseyer, "Those Japanese Firms with their Disdain for Shareholders: Another Fable for the

Academy," 74 *Washington University Law Quarterly* (1996), reprinted by permission of the Washington University Law Quarterly and Steven Kaplan.

Scholarship is important and fun, but we dedicate this book to the people who remind us every day what really matters—to Norma Wyse and Emi Nakazato—and what real fun is—to Jennifer and Geoffrey Ramseyer and to Mari and Mao Nakazato.

CAVEATS

Cases

Why so many cases, you may ask, for we do rely heavily on court opinions in this book. Partly we do this to help readers understand the scope of the statutes. Partly we do this to help readers compare Japanese law with U.S. law, which is always presented through cases. And partly we do this simply because the rules the courts enforce *are* the law, and those court-enforced rules structure the contours of the bargains people reach in Japan. For reasons we explain throughout this book, the popular notion that Japanese behave in ways uncorrelated to judicial outcomes is flatly false.

Some readers of earlier drafts asked why we sometimes used lower court opinions when there were Supreme Court opinions on point. Others asked why we used old opinions when there were more recent ones available. And the most candid asked why we persistently chose cases involving love affairs, movie directors, prostitutes, mobsters, tax cheats, crooked politicians, and pyramid schemes when surely (they argued) we could have found cases more central to Japanese society.

We shall be candid in reply. We used the cases we did because we wanted a book that you would read. We could easily have used only the most recent cases, the cases from the highest courts, or the cases involving disputes central to the business community. We could easily have written a book with high court cases over soybean futures, over magnesium ore F.O.B. contracts, over standby letters of credit, over automobile accidents. But you would not have read it.

Perhaps you do *buy* books that deal with soybean futures, magnesium ore F.O.B. contracts, and standby letters of credit. Perhaps you even promise yourself you will read them. Somehow, though, we suspect you always find other more pressing, more urgent, or simply more intriguing things you need to do. You may eventually consult the book. But read it, never. Or aren't you, as Richard Blaine famously asked, the kind that tells?

Rest assured, except where otherwise noted, we use cases that are good law. Given a choice between a Supreme Court case involving breach of contract for the delivery of steel ingots and a lower court opinion on breach of contract to hush up a passionate affair, however, we have consistently chosen the affair. Call it unprincipled, call it pandering—we are not proud. Most ordinary mortals we know enjoy reading about the foibles and weaknesses that plague other ordinary mortals. In this book, we pander to those ordinary readers.

Other Countries

We skip the European and South American parallels. Several readers urged us to make those comparisons. Given the French and German antecedents to much modern Japanese law, we agree that the comparisons could be interesting.

We nonetheless avoid the Continental parallels for simple reasons of expertise. Between the two of us, we are fairly certain we know U.S. and Japanese law. We have less confidence about anywhere else. As we show throughout this book, however, even civil-law regimes like Japan depend crucially on the case law, and many commonly held stereotypes about empirical law-related phenomena are flatly wrong. Although we could rely on secondary sources for information about other civil-law systems, we have no reason to think the secondary materials about those systems are any better than the materials about Japan. Put most bluntly, we have seen too many comparativists use bad secondary sources to rape Japanese law for us to try the same thing on Europe or South America.

Names

Throughout the book, we give Japanese names in the American format: given name first, family name last.

We have tried to render Japanese names in their most common readings. Because many Japanese names have multiple readings, we cannot claim that the reading we assign is necessarily the one the person himself uses.

When a case involves potentially embarrassing material in Japan, the court reporter often includes only pseudonyms. Names like Tarō Kōno and Hanako Otsuyama are the Japanese equivalent of John Doe and Mary Roe.

Citation Format

Many Japanese reported opinions appear in several reporters. Paralleling its rules for U.S. opinions, the *Bluebook* mandates primary citation to the official reporter. Unfortunately the rule is perverse in the extreme: far more U.S. libraries carry one or both of the principal private reporters (the *Hanrei jihō* and *Hanrei taimuzu*) than carry any official source. Accordingly, we ignore the *Bluebook* rule and cite cases by the most commonly available source in which it appears.

In most other respects, we cite cases in a way that tracks the *Bluebook* rules for U.S. cases: party names, the court reporter with volume and page numbers, the court, and the date. Because Japanese scholars often cite cases by the exact date decided, we give the month and date as well as the year. We ignore those *Bluebook* rules for Japanese material that (perversely again) track European citation practices rather than U.S. practice.

In translating from the Japanese, we believe in using English. For that reason, we have consistently tried to convert our translations into ordinary, idiomatic English. And, again, for that reason, we translate *hō* as "Act" rather than "Law" when part of the title of an act (who's heard of the "Sherman Law" after all?), and *jō* as "section" rather than "article" when referring to a section of an act (is the definition of income in article 61 of the IRC?). As to why so many Japan experts have so steadfastly done the contrary for so many years, we have not a clue.

Dollar Exchange Equivalents

Given the fluctuations in foreign exchange rates during much of this century, we keep all references to money in their original nominal amounts. To estimate dollar equivalents, turn to the following exchange-rate table.

EXCHANGE RATES

Year	¥/$	Year	¥/$	Year	¥/$	Year	¥/$
1891	1.25	1917	1.98	1943	4.25	1969	358.05
1893	1.65	1919	1.98	1945	*	1971	315.70
1895	1.98	1921	2.08	1947	*	1973	281.00
1897	2.01	1923	2.05	1949	*	1975	306.15
1899	2.02	1925	2.45	1951	361.05	1977	241.05
1901	2.03	1927	2.11	1953	360.80	1979	241.00
1903	2.02	1929	2.17	1955	360.80	1981	221.10
1905	2.02	1931	2.05	1957	360.80	1983	233.45
1907	2.03	1933	3.96	1959	359.80	1985	201.35
1909	2.02	1935	3.50	1961	361.80	1987	151.00
1911	2.03	1937	3.47	1963	362.40	1989	130.00
1913	2.03	1939	3.85	1965	361.40	1991	135.00
1915	2.05	1941	4.26	1967	362.20	1993	118.00

Sources: The rates are from Nihon tōkei kyōkai, ed., *Nihon chōki tōkei sōran* [Long-Term Japanese Statistics] (Tokyo: Nihon tōkei kyōkai, 1988), vol. 3, table 10-11, and supplemented by Sōmuchō tōkeikyoku, ed., *Nihon tōkei nenkan* [Japanese Statistical Yearbook] (Tokyo: Sōmuchō, 1996), table 12-16.

*Hyperinflation in Japan.

Note: Each rate is the average for the year where available; otherwise, it is the mean of the high and low for the year.

1 INTRODUCTION

> A was in a dispute with a criminal gang. To protect himself, he car-
> ried a hunting knife. While A was walking home one evening at dusk,
> B suddenly came from behind and raised his right hand to block his way.
> Thinking that a gang member was about to attack him, A panicked. With
> intent to kill, he stabbed B in the stomach. B spent three months recover-
> ing from the wound. Apparently B had mistaken A for a friend of his and
> had jumped in front to surprise him.
>
> Discuss the propriety of convicting A for attempted murder.

For American lawyers, it has all the trappings of a sick dream. In three
years of law school, they read too many such questions to want to read still
more. Yet it is not an American law school question. Instead, it is one of
the questions on the 1994 entrance exam for the Japanese Legal Research
and Training Institute (LRTI).[1]

If that question seems simple (it is not), mathophobic U.S. law students
should take particular care. Would-be entrants to the LRTI must also take
exams in nonlaw subjects. One of the economics questions a few years earlier was

> Describe the characteristics of the Cobb-Douglas production func-
> tion, and use it to explain the distribution of income. . . .

As explained in a model answer by Professor Takashi Iga of Kobe Univer-
sity, the right answer would first have reproduced the function itself: $P = aL^kC^{1-k}$, where $(0 < k < 1)$. A couple of partial derivatives later it would
have noted that $\partial^2P/\partial L^2 = ak(k-1)L^{k-2}C^{1-k}$. After a graph showing
the intersection of P and C/L, not to mention some more partial derivatives
and an optimization, it would finally have derived the distribution of income as $kP/L = w$ and $(1-k)P/C = r$.

This entrance exam to the LRTI is the effective bar exam in Japan, for
primarily only LRTI graduates can litigate. Yet it is the bar-exam equivalent with a catch: in the United States, almost everyone passes the bar—if
not on the first try, at least on the second. In Japan, almost no one does. In
this chapter, we trace the impact that this restrictive regulatory environment has had on the legal services industry generally. We also speculate on
the effects that the courts have had on the Japanese economy and that politics have had on the Japanese courts. We begin by exploring the function

no one passes the LRTI test

law plays in economic growth (section I). We then turn to the legal services industry (section II) and the courts (section III).

I. Law and Economic Growth
A. The Role of Law
1. *The Theory*

Growth depends on incentives, and incentives partially depend on the law. More precisely, economic growth occurs at efficient levels when people face legal and other institutional incentives that align the social and private rates of return to their activities. As Douglass North and Robert Paul Thomas put it in their breakneck history of the West, growth depends on "the establishment of institutional arrangements and property rights that create an incentive to channel individual economic effort into activities that bring the private rate of return close to the social rate of return."[2]

In theory, the private return could exceed the social return, or the social return could exceed the private, and in either case, inefficient growth rates would ensue. If people can freely impose costs on others, then their private rates of return will exceed the net social rate. Through their activities, they will cause the economy to grow at a rate that is inefficiently high. Yet modern problems with environmental pollution notwithstanding, some problems are trivial, and for most of the world and through most of history, this has been one.

More commonly, the social rates of return to economic activity exceed the private rates of return. People may consider dredging a river, for instance. But if others will benefit from the effort, too few rivers will be dredged. People may consider planting corn. But if others can steal the harvest at night, too little corn will be planted. In either case, because the people embarking on the project will capture only part of the good they do, they will undertake the project at suboptimal levels.

This problem is not trivial. Instead, through history and across continents, people have failed to capture anywhere near the full returns to the investments they make. Only exceptionally have institutional arrangements raised private rates of return to levels approaching the social rates of return. Only then has rapid growth followed.

In a world free of transactions costs, this problem would disappear. Parties would make the deals and side payments they need to align the social and private returns.[3] True as it is, however, the point (called the Coase Theorem) does little to explain the role law has played across the world and through history. For that comparative and historical inquiry, the question that matters is which legal institutional arrangements cause private returns to which activities most closely to track their social returns.

With at least two decades of research now in hand, part of the answer is clear: an economy will probably grow at nearly efficient levels when the law accomplishes several goals. First, it clearly defines claims to labor and scarce assets. Second, it gives people the right to exclude others (including the state) both from those assets and from the returns to economic activity. Third, it gives people the right freely to transfer claims to labor and assets. Last, it gives people the ability cheaply to enforce all this in court.

More simply put, the economy will grow at relatively efficient levels when people can work and invest with the assurance that they will capture most of the returns they earn. If neighbors capture the gains, if bandits can steal, if the government can expropriate—if any of this occurs, they will work and invest suboptimally. And if they work and invest too little, growth rates will remain inefficiently low.[4]

All this matters because the focus on property rights helps clarify why Japan has done as well as it has. It has done well because—for most of the past century and a half—the government has used the law to define and enforce private claims to scarce resources. In doing so, it has brought the social and private rates of return to economic activity closer together. Elsewhere one of us discusses the effect all this had on prewar Japan.[5] In this book, we examine modern Japanese law in light of the same dynamic.

In any detailed legal analysis, one can miss the forest for the trees. Given the many inefficient details to modern Japanese law (details to which we devote considerable attention in the chapters to follow), one can miss the usually sensible approach it takes. At root, it clearly defines and enforces most important claims to scarce resources. It does not do so perfectly, and throughout the book, we explore many of the problems that follow. We stress here, however, the basic way it tends to "get it right."

2. The Outline

We proceed as follows. For efficient growth to occur, people must have clear and enforceable rights to scarce resources—and in chapter 2, we explore how courts (with error, to be sure) define and enforce those property rights in Japan. People must also be able cheaply to transfer those resources—and in chapter 3, we explain how Japanese courts enforce such transfers. In the course of their economic activities, people must have incentives to engage only in cost-justified endeavors—and in chapter 4, we outline how Japanese courts police negative "externalities." And people must be able cheaply to coordinate their activities—and in chapter 5, we explain how Japanese courts facilitate joint production.

In chapters 6–10, we examine more explicitly the role the state plays in Japan. Given the economies of scale to some enforcement activities, in a relatively efficient regime the state will often do two things. First, it will let people enforce their claims to scarce resources through a civil judicial system (chapter 6). Second, it will enforce some claims at its own initiative through the criminal justice system (chapter 7). Unless it also credibly promises people that it will limit its intrusions into their private lives, however, it can easily stifle initiative. In chapter 8, we examine how it uses the law to limit its regulatory activity. In chapter 9, we examine how it uses the law to limit its extractive activity.

B. Constitutional Constraints
1. Guarantees

Imperfectly, to be sure, the Japanese Constitution helps the government commit to maintaining a limited role in human affairs. The first constitution dated from 1889. Based on a Prussian model, it generally required the state to act through statute. In a variety of other ways, it limited the way the state would intervene in private affairs. Not only did this include some protection against arbitrary arrest and arbitrary intrusions into matters of thought and speech, but also it included protections against expropriation. As one court put it in 1918, "[T]he inviolability of the right to property is one of the fundamental principles of the Imperial Constitution." [6]

In part because the 1889 constitution placed sovereignty in the emperor, in part because it limited the government less rigorously than did the U.S. Constitution, and in part simply because Douglas MacArthur had just won the war and saw no reason not to remake Japan in his own image, the United States (technically the allied occupation) imposed a new constitution on Japan in 1947. Through this document, it transformed Japan into a constitutional monarchy (arts. 1, 4). The constitution formally transferred sovereignty to a democratically elected parliament (art. 41), kept the judiciary independent (art. 76), and banned the military (art. 9).

This constitution also guarantees most civil rights U.S. readers consider fundamental, and a few others to boot. More specifically, it provides

- bans on race, sex, social, and religious discrimination (art. 14), and on the government's taking property without paying just compensation (art. 29)

- guarantees of universal adult suffrage (art. 15); of freedom of thought (art. 19), religion (art. 20), assembly, speech, and press (art. 21); of education (art. 26); of collective bargaining (art. 28); and of the right to hold property (art. 29)

- various criminal procedural rights: a guarantee of due process (art. 31); protections against arbitrary arrest, search, or seizure (arts. 33–35); a right to counsel (art. 34); a ban on torture and other cruel punishments (art. 36); a right to speedy trial (art. 37); a privilege against self-incrimination (art. 38); and protection against ex post facto laws and double jeopardy (art. 39)

The constitution omits a few rights dear to some American readers: e.g., the right to bear arms and the right to a jury trial. It includes some that the courts limit by interpretation (as we discuss elsewhere in this book). And it adds a few hortatory provisions as well: the right to work (art. 27), the right to public health (art. 25), and the right "to wholesome and cultured living" (art. 25).

Because constitutional law structures the way courts handle other questions, we do not include a separate chapter on it. Rather, we incorporate the constitutional analysis into our discussions of specific subjects. We explore the constraints on the government's ability to take property or to limit its use in chapters 2 and 8. We explore the constraints on the criminal process in chapter 7. And we explore the procedural limits to the way the government regulates in, again, chapter 8. To keep this book manageable, we omit questions concerning the military, legislative districting, and freedom of speech. We refer interested readers to other sources instead.[8]

2. Structure and Process

Traditional legal questions aside, constitutions also shape courts in an indirect, but more fundamental, way. At root, they shape courts by structuring how laws are made, for in structuring the lawmaking process, they effectively determine how closely legislators control the courts.

By creating a unitary parliamentary government, the Japanese Constitution radically constrains judicial discretion. For comparison, take the U.S. system. Under that system, a bill becomes law only if it passes both legislative houses and avoids a presidential veto. In effect, it becomes law only if it moves policy closer to the preferences of both houses and the president.[9] Suppose a court interprets a law in a way some legislators dislike. Those legislators will be able to reverse the court by statute only if they can identify a new policy (or organize a larger logroll) that both houses and the president will prefer to the policy the court chose.

By contrast, in the Japanese parliamentary system a bill will generally become law whenever it moves policy closer to the preferences of the leaders of the party dominating the lower house. The bill will only sometimes face a potential veto from the upper house, for the upper house has significantly less power under the constitution. It does not face an independent veto from the prime minister, for the prime minister is merely the leader of the lower house. Where bills in the United States face three veto gates (more, if one counts committees), a bill in Japan faces one. The result, as John Ferejohn explained, is courts with less discretion to pursue their own policy goals:

> [N]ations with traditions and practices of unrestricted parliamentary sovereignty would tend to have judges that are more or less neutral appliers of received law to cases. Conversely, those nations that restrict parliamentary sovereignty [like the United States] might be expected to develop traditions of judicial independence and power.
>
> Judges in parliamentary sovereignty systems would not emphasize or even notice the discretionary or interpretive elements of their decisions. They would see themselves, instead, as we see our agency heads: charged with carrying out parliamentary directives. This tendency would be strongest in those nations with pure majoritarian practices [like Japan]. One would also expect this to be true regardless of the history of the legal system.[10]

In effect, the Japanese parliamentary structure indirectly, but necessarily, cuts the discretion courts enjoy. Courts in the United States have broad discretion because Congress and the president find them so hard to reverse by statute. Japanese courts have less because the Diet finds it so easy.

II. The Legal Services Industry
A. Entry Barriers only 16,000 lawyers

Americans recite few facts about the Japanese bar more often than the raw numbers. To Americans, those numbers seem bizarre indeed. With a population of about 220 million, the United States has perhaps 700,000–900,000 lawyers. With about half the population, Japan has 16,000.

This dearth of lawyers results from government policy. The government controls entry to the bar and annually limits new lawyers to 700–800

Table 1.1 Overall LRTI Exam Pass Rates

	Number Passing	Pass Rate
1965	526	3.8
1970	507	2.5
1975	472	1.7
1980	486	1.7
1985	486	2.0
1990	499	2.2
1991	605	2.7
1992	630	2.7
1993	712	3.4
1994	740	3.3
1995	738	3.0
1996	768	3.0

Source: Shihō shiken hikkei [Judicial Exam Handbook] (Tokyo: Hōgaku shoin, 1996 (as updated)), 96–97, 223–227.

(table 1.1). In the United States, state bars admit some 50,000 every year. In Japan, 22,554 people sat for the 1994 LRTI entrance exam, and only 740 (157 women) passed.[11] The U.S. state bars pass 70-odd percent of the people who take the exam. The Japanese government passes perhaps 3 percent. Even among those from the very best universities, fewer than one in ten pass (table 1.2).

Run under the auspices of the Supreme Court, the LRTI gives two years of training. The students study in classrooms and work in law firms, judicial chambers, and prosecutors' offices. Throughout the period, as nominal government employees they pocket a modest salary. Because only LRTI graduates (and a few others) can join the bar (Attorneys Act, §§4, 5),[12] by restricting entry to the LRTI the government effectively restricts entry to the profession itself.

On average, those who pass the LRTI entrance exam pass it in their mid- to late twenties (table 1.3). They pass it then not because the late twenties trigger midlife crises among Japanese junior executives, but because they flunk it several times first. Often they start taking the LRTI entrance exam while still in college. There they majored in law and, during their studies, sat for the exam. For those determined to become lawyers, it was the first sitting of many. In 1994, only 47 of the 740 who passed were 22 or younger (table 1.3). The less fortunate take the exam year after year until they eventually pass or (more often) despair.

7

Table 1.2 1995 Pass Rates by School Attended
(All Schools with Ten or More Applicants Passing)

University	Number Passing	Pass Rate
Tokyo	166	8.2
Kyoto	74	7.8
Nagoya	15	5.4
Kobe	12	4.4
Hitotsubashi	21	4.3
Hokkaido	11	4.3
Osaka	16	4.3
Keio	61	4.2
Doshisha	22	3.7
Kyushu	11	3.2
Waseda	104	3.2
Jochi	10	3.1
Chuo	87	2.3
Meiji	28	2.1
Ritsumeikan	11	1.9

Source: *Shihō shiken hikkei* [Judicial Exam Handbook] (Tokyo: Hōgaku shoin, 1996), 96–97, 223–227.

This LRTI exam is a different beast from the Princeton-based Educational Testing Service (ETS) affairs to which so many U.S. lawyers owe their careers. Americans can raise their ETS scores a bit by preparing, but not by much. With substantial error, to be sure, the tests primarily measure IQ, and IQ is largely fixed by age six. By contrast, the LRTI exam tests accumulated knowledge as well. For passing it, preparation is not just helpful; it is essential.

As a result, the pass rate on the LRTI increases with the number of times a person has taken it. For the U.S. bar exams, the opposite is true. Because so many Americans pass the bar the first time, the second-time cohorts disproportionately include congenitally bad test-takers. They, in turn, usually pass at lower rates than everyone else—a point reflected in the lower February pass rates (65 percent nationally in 1993) when compared to the July rates (75 percent in 1993). Not so in Japan. The pass rates are so low that the remaining repeat takers still test well. As a result, second-time takers have a better chance of passing than the first (1.1 percent compared to 0.1 percent in 1987), and the third- and fourth-time takers do even better (1.8 percent and 2.3 percent).[13]

During their many years studying for this exam, would-be lawyers make

Table 1.3 LRTI Entrance Exam Passers:
Age and Years from First Attempt (1994)

Age				Years from First Attempt	
	Number Passing	Pass Rate	Percentage of Total	Number Passing	Percentage of Total
≤21	12	1.51	1.62	New	24	3.2
22	35	2.19	4.73	1	49	6.6
23	75	3.90	10.14	2	110	14.9
24	107	5.78	14.46	3	107	14.5
25	73	4.50	9.86	4	97	13.1*
26	71	4.91	9.59*	5	67	9.1
27	55	3.97	7.43	6	49	6.6
28	50	5.07	6.76	7	62	8.4
29	42	3.87	5.68	8	39	5.3
30≤	220	2.25	29.73	9≤	136	18.4

Source: Setsuo Miyazawa, "Shihō shiken ni okeru tōmen no kadai [Urgent Issues Regarding the LRTI Entrance Exam], 481 Hōgaku seminaa 76, 77 (1995).
    * Median.

ends meet as best they can. Some intentionally avoid graduating from college for a year or two so they retain access to the university library and keep open their chance to apply for ordinary corporate jobs. When continued undergraduate status becomes implausible, many enroll in graduate degree programs, again to keep access to the library. Although they will now find corporate placement harder, they at least maintain a socially respectable cover for their persistent failure.

Because the low pass rates induced many of the smartest students to take lucrative corporate jobs rather than focus on the risky chance of passing the bar, in 1996 the Ministry of Justice changed the rules. Of those it passed, it now chose 25–30 percent from applicants taking the exam within three years of their first try; the rest it selected from the highest scoring applicants generally. Although controversial, it was not a large change: in 1995, 24 percent of the successful applicants would have passed within three years of their first try even without the policy change.[14]

In 1993, Douglas Freeman became the first U.S. citizen to pass the LRTI exam. Koreans living in Japan had passed it routinely (six passed in 1993), but never before had an American. Freeman was twenty-seven and passed on his second try. Born in Japan, he had attended a Tokyo public high school and the University of Tokyo law faculty and had already worked several years at a securities firm.[15]

B. Practice

Once admitted, many Japanese lawyers live lives that resemble nothing so much as the frontier lawyer roles Jimmy Stewart played. They have little in common with any modern American lawyer or law student cosmopolitan enough to read a book on Japanese law. Of the 16,000 lawyers, 56 percent practice alone, and another 19 percent work in offices run by a single lawyer.[16] Only 8 percent work in firms with more than five. Most work modest hours, the mean being 46 hours per week.

Most also make do with minimal resources. As of 1990, 86 percent worked in an office with the leading private case reporter. Yet the reporter is far from complete, and only 36 percent had access to its closest competitor. Nor did they buy much else in print or use newer media. Although they could have used modems or CD-ROMs to reach the Japanese Lexis equivalent, fewer than one in ten did.

Most Japanese lawyers focus on litigation. In any given year, they generally start with 30-odd active matters. During the year, they add 30-some more and dispose of the same number. Of these matters, only about a fifth are noncontentious. About 90 percent are civil: some 25 percent concern contracts, 16 percent torts, 13 percent family law, 11 percent landlord-tenant disputes, and 10 percent real estate. About half the clients are individuals.

Although most lawyers spend their time litigating, they seldom specialize much further. Again as of 1990, 59 percent claimed no specialization. Of the minority who did specialize, 33 percent cited real estate, 24 percent corporate law, 24 percent inheritance matters, 22 percent traffic accidents, and 15 percent family law.

C. Lawyer-Substitutes

Attorneys are not the only people selling "legal services." Instead, a wide variety of experts openly sells such advice. Of these lawyer-substitutes, the most important may be the weirdly named "judicial scriveners" (*shihō shoshi*). Traditionally they maintained offices outside government offices and helped those without lawyers file the right papers. In the process, they sometimes also advised them on litigation strategy.[17]

For decades, judicial scriveners did low-level work. Times have changed. Many of the 16,000 scriveners are now people who had a plausible shot at passing the LRTI exam, but who eventually abandoned hope. Increasingly they are smart (they face a qualifying exam with a 3 percent pass rate),[18] ambitious, and well educated. Sometimes they maintain a sophisticated and aggressive practice in areas like real estate conveyancing.

Attorneys also face several other competitors (even if they may not subjectively consider them competitors). Some 500 "notary publics" (*kōshōnin*—again, an unfortunate translation) draft legal certification papers (certifying debts, for example) and other documents for individuals and corporations (like wills and charters). The government limits notarial posts to about 600 and fills them with retired prosecutors, judges, and Justice Ministry bureaucrats. They are wonderful sinecures: in 1988, over half the Osaka notaries reported taxable incomes above ¥30 million.[19]

In addition, some 63,000 tax agents (*zeirishi*) answer tax questions. Another 3,000 patent agents (*benrishi*) handle intellectual property matters. About 8,400 CPAs (*kōnin kaikei shi*) handle assorted accounting and tax issues. And over 30,000 administrative scriveners (*gyōsei shoshi*) sell simple services in real estate and regulatory matters.[20] Except for the notaries and administrative scriveners, all of these lawyer-substitutes faced licensing or certifying exams with pass rates of under a tenth.

The most common legal service providers, however, are none of these. They are the men and women who staff the corporate legal departments. Increasingly, large firms (particularly those affiliated with foreign corporations) have been hiring licensed attorneys in-house. The rest hire people who studied law in college and join these firms upon graduation. Some of these men and women stay in the legal department for most of their lives. The rest work there a few years and then climb the corporate ladder.

That legally trained executives run the legal affairs at Japanese corporations kills any notion that the Japanese make do without many legal specialists. Exactly how many executives do this legal work is hard to know. Many legally trained American corporate executives give informal legal advice even if not official corporate counsel. Similarly, many legally trained Japanese executives handle legal matters even if outside the legal departments. Conversely many licensed American lawyers do nothing legal at all, and so, too, do many legally trained Japanese.

Notwithstanding, the total number of legally trained personnel is easy to estimate. Where about 50,000 pass the bar exams in the United States each year, about 36,000 graduate from university law departments in Japan. Recall that the United States has about twice the population of

Japan. In effect, Japan has perhaps half again as many legally trained people per capita as the United States.

D. The Scope of the Practice

What constitutes the unauthorized practice of law in Japan remains in many ways fundamentally unclear. Judicial and administrative scriveners forthrightly and legally compete with lawyers for real estate work. Nonlawyer university graduates forthrightly and legally compete (as in-house staff) for corporate work. Thus, in two of the most lucrative segments of the legal services industry, lawyers face straightforward competitors. In tax and intellectual property work, they face yet more.

Effectively, Japanese lawyers have a legal monopoly only on litigation. As one might expect, they have gravitated toward it as the one segment of the market where their potential competitors face high barriers to entry. Only the Tokyo international law firms contradict this rule.

The various scriveners can legally do what they do not because the unauthorized practice ban clearly exempts what they do, but because other statutes explicitly authorize their work.[21] Similarly the legal department employees can give their legal advice not because the ban clearly exempts corporate legal advice, but because they do not hold themselves out to the public.[22] The ban itself (Attorneys Act, §72) provides:

> A person who is not an attorney may not have, as his profession, for the purpose of obtaining compensation, the handling or intermediation of advice, agency, arbitration or compromise and, other legal affairs concerning litigious cases [*jiken*], non-litigious cases and petition of exception cases to an administrative agency, such as a review claim, objection petition and re-review claim, and other legal cases in general.[23]

Note that the ban does not cover just litigation. It also covers "nonlitigious cases" and "other legal cases." To be sure, some observers argue that the word *cases* (*jiken*) limits the ban to disputes. Would that it were so clear. When Japanese researchers recently asked lawyers what sort of work they did, they used the term *jiken* for everything a lawyer might do. Consulting with corporations on retainer, drafting wills, transferring real estate—all such jobs they called *jiken*. The right translation for *jiken* is probably not "case" at all; it is "matter."

When Japanese courts construe section 72 of the Attorneys Act, they describe the ban broadly. According to one typical formula:

[t]he phrase legal case [*jiken*] covers a broad range of matters . . . .
It includes both situations where a dispute or an ambiguity exists
regarding legal rights and duties, and situations where new rights
and duties will arise.[24]

"New rights and duties will arise," of course, not just from disputes over
existing contracts. They will also arise from negotiations over new contracts. Unfortunately for American international lawyers, those negotiations are exactly what they would like to do in Japan.

Straightforwardly enough, courts hold that the unauthorized practice
ban applies to those who sell services related to litigation. They also hold
that it applies to fixers whom landlords hire to rid a building of unwanted
tenants, to professionals who register real estate, to bill collectors who recover bad debts, to specialists who draft documents for government offices,
and even to people who negotiate (uncontested) divorces. What courts
apparently have not directly adjudicated is whether those who give legal
advice in contract negotiations violate it, too.[25]

E. Fees and Incomes

Still, 16,000 is a small number, even if it merely represents all litigators in Japan. As a result, one might think that this regulatory scheme
earns Japanese lawyers large monopoly rents. Japanese bar associations do
maintain fee schedules. According to these schedules, upon taking a case
lawyers should charge 2 percent (for the largest cases) to 8 percent (for the
smallest) of the amount in controversy as a nonrefundable retainer. As a
contingent fee, they should then charge an additional 4 to 16 percent (depending again on the stakes) of the amount they actually recover. The
schedules contain a variety of exceptions and are not binding anyway.[26]
Successful lawyers also collect monthly retainers from corporate clients.

Unfortunately these schedules do not tell us whether Japanese lawyers
do charge monopoly prices because we do not know the riskiness of the
cases lawyers take and we have no reason to think lawyers follow the
schedules in any case. First, the greater their monopoly power is, the more
Japanese lawyers should take only the least risky cases. There, after all, is
where the expected value of the contingent fee will be highest. Second, the
greater their monopoly power is, the less lawyers should chisel on the fee
schedule. Some evidence exists, however, that they do chisel. In one recent
anonymous survey, over a quarter of the lawyers reported that they
charged less than the scheduled fees.[27] To know whether Japanese lawyers

charge monopoly prices, we need to know both how risky the cases they took are and how high the fees they charged are. Unfortunately, we know neither.

Although we do not know fees, we do know incomes—and the level of Japanese lawyer incomes suggests that any monopoly rent is small. According to American Lawyer, partners at the 100 highest grossing U.S. law firms in 1996 averaged per capita profits of $492,000.[28] They earned the most per partner at New York's Cravath, Swaine & Moore: $1.52 million. Even at the least profitable firm in the group (Cleveland's Baker & Hostetler), they made a respectable $205,000.

As everyone in practice knows, however, American Lawyer samples firms at the high end of the income distribution. Most American lawyers make nowhere near that much money; the lawyerly median may be high, but so is the variance. In their classic study of the Chicago bar, John Heinz and Edward Laumann did find that the median income in the bar was over double the median national family income. They also found, though, that the highest paid 17 percent of the lawyers earned double that lawyerly median.[29]

Given the dearth of Japanese lawyers and the feverish competition for LRTI spots, one might think Japanese lawyers earn incomes closer to the American Lawyer figures than to the U.S. national lawyer median. Yet recall what Japanese lawyers do: mostly mundane work. And according to an anonymous 1990 survey,[30] most also earn mundane incomes: an annual median of ¥11,030,000 and a mean of ¥15,440,000. Compared to the other jobs these lawyers might have taken, these are modest numbers—only slightly more than what their white-collar peers earned: corporate branch managers (average age fifty) could expect a mean of ¥12 million, for example, where a lawyer could expect ¥14 million in his forties and ¥20 million in his fifties. And lawyers seem to earn less than physicians: doctors running private clinics earned a mean of ¥32 million, and a doctor working for others (average age thirty-seven) earned ¥13 million.

As the difference between the ¥11 million lawyer median and ¥15 million lawyer mean implies, a few Japanese lawyers do make a killing. These are the partners in the multilawyer firms. They constitute 8.6 percent of all lawyers, but dominate the Tokyo international practice. In 1990, they made a median of ¥25 million and a mean of ¥32 million. Indeed, 42 percent of the partners made more than ¥30 million, and 17 percent made more than ¥50 million.

F. Foreign Lawyers

At one time, Americans dominated the international legal scene in Tokyo. But that was a time long ago. During the occupation, foreign lawyers in Japan could set up firms to handle the international legal business. When the occupation ended and the Japanese Diet revised the Attorneys Act, it grandfathered these men. There were about seventy of them, and though they were a diverse group, the best were very good. To them, the Japanese market promised a brilliant career.[31]

The grandfathered lawyers are largely gone now. But many of the firms they founded remain, run under Japanese management. Since the 1950s, other Japanese lawyers have started their own international firms, and some foreign firms have opened Tokyo offices to boot. As a result, a corporation wanting international legal advice in Tokyo effectively has a choice among three groups: the successor firms to the occupation-era foreigners, the indigenous international firms, and a perennially changing mix of foreign (mostly American) firms.

The most recent chapter in the story of the competition among these firms began in the 1970s, when one Chicago-based firm arrived in Tokyo.[32] It already ran a broad array of international operations, and it saw Japan as an additional opportunity. In Tokyo, it would establish a business that complemented its work in the rest of its offices. It set up a Tokyo office, and within a few years, several other firms tried to follow. Yet though the government gave the partner to the first of these later firms a work visa, when a partner in the second applied, it balked. Other American firms began to eye the Tokyo market, too, but with no new work visas the process had stalled.

The resulting quandary stumped American government officials. Some observers urged them to rely on the bilateral Friendship, Commerce and Navigation Treaty.[33] Article VIII did specify that American professionals could advise American firms in Japan. Unfortunately it said nothing about offices (and the American lawyers did not want to live in hotel rooms), and many American lawyers wanted to solicit business among Japanese firms anyway. In any case, it was an approach the American negotiators rejected. Instead, they demanded and obtained a new Japanese regulatory statute: the Foreign Lawyers Act (FLA), effective 1987.[34]

For a law that supposedly liberalized matters, the Foreign Lawyers Act did very little. By its initial terms, foreigners could now advise firms only on the law of their home jurisdiction (FLA, §3(a)). They could not handle litigation, government filings, real estate, or intellectual property work (FLA, §3(a)). They could not do anything at all in Japan until they had practiced at home for at least five years (FLA, §10(a)). And lest they become too effective a competitor notwithstanding all this, they could not hire or form partnerships with any Japanese attorney (FLA §49—a rule changed by the mid-1990s, §49-2). A more illiberal liberalization would have been hard to design.

The puzzle is why American negotiators settled for such a meager deal. Some observers suggested simple bad lawyering.[35] In fact, though, the outcome is equally consistent with the way firms routinely manipulate government regulators. On the Japanese side, the strategic considerations were simple: Japanese international lawyers earn high incomes and sought to exclude potential competitors. Granted, as potential consumers, Japanese business firms wanted a more competitive legal market. Yet in democratic regimes in most countries, governments often find it politically advantageous to cater to producer demands over more broadly based consumer preferences. Apparently the Japanese government did that here. In doing so, it did not behave unusually—governments around the globe have routinely excluded foreign lawyers.

The American strategic picture was more complex. Many of the most prestigious and politically influential U.S. firms wanted to enter the Tokyo market. Yet they found the market dominated by less prestigious competitors. These competitors generally had linguistically sophisticated U.S. lawyers on staff and maintained close working relations with Japanese firms.

By obtaining the statute that they did, the more prestigious firms knocked their innovative Tokyo competitors out of the lead. Because many of the American lawyers already in Tokyo had not spent five years in an American office, they now had to leave the Tokyo market and their Japanese clients. Because the statute banned integrated United States–Japan offices, they had to sever their ties with their Japanese colleagues. The statute may not have been much of a liberalization, but to the most sophisticated firms, pure liberalization probably was not their first choice. Their first choice was to knock out their most successful competitors—and that the statute did in spades.

III. The Courts
A. Court Structure

The 700-odd people who enter the LRTI do not all become lawyers.[36] Rather, each year some 80–100 become judges, and another 40–80 become prosecutors. In Japan, judging is a job people take when they finish the LRTI. They generally stay judges until about age sixty. That said, they do not hold lifetime appointments. Instead, they hold ten-year appointments and face mandatory retirement at age sixty-five. Whether to renew their ten-year terms is a power the Cabinet holds. Only twice since World War II has it chosen not to renew.

The 2,000-plus (non–Supreme Court) judges sit where their judicial betters tell them to sit. Where an American judge might be appointed to the Northern District of Illinois, a Japanese judge is not appointed anywhere. Instead, he is simply appointed a judge (technically an assistant judge for the first ten years). He then receives a new assignment every two or three years. With each, he bounces up or down the judicial hierarchy and all around the country.

For example, judge A might first find himself assigned to a district court. After three years, he might move to a high court and then to a family court branch office. He might also find himself moved in three-year intervals from Miyazaki to Osaka to Okinawa. Occasionally he might even be seconded to another government job, named to the court's administrative office (the Secretariat), or made a "law clerk" to the Supreme Court.

The Supreme Court is different. The fifteen justices are appointed by the prime minister specifically as Supreme Court justices. Of these, a plurality are unusually distinguished career judges. They receive the appointment in their sixties, usually as the capstone to their career. Others are typically law professors, prosecutors, or lawyers. They face periodic reconfirmation by the electorate, but no sitting justice has ever lost an election. As they face mandatory retirement at seventy, they seldom face more than a few elections anyway.[37]

B. Career Incentives

This institutional structure radically shapes the incentives judges face: fundamentally it gives judges an incentive to act in those ways that the people deciding their transfers consider appropriate. After all, judges do not consider all posts equal. Most prefer assignments up the court hierarchy (a high court or a district court post) to down (a branch office or a family court post). Most also prefer living in the large cities (particularly Tokyo) to the small ones.

In such a world, the people who control assignments control incentives. Most directly, that power over assignments lies with the Supreme Court Secretariat—the administrative center of the courts. It is staffed by professional judges (itself a two- or three-year posting) and is considered a prestigious post. Indirectly, however, that power over assignments lies with the ruling party in the Diet (for most of the postwar period, the Liberal Democratic Party (LDP)). It lies indirectly with the LDP because the head of the Secretariat answers to the Supreme Court, and the Supreme Court includes only recent LDP appointees. By naming appropriate people to the Supreme Court and by giving those justices power over the personnel office, the LDP potentially controls lower-court judges.

We emphatically do not claim that the LDP visibly intervenes in the courts, for to cause courts to decide cases in ways it prefers it need not visibly intervene at all. Rather, judges who share LDP policy preferences will disproportionately self-select into judicial careers, and those who do become judges will generally anticipate what the LDP wants at the outset. Suppose, for example, an LRTI graduate takes his Marxism seriously. He knows (as we explain below) that if he becomes a judge, he will be able to indulge his Marxism only at considerable risk. All else equal, he will be less inclined to take a judgeship than will someone who shares LDP policy preferences.

Supreme Court appointees generally share LDP policy preferences. After all, the LDP appointed them as prominent sixty-something judges, statesmen, or academics on the basis of their long careers. These justices control the Secretariat, and the Secretariat controls judicial careers. Given this structure, the Secretariat will seldom need to punish judges—for sensible judges will anticipate what it wants. The LDP will seldom need to complain about the Secretariat—for the Supreme Court will already have enforced LDP preferences on the Secretariat.

To say that courts generally enforce LDP policy preferences is not to say anything pejorative. In Japan, as elsewhere, most cases involve traffic accident or debt collection disputes. In such cases, the LDP merely wants judges to decide the cases quickly, uniformly, and efficiently. That a judge does what the LDP wants him to do in most cases means only that he does what anyone sensible would want a judge to do.

This does not make partisanship irrelevant. In a minority of cases, judges do face incentives with a distinctively partisan bias. Take a 1997 study by Ramseyer and Eric Rasmusen.[38] They first examined the careers of judges who joined a prominent left-leaning organization of lawyers, law professors, and judges in the 1960s (think of it as the Japanese National Lawyers Guild). Holding constant other indices of intellectual ability (e.g.,

Table 1.4 Effects of Section 138 Opinions on Judicial Postings

	Later Branch	Later *Sōkatsu*
Constant	−.67**	.24
Prior Branch	.97	
Prior *Sōkatsu*		.88**
Prior Opinions/Yr	.06	−.22
§138 Decision	.80***	−.47*

Source: J. Mark Ramseyer and Eric B. Rasmusen, "Judicial Independence in a Civil Law Regime: The Evidence from Japan," 13 *J.L. Econ. & Org.* 259 (1997).

Variables:

PRIOR BRANCH: Percentage of years a judge spent in branch offices during the ten years before the section 138 decision.

LATER BRANCH: Equivalent of PRIOR BRANCH for the ten years after the section 138 decision.

PRIOR *SŌKATSU:* Percentage of years a judge spent with *sōkatsu* duties during the ten years before the section 138 decision.

LATER *SŌKATSU:* Equivalent of PRIOR *SŌKATSU* for the ten years after the section 138 decision.

PRIOR OPINIONS/YR: Average number of published opinions per year on bench for the ten years before the section 138 decision.

§138 DECISION: 0 if the judge held the canvassing ban constitutional; 1 if otherwise.

Notes: *** Statistically significant at 1 percent level.

** Statistically significant at 5 percent level.

* Statistically significant at 10 percent level.

Program: STATA, running tobit.

the school the judge attended),[39] they found that these judges were still receiving systematically inferior posts in the 1980s.

Second, Ramseyer and Rasmusen found that judges who decide individual cases against the government receive worse assignments than other judges. For this, they examined cases where the government is a party (criminal, tax, public-sector labor, and administrative law cases). Again holding all else constant, they found that a judge who decides a case against the government tends to receive a worse job.

Last, Ramseyer and Rasmusen picked a distinctly partisan issue: the constitutionality of the ban on door-to-door canvassing (Elections Act, §138).[40] Because incumbents obtain free air-time by virtue of being incumbents and the LDP had more incumbents than anyone else, the LDP consistently favored the ban. Because they had almost no incumbents, the Communists consistently opposed it. Ramseyer and Rasmusen then examined the impact that cases involving the ban had on a judge's career.

The results appear in table 1.4: regressions estimating the percentage of a judge's career in branch offices (considered undesirable posts) during the ten years after he decided a section 138 case and the analogous percentage of time with administrative responsibilities (specifically, *sōkatsu* duties—considered a desirable assignment). To hold judicial quality constant, Ramseyer and Rasmusen accounted for both the average number of opinions a judge published per year and the quality of his post prior to the decision.

On average, judges who held the canvassing ban unconstitutional (those who took the Communist position) did worse than did those who held it constitutional. As the positive coefficient on §138 DECISION for the dependent variable LATER BRANCH implies, those who held the ban unconstitutional spent longer in branch offices for doing so. As the negative coefficient on §138 DECISION for the dependent variable LATER *SŌKATSU* implies, they spent less time with administrative responsibilities.

Conclusions

It is a truth universally acknowledged, Jane Austin once almost observed, that a man in possession of a good fortune must be in want of a lawyer. And it is a truth regularly repeated among American lawyers, as much to ourselves as to anyone else who would listen (of which there are not many), that an economy in possession of significant wealth must be in want of quite a few lawyers. Others have never been so sure. Economists sometimes use the number of lawyers as a proxy for the dead-weight loss in the economy. Noneconomists sometimes suggest in the *New York Times* that we trade lawyers for cars with Japan, one lawyer for one car.

Japan seems to disprove our lawyerly myths. With scarcely 16,000 lawyers, but a functioning democracy and a successful economy, it threatens our own lawyerly pride just as it fuels our clients' antilawyer prejudices. "We can do just fine, thank you," Japan seems to be saying, "without your complement of lawyers. Perhaps you could do just fine without them, too."

In fact, it is not quite clear what myths Japan disproves, for it is not at all clear it makes do without legal services. True enough, it has barely 16,000 lawyers. But it has barely 16,000 only because the government flunks 97 percent of the people who would be lawyers. And while it may have few lawyers, it has a huge number of legal specialists. Indeed, every year its universities graduate significantly more legal specialists per capita than do American universities.

Judges in Japan have the same training as do lawyers. In general, they do their work efficiently and effectively. That they do so is no accident. To induce them to work hard, the administrative office of the courts maintains an elaborate incentive system through which it rewards judges by the work they do. Judges circulate through a wide variety of posts during their careers. Disproportionately, those who work as the administrative office would like them to work obtain the best jobs.

2 PROPERTY

Giichi Kō had clout. Head of a local crime syndicate branch, he operated out of a building in central Akita city in northern Japan. About a mile from the train station, his office was also near a residential area, various shops, a hospital, and an elementary school. He made no bones about who he was or what he did. Prominently on the front of the building, he displayed the syndicate's symbol and a sign announcing the branch headquarters.

In June 1990, several members of Kō's branch defected to the Yamaguchi-gumi, the largest and most powerful of the Japanese *yakuza* (see subsection 7.II.C). Once they left, Kō knew it would be war. His men fastened steel plates to the walls, installed spotlights, and replaced the windows with bulletproof glass. To the neighbors, it was bad enough when the rivals started shooting at each other and each other's homes. It was beyond the pale when they made mistakes and starting shooting at other people's homes besides.

With no interest in playing target to the Yamaguchi-gumi, the neighbors sued. Kō may have had an apparent legal right to the office, but they wanted him out anyway. Applying general nuisance law principles, the court enjoined him from using the building as his headquarters.[1] In the process, it faced a central and perennial tension in property law: how generally to enforce an owner's interests in his property (as Kō asserted), yet sometimes to limit the use to which he can put it (as Kō's neighbors asserted). The story of this chapter is the story of that tension.

Basic to economic growth is a legal regime that effectively lets people capture and transfer the returns to scarce resources. In most respects that matter (tenancy law being a disastrous exception), Japanese property law provides such a regime. Based on the Prussian-based Civil Code enacted in the 1890s[2] and embroidered through the case law and occasional statutes, it defines rights to scarce resources, it lets people control those resources and exclude others from them, and it lets people transfer them.

In many respects that matter (though with a series of exceptions that we note), Japanese property law also resembles property law in the United States. In order to clarify where Japanese law does and does not resemble the law in the United States, in section I we follow the ordering of legal doctrine generally used in U.S. texts. As practicing lawyers will quickly note, this obviously has little relation to modern business practice—but that is another issue. We start with ownership through possession (subsection A): of animals, of lost property, and through adverse possession. We catalog the various Civil Code estates, contrast them with the Anglo-American estates, and explain joint ownership arrangements (subsection B). We explore easements (subsection C), water law (subsection D), zoning and eminent domain (subsection E), and recordation rules (subsection F). We conclude by studying the bizarrely distinctive Japanese landlord-tenant law (section II).

I. The Law
A. Possession as the Root of Title
1. Animals

Title to animals depends on possession. Yet it depends in a way that varies with the animal at issue. Suppose an animal is wild. Because it is free until caught, the rules on unowned property apply (see subsection 2) and track the famed fox in *Pierson v. Post:*[3] he who first captures the animal acquires title (Civil Code, §239). One Japanese hunter chased a badger into a cave. To stop it from running away, he blocked the entrance with a rock. Title follows possession, capture gives possession, and the hunter here had captured the hapless badger. The badger was his.[4]

Suppose the animal is of the sort people usually keep as pets. The rules that govern lost property (see subsection 2) now apply instead. One day in the late 1920s, claimed Sōtarō Sone, a mina bird flew into his house. He caught it, fed it, and asked around if anyone knew who owned it. Hearing no claimants, he and his wife kept and loved the bird. In 1930, Umetarō Inagaki's wife arrived at his house with three policemen in tow. The bird was hers, she claimed, and she demanded it back. Sone's wife refused, but Inagaki and the officers took the bird away anyway.

Sone sued to recover the bird and litigated all the way to the Supreme Court. In the end, he lost. According to the court, in Japan mina birds seldom live in the wild. As a result, title does not follow possession. Instead, it follows the rules over lost property, and Sone should have reported the bird to the police. As he did not do so, he could not now claim it as his own.[5]

Suppose, finally, the animal is a weird pet—one that usually runs wild, but that someone had in fact tamed. For these, the Civil Code effectively gives the original owner a month to find his lost pet. If he finds it during that month, he can retrieve it. If he does not, then the finder who believes in good faith that the animal is wild acquires title (Civil Code, §195).

2. Lost and Stolen Property

Consider lost property more generally. Suppose one finds a piece of moveable property. If the thing had never been owned, then the finder acquires title (Civil Code, §239). In keeping it, he runs a risk, though. If a court later finds that the thing had been lost or stolen, then it will hold that he had a duty to take it to the police station (Lost Objects Act (LOA), §1).[6] If instead he kept it for his own, he loses the right to claim title (LOA, §9). Suppose now someone finds a piece of lost property (or buried treasure (LOA, §13)) and reports it to the police. The police will issue a public notice, and if no one claims it after a significant interval, the finder (if behaving in good faith) will acquire title (Civil Code, §§239–241). If the original owner does claim it in time, he will need to pay the finder at least 5 percent of its value (LOA, §4).

For bona fide purchasers of property that has not been stolen or lost, somewhat different rules apply. In 1953, Naigai kōgyō K.K. imported a jukebox. It was new, it was rare, and it was expensive. Along with the assets to the Club Flamingo, Naigai rented it to a foreigner, apparently a Frenchman. Business was bad, the club's employees went unpaid, and the Frenchman vanished. A manager named Kawase took over the club. He had spent years running cabarets, hotels, and nightclubs in the international sector, but even he could not turn Club Flamingo around. Desperate, he sold off the club's assets. The jukebox he sold to one Hondō.

The problem, of course, is that the jukebox was not Kawase's to sell. Had it been stolen or lost, Naigai could have recovered it from Hondō within two years (Civil Code, §193). Unfortunately for Naigai, it was neither. Provided Hondō acquired it in good faith and without negligence, the machine was his to keep (Civil Code, §192). Hondō had examined documents relating to the machine, and even had he been able to find the Frenchman, the court doubted the Frenchman would have denied ownership. Accordingly the court concluded that Hondō had done everything one could reasonably expect, and gave him title.[7]

3. Adverse Possession

A squatter acquires title to real estate by adverse possession if he possesses it openly and notoriously with intent to own for twenty years. If he begins the term with a good-faith nonnegligent belief that he has title, he acquires it in ten (Civil Code, §162).[8]

In 1942, Pu Yi's puppet regime of Manchukuo (of Bertolucci's *Last*

Emperor fame) acquired land for an embassy in Tokyo. When the regime disappeared three years later, by international law title to its assets passed to Chiang Kai-Shek's Republic of China (ROC). In 1949, Mao's Red Army overran China, and Chiang hopped the straits with his cronies into Taiwan. Pu Yi went into "self-criticism," and title to his Tokyo embassy seemed to fall to Taibei.

The Great Leap Forward and the Cultural Revolution came and went; Pu Yi lost his wives and weathered his prison stint to live quietly and modestly (at least so Bertolucci tells us). Then in 1972, Pat and Richard Nixon flew to China. With fanfare galore, they announced they were switching diplomatic ties from the ROC to the People's Republic of China (PRC). In their wake, Japan switched ties, too. For Pu Yi's Tokyo embassy, this arguably meant title now passed to the PRC.

During the several postwar decades, the Japanese government had managed the embassy as trustee for the ROC government. In fact, the ROC had not wanted it, and Japan had not done anything. Instead, it had let a series of squatters occupy and use the land. By the mid-1970s, the property was worth real money. Located in the hyper-posh Motoazabu section of Tokyo, the 13,000-square-foot lot was pricy even by the rarified standards of diplomatic enclaves. The Beijing regime wanted it back, but to avoid an international scene, the Tokyo government first had to remove the squatters of three decades. It sued to evict, and the squatters claimed title by adverse possession.

Perhaps the squatters had been too nice for their own good. Then again, perhaps the government had let the squatters be only because they assured it they would cooperate when necessary. The Japanese government had delegated its nonmanagerial management to the Yasuda Trust Bank, and the bank had shown a similarly pronounced indifference. Yet in 1958, the squatters had explicitly told the bank that if the government ever wanted the property back, they would leave. In 1971, they considered putting up an apartment building, but asked for a lease first. To the court, all this obviated any claim that they had possessed the property "with intent to own." Absent that intent, they could not claim title by adverse possession.[9]

B. Title
1. *The Civil Code Estates*

The Japanese Civil Code catalogues nine estates—nine types of interests in property. Under the Code, if a person holds one of the nine (and has recorded it when necessary), he can assert his interest not just against those with whom he deals, but against third parties as well (Civil Code, §177). By contrast, if he holds a right that arises by contract (or tort), he can assert it only against the promisor (or tortfeasor).

For our purposes, the important three of the nine estates are the rights to possession (Civil Code, §§180 et seq.), to ownership (§§206 et seq.), and to an easement (§§280 et seq.). The others are (1) rights to use someone else's land to construct a building or plant trees or bamboo (sometimes translated "superficies"; Civil Code §§265 et seq.); (2) long-term (twenty- to fifty-year) agricultural leases (sometimes translated "emphyteusis"; §§270 et seq.); and (3) various creditors' rights—mortgages (sometimes translated "hypothecs"; §§369 et seq.), liens (§§295 et seq.), pledges (§§342 et seq.), and certain other priority rights (§§303 et seq.).

The Code states that the list is exclusive unless otherwise provided by statute (§175). By special statute, lessees have rights close to those enjoyed by the holders of Code estates (see section II). In addition, however, courts have effectively given similar rights to customary holders of interests in water and steam (see subsection D).

2. Future Interests

Contrast all this to the standard list of Anglo-American estates. A typical catalogue of the classic possessory estates in the English tradition would list the fee simple, fee tail, and life estate as freehold estates and the leasehold as a nonfreehold estate. As nonpossessory estates, it would then list the reversion, the possibility of reverter, and all those other future interests that law students have learned to love and, upon passing the bar, have promptly forgotten.

Essentially the two legal regimes divide estates along fundamentally different lines. The classical Anglo-American estates represent attempts by grantors to control the future: what happens to the property if a given event occurs (e.g., a lineal descendant does not have a son). The Japanese estates represent attempts to carve out contemporaneous rights to do specified (and only specified) things to land (e.g., to plant trees).

The obvious comparative question is what happens in Japan if parties do try to control future land use: What happens, for example, if A sells land to B "so long as used for educational purposes"? Under traditional English property law, B would acquire a fee simple determinable, and A would retain a possibility of reverter. Under Japanese law, title to the land would generally pass to B upon recordation. At that point, B would own the land freely. Should he sell it to a shopping center, A probably could not reclaim it. What *A* would retain instead is a contractual right: a right to sue *B* for money damages.

And yet, as basic as these differences may seem to textbook Property, none has much to do with the world of real estate practice. What matter in both Japan and the United States are possession, title, easements, and leases. The possibility of reverter does not figure prominently (if at all) in modern American legal practice—if it did, more readers of this book would have remembered what it was. Emphyteusis does not figure prominently in modern Japanese legal practice—if it did, translators would not have used a word that most American lawyers will confuse with a lung disease. The visible differences in estates mask a more fundamental similarity: on possession, title, and easements (but not leases—see section II), American law and Japanese law take relatively close approaches.

3. Joint Ownership

a. General Rules. Joint owners share the whole of the property (Civil Code, §249; Japan dispenses with distinctions among joint, in-common, and by-entirety tenancies). To alter the property they must agree unanimously (Civil Code, §251); to make lesser managerial decisions, they must take a majority vote (§252). They share expenses proportionally to their ownership interests (Civil Code, §253). Unless they otherwise provide, a court will presume that their interests are equal (Civil Code, §250). Each may sue to partition the property (Civil Code, §§256, 258).

Mokichi Morimiya fell ill in 1962. He had a wife, two children, and a mistress of 35 years. Reasonably enough, he feared that the four would quarrel over his estate when he died. Unreasonably in the extreme, he thought he could solve the problem by leaving each an undivided quarter interest in his real estate. He did, he died, and—predictably enough—the four fought bitterly. When finally his mistress and one of the children sued to partition the property, the court was only too happy to oblige.[10]

b. Condominiums. Perhaps the most common disputes in joint ownership involve condominiums. Granted, nuisance law mitigates many of the more egregious problems that arise when people live and own property close to and on top of each other. In applying that law, moreover, Japanese courts do use a sensible cost-benefit analysis that closely tracks the Hand formula (see subsection 4.I.C) often used in the United States.[11] Take the (noncondominium) mob case that opened this chapter. According to the court, the adverse effect of operating a mob office on the surrounding neighborhood overwhelmed any interest the mob boss might have. As a result, by that nuisance law analysis it could enjoin him from using the building as his office.[12]

Condominiums raise a variety of peculiar legal issues, however, and Japan—like most American jurisdictions—deals with these questions through a special Condominium Act.[13] Particularly interesting are those provisions governing antisocial occupants. Under the act, if an occupant engages in conduct that harms the common interests of the owners, those other owners may demand that he desist (Condominium Act, §57). To sue on the demand, they will need the support of a majority of the owners and of the voting interests. Unless they otherwise provide, they will have voting interests proportional to their floor space (Condominium Act, §§14, 38).

If the dissatisfied owners can show that the antisocial occupant is hard to live with and that a simple injunction against his offending conduct will not do, they can take more drastic measures. If they can muster a three-fourths vote of both all owners and all voting interests, they can vote to evict him, whether he owns the unit (Condominium Act, §58) or rents it (§60). If they want, they can even auction off his unit (Condominium Act, §59).

Consider first the simple injunction. *Karaoke* is big business in Japan—in the mid-1990s, nearly a ¥1 trillion industry with a clientele of 60 million. In order to shed its dependence on adult male patronage, over the past decade it has moved out of the bars. To Western visitors, it seems to have moved into everything: to the occasional McDonald's (they call their *karaoke* MacSong); to a commuter train near Osaka; even to at least one entrepreneurial taxi.[14]

For singers who would practice first in private, there are *karaoke* studios. In them, would-be Elvis or Madonna or Hachirō- Kasuga look-alikes can practice their solos about love; about sex; or (in the Japanese analogue to country music for the fifty-something crowd) about how he left his mother in the country to catch the night train to Tokyo, how it rained all night in the harbor when he left his true love last, or how he held his dying buddy on the plains of Manchuria while the blood from his wounds faded into the glow of the setting sun.

The *karaoke* studio Fortissimo gave its customers those private rooms in a ground-floor unit of a nine-story condominium complex. When bored, they could apparently play computer games, eat curry rice, or drink coffee. They did all that, but according to neighbors, they also chatted, shouted, and raced their engines in the parking lot. Neighbors complained about the noise from the parking lot, the wind from the air conditioning units, the smells from the kitchen, and the tastelessness of Fortissimo's lighted sign. Certainly not least (perhaps the studio's name was no thoughtless choice), they complained about the noise and vibration from the *karaoke* machines themselves.

The court enjoined Fortissimo from operating between midnight and 4 A.M. on weekdays and between 1 A.M. and 4 A.M. on Sundays and holidays. Although the residents had sued under §57 of the Condominium Act, the court used a straightforward nuisance law analysis. On the one hand, the Fortissimo owners had invested large amounts in the equipment; the condominium by-laws allowed owners of first-floor units to use them for commercial purposes; and located as it was on a major highway, the building was not a quiet place anyway. On the other, sleep is important, and by operating late at night, Fortissimo greatly irritated its neighbors. Weighing the competing interests, the court enjoined Fortissimo from operating at night.[15]

Consider, too, the more drastic remedies condominium associations can take against antisocial occupants. The most prominent cases involve— again—the mob. Japanese *yakuza* groups regularly buy or rent condominiums to use as offices. When they do, they regularly bully their neighbors into silence. Occasionally, however, those neighbors refuse to defer. When they complain and sue, they routinely win.

In 1983, Sakae Harami rented his Yokohama condominium to Yoshio Masuda. Masuda was a central figure in the Yamaguchi-gumi. He controlled upwards of 400 men and was once the rumored successor to the entire syndicate. His neighbors, though, were not an easily intimidated bunch. They sued to evict him and cited a laundry list of complaints. Many are common to condominium suits against the mob generally: in using the apartment as an office, he broke the by-laws allowing only residential use; his men were rude; they violated parking rules; they put the garbage out improperly.

Obviously, if home offices, rudeness, parking violations, and misplaced garbage were grounds to evict, then evictions in Japan would number thousands a day, and most Americans (at least most New Yorkers) would last four days at most. Critical to Masuda's neighbors, when the Yamaguchi-gumi head died in 1981, the gang split over his successor. Masuda's faction stayed, and the dissatisfied left to form the Ichiwa-kai. Tensions stayed high and, in 1985, turned into war. From late January through mid-May 1985, police tallied 67 shootings and 14 deaths relating to the dispute. For those of us used to the drug wars on the south side of Chicago, it all seems a day's work. In Japanese mob history, it was the bloodiest rivalry ever. To the other members of the condominium, all this meant they now lived in the combat zone. It meant the risk of stray bullets. It meant large numbers of hoodlums milling around. It meant closed-circuit TVs. It meant steel panels on the building. It meant body frisks and aggressive questioning when they tried to enter their own building. Obviously it meant dramatically lower property values.

When the condominium association voted to oust Masuda, the court enforced the vote: it vacated his lease and ordered him out of the building.[16] The illegal activity was egregious, the harm to the neighbors was obvious, and the court saw no other way to solve the problem. In other similar cases, sometimes the mobsters have owned (rather than rented) the unit. When they did, the condominium associations have still sued. Routinely—and successfully—they have evicted them from their own units and sometimes auctioned the units to the public as well.[17]

C. Easements

One can acquire an easement by virtue of the location of one's land, by contract, or by use. If an owner needs to walk onto a neighboring plot to repair the fixtures on his own land, he may do so (Civil Code, §209). If his land is completely enclosed, he may cross his neighbor's plot to reach a public road (Civil Code, §210; though he may owe compensation for this).[18] Whatever the situation, he may always negotiate an easement by contract. And if he uses a neighbor's land openly and notoriously for twenty years (ten years if in good faith), he acquires an easement by adverse possession (Civil Code, §§283, 163). Any easement he has runs with his land and may not be transferred independently (Civil Code, §281). If he does not use it for twenty years, it disappears (Civil Code, §§291, 167).

From 1951 to 1955, Ichirō Kōno had been a member of the Shinjuku Ward Council. He acquired some notoriety when newspapers reported that he had walled off city land and started using it as his own. Eventually, however, his wife, Hanako, bought the land from the city and resold it to their oldest son, Tarō. Meanwhile, Ichirō had moved out of the house, taken up with a mistress, and started another family.

Ichirō owned a piece of land next to the plot Hanako had sold to their son Tarō. In part in order to gain access to the road in front of his son's land, he had paved and walled off some of his son's property and used it as a passage. Eventually Tarō decided he wanted the land for a parking lot and decided not to humor his father any longer. He had consistently sided with his mother in the divorce and, in 1981, sued Ichirō to remove the wall. Ichirō claimed title by adverse possession.

Ichirō did not have title. As with the squatters at the Manchukuo embassy, the court found he lacked any intent to own the property. He did, however, have an easement. Under section 283 of the Civil Code, he acquired an easement simply by using the land openly and continuously—and intent was irrelevant. Accordingly Tarō could force Ichirō to remove the wall, but could not stop him from using some of the land as a passage.[19]

D. Water
1. Flowing Water

For rivers and streams, Japanese courts use rules that closely track the prior appropriation regime in the western United States.[20] They did not find the rules in the Civil Code. Imported from water-rich Prussia, the Code does not partition rights to rivers. Instead, it largely treats water as an unlimited resource and lets riparian owners use rivers as they please. For Japan, it introduced a scheme that never would have worked.

In Japan, water is scarce. It is not scarce by any measure of aggregate rainfall, but it is scarce when most needed. At the start of the twentieth century, most Japanese farmed. More than anything else, they raised rice, and they raised it in irrigated paddies. For this, they needed water in precise amounts, at precise times. During several of the months they needed the water, it could be scarce indeed.

This mismatch between the Code and agricultural practice became clear even before the Code officially took effect. Take a Supreme Court case from 1896. The thirteen plaintiffs were downstream farmers; the defendants apparently were an upstream family that had diverted water to open a new paddy. By custom, the plaintiffs had used the stream to irrigate their paddies, but in diverting the water, the defendants now threatened to leave the plaintiffs' downstream paddies dry. The plaintiffs sued, and the Supreme Court held in their favor. Water above ground, it explained, belongs to those who have been using it. Once they acquire a customary use, they can enforce in court a right to continue to use it, subject only to whatever customary limits bound them in the past.[21]

2. Underground Water and Steam

a. General. Subterranean water created a harder problem. Because the Civil Code largely ignored water above ground, it left the Supreme Court room to invent a rule that worked. Water underground it

31

seemed to cover explicitly: by section 207 of the Code, he who held title to land held title to everything below the surface. By implication, he could use subterranean water as heavily as he wished.

Yet underground water feeds aboveground streams. A court can try as hard as it wants to apportion aboveground water, but it will accomplish little if it lets landowners use underground water as they please. To let riparian farmers use the water at customary levels, it needs somehow to limit the way people use subterranean water as well.

Toward this problem, the courts took two approaches. In some cases, particularly those involving hot springs, they added a customary gloss: an owner could use underground steam as he wished, but only if local custom did not ban that use. In others, they turned to the abuse-of-rights doctrine: an owner could use underground water only if he did not abuse the right. As explained in subsection 4.I.A.3, Japanese courts imported the abuse-of-rights doctrine from European courts. Through it, they limited apparently unrestricted legal rights to "reasonable" levels—often determined using, again, a Hand-style cost-benefit analysis. In the context of underground water, they limited a fee owner to that use which did not unreasonably harm his neighbors.

   b. Custom. To explore the customary gloss approach, take a case involving the tiny seaside resort of Kinosaki.[22] Just over the mountains from the metropolitan centers of Kobe, Kyoto, and Osaka, Kinosaki faced the Japan Sea. It enjoyed several veins of underground steam and by legend could claim for them medicinal value. After all, the springs had cured the seventh-century emperor who initially found them when he spotted a stork enjoying the water. Presumably the town also enjoyed the "personal services" industry, in which hot-springs communities traditionally specialized and which the mob now controls.

   At the turn of the century, Kinosaki had six public baths (at least one of them an open-air affair) and 60-odd bathless inns. It also boasted several villas for the rich and famous, and these villas enjoyed private, piped-in steam baths. In 1909, the train arrived. What had been a long trip for the leisure class now became a convenient vacation for the several million hoi polloi across the mountain. To cater to the relatively more affluent among them, a number of developers built new hotels with indoor baths. In doing so, they precipitated a crisis, for they threatened to run the six public baths dry. If the baths went, so would the 60-odd bathless inns that sent their patrons to them.

The fight proceeded in the courts, and it proceeded in the streets. The bathless innkeepers sued the owner of the new hotel in court. But they also boycotted merchants who dealt with him. Their children harassed his children. And in 1933, they even tried to shut off the electricity to the town and use the chaos to storm the hotel.

The court battle was one the bathless lost, and the street battle was one they then abandoned. To the courts, any customary ban against indoor baths had long since disappeared. The town had for decades tolerated the occasional villa with piped-in steam. As a result, by the time it sued the hotel in the 1930s, no customary ban remained. Without it, the court could turn only to the basic right fee owners enjoyed to use underground resources freely.

Yet catastrophe did not ensue, even for the bathless inns. The reason was technological: engineers soon discovered how to increase the volume of steam extracted. Today Kinosaki claims both public and private baths, and with the baths has come extravagant tourist potential. Developers long ago turned the surrounding mountains into a ski resort. They ran cable cars up to the local "hot springs temple." By the 1960s, the town could boast 1.5 million visitors a year.

c. Abuse of Rights. To explore the abuse-of-rights doctrine, take the dispute over a suburban Tokyo restaurant named Komatsuen (Small Pine Garden). Kiku Honda opened the lavish establishment in 1932. She built a classical Japanese garden, and in it, she planted trees, ran a fountain, and stocked a pond with carp. To supply the water it needed, she sank two wells.

Kamenosuke Samejima ran a trout farm nearby. Because trout thrive in flowing water, he needed enormous quantities. During 1933 and 1934, he dug six wells. In the process, he ran one of Honda's wells dry and threatened the other. When Honda complained and dug a third well, he ignored her pleas and dug his wells deeper still. All of Honda's wells went dry. Her fish died, her customers went elsewhere, and her profits vanished.

When Honda sued, Samejima noted that he owned his land. As owner, he could use underground water as he pleased. The Supreme Court disagreed. In using so much water that he destroyed Honda's business, he abused his right. As fee owner, he could use underground water—but only reasonably. How much water was reasonable water depended in part on the damage he caused others, and it was a line he here crossed.[23]

E. Government Power

Zoning in Japan involves multiple tiers of government. At a national level, the City Planning Act (CPA, §8)[24] defines several categories of urban districts (e.g., residential, commercial, industrial), and the Construction Standards Act (CSA, §48)[25] limits the ways residents can use land within each. More locally, the prefectural governor designates the actual districts (CPA, §5(a)), and a construction manager appointed by the mayor enforces this legal structure (CSA, §4). The CSA also limits the height and footprint of a building (CSA, §43) and the extent to which it can block the sunlight to neighboring units (CSA, §56-2).[26] A separate statute restricts the areas within which businesses can provide adult entertainment.[27]

The Japanese government can and does buy property by eminent domain. Although the constitution requires it to compensate the owner when it does (Art. 29),[28] the Americans (technically the Allied occupation) gutted the requirement when they forced through "land reform" after the war. Under the scheme the Japanese government eventually adopted, it bought the land from the owners of relatively large farms through eminent domain. It then resold it to their former tenants.

Effectively, however, the government took from the rich and gave to the poor. It paid for the farms in 1947 or later, but paid in 30-year bonds bearing 3.6 percent interest according to a compensation formula that used 1945 prices. These were days of rampant inflation: from 1945 to 1947, indexed price levels rose from 100 to 1,364 and by 1949, to 5,915; by 1977, they had obviously risen much farther.[29] By 1948, one acre of good paddy went for 13 packs of cigarettes, and the typical tenant-turned-owner paid for his farm within one or two years.[30] The result was wildly haphazard redistribution: those rich Japanese who happened to have invested heavily in rural real estate lost their wealth; those poor Japanese who happened to have worked on large farms found wealth thrust upon them.

In 1953, the Japanese Supreme Court dutifully held the scheme constitutional. Quickly the newly propertied farmers became the backbone of the conservative politicians who would in 1955 form the Liberal Democratic Party. Perhaps not coincidentally all five justices appointed by conservative governments voted to uphold what one might otherwise have thought a very socialist plan. Four of the ten justices appointed by the 1947–1948 Socialist government thought it an unconstitutional taking.

As the land reform case suggests, Japanese courts have not traditionally viewed constitutional challenges under the takings clause sympathetically.

In eminent domain cases, they have generally required only that the government have a plan for providing reasonable compensation. According to the 1953 case, compensation paid with hyperinflated money is still reasonable. Because the facts of the case are so egregious, however, one might reasonably ask whether the Supreme Court today would still find the same scheme constitutional.

In zoning challenges, courts have asked whether the restrictions reasonably furthered a valid public policy. If they did, the courts require no compensation. Consider two illustrations. Since 1969, Yuriko Nakasako had been running a motel. Called the Yuriko Car Hotel, hers was not quite what Americans would envision. Discreet in the extreme, she ran a motel where each room had its own private garage and was accessible only through a door not visible to the outside.

In 1972, the local assembly decided (under the national statute governing adult entertainment) to ban all motels with attached private garages from her neighborhood, effective October 1973. Nakasako ignored the rule, continued to operate as before, and argued that the zoning change was an uncompensated taking. The court disagreed. Motels with private garages functioned largely as avenues for illicit sexual liaisons, it explained. The assembly had a valid reason based on public policy to limit them, it wrote a regulation sensibly related to that reason, and it did not exceed the scope necessary to do what it needed to do. Given the reasonableness of the restriction, Nakasako could not demand compensation.[31]

Or consider the dispute over the new Tokyo airport at Narita. At 3 A.M. on the morning of May 6, 1977, police approached two steel towers that protestors had built at the ends of runways. They wore helmets and carried shields, water cannons, and tear gas. The protestors, most from the Japan Revolutionary Communist League, knew the police were coming and had been mobilizing through the night. When the police finally attacked, some threw rocks and Molotov cocktails. Others tried to beat the police with steel bars. The battle lasted hours, but by noon the next day, the police had reached and demolished the towers.

Nonetheless, skirmishes (involving eventually up to 4,000 police and nearly as many protestors) continued for several days. Many of those involved were blinded, burned, or otherwise injured. One protestor—a medic in the protestors' field hospital—was killed, apparently shot in the back of the head at close range with a tear gas canister.

The towers themselves were ramshackle affairs. The government had planned to open the new airport on March 30, 1978, and the fringe left had made opposition to it the cause of the day. To stop training flights into and out of the airport, they had posted towers at the end of the runways. Crucial to the legal questions involved, the towers violated local zoning rules.

Both in the government's initial (preattack) suit to enjoin the towers and in the protestors' later (postattack) suit for damages, the protestors contested the constitutionality of the zoning. They owned the land. With the land, they owned the air above it (Civil Code, §207). As the zoning statute limited their rights to that air space without compensation, it violated the constitutional ban on uncompensated takings.

Again, the court disagreed. The government could properly set reasonable limits on what individuals could do with their property. Given the public need for the airport, the importance of flight safety, and the limited scope of the restrictions, the ban on towers harmed the neighbors only by amounts that a government could properly demand of its citizens. Accordingly it did not need to compensate the neighbors.[32]

F. Recordation
1. The Statute

If one buys real estate in Japan, one can enforce one's interest against third parties by recording the purchase.[33] As discussed below, in form the system is a "race" regime; as enforced, it is "race-notice." If one rents land and puts a building on it, one can enforce the leasehold against third parties (such as purchasers of the land) by registering the house (Land and House Lease Act (LHLA), §10).[34] And if one rents a house (or an apartment), one can enforce the leasehold against third-party purchasers even if one never registers it (LHLA, §31).

2. Race

At stake was piece of mountain land. The village had long held it in common but, in 1948, sold it to Tsuguyoshi Hara. He, in turn, sold it to defendant Ōtsu. Ōtsu duly recorded his purchase. In fact, however, the Kimura family had been using the land continuously since 1895. That year Kyūshirō Kimura had bought the neighboring parcel and had mistakenly concluded that his new plot included the tract Hara eventually bought from the village a half-century later. Hisashirō passed the land to Aijirō Kimura, and Aijirō passed it to Keikichi Kimura. Since the Kimuras assumed all along that they owned the land, they never recorded what would otherwise have been valid title by adverse possession. When Ōtsu sued in

1972 to evict them, they lost. According to the court, even successors in interest to claimants by adverse possession must record their interests to prevail against a later buyer who records.[35]

3. Race-Notice

As in many American jurisdictions, Japanese courts have never had the heart to enforce their race statute by its terms. Instead, through judicial interpretation they have effectively converted it into a race-notice regime: he who records first may usually win, but often not against a prior unrecorded claim of which he has notice.

Iseji Nagano, for example, had bought a plot of forest land from Sadayoshi Ōkubo's father in 1927. Critically, he failed to record the purchase. Later he quarreled with Katsuji Takahashi, who discovered Nagano's earlier failure. Itching for revenge, Takahashi paid Ōkubo a small sum, in return for which Ōkubo sold him the land his father had already sold Nagano. His purchase complete, Takahashi recorded his transaction and sued to evict Nagano.

By the express terms of the Japanese statute, Takahashi would seem to win. To the Supreme Court, however, his scheme stank. It violated, the court reasoned, the "public order and good morals" of section 90 of the Civil Code (see subsection 3.I.D.4). His purchase void, Takahashi lost, and Nagano could keep his forest.[36]

II. Landlord-Tenant Law
A. Introduction

It is a common enough sight in Tokyo. In the middle of the block stands a Hermes and Gucci boutique. A few buildings away is a shack. The shack can hardly cover more than 400 square feet and probably dates from the early postwar years. For a roof, it has two simple sheets of rusted corrugated steel. At one time, its walls were creosoted wood, but they have long since rotted through. To keep out the rain, someone has nailed corrugated steel to the sides, too.

The jarring juxtaposition results directly from Japanese law. We all know the problems that rent control caused in New York and Santa Monica. In Japan, landlord-tenant law is different in form, but no less disastrous in effect. The shacks next to Hermes boutiques, the virtual absence of comfortably sized rental units, the use of large nonrefundable deposits by landlords, the extraordinarily long commutes, the role of the mob in evicting tenants—these are not the cause of Japan's housing problem. They are

37

merely evidence of it. The cause lies instead in a legal regime that prevents landlords and tenants from negotiating fixed-term leases.

B. The Law

By judicial interpretation, almost all leases in Japan—no matter how many recitals to the contrary—give the tenant an interest close to a life estate.[37] If a lessee puts a building on rented land, for example, a court will renew the lease for as long as the building stands (LHLA, §5). Regardless of what the contract may say, the lessor will be able to refuse to renew only if he can show "just cause" (LHLA, §6)—a right courts interpret narrowly. If a lessee rents a house or an apartment, the lessor may again refuse to renew only if he can show "just cause" (LHLA, §§26–28). If the rent deviates from market rates over the course of a long tenancy, either party can demand (unless they have agreed to the contrary) an adjustment (LHLA, §§11, 32).

The plaintiff had lived in the building until 1974, when he moved to a new house in Kobe. He wanted to rent his original house, but only temporarily. His son would marry soon, and he wanted him to be able to use it when he did. Accordingly the plaintiff negotiated a two-year lease with the defendant for ¥50,000 a month. He explicitly told the defendant that he wanted his son to use this house when he married; that this meant that he could probably rent it only five years; and that at the end of those five years, he wanted the defendant out. To all this, the defendant expressly agreed.

In 1979, the plaintiff's son finished graduate school and took a job with the Osaka government. It was time for him to marry, so the plaintiff asked the defendant to leave. The defendant, however, liked where he was and refused. When the plaintiff sued, the court looked not to the terms to which the two had expressly agreed, but to the extent to which they each "needed" the house. "While we cannot deny that the plaintiff needs to use this building," it reasoned, "his need is not greater than the defendant's. Accordingly, the plaintiff has not yet shown just cause" to evict the defendant. Nonetheless, the plaintiff wanted his house badly enough that he offered to pay the defendant to move. The plaintiff made ¥345,000 per month and the defendant made ¥250,000; recall that the rent had been ¥50,000 a month (later raised to ¥60,000). If the plaintiff would pay the defendant ¥5 million, the court declared, it would let him evict the defendant after all.[38]

K.K. Gotō Building owned a building in Roppongi, the high-fashion night-life section of Tokyo (and some 800 yards from the former Manchukuo embassy). In 1969, it rented space for a disco to Mandarin Trading, K.K. In the lease, it included two clauses of moment: (1) that Mandarin would not change its representative directors without notifying it and (2) that Mandarin would not modify the building without its advance consent. In fact, in 1981 Mandarin changed its representative directors without notifying Gotō and, a few years later, made major alterations to the building over Gotō's adamant objections.

Gotō sued to evict. It was not just that Mandarin had violated the lease. Mandarin had several times been ordered to close the disco for breaking adult entertainment law. Moreover, the building itself—dating as it did from 1956—was a catastrophe waiting to happen. In their inspection, government engineers had given it their worst rating possible. It would not withstand earthquakes. It had neither appropriate plumbing nor appropriate wiring. It was a fire trap for the residential units on the upper stories. It no longer had an elevator, as the city inspectors had ordered it shut down. Gotō apparently met all the contractual terms for terminating the lease. It was high time to do so, it reasoned, and demolish the building.

To the court, Gotō lacked the right to evict. If it wanted Mandarin out, it would have to pay it besides. The contract included no such requirement. The court simply invented it from whole cloth, just as it had for the father who wanted his house back for his son. If Gotō wanted to evict Mandarin, it would first need to pay Mandarin ¥400 million.[39]

C. The Problems

Effectively Japanese courts give every tenant the right to stay in a unit as long as he likes, provided only that he pay rent at a rate a court approves. The result is not quite rent control. The courts do approve rent increases, though how closely they track the market remains unclear. At least according to some, they approve them only haphazardly. Economist Yukio Noguchi, for instance, claims that "actual rents are left at irrationally low levels."[40] To the extent Noguchi is right, the Japanese regime will in fact create the usual rent-control problems.

Yet in crucial ways, the Japanese regime is much worse than rent control. Ordinary rent control one can at least evade through condominium conversions. The Japanese regime is far harder to avoid and rigidly prevents owners from putting land to its highest use.[41] The most painful evidence comes from commuting times: on average, Tokyo residents commute to work over an hour each way.[42] Despite that trek, they still do not find

Table 2.1 Indexed Housing Patterns: An International Comparison

	Population Density	Rental Charge	Household Income	Rental Unit Size
Hong Kong	1,159	123	59	133
Madrid	268	82	100	200
Taibei	172	75	79	166
Seoul	171	56	63	150
Tokyo	100	100	100	100
Toronto	83	85	130	172
Milan	58	60	102	133
New York	49	53–71	120	250–333
Sydney	43	60	102	166

Source: Nihon jūtaka sentaa, ed., *Jūkyohi no kokusai hikaku* [An International Comparison of Living Costs] (Tokyo: Nihon jūtaku sentaa, 1992), 44.

large rental apartments. Even residents of Hong Kong (with eleven times the population density) rent bigger units.

The binding constraint in Japan is not the high population-land ratio. That ratio is higher in Tokyo than in most American cities, but hardly high in international terms. Several cities with roughly comparable incomes are more crowded, yet supply cheaper and bigger rental units (table 2.1). According to the National Land Agency, the twenty-three wards of Tokyo have enough land to house—at 900 square feet per household, with parks and wide streets—not just the present 8 million people, but 5 million more besides.[43]

Neither is the binding constraint the earthquake risk. There was once a day when that risk stopped construction firms from building skyscrapers in Tokyo. That day is several decades past. Neither is the constraint the building codes. With a mean height of 2.7 stories, Tokyo stands at only 40 percent of its authorized capacity.[44]

Rather, the constraint that binds is the legal regime that prevents landlords and tenants from negotiating fixed-term leases. Consider its predictable effects. First, landlords find it harder to redevelop their property. If they think they can make better use of the land in another form, they will want to redevelop. To do so, they need the present tenants to leave. In Japan, however, they cannot evict. To redevelop, they will need either to wait till the tenants leave voluntarily or to pay them extremely large amounts.[45]

Second, landlords are less likely to improve existing rental units. Unless a tenant leaves, they cannot make major renovations, and they cannot make him leave. As a result, they can do only those renovations that their tenant will welcome, and a low-income tenant will not welcome upscale renovations that move rents upscale besides.

Third, once a tenant dies or moves, a landlord will be more likely to keep the unit off the market. In 1993, 9.8 percent of Japanese housing units were empty.[46] That figure obviously did not include the *potential* units developers might have built on parking lots and vacant land, and "[e]ven in the urbanized areas," observes Noguchi, "plenty of land is still underused or left idle."[47] Over half of the empty units, moreover, were ones where the landlords were not looking for tenants. These units were often on prime real estate: the mean walk from a vacant unit to a train station was 9.6 minutes. Landlords kept these units empty because they wanted eventually to renovate them or to redevelop the property.[48] In an unregulated regime, they could have rented them while they prepared to redevelop. In Japan, if they did so, those new tenants could have held up the entire project. Rather than run that risk, landlords kept the units vacant.

Fourth, landlords charge huge up-front fees. In effect, a tenant in Japan obtains not just a right to use the unit month to month, but also an option to continue that use indefinitely. Consequently landlords couple term payments for the month-to-month right with a lump-sum charge for the option. For rental apartments, Tokyo landlords typically charge two months' rent as a refundable deposit and an extra two months' rent as a nonrefundable fee. For rental land (if one can even find a landlord willing to rent development land), a "renter" will need to pay as an up-front "rental" fee a whopping 60–90 percent of the sale value of the property.[49]

Fifth, most developers supply only rental units that tenants will use for short periods. New rental units in Japan, as Noguchi put it, are almost all "for students, single persons, or couples without children who will not occupy the [unit] for a very long period."[50] Other than the apartments for the foreign market, these rental units are minuscule: in 1995, new privately owned houses averaged 1,478 square feet, new condominiums 975 square feet, but new rental units only 562 square feet.[51] Of the 10.8 million households living in the private rental units, 5.1 million were single individuals, and 2.8 million were childless couples. Although such households were only 44 percent of all households nationally, they were nearly 70 percent of the households in private rental units. Conversely, although households with four or more members were nearly 40 percent of the national total,

41

they were barely 17 percent of the households in private rental units.[52] Because most Japanese eventually marry and have children, by supplying only minuscule units landlords ensure that tenants stay only a few years.

Conclusion

Akira Saitō had a theory or two. He knew he was right and had written several books explaining why. Casting himself as a "scholar of sexual sensibilities," in the early 1930s he published *The Simple Principles of the Copulation of Mind and Matter, The Errors of Theoretical Physics,* and *The Sun Is Not a Hot Mass.* Generous besides, he sent free copies to what was then the Tokyo Imperial University. The ungrateful university, however, declined to enter them in its library. When it refused to apologize and refused even to let him publicly debate the faculty, Saitō sued.

To the Tokyo Court of Appeals, Saitō had no case. "No matter what type of book he writes, no matter how good it might be, no matter how innovative he may seem," explained the court, "a private individual does not have a legal right to demand that the Tokyo Imperial University keep a book he donates." Saitō had framed his claim in tort, but in fact the basic issue lay in property. A government institution it may be, but the Tokyo Imperial University owned its land, its lecture halls, its library. Consistent with that property right, it could properly exclude. That is all it did here, and to the court, that was fine.[53]

As Saitō's case suggests, in most areas Japanese courts define and enforce the right to control scarce resources. They let people who hold those rights exclude others (and their books). They let them keep the returns to any investments they make. They let them transfer any interests they hold. Such basic property rights are fundamental to economic growth. With exceptions to be sure, Japanese courts define and enforce them.

3 CONTRACTS

By tradition, Japanese contracts could be short:

I Gohei, Kobayashi village, permanently convey to you my son Tora. I have surely received in exchange and deposited 50 *me* in silver.

Should Tora escape, I shall locate and return him. If I do not find him, I shall procure a replacement for you.

You should enroll Tora in your own religion.

I hereby produce this document as provided above.

[Promisor:] Kobayashi village, parent Gohei

Second day, third month, 1673

To: Kyūemon, of Shimo-kawarabayashi[1]

Or they could be long:

I hereby agree to send my daughter Riku, age 17, to your establishment to work as a prostitute. She shall work for a period of nine years, from the 19th day of the eleventh month of this year of the monkey to the 19th day of the eleventh month of the year of the serpent. In exchange for this work, I have surely received 45 *kanme* in silver currency.

No matter what happens, I shall not ask for time off for Riku during this period.

Neither I nor anyone else has any objection to this arrangement.

If you find Riku unsuited for service as a prostitute, you may assign her elsewhere as a servant. Should Riku show bad manners or act rudely, you may punish her as you see fit.

Should Riku steal anything or escape, you need not search for her. Instead, I shall immediately search for her, make good to you the stolen items, and return her to you.

Provided that Riku is released from service at the end of the above term, I shall not object to either of the following measures: first, that in order to raise silver currency you pledge her as security for any amount of silver; or second, that you transfer her to any business establishment in any province. . . .

And on it went for eight more elaborate clauses before ending with the standard:

Whereupon as a record for later occasions, I hereby produce this loan document as provided above.

[Promisors:] Guardian, Hisa
(wife of the late Rikitarō, Nishi-furukawa-chō)
Daughter of the above and laborer, Riku
(prostitute a.k.a. Ōzan, of the Hozenya, Yoriai-chō)
Eleventh month, 1836[2]

Japanese have for centuries used contracts to transfer economically valuable goods and services. The point is important, for to foster economic growth, the law will need not just to define property rights (chapter 2). It must also let people transfer them.[3] As with the law of property, modern Japanese contract law follows the late-nineteenth-century Prussian-based Civil Code. By largely (there are exceptions to be sure) enforcing voluntary agreements to transfer such rights, it facilitates welfare-increasing transfers.

With some obvious formal differences (the absence of a consideration requirement, for one), Japanese contract law tracks much of the substance of U.S. contract law. To facilitate that comparison, in section I we explore issues of consideration (subsection A), offer and acceptance (subsection B), formalities (subsection C), defenses (subsection D), and remedies (subsection E). We then discuss the role that contracts play in the business environment (section II) and examine the impact that the legal restraints on private contracts have had on medical malpractice law (section III).

I. The Law
A. Consideration
1. Its Absence

As in many, if not most, advanced capitalist countries, parties to a contract in Japan need no consideration to bind themselves. According to the Civil Code (§549),[4] they can enforce their promises, money or no, reliance or no, promissory estoppel or no. For them, a gratuitous promise is as good as any other.

It was love at first sight. Or at least it was lust. Hanako Otsuyama was tending bar in the Ginza, and Tarō Kōno was on his way home. He saw her, fell for her, and begged her for a date. Several dates later they turned their romance into an affair. Love is nothing if not indiscreet, however, and Kōno eventually gave Otsuyama his bank card. Worse, he gave her some film and asked her to have prints made, and the prints showed him with his wife. A year into the affair and contrary to all his protestations, Otsuyama

now found he had been married all along. Faced with his full
plicity, she promptly went to the bank and gutted his accou
¥2.8 million.

When Kōno sued for the money, the court let Otsuyama keep it. Giving
her the card, it explained, was equivalent to promising her cash. Within a
sexual relationship, if a man gives a woman a cash card, she can reasonably infer that he authorizes her to withdraw money when she wants, and
a gift under Japanese law is as good as a bargained-for exchange. Unless
he says otherwise, in giving her the card he promises her the money she
wants.[5]

2. Renegotiation and Fraud

If the opinion in *Kōno v. Otsuyama* seems odd, it was not the issue of consideration that made the court do it. Even absent a consideration
requirement, the court could have held the bar maid liable by proposing a
less dubious psychology about what philandering men intend. And even
with a consideration requirement, it could have held her not liable by in-
terpreting the transfer of the card either as payment for sexual services or
as an immediate gift of cash. In exploring the concept of consideration, the
interesting analytic questions less concern cases like this than issues of
how Japanese courts handle two real problems American courts address
through the consideration rule: opportunistic renegotiation and fraudulent
claims.

The renegotiation problem is the one sailors posed in classic form
when—part way through their voyage—they refused to work unless their
employer raised their pay.[6] If he agreed, but then later reneged, American
courts could refuse to enforce the raise. Formally they did so on the ground
that the sailors' preexisting duty to work obviated the consideration. Sub-
stantively they did so to prevent the sailors from holding up the firm in the
middle of the contract. Absent a consideration rule, Japanese courts face
the same substantive problem without the same formal solution. To deal
with the problem, they manipulate doctrines like duress instead, as the discussion in subsection D.4.c shows.

The fraudulent claims problem derives from the fact that real people
only rarely give away their money with no thought for an exchange. As a
result, any court that freely enforces donative promises invites two problems. First, it gives people an incentive to lie and falsely claim that others
promised them gifts (a particularly vexing problem when the putative
donor is dead). Second, it raises the risk that a court faced with a formally

45

donative gift will enforce it without noticing the implied reciprocal promise.

Japanese courts deal with lying claimants by refusing to enforce a donative promise unless in writing (Civil Code, §550), a requirement they do not impose on bargained-for promises. They deal with the second problem (implied reciprocal promises) by converting what the parties formally designated a donative promise into an explicit bargained-for exchange.

To see this second judicial strategy, take the husband who promised his wife land, but died before registering the transfer. Because he died with the title, some of the promised land passed to his daughter by an earlier marriage. When the stepmother asked the daughter to record the transfer, the daughter and her husband instead revoked the gift. The stepmother, they told the court, had been robbing the father blind. Indeed, the stepmother had refused to let his doctors treat him, had stopped his nurse from giving him his heart medicine, and had deliberately tried to poison him. The court agreed that their claims would entitle them to revoke the gift if true, for the stepmother would have violated her implicit promise to care for her husband. It just did not believe their claims were true.[7]

If matters turn bad enough, courts let donors revoke gifts made years before. When he left home, claims Professor Robert Cooter, his father took him aside and gave him advice: "Son, you only get two chances in life to get rich: once when you're born, and once when you're married. Don't blow your second chance." Matsuko Kōno did not blow her second chance. In 1919, she married into the richest family in the village. As her mother-in-law was chronically ill, she cared tenderly (the court so found) both for her parents-in-law and for all eight of her husband's siblings. Among the latter, she was particularly fond of young Saburō. She doted on him. She nursed him when he fell sick. She paid his bills when he went to medical school. She befriended his wife when he married. And because she had no children of her own, she hoped to spend her last years with him and his family. By all outward signs, they seemed to hope so, too—seemed, that is, until she gave Saburō everything she owned in 1968.

Once Saburō had title to Matsuko's assets, the relationship unraveled. When a former family servant asked Matsuko for some wood to fix his roof, she agreed. Saburō, however, went to the police and told them that she and the servant had stolen wood. Matsuko, already in her mid-seventies, found herself hauled into the police station for interrogation. Because Matsuko had given Saburō everything she owned, she now depended on him for a monthly allowance. By 1972, he had quit paying. When she begged her neighbors for loans, he warned them that he would not pay her debts. When she went to a village ceremony in honor of her husband, he entered her house (he had title, after all) and took her telephone. When she checked into the hospital, he encircled her house with barbed wire.

Enough already, said the court. Matsuko (or her heir, as she died during the trial) could revoke the gift. She had given Saburō her property in the context of a continuing relationship, and he had breached that relationship. She had given him her assets with the thought that he would love and care for her in return, the court implied, and he had accepted the assets knowing she thought he would. In behaving as badly as he did, he breached the promises he implicitly made in taking the gift.[8]

B. Offer, Acceptance, and Third Parties

Issues of offer and acceptance seldom present major conundrums in ordinary business contracts, whether in the United States or in Japan. The Japanese rules on point are relatively straightforward: a sales contract arises when A agrees to sell something for a price and B agrees to buy it at that price (Civil Code, §555); if A sets a time limit on his offer, it expires after that time (§521), but if he sets no limit, he may revoke it after a reasonable time (§524); if B sends A an "acceptance" giving different terms from those in A's offer, the "acceptance" is not an acceptance, but a new offer (§528).[9]

When conundrums arise, they do so in very odd situations. In 1961, Hitomi Okazaki was nineteen years old and working evenings in her mother's coffee shop. Because she worked late, she sometimes went home by cab. If Masaaki Nishio of the Nankai Taxi Company drove her home, however, he often let her ride free. Increasingly she called only Nankai and asked specifically for Nishio when she did.

On April 5, Okazaki went to visit a friend in a hospital. At 10 P.M., she wanted to go home, so she called Nankai and asked for Nishio. When he arrived, she hopped in the front seat. Nishio left the meter off and drove her home. Once there, though, he suggested they go for a drive. It was too late, she replied, but he took her to an abandoned army base anyway and raped her.

Okazaki sued Nankai in contract. She could have sued in tort, of course. Yet the independence with which cab drivers do their work and the lack of any supervisory negligence by Nankai probably made proving respondeat superior hard (see subsection 4.I.E.2). Okazaki argued instead that Nankai had promised to transport her home safely and, by subjecting her to a rape, had breached that promise.

To the court, the problem with Okazaki's contractual theory was factual: whether Okazaki, given how she had hoped Nishio would again cheat Nankai of her fare and sneak her a free ride, had made any contract with Nankai. The court held she had. When she asked Nankai for a cab and Nankai agreed to send one to the hospital, they entered a contract. That she intended to renege on her duty to pay did not obviate the contract, and Nankai's duty of safe carriage followed.[10]

Courts enforce contracts for the benefit of a third party. Suppose S sells a car to B. If S owes money to third party T, S may want to have B pay the price to T. If S and B explicitly note those terms in the sales contract, then when T agrees to the contract, T will acquire an independent right against B for the purchase price (Civil Code, §537). B can, however, assert against T its defenses against S (Civil Code, §539).

C. Form and Interpretation

Japanese courts enforce neither a general statute of frauds nor a parol evidence rule. Instead, they let parties sue on oral agreements and quarrel about supposed side agreements that contradict any contractual text they do have.

Like the lack of a developed set of evidentiary rules (see subsection 6.I.B.8), the fact that Japanese courts stand willing to referee these swearing contests stems from the absence of juries. Courts in the United States maintain evidentiary rules because they cannot trust juries to know up from down. They use the Statute of Frauds and the parol evidence rule for the same reason—they simply cannot assume these amateurs will get it right. Judges, by contrast, have heard it all before. They understand that sensible business executives usually put important terms in writing. More important, even when sensible business executives do not, judges generally understand the importance of ex ante incentives: that the world will usually be a better place if parties put most important agreements in writing and realize that courts will hold them to that text.

Because U.S. courts cannot trust their fact-finders to understand all this, they ban lawyers from making certain arguments to the jury. The rules of evidence, the Statute of Frauds, and the parol evidence rule are all variations on that same phenomenon. With sophisticated judges handling all the issues, Japanese courts do not need those blanket rules (though even they retain some writing requirements; see subsection A.2). Rather, they can leave the issue open in form and trust a judge to take the sensible course in practice.

D. Defenses
1. Indefinite Contracts

Although Japanese courts will refuse to enforce a contract if too indefinite, they work hard to avoid that result. For example, if the parties do not specify the quality of a good the promisor should deliver, the courts will mandate intermediate-quality goods (Civil Code, §401(a)). If they specify interest, but not the rate, the courts will order 5 percent interest (Civil Code, §§404–405). If they specify several ways to perform, but not who will choose among them, the courts will let the obligor choose (Civil Code, §406). If they do not specify the time of performance, the courts will look to the time of the obligee's demand (Civil Code, §412(c)) or, in sales contracts, require payment upon delivery (Civil Code, §573). If they do not specify who bears the cost of performance, the courts will place the costs on the obligor (Civil Code, §485). If they agree on an approximate, but not exact, price, the courts may find that approximate is definite enough.[11] And if they simply agree to talk price later, the courts may conclude that they intended to sell at a reasonable price, set that reasonable price, and enforce the contract.[12]

If anything is indefinite, one might think it is matters of the soul. Yet to the Tokyo District Court, even a contract to pray for all eternity was enforceable. Several generations back the head of the Sakabe house had given land to a local temple. In exchange, the temple had promised to say prayers in perpetuity for the family's ancestors. Why the temple quit praying the court does not say, but come 1913 the new family head decided to sue on the promise. Affairs of the heart were beyond its power to dictate, the court admitted. It would not try to determine whether the priests said their prayers with feeling. Affairs of form, however, were issues it knew how to adjudicate. It could and would require the temple to recite its promised prayers (with feeling or no), to make its ritual offerings, and to light the requisite incense.[13]

2. Mistake and Changed Circumstances

a. Mistake. By section 95 of the Civil Code, a mistake underlying an agreement—if sufficiently basic—renders the contract void unless the mistaken party is grossly negligent. Shōkichi Yoshida agreed to buy a horse

49

from Satoharu Hashimoto, but in part because Hashimoto said the horse was pregnant. Yoshida believed him, bought the horse, and apparently found she was simply fat. He sued to rescind. For reasons not clear, on appeal he did not claim fraud or guarantee, but instead argued mistake. Think of it as reverse–*Sherwood v. Walker*[14] for a horse: apparently, rather than contracting for what was a pregnant cow, thinking she was fat and barren, the parties contracted for what was a fat and barren horse, thinking she was pregnant. As in *Sherwood,* the contract was void, and the disadvantaged party (here the buyer) could recover.[15]

Or consider the more recent dispute between Miyamoto sangyō, K.K. and K.K. Nakagawa sōgyō. Miyamoto sold scrap steel. Business was bad, so it wanted to enter the hotel business—but not just any segment of the market. It wanted to enter what in Japan passes as the "love hotel" market—the by-the-hour hotels. Having no experience, Miyamoto decided to buy the existing hotel Angel from Nakagawa. Miyamoto paid one-tenth down and then discovered that it would not be able to operate the hotel on an hourly rental basis. Prefectural regulations prohibited hourly rental hotels within 200 meters of schools, libraries, and hospitals, and Angel was 175 meters from a hospital. Nakagawa was apparently grandfathered, but the government would not license a new owner. Miyamoto rescinded. The court let it do so, inter alia, on the ground that the mistake went to a basic element of the contract.[16]

b. Changed Circumstances. Only rarely do Japanese courts let a party escape its contractual duties because of changed circumstances. To do so, according to the classic judicial formula, it must show (1) that circumstances have changed drastically since it made the contract, (2) that it did not foresee and could not have foreseen the change, (3) that it was not responsible for the change, and (4) that enforcing the contract would egregiously violate notions of truth and equity.[17]

The case that established the formula concerned a lease to a modest house in Osaka. In late 1943, the tenant had agreed to vacate it by the end of 1944. When the landlord tried to evict the tenant after the war, the tenant cited changed circumstances. The court agreed that the circumstances had changed, but refused to let the tenant stay (a particularly surprising result given the general pro-tenant judicial bias, see section 2.II). In late 1943, Osaka tenants could still find plenty of housing. By the end of the war, Allied bombers had leveled the city. Neither party could have foreseen the resulting shortage, and obviously enough, neither side caused it. Crucially, however, the tenant had simply gambled and lost, and to the court, enforcing a gamble was not unfair. Imperfectly informed as they may have been, the parties had rationally made a deal. The fourth requirement for voiding a contract (that enforcing it would violate notions of truth and equity) was not met, and the court would now enforce the deal.[18]

3. Impracticability

Japanese courts maintain a detailed set of rules to handle questions of impracticability. If performance is obviously impossible from the outset (e.g., a promise to deliver Martian rocks), it is void. If performance was initially possible and becomes impracticable for reasons attributable to the obligor, then (absent an agreement to the contrary) courts will let the obligee cancel the contract (Civil Code, §543). If performance of a duty to deliver a specified good becomes impracticable for reasons not attributable to the obligor (seller), then (absent an agreement to the contrary) courts will place the risk of loss on the obligee (buyer). In all other cases of impracticability (again absent agreement), courts will place the risk of loss on the obligor (seller) (Civil Code, §§534, 536).

It was June 5, 1945, two months before the Bomb. The Yamanaka Aircraft Company needed money to stay alive. It was not alone, of course. With the economy a mess, everyone needed money, and no one had it. Unable to find funds through ordinary channels, Yamanaka turned to Okuzō Kobayashi. At least Kobayashi owned 40 packages of mosquito-repellent incense coils. If Yamanaka would find a buyer for his coils, he would lend it the proceeds. Toward the goal of finding a final buyer, Yamanaka contracted to buy them from Kobayashi for ¥24,000. Ten days later Allied bombers incinerated the coils. Kobayashi's successor in interest sued Yamanaka for the purchase price, and the court ordered Yamanaka to pay. As the coils were specified goods, their loss fell on the buyer.[19]

4. Public Policy

a. Immorality. Predictably enough, Japanese courts refuse to enforce contracts that they believe violate "the public order or good morals" (Civil Code, §90); equally predictably, what they think violates that standard is sometimes obscure. For example, prewar courts did enforce contracts for prostitution. It was not a job blessed "in the sutras," the Supreme Court noted, but it was a job explicitly allowed by statute.[20] They also enforced a brothel's claim for any money it had advanced a prostitute. Simultaneously, however, they refused to enforce the employment contract where the prostitute agreed to work at the brothel to repay that advance.

Such a multiyear contract, the courts explained, constrained her freedom too egregiously.[21] Similarly, if A agreed to marry B, but then changed his or her mind, courts would often let B sue A for damages. If either of them was already married to someone else at the time they entered the contract, however, the courts declared the contract void.[22]

In some cases, the distinctions could become subtle indeed. Everyone agreed in court that Chūjirō Shimizu came home one day in November 1904 to find his wife in bed with Harukichi Onda—apparently known in the community as a shiftless philanderer. They told different stories about what happened next. According to Onda, Shimizu grabbed a butcher knife and threatened to kill him unless he promised to pay ¥20. He promised to pay. According to Shimizu's witness, things happened more deliberately. Later that day Shimizu visited Hansaburō Ozawa to discuss what to do. Shimizu wanted to leave his wife, needed money for child support, and thought Onda should pay. Ozawa then relayed the problem to another acquaintance, Ichitarō Nakamura, and through their intermediation, Onda eventually agreed to pay ¥20 in four monthly installments with 20 percent interest. For reasons the court does not detail (though P. T. Barnum's motto does come to mind), Nakamura then agreed to guarantee Onda's debt. Onda reneged (of course), Shimizu sued Onda on the note, and—Onda being broke—Shimizu then sued Nakamura on the guarantee.

Nakamura raised two defenses. First, he argued duress: Onda only agreed to pay when Shimizu attacked him with a knife. If true, the story would have made a valid defense (see subsection c), but the court did not believe it was true. Second, he argued "public order and good morals": Onda promised the money as the price for sex with Shimizu's wife, and contracts to sell adulterous sex violated public policy. Not quite, said the court. If Onda had promised ¥20 for the right to commit adultery, the promise would have been unenforceable. But Onda did not promise ¥20 for the right. He promised ¥20 to apologize for an earlier wrong, and apologies are fine. As guarantor, Nakamura was now liable.[23]

    b. Unconscionability: Harsh Clauses; Choice of Law and Arbitration. Much as in the United States, notions of unconscionability add considerable uncertainty to the law. On the one hand, the basic rule remains that courts enforce contracts. Indeed, they can sometimes take the rule quite far. The Sanwa Shipping Company, for example, had a policy of refusing to pay for any unusually valuable goods it lost unless the shipper told it about the goods in advance. In 1952, Tsujikichi K.K. shipped a package of valuable silk with Sanwa without disclosing its contents. While the Sanwa driver was on his delivery route, someone stole the silk. Sanwa pleaded its standard policy—but had no evidence that Tsujikichi had ever agreed to the terms. Instead, its loss limitation was merely part of the form contract it had posted on the wall. That was notice enough, the court said, and enforced its terms.[24]

On the other hand, from time to time courts also ignore contractual provisions they do not like. Usually they argue either that the clauses violate public policy or that the parties did not intend what they wrote. When insurance companies try to limit their liability, for example, they run the risk that a court will ignore the limit.[25] Similarly, take what was a typical lease at the turn of the century. Commonly a person rented land and then built a house on the plot. When the tenant did so, the lease term raised obvious problems of opportunism. If the court enforced the contract, the landlord could hold up the tenant for the value of the house (e.g., insist on rent in the renewal contract so large as to represent most of the value of the house). If the court instead ignored the lease, by building a house the tenant could convert a rental contract into something closer to fee simple. Whether the courts recognized the second risk is unclear, but they thought they knew the first when they saw it. Kanzaburō Namekawa rented a plot of land in Kobe from Ichimatsu Fujita in 1899 for three years. Shortly before the lease expired, he build a two-story building on it. When Namekawa sued to evict, the Kobe District Court refused to let him. Fujita could stay.[26]

The Kobe court's reaction was standard, and it contributed to the disastrous real estate market in Japan today (see section 2.II). Had the courts been willing to evict tenants at the end of the leases, the immediate defendants would have suffered large losses. The market, however, would have corrected itself as people who wanted to build houses began negotiating fee purchases or longer-term leases. Because the courts instead ignored the lease terms, they killed the market for fixed-term rentals. Landlords would no longer rent on fixed-term contracts at the market rental value, for they had no assurance that they could retrieve the property at the end of the lease. Instead, they either took the property off the rental market or coupled the rent with stratospheric nonrefundable deposits.

Notwithstanding unconscionability concerns, Japanese courts typically enforce both clauses choosing foreign law and clauses mandating arbitration. By statute, parties to a contract may generally choose the law that will govern their disputes.[27] Simultaneously (though not by statute) they may also elect to submit any disputes to arbitration, even by foreign arbitral fora.[28] There are exceptions: real estate (and all registrable personalty) is always governed by the law of situs, torts (and all unjust enrichment claims) are always governed by the law of the place where the tortious act occurred, and domestic relations are governed by a broad set of special rules.[29]

Predictably, however, courts sometimes cite public policy to trump even these principles. Some courts apply Japanese labor law to employment contracts negotiated in the United States among Americans and picking U.S. law as the governing law, for example.[30] And in noncommercial contexts, the problem can be particularly acute. Alfred Brooks was an occupation lawyer assigned to the Tokyo war-crime trials. Reiko Yuzawa was a classical Japanese dance student who in the chaos of 1945 became a waitress. They met when Brooks stopped at her restaurant and soon started an affair.

In 1947, Brooks convinced Yuzawa to live with his family on the pretext of teaching his children dance. By 1948, she was pregnant, and he sent her away. After she gave birth to a son, Jōji, she sued Brooks in Jōji's name to establish paternity. Brooks argued that he was a Missouri citizen, that under Japanese choice of law rules Missouri law governed, and that Missouri law did not permit such paternity suits. Never mind, said the Tokyo District Court. Missouri law might indeed normally govern, but the notion that a court would deny a paternity suit was preposterous. Jōji could proceed.[31]

c. Fraud and Duress. According to section 96 of the Civil Code, one who agrees to a promise through fraud or duress may (absent an innocent third party) rescind the promise. The simplest cases are obvious. Take a dispute between two firms over a shipment (again) of mosquito-repellent incense coils. The representative of one of the firms agreed to settle the dispute by paying cash, but only after a mobster had (with the other firm's knowledge) yelled at him, sent violent threats, and pulled a knife. Theirs was not to reason why, the representative apparently (and reasonably) concluded. Theirs was but to pay or—well, Tennyson would not have phrased it thus, but theirs was but to pay or sleep with the fishes. The representative duly agreed to pay. When the other firm sued on that agreement, the court let the promisor refuse. Offers about sleeping with fishes are offers one cannot reasonably refuse, and offers one party cannot refuse are offers the other party cannot enforce in court.[32]

Or consider the wife who told her husband she wanted a divorce because she was too weak to do her work. Her husband tried to convince her

otherwise, but when she insisted, he agreed to the divorce, paid her
¥50,000, and promised to pay another ¥100,000. In fact, she had been
having an affair and wanted simply to live with her lover. When the ex-
husband discovered the lover, he refused to pay. She sued, and the court let
him keep his money. She had lied, and he would never have agreed to pay
the ¥150,000 if he had known of her lover. Having agreed out of fraud, he
could validly rescind.[33]

Duress can be ambiguous, of course, as threats of adverse publicity illustrate. Successful film director Kinji Fukasaku had patronized a basement
Kyoto bar for years. In 1979, the manager of the bar decided to have cosmetic surgery on her eyes and nose. Soon thereafter she and the director
found themselves alone in the bar, late at night. Exactly what happened the
court left unsaid, but in searching for the manager's lips, the director acci-
dentally banged her nose. In the ensuing confusion, some of the manager's
stitches came undone, and the silicone implant in her nose came unstuck.

The manager's mother visited the director to talk restitution, and he
agreed to pay ¥3 million. But the manager wanted more, much more. She
wanted ¥100 million, she declared, and if he refused, she would call her
friends at the scandal magazines. She had told about her love life with the
stars before, and she could tell about it again.

Fukasaku was busy. He was shooting the biggest movie of his career. He
called it *The Day of Resurrection,* and it had a plot to match the budget:
several spies would steal unkillable bacteria from an East German lab, but
crash their plane in the Alps; the bacteria would escape and circle the globe
on the trade winds; everyone everywhere (including the U.S. president,
played by Glenn Ford) would die, except a hardy few living at the South
Pole. When things looked as bad as could be for the Antarcticans, they
would turn worse still: a chill would send global temperatures plummeting
and trigger earthquakes around the world; the earthquakes would launch
the U.S. ICBMs against the Soviets; the Soviets would fire their missiles in
response—but the Soviets were known to have aimed some of their missiles
at Antarctica. Hence the climax: could an American press officer and a
Japanese scientist (in love with Olivia Hussey back at the South Pole) save
Antarctica from annihilation?[34]

Battleship Potemkin it was not, but it was a good bit better than what
its producer Haruki Kadokawa usually made. The next year, for example,
he would produce *Sailor Suit and Machine Gun,* remembered mainly for
the scene where a high school girl in a sailor outfit mows down gangsters
with a machine gun in slow motion, all the while mouthing "ecstasy."[35] In

any case, at ¥2.5 billion *Resurrection* had the biggest budget in Japanese film history. The last thing Fukasaku needed was a scandal about what he did, drunk, at 5:30 A.M. in a basement Kyoto bar. In exchange for the manager's agreement to keep quiet, he agreed to pay another ¥10 million. He then defaulted, and she sued. According to the Osaka High Court, her threats to tell all constituted duress. By section 96 of the Civil Code, he could properly refuse to pay.[36]

The interesting question is not only whether publicity constitutes duress, but also whether the case is about duress at all. Arguably the court was just enforcing the initial ¥3 million settlement. She had agreed to keep quiet, but now threatened to renege. Given her contractual duty of silence, an American court could have enforced the initial deal by noting that the second promise lacked consideration. Without a consideration rule, the Japanese court could not do that. By citing duress, however, it could accomplish the same result—it could prevent the manager from opportunistically renegotiating the initial bargain.

E. Remedies
1. Introduction

Suppose *S* contracts to sell steel to *B*. When the spot market price of steel falls, *B* rejects delivery. Under Japanese law, *S* has a choice. He can either (1) force *B* to accept the steel and sue for the contract price plus interest or (2) rescind the contract, sell the steel on the spot market at the lower price, and sue for his lost profits. Conversely suppose the spot price rises and *S* refuses to deliver. *B* has the analogous choice. He can either (1) sue for specific performance plus interest or (2) rescind, buy steel on the spot market at the higher price, and sue for the price difference.

This general remedial scheme raises at least the following issues of detail: exactly when can parties rescind, how much can a nonbreaching party collect in damages, and when can a party demand specific performance? Below we consider each, in turn, and conclude by discussing liquidated damages.

2. Rescission

Again, take contracting parties *S* and *B*. If *S* refuses to perform, subject to a variety of qualifications *B* can rescind. When *S* agrees to sell, but reneges because the spot market price has risen, his breach is clear enough. Yet other situations are less clear and raise the predictable issues of substantial performance. On those issues, Japanese courts usually take the sensible course. If B cannot use S's performance unless S performs completely, then when S performs partially, B may treat it as a breach and rescind. If nearly complete performance largely meets B's requirements, then when S performs partially, B may sue for the cost of cure, but not rescind. If the value to B of partial performance is linear to the extent of S's performance, then B may demand only damages proportional to the uncompleted portion of the contract.[37]

If B rescinds, courts will order a return to the precontractual status quo (Civil Code, §545(a)). Hence neither S nor B will need to follow the terms of the contract. If either has already delivered money or goods, he can demand their return. If the court-ordered return does not make a nonbreaching party whole, he can sue for expectation damages to boot (Civil Code, §545(c)).

Before rescinding a contract, B must formally demand that S perform and give him a reasonable time to do so (Civil Code, §541). How long he must give depends on the facts, but he can validly (even if counterfactually) assume that S has been preparing to perform all along.[38] Sometimes B can dispense with the reasonable time requirement entirely. Take Y.G. Maruichi shōkai. The hula hoop craze had hit Japanese shores on October 20, 1958 (at least so said the Osaka High Court). By mid-November, Maruichi needed at least 500 hoops a day. Dainichi claimed already to be making 2,000 a day, so it agreed to sell Maruichi 200 hoops daily beginning November 17. The day arrived, but no hoops. When Maruichi checked, it found that Dainichi had placed an order for hula-hoop-making machines, but had yet to make a single hoop itself. Without bothering to give Dainichi another chance to perform, Maruichi rescinded the contract.

The court agreed that Maruichi could rescind immediately. By the terms of the Civil Code (§542), whenever time is of the essence, a nonbreaching party can rescind without giving the other time to perform. It was of the essence here, since the craze had already abated by late November. But the court gave another reason: in a contract that requires ongoing performance, substantial dishonest conduct justifies immediate rescission. The issue typically arises in leases,[39] but here, too, Dainichi had agreed to ongoing delivery. It had lied about its manufacturing history, and Maruichi could immediately rescind.[40]

3. Damages

a. Generally. Should a party to a contract breach, the nonbreaching party can generally demand expectation damages.[41] If a seller reneges when the price of its goods rises, for example, the buyer can demand the difference between the contractual price and the market price. In October 1946, Hideo Ōsumi (on the southern island of Shikoku) contracted to buy from Asahikawa Power Textiles (on the northern island of Hokkaido) materials he needed to make the wooden sandals (*geta*) that were the occasional plebeian footwear of choice. Their contract specified ¥25,000, F.O.B. the Nittsū Shipping Firm in Hokkaido in November. When Asahikawa failed to deliver, Ōsumi several times demanded performance. Eventually he despaired and rescinded the contract. By then, the market price of the goods had climbed to ¥80,000 to ¥90,000. According to the Supreme Court, Ōsumi could collect the difference between the contract price and the market price:

> Where (as here) the buyer rescinds a contract because the seller has not delivered the goods, until he rescinds that contract he has the right to demand delivery. Upon rescission, he loses that right but gains the right to demand damages instead. Conversely, until the buyer rescinds the contract, the seller has the duty to deliver the goods. Upon rescission, it escapes that duty, but acquires the duty to pay damages instead. Accordingly, the damages which a buyer can demand are set by the conditions at the time he rescinds a contract.[42]

When a buyer reneges because the market price has fallen, the seller can, of course, demand the converse. In March 1914, a Japanese buyer contracted to buy 9,000 pounds of Chinese cowhides at ¥.53 per pound. When the buyer defaulted, the Chinese seller rescinded the contract and sold the hides at ¥.34 per pound. The seller sued, and the court awarded him the difference between ¥.53 and ¥.34 per pound.[43]

  b. The Hadley *Rule.* On the scope of damages a plaintiff can demand, Japanese courts follow the *Hadley v. Baxendale*[44] rule (an odd legal import, of course, for a Prussian-based statute): plaintiffs can demand the "damages that would ordinarily arise" from breach (Civil Code, §416(a)), together with the "damages that arise from special circumstances" if, but only if, the parties could or should have foreseen those circumstances (§416(b)). Crucially the rule induces contracting parties with private information about the amounts at risk to disclose that information. That disclosure, in turn, will tend to induce the other party to take more appropriate levels of care.

  Recall the dispute between Ōsumi and Asahikawa Textiles. The difference between the contract and eventual market prices stemmed from the early postwar hyperinflation. That hyperinflation, claimed Asahikawa, was an extraordinary factor not within the ambit of section 416's ordinary damages. Not so, said the high court. First, when the parties negotiated their contract "around October 13, 1946, the economy was pervaded by the post-defeat hyper-inflation. Consequently, any inflationary damages did not result from special circumstances." Second, even if the hyper-inflation did result from such special circumstances, "the circumstances already existed at the time of contracting." As a result, a commercial firm like Asahikawa readily "should have foreseen them." The point of the *Hadley* rule, as noted, is to force parties with private information to disclose. Here neither party had private information, and the court sensibly refused to apply it.[45]

4. Specific Performance

On questions of specific performance, Japanese courts distinguish between what one could call contracts "to transfer" and contracts "to do." They award specific performance in the former, but not in the latter. Unlike Anglo-American courts, they do not require that a contract involve idiosyncratic goods before ordering specific performance.[46]

To illustrate the Japanese rules, take nonbreaching party N and breaching party B. If N and B negotiated a contract "to transfer"—to sell a car, for example, or to convey real estate—N can obtain specific performance (Civil Code, §414(a)). If instead they negotiated a contract "to do"—to design a building or to fix the kitchen sink—N cannot. Instead, N's remedies will depend on whether the service is something any number of others can do (like fixing the sink) or something only B can do (like designing an architectural marvel).

If B had agreed to perform a widely available service, then N can hire another person to do the job and charge B for the additional cost (Civil Code, §414(b)). That remedy does not help if B is I. M. Pei, of course, and N hired him to design the local masterpiece. Should that be the case, N cannot use substitute performance. Indeed, N will not want a substitute. He wants Pei. Accordingly he can ask the court to order Pei to pay N a fee for every day he refuses to perform (see section 6.II).

The availability of these remedies does not preclude a claim for damages instead. Moreover, even if N obtains specific or substitute performance, he can still sue B for any amount by which that remedy does not make him whole (Civil Code, §414(d)). A tenant, for example, must return the rented premises (subject to normal wear and tear) in their initial condition. Yet in one 1983 case, the tenant had left the hospital and died alone in her apartment. By the time others found her, the unfortunate woman's body was badly decomposed. Blood and other bodily fluids had seeped through the floor, and the smell had permeated the entire apartment. When the landlord called a contractor, the contractor found he could remove the smell only by replacing all walls, ceilings, and floors. Even after the renovation, the smell lingered for another month. According to the court, the lonely woman's heirs and guarantors were liable both for the cost of renovation and for the lost rent.[47]

5. Liquidated Damages

The Civil Code (§420) explicitly allows parties to set liquidated damages:

> The parties to a contract may specify in advance the damages payable upon breach. If they do, the court may neither increase nor decrease that amount.

Notwithstanding the straightforward language, in the name of public policy Japanese courts still refuse to enforce such damage clauses when they consider them excessive.

Whatever his talents, Motoharu Itō had ambition. He would be a crooner. He had finished technical high school. He had found a job at a textile factory. Now he had a one-year contract with Nihon Grand Record, K.K. He would sing for them, and they would find him gigs and sell his records.

Alas, with paid-in capital of ¥2 million, a 390-square-foot office, and a 160-foot rehearsal room, Grand had more name than substance. For Itō's services and dreams, it paid ¥3,000 up front, ¥2,000 each month, ¥1,500 to ¥2,000 per recording, and ¥2,100 to ¥2,500 per nightclub stint. For him, it recorded three 45 r.p.m. records and found perhaps a dozen gigs. In exchange, however, Itō had not just agreed to sing for Grand. He had also agreed to sing for no one else and to pay it ¥5 million if he did. When toward the end of his year he appeared on TV in a singing contest, Grand sued for that ¥5 million.

Much to Grand's chagrin, the trial court apparently analogized it to a prewar brothel.[48] The brothels had sometimes added liquidated damage clauses to their indentured servitude contracts, and the courts had sometimes refused to enforce them when they did.[49] The high court spared

Grand the analogy, but refused to enforce the ¥5 million clause anyway. The more established studios used liquidated damage clauses that ranged from ¥100,000 to ¥70 million. Given Grand's scale, how little it did for Itō, and how new and unsuccessful Itō was, the court found the ¥5 million excessive and refused to enforce it.[50]

II. Long-Term Relations

Of peculiar theories about when Japanese executives negotiate contracts, about what they put in them, and about when they keep them, it seems there is no end. Many decades ago some academics looked for national personality traits. In time, they gave up and for good reason: the intranational variation swamped any generalizations they might make about differences in the cross-national means. Stereotypes about national corporate personalities are something else. Like Jason and Freddie Krueger, they just will not die. Unfortunately, even if not dead, most are dead wrong: they misdescribe Japanese behavior, they compare it to a misperceived U.S. standard, and they ignore the huge variation within Japan itself.

A. Japan

Japanese negotiate and write extensive contracts. Their contracts are not necessarily vague. Neither are they necessarily short. To be sure, some are vague and short. And at least on the margin, one might expect Japanese contracts to be shorter than U.S. contracts—simply because one would expect them to be less completely specified; one might expect them to be less completely specified—simply because on this dimension the Japanese legal system is better. Japanese courts dispense with novice juries. They keep uniformly high professional standards among their judges. And they skirt the choice of law problems that a federal system produces and the unprincipled Restatement (Second) of Conflict of Laws exacerbates. All this should help Japanese firms predict the default rule of Japanese contract law. It may also make them more likely to find it acceptable. If so, then they may have less incentive to negotiate a private legal regime by contract.

Whatever happens on the margin, though, parties to repeat deals in Japan generally do specify the important terms of their deal. Take the automobile industry, where by standard accounts large manufacturers deal with small suppliers on a long-term basis, where contracts are short and vague, where honesty is the rule and opportunism nearly unknown. First, the contracts are not brief. Granted, the manufacturer and supplier often sign a short "Basic Contract." Yet that Basic Contract is just the start. The parties follow it with a host of documents, and those documents specify the monthly production schedules and a panoply of other details. Notwithstanding the repeated nature of their relations, the parties talk specifics.[51]

Second, manufacturers and suppliers protect their interests through the basic contractual structure. Most obviously, they diversify their business ties. The manufacturer knows that if it buys all its requirements from one supplier, that supplier can extract large price adjustments and will feel little competitive pressure to perform. Accordingly it duplicates its deals with multiple vendors.[52] The suppliers know that if they sell all their goods to one manufacturer, that manufacturer can play the same game to boot. Accordingly they, too, diversify. Of the 162 suppliers in the Toyota suppliers association, 45 also belong to the Nissan association, and the approximate converse holds as well. Some of the largest suppliers, like Akebono Brake and Koito, belong to the suppliers associations of all five car makers (Toyota, Nissan, Honda, Mazda, and Mitsubishi).[53] Manufacturers do not trust in the suppliers' loyalty, in short, and neither do suppliers trust in the manufacturer's benevolence.[54]

Much the same story describes the banking industry. Again, observers paint a world dominated by long-term relations, a world where firms borrow repeatedly and regularly from their "main bank" and where main banks save their embattled clients. Yet here, too, parties negotiate detailed contracts. Lest a borrower renege, on long-term loans banks typically demand security interests or guarantees. Lest a bank act opportunistically, borrowers typically diversify. In most cases, major borrowers obtain only 20 to 35 percent of their borrowed funds from their "main bank."[55]

At least as important, borrowers routinely default, and when they do, banks routinely "kill" them. Through their clearinghouse, banks maintain an iron rule by which they stop all checking and discounting services to firms that default on two notes within any six-month period. By placing the defaulting firm on a cash basis, they effectively force it into liquidation.[56] Even before the banking crisis of the late 1980s and 1990s, they enforced the rule regularly and brutally (see table 3.1).

B. The United States

Many of the observers who contrast national contracting styles do not just misdescribe Japan. They also get the United States wrong. Perhaps their most common mistake is to assume that U.S. firms negotiate everything to the tee and enforce the terms they negotiate to the letter. We have known (or been on notice) at least since Stewart Macaulay's 1963 article

Table 3.1 Bank Suspension of Business

Year	Firms Suspended
1980	62,766
1981	59,024
1982	50,621
1983	48,429
1984	48,283
1985	39,949

Source: J. Mark Ramseyer, "Legal Rules in Repeated Deals: Banking in the Shadow of Defection in Japan," 20 *J. Legal Stud.* 91, 111 (1991).

on Wisconsin businessmen that American firms often ignore legal rights in repeated deals.[57] We have known at least since then, as Lisa Bernstein put it, that in "many contexts, transactors accept late payment, vary quantity terms, assume new obligations, wave covenants, and adjust prices in ways that their written contracts do not require."[58]

More recent studies make the same point. In his justifiably famous study of rural California, Robert Ellickson found that people widely ignored the law.[59] In his account of Statute of Frauds cases, Jason Johnston found oral agreements common in repeated transactions.[60] In his research into the shipping industry, Thomas Palay found that parties with relationship-specific capital at stake often made adjustments they did not legally need to make.[61] And in the modern software industry, Bernstein found that firms regularly disclaimed liability in their shrink-wrap contracts and then proceeded to make good the very liabilities they disclaimed. As one manufacturer put it:

> [M]ost software houses are willing to be less restrictive in practice, but with suits being brought for almost any reason, valid and otherwise, and with such suits being expensive to defend . . . [s]oftware houses will probably continue to use similar wording in warranties and licenses, if for no other reason than to avoid attorneys fees rather than responsibility.

They refuse a legally enforceable promise because, in Bernstein's words, "litigation is costly, prone to delay, and subject to judicial error." They make the same promise outside the law because consumers want it and are willing to pay. Rather than bond the promise with a court-enforceable right, they bond it with their reputation.[62]

American executives even include in their contracts those vaunted let's-adjust-price-later-to-be-fair clauses said to be so peculiar to Japan. In his account of the (necessarily long-term) contracts between utilities and coal mines, Paul Joskow found that a majority of the contracts let one or both parties reopen the terms if the original deal became "a gross inequity."[63] Fixed-price contracts may allow the risk-averse party to transfer risks to a risk-neutral partner. But parties also recognize that a large divergence between the spot market and contract prices can give parties a variety of inefficient strategic incentives. Rather than face those problems, they renegotiate.[64]

If U.S. and Japanese executives generally draft elaborate contracts, but then sometimes ignore the very terms they negotiated, they do so for a reason. By far the best analysis of their strategy appears in Bernstein's study of the U.S. feed and grain industry.[65] Bernstein observes that (1) on the one hand, parties to long-term contracts regularly make adjustments and concessions they need not legally make and (2) on the other, the industry's arbitration officers take a brutally formalistic approach to contracts.

That arbitration officers (rather than judges) take this formalistic line is important because the industry need not use arbitration unless its members find it better than the courts. It provides these private judicial services only because its members find them a cost-effective substitute for the courts. The puzzle is why industry members want their arbitrators to use principles so different from the approach they themselves take with their partners.

The answer, according to Bernstein, is that firms use different rules for end-game disputes than they do for ongoing relations. During an ongoing relationship, firms A and B often can bond their promise either with their reputations or with their prospects for future gains from their relationship. In the end-game, they cannot.

As a result, during the course of a continuing relationship, A and B can rely on signals that are observable, but not verifiable—signals that everyone can see, but that no one can cheaply prove to a court. As long as their relationship continues, they will seldom need verifiable signals—both because others will see how they act and dock their reputational capital if they cheat and because their future profits from dealing with each other will bond their behavior.

A and B do need verifiable signals if their relationship collapses, particularly if either is near insolvency. At that point, A cannot depend on what B will do to preserve its reputation or future business, for B will have little reputation or future business to preserve. Instead, A can depend only on what a court can force *B* to do. For that purpose, it cannot use observable, but unverifiable, promises. Instead, it needs clear, brutal, verifiable rules.

The result (one that explains business practice both in the United States and in Japan) is a two-tiered contracting scheme. On the one hand, so long as the relationship continues, the parties structure their interaction by nonbinding terms. To prevent each other from behaving opportunistically, they rely on future profits and reputations. On the other, they also recognize that all relations may sometime end and that when they do, reputational sanctions will offer little protection. Accordingly, in addition to the informal nonbinding deal, the parties draft a parallel, legally enforceable contract that governs the terms of the end-game. Their arbitrators implicitly recognize this two-part structure and determine the outcome of the end-game by the formal contract rather than the informal arrangement.

C. Intranational Variance

The point is not that Japanese and U.S. contracting practices are the same. The point is that we do not know—and that no one has even begun to collect the data we need to tell. We know that U.S. firms often (particularly with long-term partners) make do without detailed contracts, but sometimes draft them. We know that they often keep their promises, but sometimes renege. We know that they often ignore their contractual "rights," but sometimes enforce the contractual letter. That much we can also say about Japan. To date, the comparative inquiry has gone no further.

We also have good reason to think that the *intra*national variance will swamp any *cross*-national difference in the means. Whether in Japan or in the United States, how much firms *A* and *B* use and rely on legally enforceable contracts will depend on several often closely related factors:

- the extent to which *A* and *B* are tied to a small, closely knit community

- the speed and accuracy with which information travels among the firms with which *A* and *B* deal

- the number of other firms with which *A* and *B* do business

- the degree to which *A* and *B* have invested time and resources in their reputations for integrity

- the extent to which *A* and *B* can use assets, guarantees, or controlling stock interests to secure their performance

- the degree to which, wholly aside from these factors, *A* and *B* can credibly convince each other that they can rationally expect to continue to do business with each other in the future

Firms in the United States vary widely along these lines, as recent scholars have shown. But Japanese firms vary widely, too. American lawyers usually see only a tiny segment of Japanese society: during law school, they meet fast-track Japanese lawyers in the United States for an LL.M. degree. During business trips, they visit the offices of firms successful enough to compete in the international market and negotiate with lawyers successful enough to capture those firms' business. These are men (and a few women) who have largely attended the same elite universities, who patronize the same restaurants and health clubs, and who sometimes even marry each other's relatives. Within their small world, information travels quickly, repeat interactions are the norm, and reputations are crucial.

The vast majority of Japanese live and work outside these circles. If they go to college at all (and not all do), they attend massive, anonymous universities. They live in the suburbs in condominiums in large apartment complexes where no one knows more than a half dozen neighbors. They work for small firms with no substantial reputation, a handful of clients, and only a haphazard chance of survival. It is not a world to which models of strong social norms and repeat interaction much apply. But it is the world where many—if not most—Japanese live.

III. Medical Malpractice
A. Introduction

In medical malpractice cases, U.S. courts impose nonwaivable tort standards on what is fundamentally a contractual relationship. The patient is buying medical services. The doctor and hospital are selling them. Given the consensual nature of the bargain they strike, the efficient rule is the same as for any other consensual deal: enforce the terms the parties negotiate.[66]

At one time, U.S. courts imposed just such a rule. Witness *Hawkins v. McGee*,[67] the first contracts case for generations of law students and the case with which John Houseman harassed Timothy Bottoms of *Paper Chase* fame: the doctor promised a perfect hand, but delivered a hairy hand, and the court awarded his patient the difference in value between the two. No longer do U.S. courts apply that approach. Instead, they cite tort principles and apply terms that have nothing to do with the bargains the parties strike.

Japanese courts impose tort duties on malpractice disputes too, but without formally supplanting contract. As a result, nominally a claimant can choose whether to sue under contract or in tort. That alone would be reason to discuss malpractice in this chapter rather than the next. But there is another: claiming levels are low in Japanese malpractice, and those low levels may result from the way the government regulates the initial patient-doctor contract itself. To explore all this, we begin by outlining malpractice law (subsection B) and estimating aggregate claiming levels (subsection C). We then explain the potential tie between the regulation of medical contracts and the low level of claiming (subsection D).

B. Malpractice Law

Formally a Japanese malpractice claimant may sue either under contract or in tort. If he sues under contract, he initially need show only that his doctor did not achieve the result for which he hired him (e.g., he contracted for a perfect hand and obtained a hairy one). Thereupon, however—and here the formal contract regime shifts to tort—the doctor defends by showing that he exercised "due care." On this, he bears the burden of proof.[68]

If a malpractice claimant sues in tort, the case proceeds along much the same lines. Although tort plaintiffs must usually prove causation and lack of care, in malpractice cases courts deliberately switch the burden. As a result, to defend, a doctor will need to show that he met the standard set by other doctors in his specialty in his community. As the Tokyo District Court explained:

> The plaintiffs have neither asserted nor proven that the surgeon violated his duty of care. The case involves the highly specialized field of medicine. . . . In such cases, a plaintiff must show (i) that there was a mishap in his procedure [here the doctor punctured him twice rather than once], and (ii) that his symptoms thereafter worsened. Once he does so, a court may properly infer both negligence and the resulting injury.
>
> The defendants are the ones who hold the specialized medical knowledge and data. Once a plaintiff has made his preliminary showing, therefore, a defendant must prove either: (a) the absence of negligence . . . , or (b) the lack of causation between the mishap and the symptomatic worsening. Unless he does, the court should hold him liable.[69]

Table 3.2 Malpractice Cases and Claims

	Litigated Cases (All Japan)		Claims (Kyoto Pref.)
	No. Filed	P Win	
1978	238	34.7	42
1979	252	39.3	44
1980	310	30.3	39
1981	195	39.0	27
1982	270	32.6	44
1983	271	35.3	32
1984	255	26.6	45
1985	272	31.7	42
1986	335	30.0	39
1987	355	17.6	45
1988	352	21.3	51
1989	369	27.6	46
1990	364	30.3	32

Source: Tachiaki Azami and Tomio Nakai, *Iryō kago hō* [Medical Malpractice Law] (Tokyo: Seirin shoin, 1994), 6–11.

Hence the irony: a claimant may choose whether to sue in tort or under contract, but seldom will it make much difference. Even under contract, the effective regime will resemble tort.

C. Claiming Patterns
1. Cases Filed

Each year Japanese patients file scarcely 300–400 medical malpractice cases and win perhaps 30 percent (table 3.2). According to one survey of 1988–1991 malpractice cases, when they win cash, they recover a mean of ¥41 million. In 15 percent of the cases, they recover ¥5 million or less, and in only 5 percent do they recover more than ¥100 million.[70]

2. Claims Asserted

Not only do patients not sue, but also they do not assert their claims out of court. Although we know of no national data, local figures suggest some rough comparisons. According to the Kyoto medical association, patients or their families bring about 40 malpractice claims a year against local doctors (table 3.2). This constitutes 7 claims per 1,000 physicians a year. As of 1985, the comparable figure in the United States was 101.[71]

Consider the implications these local figures pose for national estimates.

About 2.6 million people live in Kyoto prefecture, and about 5,700 doctors practice there. If Kyoto claiming practices are typical and malpractice claims track the patient population, patients must bring about 2,000 claims nationally. If claims instead track the physician population, they bring about 1,500 claims.

We can replicate these estimates for other areas. Take claims in Osaka and Hyogo for 1989–1992:[72]

	Claims/yr	Dr Pop	Gen Pop	Est A	Est B
Osaka	160	14,000	8.7 million	2,300	3,700
Hyogo	34	7,200	5.2 million	940	790

In estimate *A*, we estimate the annual number of malpractice claims nationally by extrapolating local data on the basis of physician population ratios. In estimate *B*, we do the same with general population ratios. All told, the figures suggest a range for national malpractice claims of about 800 to 3,700. The comparable figure for the United States would lie in the 70,000 to 110,000 range.[73]

3. Compensation Paid

To estimate the aggregate compensation paid, turn to insurance data. Japanese doctors buy malpractice insurance either from the Japan Medical Association (JMA) or directly from private carriers. The JMA offers several policies, and the variation depends primarily on whether the doctor is buying the policy for himself or for his hospital or clinic.

Typically the Japanese policies for individual doctors have a ¥100 million per claim cap and a ¥1 million deductible. They cost about ¥40,000 to ¥50,000 a year. By contrast, in 1986–1987, U.S. doctors paid annual premiums averaging $24,000. The mean disguised an exploding crisis, of course: internists in Arkansas paid $1,900, while obstetricians in parts of Florida paid $59,000 in 1986 and $165,000 by 1987.[74] Even the relatively modest $24,000 mean, however, represented seventy to ninety times the Japanese figure.

Now consider some back-of-the-envelope arithmetic. Suppose all Japanese policies are for individual physicians (in fact, hospitals and clinics buy insurance for the malpractice of other staff) and that all compensation payments come from insurance policies (in fact, many payments are below the ¥1 million deductible). From 1976 to 1986, U.S. insurers paid on claims 87.5 percent of the malpractice premiums they received. At similar pay-out rates, Japanese insurers (with ¥45,000 premiums and perhaps 220,000 physicians) would pay claims of about ¥8.7 billion a year. From 1991 to 1995, U.S. insurers paid on claims 114 percent of their malpractice premia; at that rate, Japanese insurers would pay ¥11.3 billion. Compared with a U.S. pay-out of $5.1 billion, these estimated Japanese payouts represent a per capita figure of about 4 percent of the U.S. numbers.[75]

D. The Impact of Price Regulation
1. *The Puzzle*

To explain these low claiming levels, observers often point to a putative Japanese reluctance to sue people in power or to procedural hurdles. While not impossible, these hypotheses mask a reason tied to the very structure of competition in the industry. Before patients will file claims in large numbers, courts must be able to set a quality standard that a significant minority of doctors will not meet. As a result, before there will be widespread malpractice claims, there must first be a dispersion in the quality of services sold. In the Japanese medical services industry, the dispersion is small.

2. *Price Regulation and Malpractice*

Under a tort-based regime, judges will set a minimum standard of quality. Doctors who sell services below the standard will then be liable for any unfavorable consequences. Typically judges will want a standard that catches the bottom tail of the quality distribution—a standard that most, but not all, doctors will meet.

In turn, all this implies that the amount of legally cognizable malpractice under a tort-based regime will depend on the distribution of service quality. If the quality variance is large, courts can readily define malpractice at levels that exempt the majority of services doctors provide, but still catch substantial amounts in the bottom tail. If the quality variance is small, they will find it harder to do so. Instead, most standards will either exempt all doctors or catch all.

In most unregulated markets, sellers provide a broad range of services. Some consumers will prefer to spend less and buy the lower quality. Others will spend more and buy the higher. Under a true contract law regime, whether the variance in quality promised is wide or narrow would not affect claiming patterns. Either way, patients could collect when a doctor fails to deliver what he promises. If he promised high quality but delivered middle quality, he would incur liability. If he promised low quality and delivered low, he would incur none.

Tort law imposes on this universe a legal minimum. Under tort, a doctor who sells services below the minimum is liable whether he promised high or low quality. As a result, the number of patients with malpractice claims will depend not on what doctors promised, but on the minimum level the law imposes and the range of quality sold. Given a constant quality distribution, the higher the tort standard, the more malpractice. Given a constant tort standard and a constant quality median, the wider the variation in quality sold, the more malpractice.

Consider now the effect of price regulation. If the government sets the regulated price sufficiently high, some doctors will sometimes sell lower quality out of a simple inability to perform at the high level. If it sets prices low, however, all doctors will sell services that clear the market at the lower, regulated price. Those who would otherwise sell high quality will generally sell lower quality, for they earn no financial return for their higher efforts. Instead, virtually all doctors will be able to meet the quality standard that clears the market, and no doctor will have an incentive to do any better.

Because price regulation (particularly at a low price) will cause service quality to converge on the level that clears the market at the mandated price, it necessarily narrows the variance in quality sold. To a court setting a malpractice standard, this creates a problem, for it means that minuscule shifts in the legal standard near the market-clearing quality level will produce enormous changes in the amount of malpractice. More colloquially, it means that a court effectively can choose only between two legal regimes: one in which all doctors potentially commit malpractice all of the time and one in which no one ever commits it. Unless a court is willing to impose a standard virtually no doctors meet, it has little choice but to impose one that everyone clears.

3. Quality in Japanese Medicine

Despite rules that superficially facilitate malpractice claims, Japanese courts have apparently chosen standards all doctors meet. Effectively government regulators have probably given them no choice. By setting prices for medical services so low, regulators have reduced the quality variance to the point that courts cannot impose tort standards that catch a substantial minority of doctors.

Japanese patients pay for medical services through a nationally mandated insurance system. Everyone must join it, and everyone must trade at the prices set by the national regulatory board. Patients who want to buy high-quality services may not legally pay more, even in cash (though many

Table 3.3 Relative Medical Service Fees (1984)

	Japan (¥)	United States	Belgium	Germany	France	Luxembourg	Netherlands	Switzerland
		Relative to Japan						
First consultation with internist	1,350	10.3	2.6	1.4	2.1	4.4	3.1	4.9
Hysterectomy	61,000	5.8	0.8	0.5	0.6	0.7	0.6	1.4
Appendectomy	37,500	6.1	0.7	0.4	0.5	0.6	0.4	1.5
Electroencephalography	5,000	5.0	2.2	1.3	5.2	1.1	1.5	4.5
Electrocardiology	1,500	6.4	2.0	2.0	2.1	2.0	—	5.6
Bronchoscopy	3,200	25.8	3.1	2.1	3.5	4.1	4.1	6.1
Rectosigmoidoscopy	900	18.0	5.3	12.2	4.8	5.8	12.5	27.0

Source: Calculated on the basis of data found in John K. Inglehart, "Japan's Medical Care System (pt. 2)," 319 *New Eng. J. Med.* 1166, 1169 (1988).

Note: Japanese prices are in yen. Figures for other countries are stated as a multiple of Japanese prices, adjusted for purchasing power parity.

pay illegal bribes). Doctors who want to sell high-quality services may not legally charge for them. Good doctors, bad doctors, high-quality hospitals, low-quality mills—all must contract for all services at the mandated price.[76]

With few exceptions, regulators have set the fees at extremely low levels (see table 3.3). Predictably enough, massive, uniform quality degradation has ensued. Observers routinely miss the consequences of the regulation only because they somehow deny that doctors are like everyone else. If the government set a maximum $8,000 price for new cars, one would not see many air bags, antilock brakes, or five-year warranties—much less leather seats, cruise control, or 0-to-60-in-5-seconds performance. So, too, with medicine. Here, as elsewhere, people get what they pay for, and when the government limits what patients can pay, it necessarily limits what they will receive.

The horror stories are common, and largely uncontested. Routinely, patients wait an hour or more to see a doctor and then obtain an exam that lasts no more than a few minutes. The popular aphorism in Japan is that one waits three hours to see a doctor for three minutes; according to one recent study, internists see an average of 64 patients a day, for an average of 5 minutes each.[77] By comparison, U.S. internists spend an average of 12 minutes. Draw your own conclusion on quality—those 300 seconds include, presumably, the time to review the patient's file; to talk with him; to examine him; to diagnose the problem; to prescribe treatment; to explain the diagnosis, treatment, and prognosis; and to write up the results on the patient's chart.

Because the mandatory fee schedules limit the fee per visit, but not the frequency of visits, doctors routinely make their patients return time and again. Where an average U.S. citizen sees a doctor five times a year, a Japanese visits one 15 times a year. Anthropologist Emiko Ohnuki-Tierney captured the scene well:

> [A]t hospital X, during three morning hours on May 19, 1979, two doctors at the internal medicine clinic saw 100 outpatients who were there for the first time, in addition to 102 patients who had been seen there at least once before. During the same period, the one doctor on duty at the eye clinic saw 48 patients, and the doctor at the ear, nose, and throat clinic saw 45 patients. The obstetric/gynecology clinic . . . usually had one doctor on duty who was occasionally joined by a resident, and the average number of patients each morning was between 40 and 50. . . . These figures

were checked with several doctors working elsewhere in Japan, and are not at all unusual. Obviously, the average time a doctor spends with each patient is very short indeed.[78]

Obviously indeed.

Readers of earlier drafts suggested that quality degradation this massive should lead consumers to cheat on the regulations on a wide scale. Hypothetically they could cheat on the regulation by flying to the United States and seeing a doctor here. They are hardly likely to do that for the routine—and chronic—diseases that fill the days for most doctors. Given the ban on health insurance outside the national system, they will fly here for the non-routine specialized operation only if they can pay in cash. Perhaps some do—we have no data either way. We do know, however, that plaintiffs with cash cheat on the system by bribing the best doctors at the best hospitals to take their cases. According to one estimate, the out-of-pocket bribes paid to the better doctors in 1990 may total nearly ¥390 billion.[79]

For malpractice levels, the implications are straightforward. Because of the heavily suppressed prices, queues will be long, and (except where bribes are large) the quality will be low. Because that quality will be low, (1) even the dullest doctor will be able to meet the quality standard that clears the market, and (2) even the brightest will often have no financial incentive to do any better. Only those who take bribes will provide anything better than the norm.

The resulting compressed quality range will make it hard for courts to pick a tort-based standard that defines as malpractice a substantial minority of the services sold. Instead, courts can declare either that most doctors commit malpractice most of the time or that virtually none commits malpractice ever. According to the data on suits, claims, and insurer payments, they have apparently chosen the latter.

Conclusion

Japanese courts enforce most promises people make to buy, sell, or rent scarce resources. In doing so, they do not use a contract law that in all detail tracks the U.S. law. But the differences disguise a basic similarity: with error to be sure (in the health services industry, for example), courts in both countries allow and enforce private promises. Faced with this judicial service, Japanese use it. In the shadow of the courts, they buy, sell, and rent scarce resources.

4   TORTS

In March 1982, Sheryn Mason flew into Yokohama from New Zealand. An exchange student, she was determined to learn Japanese and arranged to stay with the Hasegawas. Mr. Hasegawa was a middle-aged English professor who had studied in the United States during the 1950s. Grateful to the Americans who had taken him into their homes (or so he said), he now invited foreign exchange students to stay with his family, always without charge.

As soon as she arrived, Mason took up with Vincent Gruser. Calling him a loner would be the charitable course. A twenty-nine-year-old Baltimore junior high teacher, Gruser was also in Yokohama on an exchange program. By the end of April, Mason was staying with him every night until 2 or 3 in the morning. As word of the rendezvous whizzed along the neighborhood gossip chain, Mrs. Hasegawa asked Mason to come home earlier. She did, but at 12:30 rather than 2 or 3. To the Hasegawas, staying out every night past midnight defeated the point of a homestay. They asked her to leave, and on July 4, she vanished without a trace.

Gruser marched over to the Hasegawas. He was mad and loud. Mrs. Hasegawa was a "bitch," a "terrorist," he shouted. All of Mason's problems were their fault. Only racists and terrorists would kick a foreigner out of their home. That they would complain about her returning late at night showed they knew nothing about American customs, violated Mason's right to privacy, proved that Hasegawa was unqualified to teach English—and on he went, yelling for thirty minutes.

After a few more exchanges, Mr. Hasegawa asked two American friends to visit Gruser at the high school where he taught. Alas, it was déjà vu all over again. Hasegawa was a liar and a racist, Gruser shouted. He did not know basic English grammar. His wife was a terrorist, an old bitch who would bed any man that came along. Enough already, decided Hasegawa, and he sued.[1]

At its best, tort law controls externalities. At least when a loss is inefficient, it forces people who impose losses on others to compensate them. In the process, it forces them more fully to internalize the costs of their activity. Battery is one such externalized cost, but when egregious enough, so is slander. Hasegawa sued Gruser for slander, and the story of this chapter is the story of suits such as his.

We begin by outlining Japanese tort law, yet another product of the late-nineteenth-century Civil Code, and one that in substance resembles much of U.S. law (section I). We explore intentional torts (subsection A), strict liability for hazardous activities (subsection B), negligence (subsection C), causation and damages (subsection D), and a few other issues (subsection E). In section II, we turn to empirical evidence of traffic accident claims and in section III to products liability.

I. The Law
A. Intentional Torts
1. *Introduction*

Most Japanese tort law stems from a short sentence in the Civil Code. The sentence is section 709:

> If anyone intentionally or negligently invades the rights of another, he must compensate that person for any damage that results.[2]

The standard intentional torts follow directly. Take assault, for example, or battery, or trespass, or false imprisonment. Because in each case one person intentionally invades the rights of another, in each case that person is liable.

Courts volunteer a variety of formulae for the requisite intent, but the gist varies little. A person commits an intentional tort if he performs an act from which an ordinary person would expect improper consequences. As the Japanese Supreme Court wrote in a 1930 defamation case:

> A tortfeasor need not intend to invade another person's rights. He need only recognize the facts that will result in the invasion of those rights.[3]

To commit a tort, a defendant need not intend to harm anyone. He need only intend to perform an act that the courts believe illegally, immorally, or abusively violates a legally protected interest.

2. *Illegally*

In this definition, *illegality* is clear enough. If *A* violates a statute and injures *B* in the process, *A* probably commits a tort.[4] Although statutes cover many of the real cases that arise, they do not cover all. From time to time, courts make ad hoc exceptions and hold that defendants "illegally" violate an interest even if they violate interests no statute protects.[5]

3. Immorally

Immorality is tougher to define, but usually straightforward. Suppose a man tells a woman he plans to marry her. If he is lying and convinces her to have sex, she can sue him for violating her chastity. In effect, hold the courts, he has intentionally harmed her through seriously immoral tactics.[6]

4. Abusively

By *abusive,* Japanese courts refer to the continentally inspired abuse-of-rights doctrine. Classically a person abused his right if he took action based on a claim of right that earned him trivial gains but harmed others egregiously. For instance, Coquerel, a Frenchman, tried to sell his land to neighbor Clément-Bayard, who launched dirigibles from his estate. Clément-Bayard refused to buy, so Coquerel built two thirty-foot-high fences on his land and punctuated them with six- to nine-foot steel spikes. When he successfully skewered one of Clément-Bayard's dirigibles, Clément-Bayard sued. Held the French Supreme Court: Coquerel may have owned his property, and owners may generally have a right to build on their property what they please, but in installing the spikes, Coquerel abused his right and was liable.[7]

In Japan, the doctrine took a similar tack. In the 1920s, Hangorō Kanamori was negotiating with the owner of a neighboring tuberculosis sanitarium.[8] The neighbor wanted to expand his sanitarium, and for that, he needed Kanamori's land. Over a million people were dying from tuberculosis every decade, and sanitaria were in short supply. Predictably, sanitaria were also unpopular, at least among those for whom the buildings would be in their backyard.

Coldly, but understandably, people everywhere shunned those with the deadly and largely incurable disease. Indeed, things were bad enough for one young tuberculosis victim that he set out one night in 1938 with an axe, three swords, and a shotgun. To spite the villagers who had ostracized him (not to mention the married women who had now cut off their affairs with him), he first severed the power lines to the village. He then methodically killed thirty of the villagers—nearly a third of the entire hamlet. Apparently to spare his grandmother the social embarrassment he was creating, he approached her in her sleep and beheaded her, too. He left a few notes describing how badly the villagers had treated him, climbed a mountain overlooking the village, and killed himself.[9]

Kanamori was not about to sell the sanitarium owner a plot of his land cheaply. He named a high price, but the owner balked. Kanamori then built a huge shed. To block the air and light to the existing sanitarium building, he placed his new shed next to the property line. And to maximize the irritation to the sanitarium patients, he told his workers to use particularly noisy and foul-smelling building procedures. They then aggressively harassed the patients besides. "We'll cook you to death in there," they yelled. "If you can't take it, go to the [nearby] Iida clinic." Because Kanamori owned the property, he had a "right" to build the shed. In doing so in a way that maximized the sanitarium's losses, but earned him few offsetting benefits, however, he abused that right. According to the court, he was liable in tort.

5. Legally Protected Interest

To find a tort, a court must find a legally protected interest. The notion cuts a broad swath. Physical integrity is a legally protected interest. At least one woman who contracted venereal disease from her ex-husband successfully sued him in tort.[10] Business goodwill and psychological health are legally protected interests—and adultery by their spouse is something most people find psychologically distressing. Hence, there being no interspousal immunity in Japan, a cuckolded spouse can sue the adulterous spouse and his or her partner for the cost of that distress.

For example, Ichirō Nakamura married Hanako Nakamura in 1947. To help make ends meet, they opened a bar. There Hanako met Tsuneo Tanaka and launched an affair. Early in 1958, Ichirō took to his bed with tuberculosis. A few months later Hanako left him and their two children and vanished. Ichirō distributed 10,000 copies of her picture to police and scoured the country. Two years later he found her in another city, ensconced with Tanaka. He begged her to come home. When she refused, he sued her and Tanaka. To the court, they were jointly liable in tort for the distress they caused him.[11]

B. Strict Liability for Hazardous Activities
1. Animals

In several areas, Japanese tort law mandates rules close to strict liability. Generally these rules concern unusually hazardous activities. City dwellers, for example, tend to love their own dogs and dread everyone else's. Hence, under the Civil Code, if an animal injures someone, the person with the possessory right to the beast is liable (§718(a)). To avoid liability, he must prove he exercised reasonable care (Civil Code, §718(a) *proviso*). Because the reasonable level of care depends on the animal's history, the law effectively gives him something close to the familiar "one free bite." [12]

2. Reservoirs

In river-streaked, typhoon-drenched, and irrigation-obsessed Japan, courts often face disputes close to the well-known *Rylands v. Fletcher*.[13] They handle them much the way the *Rylands* court did: they hold the owners of bursting reservoirs liable for the ensuing harm. Rivers can overflow, dams can crumble, and reservoirs can burst. When they do, Japanese courts cite section 717 of the Civil Code. Under section 717, the person with the possessory interest in a defective fixture is liable for any resulting injuries. The rule is not quite one of strict liability, for a reservoir that bursts is not necessarily defective. Moreover, even if a plaintiff shows that a defective fixture caused the damage, the possessor can still escape liability by showing that he exercised the requisite care (Civil Code, §717(a)). Nonetheless, the exceptions are strict. In general, to escape liability a possessor will need to show that the catastrophe was one nobody could reasonably have expected.

3. Factories

Courts apply the section 717 rule beyond broken dikes and bursting reservoirs. Even in the 1930s, if children could touch electrical wires by climbing a tree, the utility company was liable for defectively installing the wires. It was liable even if the tree had grown toward the wire after the installation.[14] By the 1960s, lower courts were expanding section 717 further. Where a propane gas tank leaked and caused a fire, for example, the court held the possessor liable. The tank was portable, but never mind. The court called it a fixture and held the firm with the possessory interest liable.[15] Where a worker lost her arm in a noodle-making machine, another court held the factory liable. It had fastened the machine to the floor, so a fixture the machine must be.[16]

C. Negligence
1. The Standard

In Japanese negligence law (based, again, on section 709), the basic standard is one of "ordinary" or "reasonable" care—what, in the Supreme Court's words, "a person of ordinary care would do in the circumstances." [17] The variations on the standard seem endless, but courts often use a test that parallels the famous three-factor cost-benefit calculus

Learned Hand applied to the barge owner in *United States v. Carroll Towing Co.*:

> (1) the probability that [the barge] will break away; (2) the gravity of the resulting injury, if she does; and (3) the burden of adequate precautions.[18]

As a famous (but somewhat opaque) example, take a 1919 railroad case.[19] The case is in effect a nuisance and early environmental case, and modern environmental law continues much of its logic.[20] The railroad had double-tracked its line past a famous pine tree and used the lines to switch cars. In doing so, it exposed the tree to far more than the usual amount of soot and smoke. Eventually it killed the tree.

As the tree was not just any tree, the owner sued. By local legend, it was the tree against which sixteenth-century warlord Takeda Shingen (immortalized in Akira Kurosawa's epic *Kagemusha*) had once rested his banner. Given the amount of soot and the proximity of the tree, the harm was foreseeable; given the ease of erecting a wall or moving the tracks, the cost of avoidance was small; and given the high foreseeability and cheap preventive costs, the railroad's actions were unreasonable. Given all this, the railroad owed the tree owner damages.

Or take a medical malpractice case. When Ichirō Hasegawa asked a doctor at the First National Tokyo Hospital about his athlete's foot, the doctor recommended x-rays. Over the next two years, he irradiated Hasegawa's feet with forty-four heavy x-ray doses. Eventually Hasegawa developed skin cancer, and doctors had to amputate his feet. He sued, and the Supreme Court found the hospital negligent. After noting the trade-off between killing the fungus and causing the cancer, it explicitly outlined the cost-benefit analysis:

> At issue is the physician's care in balancing the illness and its effective treatment on the one hand, and the attendant risks on the other. As the appellant argues, the radiation doubtless did reduce the appellee's [Hasegawa's] athlete's foot. But to increase the effectiveness of the treatment, the physician raised the dosage of the radiation to the massive levels found by the trial court. These levels indicate that he breached his duty of care (the treatment might have been appropriate in special circumstances—*e.g.*, where part of a research program undertaken with the patient's consent).[21]

2. Comparative Negligence

This negligence regime is one of comparative negligence (Civil Code, §722(b)):

> When a victim has been negligent, the court may consider that fact
> in setting the amount of compensation.

The rule applies whether the tortfeasor harmed the plaintiff negligently or intentionally. Although it otherwise works much as it does in American states, consider a few specifics.

First, Japanese courts have wide discretion in setting the comparative negligence offset. Take an early case with shades of Clementine Carter and the Earp brothers. Late one night Kichimatsu Nakatani met a young woman. Being drunk, he harassed her. Her four brothers tried to stop him, but the conversation ended in a brawl between Nakatani and the brothers. The brothers won. Beaten and insulted, Nakatani rounded up his friends. Together they regrouped, attacked the brothers, and beat one to death. In court, Nakatani argued that the decedent had himself been negligent in joining the brawl. Accordingly he (Nakatani) should be liable only for a reduced amount. Not so, said the court. Even if the decedent had been negligent, the trial court could freely decide whether to give much—if any—effect to that negligence.[22]

Second, courts may consider a victim's actions for comparative negligence purposes even if the victim would himself be immune from suit. The typical problem involves a child who dashes in front of a car. If the child is too young to be liable in tort (see subsection E.3), should his negligence reduce his recovery? After some initial hesitation,[23] the Supreme Court separated the two issues: (1) whether the child is mature enough to be liable for his own torts and (2) whether, even if he is not mature enough to be liable, he is mature enough that his negligence should offset any recovery. What the latter requires, under this bifurcated formula, is a basic "capacity to discriminate among the facts."[24] As a result, the question is not whether a twelve-year-old's carelessness will count as comparative negligence—it will; it is whether a four-year-old's will count—maybe it will.[25]

Third, the courts will impute comparative negligence among a victim's family members. Again, the issue usually concerns children hit by cars: Will a mother's negligent supervision reduce her child's recovery? Alternatively will a child's negligence reduce his parent's recovery? After some initial hesitation,[26] the courts decided to impute comparative negligence. In determining the offset for comparative negligence, the relevant measure is—in the Supreme Court's words—the negligence not just of the plaintiff, but also of "the plaintiff's side."[27]

D. Causation and Damages
1. *The Foreseeable Plaintiff*

Foreseeability remains a persistent analytic problem in Japanese tort law. The issue does not, however, involve the foreseeability of the plaintiff himself. Courts do not follow Benjamin Cardozo's *Palsgraf v. Long Island Railroad*[28] rule and ask whether the defendant owed a duty to this particular plaintiff. Rather, as the Supreme Court wrote in 1932:

> One commits an intentional or negligent tort if he can foresee (or fails to foresee because of a lack of care) that he will cause harm to someone. It is not necessary that he foresee (or fail to foresee because of a lack of care) harm to any *particular* person.[29]

2. *Special Damages*

Instead, the issue involves the extent to which plaintiffs can collect for the unexpected harm—the odd, the quirky, the bizarre. Although section 709 said only that the plaintiff could recover his damages, section 416 had introduced the *Hadley v. Baxendale* rule (see subsection 3.I.F.3.b):

> (a) An obligee may demand compensation for those damages that would ordinarily arise from the failure to perform the obligation.
> (b) An obligee may demand compensation for those damages that arose from special circumstances if the obligor foresaw or should have foreseen those circumstances.

The initial question was whether section 416 applied to tort. It being the *Hadley* rule, the drafters seemed to have intended it to apply only in contract. Nonetheless, the courts apply it in tort, too: special damages are recoverable only if foreseeable. In the words of the Supreme Court:

> As the cases have held, Civil Code §416 applies *mutatis mutandi* to damage compensation in tort. If damages arise from special circumstances, the tortfeasor must pay compensation for them only if he foresaw or should have foreseen those circumstances.[30]

By way of example, consider a cat-loving MITI bureaucrat who lived near a dog-loving physician. The young bureaucrat and his wife were childless and, the court tells us, loved their cat as dearly as any parent loved a child. The neighboring doctor kept a Doberman and a German shepherd. One day, as the doctor's servant was running the dogs unleashed, the German shepherd spotted the cat in the bureaucrat's house. It jumped the fence, bounded into the house, dragged the cat outside, and killed it. Devastated by the loss, the bureaucrat and his wife first had their beloved cat stuffed by a taxidermist. They then interred it in a special animal cemetery and paid a priest to read it sutras.

When the cat-loving couple sued the dog-loving doctor, the court held the doctor liable under section 718 (see subsection B.1). He was liable to them both for pain and suffering and for funerary expenses. They apparently did not ask for the sutra fees, but they did demand their taxidermic expenses. The court refused. "It is a special circumstance to stuff and preserve a cat," the court explained. Apparently it did not think the doctor could have known how obsessed his neighbors were with their cat. "As it is not an ordinary matter, it does not constitute ordinary damages for which the plaintiffs may demand compensation." [31]

3. The Egg-Shell Plaintiff

Applied thus, this *Hadley* analogue would seem to obviate the common-law "egg-shell plaintiff" rule (you take your victim as you find him). Yet matters are less clear. The ambiguity arises primarily from the fact that "ordinariness" is in the eyes of the beholding judge—and most judges seem to construe it broadly enough to mimic the egg-shell plaintiff rule. On the one hand, take the case of a small dog who attacked a healthy forty-three-year-old on a bicycle at night. When the dog jumped, the man lost control, crashed, and died. The court refused damages. To die from such a routine accident was, it explained, "not something that ordinarily occurs in daily life." Absent ordinariness, the dog owner escaped liability. [32]

On the other, take the seventy-three-year-old woman who met an eight-year-old girl walking an enormous, but friendly, collie. When the collie stood on its hind legs, the woman (wrongly) decided it was about to bite her. She backed off, fell down, and broke her leg. The shock aggravated her diabetes, and within two weeks, she died. Without even discussing section 416, the court found the dog owners liable. [33]

Similarly, when a dog mauled a twenty-one-year-old woman from a rich family, one 1937 court awarded high damages. "For a young woman about to be married," it reasoned, "appearance is crucial," and the dog had scarred the woman's face. That the defendant could not have expected to injure someone so prominent was irrelevant.[34] And when another woman was injured in a 1968 automobile accident, her daughter returned from her studies in Europe to nurse her. One might have thought the international travel costs unusual. Not so. The Supreme Court found jet-setting banal, declared her travel costs "ordinary," and ordered the defendant to pay them.[35]

E. Other Issues
1. Defenses

The common Japanese defenses to tort actions closely resemble the defenses in the United States. For example, consent is a defense. Even when courts give other reasons, one can easily understand those cases where courts hold children (and their parents) not liable for injuries to each other in playground games as consent cases.[36] The major limits to the defense also resemble those in the United States. Consent based on fraud, for instance, will not count. As noted earlier, a man who obtains sex through a fraudulent promise to marry is liable for violating the woman's chastity. Consent based on what judges consider "unequal bargaining power" will not count. At least one court threw out a patient's presurgery release on the grounds that it was "grossly inequitable." [37]

Similarly, protecting the person or property of oneself or others is a defense (Civil Code, §720). The limits are again predictable. Any actions one takes in self-defense should be as mild as possible. When a nineteen-year-old sailor stabbed his assailant to death in a brawl, the court refused to call it self-defense. He should, it explained, have run away instead.[38]

2. Respondeat Superior

Employers in Japan are liable for the torts their employees commit in the course of their jobs. Under section 715 of the Civil Code:

> An employer who uses another in his business must compensate third parties for harms his employee inflicts on others in the course of the business.

If found liable, an employer can sue the tortious employee for indemnity (Civil Code, §715(c)), but the employer is not liable at all if he can show that he reasonably supervised the employee (§715(a) *proviso*). Note that section 715 applies only where *A* can tell *B* how he should do the job.[39]

Much as an American court might do, Japanese courts decide whether a tort occurred "in the course of the business" by looking to external appearances: an employee commits a tort in the course of business if it looked like the course of business to third parties. If so, the employer is liable even if the employee breached his explicit orders. Take small-time fish merchant Sakuji Hodani.[40] One February morning in 1950, he rode through Tokyo in his small three-wheeled truck to buy his day's supply at the Tsukiji fish market. As he passed the center of town, the MITI minister's official Packard limousine cut him off. The three-wheeler veered onto the median strip, rolled, landed on top of Hodani, crushed his leg, and crippled him.

The Packard was not on official business. The minister and his secretary (a senior political appointee) had announced their resignation the day before. After the announcement, the secretary had told the minister's driver, Chūemon Fujinuma, that he wanted to take his children to the bicycle races (MITI-sponsored gambling affairs). Would he drive them there tomorrow? Technically it was improper, but Fujinuma was in no spot to refuse. En route to the race track, he rolled Hodani's truck.

Hodani wanted money from the government, and the government fought his claim all the way to the Supreme Court. Consistently the courts found for Hodani. This was the ministry's car. Fujinuma was the official driver. Nakamura (his resignation not yet effective) was the ministry secretary. To the courts, that sufficed. As the Tokyo High Court explained:

> Section 715 . . . applies when an employee engages in activity that—taken broadly, and objectively observed from the outside— has even the slightest appearance of being within the scope of his job. Even if he violates internal rules or commands, even if he abandons all thought of his job and abuses his position for his and his friends' private advantage, the resulting damages arise from the course of his employer's business.[41]

3. Immunities

a. Children. Tortious children have posed another intractable problem. By the terms of the Civil Code, they are liable only if they have the "capacity to take responsibility for their actions" (§712). Absent that capacity, their guardians (generally their parents) are liable in their stead unless they (the guardians) can show that they supervised the children carefully (Civil Code, §714(a)).

The analytical problem comes from the way these rules create an incentive for pro-victim judges to find that a child lacks capacity. If a court holds the child responsible, the child may be liable, but his parents escape. Take Ichirō Kōno, a routine juvenile delinquent. One night around 2 A.M., he was milling around a warehouse with seven "friends." They were sniffing paint thinner, but Kōno spilled his in his lap. One of the others noticed and started taunting him: "He peed in his pants. He peed." Kōno stood up, walked a few steps, then passed out, and fell face down on the street. Curious, another "friend" lit a cigarette lighter to see whether Kōno had in fact wet his pants. As he moved the lighter near Kōno, the thinner burst into flames.

Kōno sued the boy who had taunted him, the boy with the lighter, and the parents of both. To the court, however, the two boys were old enough to be liable in tort. One was fifteen and the other sixteen, and the fact that one may have been high on paint thinner did not negate his legal responsibility. As they themselves were liable, their parents escaped liability under section 714.[42]

On the other hand, if a court holds the child not responsible, the child escapes liability, but his parents are usually liable in his stead. Because children more often lack assets than parents, plaintiffs routinely argue that tortfeasor children are *not* responsible for what they did. Sympathetic courts often acquiesce. One court, for example, found a twelve-year-old not responsible for hitting a neighbor with a ball while playing catch. Another found a fourteen-year-old not responsible for running down a pedestrian on his bicycle.[43] And several courts have found twelve-year-olds not responsible for shooting out the eyes of their "friends" with BB guns.[44]

Given that responsibility under the Civil Code tracks the ability to understand and make decisions, the notion that twelve-year-olds are not responsible stretches the outer reaches of plausibility. To resolve the problem, courts now sometimes hold parents who negligently supervise their children independently liable under section 709. Recall the Civil Code's intended scheme: children are liable under section 709 if responsible, but their parents (unless they supervised properly) are otherwise liable in their stead under section 714. What the courts did was add another level of liability: parents who negligently supervise their children are liable for their children's torts under section 709, wholly aside from their children's liability or their own derivative liability under section 714.

Lower courts began this approach, and by 1974, the Supreme Court had adopted it. When fifteen years old, one boy had robbed a newspaper carrier. Not only did he rob him, though; he strangled him and crammed his head into the school toilet. To the Supreme Court, *both* the boy and his parents were liable. The boy knew what he was doing and was liable. But had his parents raised him better, he would not have killed the paperboy.

His alcoholic father had abused him. His mother had spoiled him rotten. They caused the murder through their negligent child-rearing. Now they were liable.[45]

b. The Government. When Japanese government employees commit torts on the job, the government is generally liable not under the Civil Code,[46] but under the National Compensation Act.[47] Subject to minor exceptions, the act's tort rules parallel those in the Civil Code. Not only is the government liable for its employees' torts, but also it is liable for damages from defective fixtures to land.

Some of the most heart-rending cases involve children abused in school. In the eighth grade, Ichirō Kōno fell in with a group of students in a heavy-metal band. They were up to no good and increasingly made him their all-purpose lackey. He carried their bags. He snuck out of school to run their errands. And in return for all this, they mocked him, humiliated him, and beat him. When a teacher caught him skipping class to buy things for them, the others dragged him to the bathroom and pummeled and kicked him. When he tried to break out of their clique, they beat him even worse.

One morning his entire class disposed of him in a mock funeral. They decorated his desk with the trappings of funerals—flowers, for instance, and incense. They left notes, but not just from other students. Several teachers signed them, too. Students wrote anything from "thanks for the good memories" to "serves you right" and "good riddance." The teachers wrote notes ranging from "how sad" to "rest in peace." It was all more than Kōno could take. Two and a half months later he left home, hopped a train, and killed himself in a distant railroad station toilet. He scrawled a note on a shopping bag:

> To my family and friends,
>   I'm sorry to disappear so suddenly. About the details, I think you'll understand if you ask Akio and Haruo [his tormentors]. I don't want to die yet, not even I. But if it continues like this, I'll be in "living hell." It'd be senseless if someone else became the next victim, of course, just because I died. So, guys, stop doing such stupid things. That's my last request.
>
>   Feb. 1, 1985
>   Ichirō Kōno

When Kōno's parents sued, the court held that his tormentors had caused him to commit suicide. Their parents were liable to Kōno's parents under section 709 for inadequate supervision. Crucially, to the court, the teachers had contributed to the disaster as well. For their part, the city government was liable as their employer.[48]

4. Joint Tortfeasors

Joint tortfeasors have placed Japanese courts in a curious dilemma. Section 719 itself seems straightforward:

> Should several people together tortiously harm someone, they are jointly and severally liable for any damages.

When two irrigation cooperatives became embroiled in a water dispute, the members of one pledged to win at all costs. A fight ensued, and one member of the rival cooperative died. According to the Supreme Court, all members of the cooperative who participated in the initial decision to fight were jointly and severally liable. All had agreed to win at all cost, and—by the straightforward logic of section 719—even those who took no direct part in the murder had to pay.[49]

The dilemma derived from the relation between the Civil Code's settlement rules and joint and several liability rules. A 1962 case presented the problem starkly.[50] Shigeo Yamaki taught high school; his wife, Michiko, worked at Toshiba. While at work, she took up with coworker Jirō Kojima and carried on an affair for nearly four years. When it ended, Shigeo and she reconciled, and Shigeo sued Kojima in tort. Under Japanese law, Kojima and Michiko had tortiously wronged Shigeo together (see subsection A.5) and under section 719 were jointly and severally liable. Under section 437, however:

> The release of an obligation owed by one jointly and severally liable obligor is effective in favor of any other obligor. . . .

In the case at hand, Shigeo had sued Kojima for ¥300,000. Had section 437 applied, in forgiving his wife he would have jeopardized the amount he could collect from Kojima. In effect, worried the courts, section 437 might dissuade victims (like Shigeo) from reconciling with tortfeasors (like Michiko). Accordingly they modified the rule. Under tort law as courts now interpret it, joint tortfeasors are jointly and severally liable, but a release of one will not reduce the liability of any other.[51]

5. Relief

a. Money Damages. Tort victims in Japan can collect damages for physical injury, for pain and suffering (Civil Code, §710), and for loss to property. They do have a duty to mitigate—a victim of one bathhouse brawl so found to his chagrin when he did not obtain reasonable medical care.[52] As noted in subsection D, courts do not award unforeseen extraordinary damages. Neither do they award nominal or punitive damages.[53]

Courts generally value a life at the present value of the decedent's expected lifetime earnings less living expenses (see subsection E.6).[54] They value a woman's life by her outside market wage, even if she worked at home.[55] Generally they use a standardized formula that varies little by the individual characteristics of the victim.[56]

b. Injunctions. The Civil Code bans injunctive relief in most tort cases (§§722(a), 417). Traditionally the only exceptions to this rule appeared in cases where a tortfeasor had sullied the victim's good name and the courts ordered newspaper notices as relief (Civil Code, §723). Increasingly, however, lower courts have begun to expand the exceptions to the cash-only rule. They do so most readily when plaintiffs claim pollution-related damages. If a plaintiff complains of dirty air from a neighboring factory, a court could just determine the present value of his expected future losses and award him cash. Increasingly they grant injunctive relief as well.[57]

6. Survival and Wrongful Death

A tort resulting in wrongful death gives rise to two types of compensable damages: net lost earnings, and pain and suffering. The right to lost earnings (theoretically) accrues to the decedent and passes as part of his estate. Although the amount nominally depends on his earning potential, in fact courts seldom vary far from the mean. From his expected gross earnings, they subtract his expected living expenses and award the remainder. In table 4.1, we employ the formula used by the Tokyo District Court to compute typical net lost earnings awards, by sex and age.

The pain and suffering awards are also highly standardized. For breadwinners, the courts award about ¥24 million. For dependents or unmarried persons, they generally award ¥17–¥21 million.

7. Statute of Limitations

A tort victim must sue within three years of when he first learns of the tort. Those three years begin to run even if he does not know his full damages, but he must at least know of the tortious action itself.[58] If he never learns of the tort, he loses his right to sue twenty years after the tort (Civil Code, §724).

Table 4.1 Calculated Decedent Lost Earnings by Age and Sex

Age	Male	Female
10	¥33 million	¥18 million
20	48	27
30	45	25
40	39	22
50	30	17
60	21	11

Source: For computation methods, see Yōji Kanda, *Kōtsū jiko no songai baishō gaku* [Damage Amounts in Traffic Accidents] (Tokyo: Jiyū kokumin, 1994), 169.

Note: Figures were calculated using standard judicial principles: (a) an expected retirement age of sixty-seven, (b) mean wages, and (c) a 50 percent deduction for living expenses. The computation method is standard to the Tokyo District Court, as used in traffic accident cases.

The three years begin to run only when the victim both (1) learns who the tortfeasor was and (2) obtains a realistic chance of suing him. In the 1930s, White Russian Victor Polosovitch had run a fox farm in Sakhalin (then under Japanese control). The police arrested him in 1942 on military charges and turned him over to the military police. They then tortured him until he confessed, and the courts convicted him on his forced confession. He spent the rest of the war in prison. During his interrogation, he learned only the family name (Ishizuka) of the man who supervised his torture.

After his release, Polosovitch scoured the country for Ishizuka. It's not the years that count—the young, but tired, Indiana Jones once replied when propositioned—it's the miles. Yet for statutes of limitations, the years are crucial—and for Polosovitch, those years covered thousands of miles besides. On March 7, 1962, barely within twenty years from the date of the tort, Polosovitch found his man and sued. Ishizuka pleaded the three-year limitation, but lost. "When factual circumstances render a claim for compensation realistically impossible," explained the Supreme Court, the statute begins to run only "when those circumstances come to an end and the victim learns the tortfeasor's name and address." [59]

II. Traffic Accidents
A. Introduction

Turn now to the single most common tort category—traffic accidents—and consider what is probably the best-known puzzle in Japanese law: why Japanese so seldom litigate.[60] We first outline three explanations for the low litigation rates: cultural differences (subsection A.1), high litigation costs (subsection A.2), and predictability (subsection A.3). We then summarize the law governing traffic accidents (subsection B) and use data on litigation and settlement to test the alternative theories (subsection C).

1. Culture

The classic explanation for the low litigation levels in Japan hinges on cultural differences and follows the research agenda pioneered by University of Tokyo law professor Takeyoshi Kawashima.[61] To Kawashima and the scores of scholars who followed him, the low litigation levels stemmed from two cultural differences between Japan and elsewhere (particularly the United States).

First, according to this theory, in Japan litigation threatens a national obsession with consensus and harmony. Japanese define themselves by reference to the network of particularistic relationships within which they live and work. Accordingly norms in Japan stress the importance of maintaining peace within those relations. By making disagreements public and compromise hard, litigation threatens that peace. Out of deference to such norms, potential claimants avoid the courts.

Second, modern law radically diverges from the social norms by which Japanese structure their relations. Where modern law imposes universalistic principles, Japanese follow what are fundamentally particularistic and status-based norms. Given a choice between law and norms, they ignore law. They order their lives instead by the rhythms of their indigenous communal values.

As vague as the hypothesis may seem, it presents a clear testable implication: if true, observed Japanese behavior will diverge from legal rules. For if the hypothesis is true, then Japanese claimants cannot credibly threaten to sue; without that credible threat, they cannot force out-of-court settlements to track legal principles. Indeed, if the hypothesis is true, most Japanese prefer cultural norms to (the very different) legal rules anyway. Given that preference, they willingly settle their quarrels by norms rather than rules.

2. Costs

Alas for Kawashima and his students, the culture-based hypothesis presented basic problems of plausibility. If social norms diverge from legal rules, then one of the parties to a dispute will usually find at least a

91

short-term (and often a long-term) financial advantage from invoking the rules. Effectively Kawashima claimed that Japanese routinely ignored that private advantage in order to follow social norms. Even when the stakes were large, they sacrificed financial gain for social conformity.

Although this profit-abandoning hypothesis surely describes some Japanese some of the time (just as it describes some Americans), as an explanation for widespread behavior it strains credibility. To virtually anyone who has lived in Japan for more than a few years, it simply does not ring true. As a result, scholars soon began to look elsewhere to explain the low litigation levels in Japan. Often they turned to institutional features of the Japanese legal system.[62]

These revisionists argued that Japanese plaintiffs avoid litigation because courts are slow and expensive. Faced with high costs and slow recoveries, they claimed, Japanese cannot realistically invoke the courts to solve their disputes. After interviewing several revisionists, in 1987 the *New York Times* announced what had almost become a new academic orthodoxy: the Japanese legal system is "bankrupt."[63]

This hypothesis, too, presents testable implications. If true, many prospective plaintiffs should be abandoning legal claims or settling them for trivial amounts. They would be doing so because they face such high costs and low returns that they cannot credibly threaten to sue. Because plaintiffs cannot threaten, defendants rarely offer more than nominal settlements. Losses, accordingly, will lie as they fall. As under the cultural hypothesis, law will not structure human affairs.

3. Predictability

a. The Logic. Japanese disputants could also settle a high percentage of their disputes because they can so readily agree about what a court would do in their case. This hypothesis carries a radical implication: Japanese settle their disputes by expected litigated outcomes, the law structures Japanese behavior, and both the cultural and the revisionist theories are wrong.

To understand this hypothesis, note that most people anywhere will prefer to settle out of court whenever possible. In Japan, as elsewhere, litigation costs (L_p, L_d, for the plaintiff and the defendant, respectively) usually exceed settlement costs (S_p, S_d). As a result, rational parties will try to settle and pocket the money they would otherwise pay their lawyers.

Whether parties to a quarrel can settle will depend in part on how nearly their risk-adjusted estimates of the litigated verdict ($E_p(V)$, $E_d(V)$)

converge. For if their estimates are close, they will usually be able to settle to their mutual advantage. Plaintiffs will take in settlement any amount that leaves them with at least their expected net gain from litigation: a reservation price equal to $E_p(V) - L_p + S_p$. Defendants will pay in settlement any amount that costs them no more than their expected total burden from litigation: a reservation price equal to $E_d(V) + L_d - S_d$. Accordingly the parties will find it advantageous to settle whenever

$$E_p(V) - L_p + S_p < E_d(V) + L_d - S_d$$

Equivalently they will find settlement advantageous whenever

$$E_p(V) - E_d(V) < (L_p + L_d) - (S_p + S_d)$$

Verbally this inequality states that settlement is possible if, but only if, (1) the total net costs that the parties expect to save through settlement exceed (2) the difference between the plaintiff's (greater) and the defendant's (lower) estimates of the outcome of suit. Whatever the mathematics, the intuition is simple: the greater the amount by which the plaintiff's estimate of the litigated outcome exceeds the defendant's estimate (the more optimistic both parties are about their own chances in court), the more likely it is they will sue.

Perhaps a simple example will help. Suppose plaintiff Peter estimates his risk-adjusted recovery in court at 100, litigation costs at 25, and settlement costs at 5. If he litigates his claim, he will recover 75 net. Because settlement negotiations will cost him 5, any settlement offer greater than 80 will put him in a better position than litigation.

Suppose defendant Diane estimates Peter's recovery at 90, her litigation costs at 25, and her settlement costs at 5. If she litigates the case, she estimates a risk-adjusted outlay of 115. Because settlement negotiations will cost her 5, any settlement less than 110 will leave her better off than litigation. With these numbers, Peter and Diane can both gain by settling for any amount between 80 and 110. If Diane estimates the likely outcome of litigation at 50, however, then she will offer Peter only $50 + 25 - 5 = 70$. Because Peter demands 80, litigation will ensue. The more nearly the parties' estimates of the outcome of litigation converge, in short, the greater the odds are they can settle.

b. Institutional Reasons. Plausible reasons why Japanese disputants might be able more readily to agree on the litigated verdict are easy to find. First, Japanese courts do not use juries (see chapter 6). Instead of arguing before amateur fact-finders, attorneys try their cases to professional judges. Unlike juries, judges take pride in uniformity across place and over time and publish past decisions for everyone to check.

Second, Japanese courts use discontinuous trial sessions spaced over a long period (see chapter 6). This, in turn, gives judges more chance to explain their views before the trial ends. Many judges even consider it their job to do so. Once a judge has tipped his hand, however, no one has much reason to finish the trial.

Third, explicitly in order to standardize their decisions, Japanese courts sometimes use detailed, clear, and public rules about damages and comparative negligence (see subsection I.E.6).[64] Although judges need not follow the formulae, most do, and sensible attorneys will use them when they negotiate settlements. Given the array of low-brow how-to books on these formulae, even lay people can use them.

c. Predictability and Variance. Each of these institutional features of the Japanese legal system raises the predictability of the litigated outcome. If all parties had identical information and made no computational errors, of course, unpredictability would not raise litigation rates. Instead, predictable or no, the parties would identically estimate that outcome ($E_p(V)$ would always equal $E_d(V)$), and all cases would settle.

Real litigants, however, will estimate the litigated value of a case in such a way that their estimates will approach the (unobserved) real value with positive variance. Some of that variance will result from computational errors, and some will result from incomplete and asymmetric information. To say that the U.S. system is less predictable than the Japanese system, however, is simply to say that the variance in the estimates by U.S. disputants of the expected litigated outcome is larger.

Recall now that in this model, litigation results from mutual optimism: the greater the optimism of the plaintiff and the defendant (the greater $E_p(V) - E_d(V)$), the greater the likelihood of litigation. Litigation, after all, results when the difference between the plaintiff's (higher) estimate of the litigated outcome and the defendant's (lower) estimate exceeds the total marginal costs of litigation. By increasing the variance in the distribution of the parties' estimates of the litigated outcome, unpredictability potentially increases the percentage of cases in which both parties estimate their own chances so optimistically as to generate litigation.

The testable implications are, again, straightforward: because the parties settle their cases by the expected litigated outcome, settlements will track litigated outcomes. Culturalists predicted that settlements would track norms that (by hypothesis) diverge from court-enforced rules. Revisionists predicted that claimants would eat their losses. This predictability thesis implies that plaintiffs recover and defendants pay amounts that track the judgments courts would issue. Unlike both other theories, it implies that parties bargain in the shadow of the law in Japan.

4. Traffic Accidents as a Data Source

a. The Potential. Because any test of these rival hypotheses would require data on settlements and litigated outcomes, it requires information that for most disputes no one has. For traffic accidents, however, we do have the information we need. We know the number of serious traffic accidents. We know the number of deaths and the number and amounts of the claims that insurers pay. And we know the size of court judgments in litigated cases. As a result, we can accurately compare both (1) the number of deaths from accidents with the number of wrongful death claims paid and (2) the average amounts paid in settlement with the amounts awarded in litigation.

b. Caveats. One could object, to be sure. Litigated cases are not a random selection of disputes. As a result, litigated amounts will not necessarily represent the amounts disputants in settled cases would have recovered in court.

Likewise, traffic accidents are not representative of all disputes. The plaintiff and the defendant in a traffic accident are unlikely to deal with each other on a repeated basis. Precisely because traffic accidents are so common and similar, moreover, the parties are more likely than other disputants to be able to use past cases to predict accurately how a court will decide their own case.

Such complaints notwithstanding, two points stand out. First, typical or no, automobile accidents are a large part of the court docket in any industrialized society. Typical or no, they are important in their own right. Second, as of the mid-1990s, we know of no one who has collected any systematic data that contradict the conclusions we reach below on the basis of these traffic accident data. If other disputes settle differently, *no one* has yet collected systematic data to prove it.

B. The Law

Traffic accident law in Japan follows general tort principles, with two major exceptions.[65] First, all drivers must carry a minimum liability insurance policy. As of the early 1990s, that minimum was ¥30 million.[66] Second, a driver is generally liable for all damage he causes unless he proves

(1) that he was not negligent, (2) that the victim or a third party was negligent, *and* (3) that his car was not defective. In effect, the law replaces negligence with something closer to strict liability.

Crucially, however, these strict liability provisions apply only when a claimant recovers against a driver's statutory minimum policy amount. Suppose he hopes instead to recover beyond that minimum, either from the defendant's assets or from his optional insurance policy. Should he assert a claim that exceeds that minimum, the normal tort rules (including negligence and comparative negligence) will apply.

Whether to claim against an optional policy thus poses a curious calculation. Suppose a male decedent was not comparatively negligent. Given the difference between the statutory ¥30 million minimum and the amounts courts award for human life (see table 4.1), his heirs will usually want to claim against the defendant's optional policy. Suppose, however, that the decedent was negligent. Although his heirs can reach a higher coverage maximum if they claim against an optional policy, they will now face a comparative negligence offset. Often that offset will bring their actual recovery back within the bounds of the statutory minimum policy anyway.

C. The Data

According to the evidence below, victims (1) aggressively assert their claims and (2) receive out of court amounts that closely track the amounts that they could receive in court. The notion that either a cultural preference for harmony or the inefficiencies of the Japanese court system induce victims not to assert their claims is simply untrue—demonstrably false.

Table 4.2 compares the number of deaths from traffic accidents (column A) with the number of wrongful death claims paid by insurers over such accidents (column B). Column C expresses the numbers in column B as percentages of those in column A.

According to Table 4.2, families of accident victims file claims and successfully recover damages in 80 to 95 percent of all deaths. Note that the deaths include both single-car accidents and multicar accidents where the victim was the only party at fault. That heirs assert claims in 80 to 95 percent of all cases involving deaths suggests, therefore, that they assert them in virtually all cases where someone other than the decedent was at fault.

In settling out of court with an insurer, heirs of decedents obtain amounts that closely track the amounts they would receive in court. To see this point, consider table 4.3, which compares average trial rulings on the

Table 4.2 Number of Insurance Claims Paid
in Fatal Traffic Accidents

	A. Deaths from Traffic Accidents	B. Insurance Claims Paid	C. Col. B/Col. A Percentage
1970	21,535	17,334	80.5
1971	21,101	18,513	87.7
1972	20,494	18,259	89.1
1973	19,068	17,990	94.3
1974	15,448	14,574	94.3
1975	14,206	12,950	91.2
1976	13,006	11,521	88.6
1977	12,095	10,687	88.4
1978	12,030	10,081	83.8
1979	11,778	10,406	88.4
1980	11,752	10,146	86.3
1981	11,874	10,132	85.3
1982	12,377	10,431	84.3
1983	12,919	10,870	84.1
1984	12,432	10,529	84.7

Claims = .876 (Deaths) R^2 = .96

Sources: Sōmuchō, ed., *Kōtsū anzen hakusho* [Traffic Safety White
Paper] (Tokyo: Ōkura shō, 1971–1987); "Shiryō hen" [Materials], 2
Kōtsū kenkyū 165, 168 table 1-3 (1972).

value of human life (net lost earnings plus pain and suffering) in disputes
over fatal traffic accidents (column A) with average insurer payments in
such disputes (column B). Column C expresses column B as a percentage
of column A.

Although table 4.3 may seem initially to suggest that victims recover less
than what they could earn in court, such is not the case. Consider the effects of comparative negligence, potential nonrecovery, and underinsur-
ance. First, column A does not represent the amount plaintiffs actually received in court. Instead, it shows how courts valued human life. Before
awarding damages to a victim's heirs from any source other than the statutory minimum policy, the courts subtract an amount commensurate with
the victim's own negligence. By contrast, column B (in cases exceeding the
statutorily required policy) shows figures net of comparative negligence.
Japanese courts appear to reduce awards for comparative negligence in litigated wrongful death cases by about a third.[67]

Second, when rational disputants negotiate settlements, they adjust the
amounts in column A for the possibility of nonrecovery. Claimants will not

Table 4.3 Court Awards and Insurer Payments
in Fatal Traffic Accidents (all insurance policies, ¥ million)

	A. Litigated Value of Human Life	B. Mean Insurer Payments	C. Col. B/Col. A Percentage
1970	7.13	5.21	73.1
1971	7.90	5.09	64.4
1972	8.89	5.16	58.0
1973	10.29	5.61	54.5
1974	11.77	8.90	75.6
1975	13.77	11.41	82.9
1976	18.29	13.21	72.2
1977	19.01	13.68	72.0
1978	23.91	14.77	61.8
1979	24.92	16.17	64.9
1980	28.95	17.02	58.8
1981	33.79	17.95	53.1
1982	37.34	18.62	49.9
1983	37.25	18.78	50.4
1984	35.81	19.49	54.4

Payments = .57 (LitigVal) R^2 = .87

Sources: Column A: Jidōsha hoken ryōritsu santei kai, ed.,
Jidōsha hoken no gaikyō [The Status of Automobile Insurance]
(1986), 61 table 21; Jidōsha hoken ryōritsu santei kai, ed., *Jidōsha
hoken ryōritsu santei kai jūgonen shi* [A Fifteen-Year History of the
Automobile Insurance Rate Determinition Council] (1981), 16; Ichirō
Katō and Takahiko Kimiya, *Jidōsha jiko no hōritsu sōdan* [Legal
Consultation on Automobile Accidents], rev. ed. (1983), 174 table;
Shōji Morooka, *Kōtsū jiko songai baishō no chishiki* [Information on
Traffic Accident Damage Compensation] (1979), 188 table. Column
B: Sōmuchō, ed., *Kōtsū anzen hakusho* [Traffic Safety White Paper]
(1971–1987); Seiichi Ishii and Susumu Yonetsu, "Kōtsū jiko ni okeru
saiban zen funsō shori" [Pretrial Dispute Resolution in Automobile
Accidents], 8 *Jurisuto: sōgō tokushū* (1977), 20, 21 table 4.

settle by reference only to what a court is likely to award if they win. They
will first discount that amount by the possibility they will lose.

Third, 40 to 50 percent of Japanese drivers buy only the statutorily required minimum liability insurance policies. In most years, the insurer's
maximum liability under these policies has fallen short of the full litigated
value of human life. As a result, insurers are often contractually liable for
much less than the amount given by column A.

Adjusted for these considerations, table 4.3 suggests that Japanese tort
claimants do very well out of court. In most years, they receive 55 to 75

percent of the litigated value of human life.[68] Discounted for comparative negligence at one-third (and with appropriate caveats about the nonrandom character of litigated disputes), these figures suggest that they recover, on average, about 80 to 110 percent of the amount they would earn if they sued and won against a fully insured defendant. As they do not always win and do not always sue fully insured defendants, the 80–110 percent figure suggests they do very well indeed.

D. Significance

For understanding Japanese law-related behavior, the point is crucial: at least in fatal traffic accidents, the heirs of victims aggressively assert their legal rights. Notwithstanding the allegedly consensual and harmonious nature of Japanese society and notwithstanding any costs and delays involved in Japanese litigation, heirs do *not* ignore the law and do not eat their losses. Instead, they settle their claims out of court for amounts that closely track the amounts they would obtain in court. Legal rules do indeed structure the nature of out-of-court settlements, for in serious traffic accidents, people generally get their just legal desserts: defendants pay and plaintiffs recover amounts close to the defendants' legal liability.

III. Products Liability
A. Introduction

The story of Japanese products liability flatly contradicts most assumptions American observers bring to the products liability field.[69] To explain, we begin with the standard rationale behind products liability (subsection B) and compare it with Japanese products liability law itself (subsection C). We turn then to what most observers conclude could never exist: the voluntary products liability regime that structured product safety claims in Japan for over two decades (subsection D).

B. The Rationale behind Products Liability Law

Modern products liability law may be well established, but it is notoriously hard to justify. Essentially it imposes on consumer sales contracts a broad panoply of nonwaivable terms. It forces sellers (or manufacturers) in specified consumer sales contracts to agree to compensate buyers (and specified third parties) for specified damages caused by specified defects in specified products. Restated, it forces sellers to bundle insurance contracts with the goods they sell.[70]

Basic theory, however, suggests that if some buyers want bundled insurance contracts, then in unregulated markets some sellers will offer them. When customized sales contracts are feasible, sellers will offer insurance contracts tailored to specific buyers. And when customized contracts are infeasible, market competition will still drive some sellers to bundle some insurance contracts with some products. Consumers who want the products liability protection will buy the bundled insurance-product package. The rest will buy the unbundled product.

As a result, a legal regime that forces sellers to bundle products liability coverage with the product sold almost necessarily lowers consumer welfare.[71] Granted, consumers who want the insurance-product bundle will still obtain it in the now-regulated market. Those who do not want it, though, will need either (1) to buy insurance worth less to them than the price they must now pay or (2) to do without the product, given the higher bundled price. Again, it is no answer to say that consumers will generally want the insurance. If they value it more than it costs, sellers in unregulated markets will offer it.

Because of this straightforward case against products liability law, scholars inclined to justify the regime turn to a series of questionable empirical claims: that given the informational and computational difficulties in determining the risk levels of complex products, consumers wildly miscalculate accident costs; that given cognitive dissonance, consumers systematically underestimate health risks; that given the small value associated with insurance coverage in any one contract, manufacturers will not find offering the coverage cost effective; that given the difficulties in distinguishing high- and low-risk consumers, adverse selection will preclude a private insurance market; or that given the need to deny the risks in their own products, firms will never convey realistic information, even about the risks of their competitors' products.[72]

To illustrate some of these arguments, take an entirely hypothetical discussion of disposable cigarette lighters. Suppose, on average, that three in every 10 million lighters explode and cause bodily injury of about $150,000. Even if rational consumers would want to protect themselves against such an injury, argue products liability proponents, they will not correctly calculate the cost of minuscule odds that gruesome accidents will occur.

Moreover, these proponents continue, a firm would earn only a trivial competitive advantage by bundling insurance with its products. After all, the cost of the risk itself is only $150,000 \times .0000003 = 4.5¢$ per lighter. No firm will undertake the managerial costs necessary to design a bundled contract when the returns are so small. Because no firm will want to call attention to the risks associated with its own products, no firm would be able cost effectively to advertise any liability insurance it did bundle.

Hence the conclusion: Even though consumers would prefer insurance against defective lighters, the vagaries of consumer irrationality and the transactions and information costs will inevitably create a world without it. Accordingly the law can improve the lot of both sellers and buyers by forcing sellers to bundle insurance. By holding sellers (or manufacturers) liable for personal injuries caused by defective products, strict products liability law does just that.[73] In subsection D, however, we shall return to exactly this issue: Do transactions costs prevent buyers and sellers voluntarily from contracting for products liability coverage? Before answering that question, we turn to the tort law of products liability in Japan.

C. Japanese Products Liability Law

Until 1995, plaintiffs with products liability claims sued under general contract or tort principles. If they sued on contract, they bypassed negligence, but recovered only if in privity. If in privity, liability for defective products could follow straightforwardly. Take the toy bow-and-arrow set that one defendant produced. Although the arrows had suction cups on the end, when seven-year-old Hiroko Onizuka played with her four-year-old brother, some came off. She then shot him with an arrow and blinded him in an eye. Reasoned the court, suction cups should not readily come off; these cups did come off; hence the defendant was liable in contract for selling defective goods.[74]

In tort, the most distinctively Japanese products liability cases have involved blowfish (*fugu*) restaurants. Blowfish carry in their eggsacks and livers a deadly poison. Unless sliced by specially trained chefs, when prepared they absorb the toxin into their meat and kill. Among the testosterone-crazed cognoscenti, however, they are popular precisely because of that risk.

Old Masaru Morita was a grand master of the *kabuki* theater, a man knighted by the government as a "Living National Treasure." He was also a gourmet who liked playing Russian roulette with his food. When he ate blowfish, he did not eat just the meat (dangerous enough as it is). He ate the deadly liver itself. If buying it violated the local health code, so much the better. In 1975, Morita's luck expired. He ate a liver, he died, and his heirs sued the restaurant. Never mind that Morita knew what he was eating. Never mind that he intentionally came to the store to eat blowfish liver. Never mind even that his friend that night warned him that "them livers is horrific things." The court deducted 30 percent for comparative negligence and billed the restaurant for the remaining value of his life.[75]

In some ways, however, this case law is history. Effective July 1, 1995, the Japanese government formally jettisoned the negligence requirement— sort of.[76] With enormous hullabaloo, it enacted the Products Liability Act and substituted strict liability for negligence—sort of. Yet the change may have been less significant than the hullabaloo would suggest. The new law apparently included in the concept of "defect" a cost-benefit approach resembling the classic Hand formula.[77] It limited compensable harms to injuries suffered through the foreseeable use of the product and included the product's price within the factors bearing on whether it was defective.[78] Accordingly readers wondering whether the courts will interpret the new law more expansively than section 709 will simply have to wait.

D. The Safety Goods System

More interesting than the nominal 1995 shift from negligence to strict liability is the products liability regime many firms instituted on their own. Unbeknownst to most Western observers, many Japanese firms had long subjected themselves—voluntarily—to a strict liability regime. Begun in the mid-1970s, the regime had four components: safety standards, testing, insurance, and a distinctive legal rule. Firms that participated in the program bought the bundled package of all four.

First, participating firms followed safety certification standards set by the Product Safety Council. The council itself was a creature of statute, though the statute did not establish the Safety Goods (SG) system. By 1994, the council had set standards for 103 products. They ranged from baby buggies to bunk beds, disposable lighters, Q-tips, and bicycles.

Second, participating firms submitted their products to the council for testing. If a product met the safety standards, the manufacturer could attach an SG label. There was nothing mandatory about this. If it failed the test, the firm just sold it without the label. The firms involved paid the costs of these tests.

Third, through a private carrier chosen by the council, the firms insured their SG products against products liability claims. In effect, those firms that wanted to bundle a products-liability insurance contract with their goods submitted them to the council and paid a fee. The council tested them and, if they met its safety standards, agreed to compensate injured users. Those firms that did not want to bundle products liability insurance with their products sold their wares independently. For these services, the council charged premiums that averaged about 0.5 percent of a product's retail price.[79]

Finally, firms used the SG system to *raise* the legal standard by which they were bound. Voluntarily they replaced the negligence requirement in tort (often presumed, to be sure) with a rule that allowed a user to recover if he could show three things: (1) that the product had been defectively manufactured,[80] (2) that he had been injured, and (3) that the defect had caused those injuries.[81] For that process, firms hired the council to serve as both adjudicator and insurer. Effectively firms joined the SG system to cater to a safety-conscious niche market.

By design, SG justice was cheap and fast. Much as under U.S. workers' compensation, claimants could recover without the costly and detailed proof a court would demand. According to most observers, victims recovered under the SG system with less evidence either of the product's defect or of causation. From time to time, observers complained about the SG system—but usually about how many products were not covered.[82] They seldom complained that the council interpreted either causation or defect too restrictively.

Again as with workers' compensation, SG claimants could collect their compensation more quickly than if they sued in court. Sometimes they even collected within the month. Indeed, if a claimant could show serious personal injury, unless he was clearly and exclusively responsible for the injury the council immediately paid ¥600,000 in interim aid. Even if he later failed to prove his claim, he kept the ¥600,000.

As of the mid-1990s, the council capped its liability for personal injury at ¥30 million and paid no compensation for property damages. The amount was low, but not egregiously so. It was the minimum coverage that automobile drivers carried. As table 4.1 shows, it let most women and some men (particularly if comparatively negligent) collect most of what a court would award.

Within a few years, firms in several industries outside the SG regime began similar systems. In 1974, the makers of large household items (e.g., kitchen cabinets and integrated bathroom units) introduced the Better Living (BL) label. As of 1992, they covered thirty-five products and paid up to ¥50 million per person and ¥500 million per accident (the actual maximum depended on the product involved). Toy makers used the Safety Toy (ST) label and paid up to ¥10 million per victim for injuries from defective toys. Fireworks manufacturers and importers began a Safety Fireworks (SF) label system in 1977 and paid up to ¥100 million per accident.[83]

Table 4.4 Claims and Payouts under the SG System

	A. Categories Labeled	B. Items Labeled (× 10 million)	C. Complaints Filed	D. Complaints Recognized	E. Compensation Paid (× ¥1,000)
1974	16	1.8	1	1	8
1975	28	7.7	12	9	525
1976	32	10.6	9	4	374
1977	38	12.7	20	12	2,186
1978	43	27.3	21	14	11,953
1979	47	50.6	33	23	5,051
1980	51	47.8	29	11	15,653
1981	54	56.3	30	21	32,142
1982	56	60.4	39	14	3,039
1983	65	64.0	70	35	9,317
1984	70	74.9	60	48	27,644
1985	72	83.7	62	21	4,481
1986	73	63.1	66	20	1,028
1987	75	74.8	62	22	2,761
1988	76	77.7	44	20	19,041
1989	80	83.5	54	20	6,245
1990	88	89.4	61	22	12,725
1991	91	96.7	54	22	1,794

Total labeled goods sold: 9,829 million
Total complaints lodged: 727
Total meritiorious complaints: 339
Total compensation paid: ¥156 million
Mean compensation paid: ¥460,000

Source: Keizai kikakuchō, ed., *Seizōbutsu sekinin seido wo chūshin to shita sōgōteki na shōhisha higai bōshi kyūzai no arikata ni tsute* [Regarding the Proper Comprehensive Measures for the Prevention of and Compensation for Consumer Harms, Centered around a Products Liability System] (Tokyo: Ōkura shō, 1993), 205.

Note: The columns represent (A) the categories of products subject to SG labeling, (B) the number of items sold with the SG label, (C) the number of complaints filed with the Product Safety Council with respect to items sold with SG labels, (D) the number of complaints in column C that were judged to be meritorious, and (E) the total compensation paid.

None of these regimes displaced the tort system. Victims dissatisfied with their recovery under these abbreviated systems could still sue under general tort law. As of 1991, however, only three SG claimants had ever done so.[84]

Table 4.4 details the claims and recoveries under the SG system. From 1974 to 1991, victims asserted 727 claims. The council recognized 339 and paid aggregate compensation of ¥156 million, or ¥460,000 per claim.

Table 4.5 SG Claims Paid as of June 1987

	Number of Claims Paid
Disposable cigarette lighters	49
Baby buggies	36
Swings	27
Metal stepladders	26
Pressure cookers	16
Bicycles	12
Roller skates	9
Baby beds	9
Slides	8
Bunk beds	7
Expanders	6
Others	36

Source: Keizai kikakuchō, ed., *Seizō butsu sekinin to baishō rikō kakuho* [Products Liability and the Assurance of Compensation] (Tokyo: Ōkura shō, 1988), 63.

Table 4.5 details the products that gave rise to these claims. The most commonly recognized complaints involved disposable cigarette lighters. Others involved baby buggies, swing sets, and stepladders.

E. Claim Levels

There is a puzzle here. In nearly two decades, the council granted only 339 claims. As table 4.4 shows, however, the harder puzzle is not the number of claims paid. It is the number of claims filed. In nearly two decades, only 727 people asserted any claims. By contrast, claimants in the United States file 13,000 products liability claims a year just in the federal courts.[85]

Initially three points seem relevant to this puzzle. First, the reason for the low claiming levels does not lie with any dramatically restrictive policies at the Products Safety Council. True, if most potential claimants knew the council demanded impossible levels of proof, then few people would file claims. Because only victims with the strongest claims would file, the 45 percent success rate (339/727) would disguise how restrictive the council has been. As noted earlier, though, in all the controversy over the new Products Liability Act, few observers of any political stripe have claimed that the council has been too restrictive.

Second, a few big tort disputes skew the American products liability data. Perhaps half of the recent cases have been asbestos cases. The Dalcon Shield and bendectin disputes stack the numbers higher still.[86]

Third the right benchmark by which to measure claiming levels is the number of victims, and for that purpose, the 13,000 federal suits are notoriously misleading. Put somewhat polemically, the right benchmark is not how many people can plausibly file claims; it is not how many can convince juries that a manufacturer ought to pay their medical bills; it is not even how many people suffer product-related injuries. The right benchmark is how many people are injured each year by *defective* products (granted, the phrase hides a thousand sins), and we have precious little reason to think the American data track that benchmark much at all.[87]

Instead of arguing before six novices culled from DMV records, suppose American trial lawyers had to make their cases to engineers from the Underwriters Lab. That, after all, is pretty much what happens in the SG system. Probably most observers would conclude that plaintiffs would file dramatically fewer claims. Probably many would also conclude that outcomes would be more accurate. Perhaps—not to put too fine a point on it—claiming levels are high in the United States because juries sympathize with accident victims and are easy to fool. Claiming levels are low under the SG system because the fact-finders know what they are doing.

Even given all this, the most important reasons why the Japanese SG claim figures fall far below the American products liability figures probably lie elsewhere. The reasons lie in the fact that the SG system (1) covers only a small segment of the Japanese economy and (2) disproportionately covers the safer products at that. After all, a *total* count of Japanese products liability claims would not just include SG claims; it would include the large number of claims against products not covered by the system. And there are many such claims. Firms in the health care and recreational products industries reported over 200 claims a year.[88] The Japan Federation of Bar Associations Product Liability Hotline handles over 1,000 inquiries annually.[89] The Citizens' Life Center (heavily concerned with consumer affairs) handles nearly 1,200 product-safety complaints a year.[90] And in 1993 alone, the restaurant industry paid ¥220 million to over 8,000 patrons.[91]

Necessarily, moreover, the SG system will disproportionately cover the safest products. To see why, ask why Japanese consumers would want to pay for SG certification. They hardly want the insurance for its own sake. Japanese citizens are heavily insured: all Japanese are covered by the national health insurance system, and many carry elaborate life insurance policies besides. Even if they wanted more insurance, why buy insurance tailored narrowly toward product-related accidents?

Instead, those Japanese consumers who want the SG certification are relatively less likely to be consumers who need more insurance than they are to be those who prefer safer products. For them, the value of the insurance lies in the way it makes credible the manufacturer's assertions about safety. Effectively, by facilitating claims against the manufacturer, the SG system helps a firm "put its money where its mouth is." Effectively, it helps the manufacturers of the safest products make their promises about safety believable and thereby gives them an advantage in the product market.[92] And precisely because the SG system covers the safest products, it generates relatively few claims.

Conclusions

At its best, tort law forces firms and people to internalize costs. More specifically, it forces them to internalize the costs they impose on third parties in situations where bargaining costs would otherwise prevent those third parties from contracting for their own protection. It does this by forcing firms and people (in some fields, everyone; in other fields, those who engage in inefficient activity) to pay for the costs they impose.

At its best, therefore, tort law deals with disputes where bargaining costs are high. Quintessentially such disputes range from traffic accidents to industrial pollution, and these disputes Japanese courts do indeed handle well. Such disputes would not include claims between parties already contracting with each other (e.g., for medical and product safety accidents), and these disputes Japanese courts handle poorly.

For the Hasegawas, what mattered was whether Japanese tort law covered malicious harms. It does. In 1986, the Yokohama District Court duly ordered the young Vincent Gruser to pay the Hasegawas ¥1 million for mental distress.

5   CORPORATIONS

Jirō Kōno's family published "newspapers" and rented potted plants. In fact, Kōno knew as much about potted plants as Vito Corleone knew about olive oil. He was a *sōkaiya* in a family of *sōkaiya,* a mobster who both kept other shareholders quiet at the firm's general meeting and blackmailed senior managers over their corporate and personal crimes and indiscretions. The newspaper subscriptions and potted plant rentals were merely the avenues through which he and his family collected their cash. As with much of the Japanese mob, they also occupied the political fringe right. Ostensibly to further their beliefs, they owned a sound truck. Presumably, every now and then they drove around town blasting prewar military marches and anti-Communist harangues.

Since the mid-1970s, the Kōno family had collected subscription and rental fees from the Chūō Sōgo Bank. In 1982, the bank announced it would no longer pay. Jirō's father stormed the bank and demanded to see the president and directors. When refused, he again ordered the bank to pay for its newspapers and potted plants. Better to pay now, said he, because he had 100 questions for the shareholders' meeting. He could easily make it last two or three hours.

When his father returned empty-handed, Jirō took his turn. Similarly rebuffed, he brought up the sound truck. "Remember," he told them, "we can take [that] sound truck over to the president's house too." Still unsuccessful, he mentioned the shareholders' meeting again, but this time raised the stakes. "That 8-hour shareholder meeting you had?" he taunted. "At the Turkish baths, we call those 'quickies.' I can spend 8 or 9 hours just on the balance sheets."

Jirō also demanded the shareholders' list. The Commercial Code[1] itself gives shareholders an unlimited right to inspect the list during business hours (§263(b)). Jirō stood on that right. He needed the list, he explained, to study "the capital circumstances of the shareholders" and "changes in shareholdings." A patent ruse, the bank replied. He did not want the list. He just wanted money. The court sided with the bank. Jirō demanded the list to extort money, it reasoned. As he had no real, reasonable purpose for wanting the list, the company could properly refuse his demand.[2]

In Japan, as in the United States, corporate law governs the relationship between a firm's shareholders (even men like Kōno) and its officers and directors. In the rest of this chapter we survey that law (section I). We begin by explaining the economic role it plays (subsection A) and outlining some preliminary detail (subsection B). We then discuss the limits on the discretion that managers owe investors (subsection C), the limits on the abuse of the corporate machinery (subsection D), the way the law facilitates corporate transfers (subsection E), and several of Japanese corporate law's more curiously inefficient aspects (subsection F). In section II, we discuss the role mobsters like Kōno play in corporate procedure, and in section III, we explore the relative importance of the stock market in Japan and the United States.

I. The Law
A. Introduction

For sustained economic growth, people need to work together. Toward that end, they need to bring to their collective enterprise diverse attributes. Some will work manually. Some will invest financially. Some will sell supplies. Some will buy products. Over it all, some will coordinate. In negotiating the way they together pursue the collective project, these men and women will negotiate—sometimes explicitly, sometimes implicitly—their relative responsibilities and returns. And in most of the advanced capitalist world, they will negotiate them in the shadow of corporate law: they will adopt the corporate law provisions they like and contract around the rest if they can.

Usually corporate law works best when it gives default rules that approximate the deals people would most often negotiate. Like much that is most basic in life, these archetypal rules are fairly straightforward. To sing the *Ring*, soprano Birgit Nilsson once explained, you mostly need a comfortable pair of shoes. To promote efficient growth, corporate law mostly needs to address the following three issues.

First, the rules should delegate discretion, yet ban managerial theft and indolence. Necessarily in group enterprises one set of people (shareholders) will invest money that others (directors and officers) will manage. Because managers manage in a world of uncertain returns, most investors will want a law that gives those managers discretion to take risks.

Because managers manage in a world where they can steal and turn indolent, however, most investors will also want limits on their managers. They will want, in short, a law that prevents their managers from absconding with the cash register or too often playing golf. Because managers cannot manage unless investors invest, most managers will want such laws, too. Both investors and managers will generally want, in short, a regime that lets corporate agents take risks and make mistakes, but that binds them from diverting funds or acting carelessly.

Second, to encourage the movement of assets to their highest valued users, the law will need generally to facilitate corporate transfers. It will need not just to let individual investors transfer their fractional interests in the firm, though it will need at least to do that. It will need also to let investors collectively transfer their productive assets.

Third, the rules should prevent people from externalizing the cost of their business. To facilitate transfers, the law will need generally to limit investor liability. Having done so, however, it will need also to prevent investors from manipulating those limitations to transfer business risks to people who cannot readily negotiate with the firm.

However imperfectly, U.S. corporate law (particularly in Delaware) does this remarkably well. With exceptions to be sure, it accomplishes all this and lets people negotiate idiosyncratic exceptions besides.[3] Largely it succeeds because of the economics of federalism. Under American choice-of-law rules, investors can choose the corporate law that will govern them by choosing the state in which to incorporate. To capture corporate franchise taxes, states can compete among themselves to offer investors and managers improved legal packages.[4]

Because Japanese corporate law is national rather than state, it faces less competitive pressure. Because it faces less pressure, it retains—for all its basic appropriateness—a substantial variety of oddly inefficient minor rules.[5] This chapter is about the law that results.

B. Preliminary Detail

Before turning to the basic contours of Japanese corporate law, skim first some preliminary (and regrettably dry) detail. As in the United States, entrepreneurs in Japan can choose from a variety of firm types. First, they can form a partnership (*gōmei gaisha*). Should they do so, each investor will be personally liable for the firm's debts (Commercial Code, §80(a)).[6] Unless they otherwise agree, each will be an agent for the firm (Commercial Code, §§70, 76) and participate equally in management (§§70, 71). They will share gains and losses according to their respective contributions (Commercial Code, §§68, 89; Civil Code, §674), but be able to transfer their interests only with the consent of the others (Commercial Code, §73).

Second, entrepreneurs can form a limited partnership (*gōshi gaisha*).

The general partners will manage the firm and have unlimited liability (Commercial Code, §146). The limited partners will be liable only to the amount of their contributions, will not share in management, and will be able to transfer their interests if the general partners consent, even if the limited partners do not (Commercial Code, §§146, 154, 156, 157).

Third, entrepreneurs can choose either a standard corporation (*kabushiki kaisha*, abbreviated K.K.) or a close corporation (*yūgen gaisha*, abbreviated Y.G.).[7] Should they opt for the close corporate form, they can use simplified procedures for their internal affairs, but will face limits on stock transfers and on the maximum number of shareholders. In most other basic respects, they will operate by the principles that govern standard corporations. Unless otherwise noted, by corporation we refer to a K.K.[8]

In a corporation, investors are liable only to the amount of their contributions (i.e., they can lose only the amount they paid for the stock; Commercial Code, §200(a)). Unless the articles of incorporation otherwise provide, they may freely transfer their shares (Commercial Code, §204(a)). To supervise the firm, they elect directors at a shareholders' meeting. At those meetings, unless otherwise provided, each share has one vote (Commercial Code, §241(a)). Should they so choose, investors may also use preferred stock—which under some circumstances need not vote (Commercial Code, §§222, 242).

Investors must hold shareholders' meetings at least annually (Commercial Code, §234(a)), the minimum quorum is one-third of the shares (§256-2), and cumulative voting is optional (§256-3). Shareholders with at least 3 percent of the stock may call a special meeting (Commercial Code, §237), and those with at least 10 percent may sue for dissolution if deadlock threatens the company (§406-2).

The board of directors must include at least three directors (Commercial Code, §255), and at least one must be a "representative director," who acts as agent for the firm (§261(a)). Directors serve one- to two-year terms (Commercial Code, §256). The minimum quorum for a board meeting is a majority (Commercial Code, §260-2).

That all this seems dreadfully familiar to American lawyers is no accident. The occupation lawyers who masterminded the revisions to the Japanese corporate law in 1949–1950 came from Chicago. They knew what they liked and liked what they knew. They presented the Japanese Diet with variations on the 1933 Illinois Business Corporation Act, and the Diet dutifully enacted them.[9]

C. Principal-Agent Constraints
1. *The Business Judgment Rule*

In many ways, both U.S. corporate law and Japanese corporate law begin with the business judgment rule: Absent fraud, illegality, gross negligence, or a conflict of interest, a court will not second-guess managerial decisions. Take the opinion in a recent derivative suit against giant Nomura Securities.[10]

The fall in stock prices at the end of the 1980s had left many Nomura clients with large losses. Whether Nomura had agreed in advance to compensate them for those losses is unclear. It denied having done so, if only because such a promise would have violated the Securities Exchange Act.[11] But such a promise would not have been irrational. In a market as heavily regulated as the Japanese securities market, rational securities firms might well have invented hidden ways to offer their largest clients bulk discounts. A promise to insure them against large losses would have done just that.

Whatever the initial deal, senior Nomura managers eventually decided to compensate several major clients for their market losses. Nomura made its largest profits underwriting new issues, and its managers apparently reasoned that the compensation would help induce those clients to keep their underwriting business with the firm. According to the Tokyo District Court, in deciding to compensate they acted within the business judgment rule:[12]

> Suppose a case raises the propriety of a director's business judgment. The reasonable approach for a court is not to decide at the outset what the director should have done, and then to compare that decision with the judgment the director actually made. Rather, the court should first examine the business judgment the director made. Then, it should ask whether the director either (i) made a careless error in assessing the factual premises to that judgment, or (ii) in making the judgment used a process that for an ordinary business executive would have been egregiously unreasonable.
>
> If a court finds that a director either did make a careless error in determining the factual premises, or did use a process that was egregiously unreasonable, then two things follow. First, it must find that the director's business judgment exceeded the scope of discretion allotted him. Second, it must hold that he violated either the duty of care of a good manager or his duty of loyalty.

The managers did not violate the Securities Exchange Act[13] and made a judgment call that they rationally thought would earn the firm large offsetting gains. To the court, that sufficed.

Or take Osamu Tezuka. A brilliant and prolific cartoonist, Tezuka was god of Japanese comics, easily the most influential artist in the massive postwar Japanese comic book industry. A rabid Disney fan, he claimed to have seen *Snow White* fifty times, *Bambi* eighty. By the time he hit his stride, as one commentator put it, he had made the "cutesy Disney look" his own.[14] Over the course of his life, he drew comics in virtually every genre—from boys' comics to girls'; from children's comics to adults'; from a series on the life of Buddha, to one on Hitler, to the perennially popular one on the boy robot Atomu. By the time he died, his life's work came to 500 volumes of 200- to 400-page books.

Artistic genius did not translate into managerial prowess, and in the early 1970s, Tezuka's animation studio fell on hard times. For revenue, it started working on cartoons by other artists, but to do that, in turn, it needed more staff. When the staff increased, Tezuka now found himself too busy managing to draw the comics he loved. He quit, but without his art the firm quickly went broke. Although Tezuka had been a director, the Tokyo District Court refused to hold him liable. Directors "have broad discretion" in matters involving "the management of the company's business," it explained. "Even if their decisions seem inappropriate *ex post*, . . . if those decisions were within the permissible scope of managerial discretion when made," then the directors "do not violate their responsibilities."[15]

Nomura could reimburse clients, and Tezuka could make bad calls, but the business judgment rule does not excuse fraudulent or illegal schemes, even when they earn the shareholders money.[16] One director of K.K. Hazama, a large construction firm traded on the Tokyo Stock Exchange, bribed a small-town mayor for ¥14 million to obtain the contract on the town's new sports facility. When the government prosecuted him for the scheme, the court sentenced him to two years in prison. When a shareholder brought a derivative suit, it held the director liable to the company to boot:

> Obviously, in doing business, companies may not use strongly anti-social tactics like bribery that violate the Criminal Code. They may not justify bribery as a business strategy on the grounds either (i) that it raises corporate profits, or (ii) that because their competitors customarily bribe they could not otherwise obtain business.[17]

113

The director was liable for the full amount of the bribe and could claim no offset for any profits the scheme earned.

2. The Duty of Loyalty

The business judgment rule governs only when a plaintiff cannot show either gross negligence or a potential conflict of interest. In the Japanese Supreme Court's words, "[A] director owes the duty of care of a good manager and a duty of loyalty."[18] Consider first the duty of loyalty, then the duty of care.

(a.) *Conflict Transactions.* Shigeru Okada was the longtime director and president of the upscale Mitsukoshi Department Store, at one time the core of the giant Mitsui conglomerate. He had joined Mitsukoshi in 1938, captured national attention in 1950 by throwing the flashiest fashion show since the war, and solidified that fame by crushing a major strike. Flamboyant to the end, he once flew guests to the Versailles to celebrate the store's fame. In 1982, however, he organized a Mitsukoshi display of Persian treasures. Too bad for him, many were fakes from a factory near Tokyo. Worse, most had come through Michi Takahisa, a jewelry designer—and his longtime mistress.

Apparently Okada had been routing Takahisa's Hong Kong trading company an increasingly large share of Mitsukoshi's imports. By 1981, Mitsukoshi bought ¥3.1 billion worth of merchandise from her firm, making it the store's eighth largest supplier. To the Tokyo District Court, Okada's breach of his duty of loyalty was clear enough: in criminal prosecution, it sentenced him to 3½ years in prison; in a civil suit, it held him liable to the firm for money he had routed his lover.[19]

Less colorfully, Yūichi Takeda was a director and department chief in an upstart computer-related firm. For his new department, he recruited a corps of software engineers and programmers. Soon, however, he quarreled with the firm's CEO over space. Angered, he began plotting a lateral move, organized a rival computer software firm, and convinced his subordinates to follow him. To the court, in enticing subordinates away he violated his duty of loyalty and owed the firm damages.[20]

b. Ratification. As under American law, directors party to a conflict of interest violate their duty of loyalty only if they do not disclose that conflict and obtain advance consent from independent directors. Hideo Fujimoto, for instance, was a representative director at one firm and owned all the stock of another. He then negotiated low-priced sales of steel rods from the first firm to the second. When a shareholder challenged his transaction in a derivative suit, the court held for the shareholder. Had the board of the first firm ratified the transaction, Fujimoto would have been safe. As it had not, he owed the firm damages.[21]

Sensibly enough, courts let shareholders use the ratification requirement against dominant insiders, but not against third parties who deal with the firm in good faith. Take the dispute between Tarō Iwasaki and a plaintiff who took an unauthorized check from an Iwasaki company. Tarō and his wife, Hanako, had together owned several firms that operated various clubs, bars, and restaurants. Both had served as directors, and Hanako had worked at the Blue as what the court called a "madam." As such, she supervised employees, ordered liquor, and paid bills.

The Iwasakis cut corners. They also got caught. Eventually a court convicted (and fined) Hanako of pouring domestic liquor into foreign liquor bottles and selling the drinks as foreign. Husband Tarō promised to repay her fine out of corporate funds. After all, he assured her, they had worked the scam together and had done it to make money for the firm. By 1964, however, he was sleeping with other women, and Hanako was having an affair of her own. With their marriage dead, Hanako doubted he would keep his word. She cut a company check to herself, discounted it with the plaintiff, and vanished.

Faced with the plaintiff's demand for payment, the payor company (now under Tarō's control) refused to honor the check. In part, Tarō refused on duty-of-loyalty grounds. His wife had cut the corporate check to herself, and that act had constituted an unratified transaction between a director (Hanako) and the firm. As such, it was void under the Commercial Code. Think again, responded the court. The plaintiff took the check in good faith. It could properly demand payment.[22]

c. Insider Trading. For securities transactions, Japan has long maintained a broad antifraud rule (equivalent to Rule 10b-5 under the 1934 Securities Exchange Act).[23] Unlike with Rule 10b-5, however, the government has not used the rule to police insider trading.[24] Its reticence should not surprise—the drafters of 10b-5 may not have intended it to apply to insider trading either.[25] Nonetheless, the Diet recently passed an explicit ban on securities trades by insiders who hold material undisclosed information.[26] With this new law available, the government has begun to bring criminal prosecutions.[27]

Japanese corporate law also includes a prophylactic rule (equivalent to section 16(b) of the 1934 act) against insider trading. Like its American counterpart, the rule requires senior officers, directors, and 10-percent-plus shareholders to disgorge to the firm any profits they make on purchases and sales within a six-month period.[28] Although the rule lay dormant for years, the (re)introduction of a requirement that insiders disclose their trades (equivalent to section 16(a)) has dramatically boosted litigation.[29]

Toward this short-swing trading ban, Japanese courts take a narrow, formalistic approach, which itself mirrors the approach U.S. courts take toward section 16(b). Consider the suit by the makers of Yōmeishu, a bizarre concoction of assorted Chinese remedies made respectable only by comparison to its competitor Seirogan, with its creosote base. The recent health food craze has boosted demand, and with sales high, Yōmeishu operates out of the swank Shibuya ward in Tokyo and trades its stock on the Tokyo Stock Exchange.

In 1989, the Yokohama hotel firm K.K. Bando Hotel began buying a big stake in Yōmeishu. When Bando sold some of that stock, Yōmeishu sued for its short-swing profits. The court held Bando Hotel liable. Yōmeishu did not need to show that Bando had "unfairly used secrets obtained from its work or status." Neither did it need to show that it had "suffered damage from [Bando's] short-swing trades." The provision was designed "indirectly to prevent insider trading," explained the court. For that, a simple prophylactic approach worked just fine.[30]

(d) Political Gifts. When in March of 1960 the directors of giant Yahata Steel donated ¥3.5 million in corporate funds to the ruling Liberal Democratic Party (LDP), shareholders brought a derivative suit. The gift was both ultra vires, they argued, and a violation of the directors' duty of loyalty. Perhaps the court's opinion reflects a political ingenuousness Japanese judges no longer enjoy. But its approach to fiduciary duties remains intact. Wrote the Supreme Court:

> Political parties are the most powerful mechanisms that exist for giving voice to the political will of the people. Accordingly, how they operate is a matter of serious concern. We can properly expect corporations—in conduct that flows naturally from their social existence—to cooperate with the healthy development of those parties.

Indeed, in Yahata's case that cooperation with the LDP was part of its "corporate social responsibility." As constraints, the court added only that the amount donated be within "reasonable levels" and that it not promote the private interests of the directors or a third party.[31]

116

3. The Duty of Care

As in the United States, directors in Japan find their decisions protected by the business judgment rule only if they exercise due care in making them. And as in the United States, the test for due care is generally gross negligence. As one court put it, the test is whether the director exercised the care of a "business executive with ordinary abilities, experience and authority in business management" or whether his or her conduct was otherwise "clearly irrational."[32]

In practice, courts let directors take large risks.[33] Consequently, in practice, directors violate their duty of care primarily when they do nothing. The director of one bathtub manufacturer, for example, violated his duty of care when he continued doing business with a buyer and extending credit to him—but he violated it because he did no credit check even though he knew the buyer was having business problems.[34]

Sometimes Japanese courts seem to impose on representative directors (see subsection B) a higher duty of care than on other directors. One defendant's father, for example, had been a representative director of a warehouse company. When his father died, its top managers asked him to take his father's post. He agreed, but found himself too busy with his full-time job. With no time to inspect either the warehouse or the corporate books, he relied entirely on others. When large losses followed, the court held he violated his duty of care to the warehouse firm. In discussing a representative director's duty, the court explained:

> A representative director owes a duty of care higher even than that owed by an ordinary director. He must loyally check to ensure that those working for the firm do not violate their responsibilities. He must stop or prevent improper firm-related activities. And he must pursue other policies to ensure the profitability of the firm.

The passage is probably dicta, given the director's complete inactivity. Indeed, the rules the court outlined seem no different from those by which ordinary directors must live. Whatever the legal line might be, however, the defendant crossed it.[35]

D. Abuse of the Corporate Form
1. Piercing the Corporate Veil

"When a corporation is a complete shell or is abused to evade the law," wrote the Supreme Court in 1969, "a court must disregard its corporate form. To recognize it would violate the very purpose behind the institutional distinctions."[36] The firm in question had run an electrical appliance store, and the owner (one man) had organized it as a corporation to evade taxes. Apparently because of his tax fraud, the court pierced the corporate veil. Although piercing the corporate veil is always an exceptional remedy, courts have pierced corporate veils where firms confused the roles of their officers, skipped required meetings, or commingled funds. As in the United States, they pierce the veil in both tort and (more dubiously) contract cases and use a heavily fact-specific inquiry.[37]

Take the 111 employees discharged when their corporate employer dissolved. Because the firm had been a wholly owned subsidiary of another, they tried to pierce the corporate veil and collect their back pay from the parent. The court let them proceed: the subsidiary's officers had been seconded from the parent, the business of the two firms had often been intermingled, and the parent firm had made all significant (and even many minor) business and personnel decisions for the subsidiary.[38]

Or take the suit by Sayoko Gotō, a former member of the Takarazuka Revue. The all-woman troupe specializes in cross-dressed actresses doing plays ranging from *West Side Story* to the *Tale of Genji* to *mon Paris*. According to one anthropologist, the "oppositional construction of gender was refracted through the Takarasiennes, who embodied the eroticized tension between sexual and gender transgression and repression."[39] Maybe so. In any case, Gotō had retired and wanted to open a "café." Quite what she planned to offer in her new establishment the court did not say. But to run it the way she wanted, she needed an adult entertainment license from the local police station.

For this "café," Gotō planned to lease space from a lawyer named Yoshikiyo Tsuchida. Tsuchida claimed to own the entire building. He used the third and fourth floors for his law office and offered Gotō the ground floor. Gotō liked it. Tsuchida explained that title was in a travel agency he owned, so she signed a lease with the agency and remodeled the premises.

When Gotō went to the police station for her license, however, she found that she needed elaborate documentation from her landlord. Tsuchida promised the documents, but never delivered. Apparently his travel agency had never obtained the obligatory construction inspections on the building. In fact, it had not even paid the contractor. Within a few months, the contractor claimed to succeed to title and evicted her.

Unable to run her "café," Gotō sued both Tsuchida's travel agency and (that firm being broke) Tsuchida himself. The court found the company liable and let Gotō pierce its corporate veil. Tsuchida had run several firms, but had made little effort to keep them distinct: he had ignored corporate formalities, his law office staff had paid corporate bills, his corporate directors had been directors in name only, and his travel agency had had no assets and had defaulted on its taxes.[40]

Although Japanese courts may pierce the corporate veil to hold shareholders liable, they also disregard the corporate form for other quite sensible reasons. Loan shark Tarō Kōno had long patronized Hanako Otsuyama at her geisha house. Business was apparently business, even if Otsuyama was very much married to Jirō Heikawa. Heikawa himself ran a tropical fish store, but ran it unsuccessfully. He was heavily in debt, and Otsuyama and her father were guaranteeing his loans. To her, Kōno now made a proposition: Divorce Heikawa and live with me, and I will repay his debts. She agreed, and they lived together at her geisha house for three years.

Kōno did not repay Heikawa's debts directly. Instead, he used his "financial services" firm. After he and Otsuyama had cut their ties, he used that firm to sue her and her father for indemnity. Their agreement with Kōno himself was irrelevant, this "firm" argued, because the firm was legally distinct from Kōno. It had paid their debt, and it had not agreed to forgive that debt; hence it could now sue for indemnity. Not so fast, held the court. One suspects it could have found more than one way to throw out Kōno's claim, but it chose to pierce the corporate veil: the firm was a one-man operation, Kōno effectively owned all the stock, he was the sole director, he was the sole employee, and he had held no shareholder meetings. Any promise he made on his own behalf bound the firm. As he had agreed to pay the debt and she had kept her half of the bargain, he could not now manipulate his shell company to escape his half.[41]

2. Directoral Liability to Third Parties

Should a firm try to externalize the cost of doing business, a third party can sometimes do more than just pierce the corporate veil. It can also sue the firm's directors.[42] Under Commercial Code §266-3, a director who damages a third party through "bad faith or gross negligence" is directly liable to him.

In a typical section 266-3 action, the Osaka High Court held San'yō bussan director Yoshinobu Kureyama liable to the firm's creditors. Kureyama had farmed full-time and trusted the other directors. They, in turn, had invested recklessly and managed lackadaisically.[43] In failing to watch them, he breached his duty of care. For that sin, he was now personally liable to the firm's creditors.

That a director is liable to third parties for "bad faith or gross negligence" does not mean he owes duties of care and loyalty toward those third parties. Quite the contrary. He owes them to the firm, but is liable under section 266-3 to third parties if his breach to the firm causes losses to them. Kureyama breached his duty to San'yō bussan and for that breach was liable to San'yō's creditors.

Much the same logic applied to Rokusaburō Mutō. He already had three jobs: patent agent, veterinarian, and prefectural legislator. But when Kikusui kōgyō, K.K., asked him to become representative director and president, he agreed. Izuo kōzai, K.K., then sold Kikusui steel rods on credit, and Kikusui defaulted. Izuo had relied on the reputation of the people at Kikusui. When it now investigated the firm, it found no office, no factory, no telephone. Mutō, it seems, had agreed to lend it his name, but had done nothing to investigate or supervise. In so doing, he breached his duty of care to Kikusui. When Kikusui's creditors lost money as a result, he owed them damages under section 266-3.[44]

E. Facilitating Transfers
1. Stock Transfers

Unless the articles of incorporation otherwise provide, shareholders in Japan may transfer their stock freely.[45] Indeed, courts enforce this rule so strongly that they will not even let firms stop transfers to the mob. Hiroshi Furukawa was a prominent *sōkaiya*. He owned stock in over 500 companies and had a criminal record that included convictions for extortion, libel, and firearm violations. When he bought stock in Teikoku sankin kōgyō, K.K., and Teisan ōto, K.K., the two firms balked. They refused to record the transfers, and Furukawa sued.

Notwithstanding Furukawa's history, the Tokyo District Court held the transfers valid:

> The exchange of property is vital both to the improvement of individual economic welfare, and to the development of culture. Their smooth exchange is—to a society based on an exchange economy—nothing short of its Magna Charta.[46]

Given the sanctity of free transferability, the need to record the sale to Furukawa followed automatically:

This court is as convinced as the appellant [firms] are of the need to prevent corporate domination by *sōkaiya*. . . . Nonetheless, if someone acquires stock and exercises his shareholder rights with an illegal motive, a court need only stop his exercise of those rights. It need not stop his preliminary acquisition of the stock itself.[47]

2. Control Transactions

a. The Absence of Hostile Bids. Although shareholders can readily transfer individual shares in Japan, hostile takeovers (deals where shareholders sell the firm against the will of their managers—quintessentially tender offers) remain rare. The puzzle is why. The puzzle is hard, for the legal barriers to hostile deals alone seem insufficient to explain their scarcity.[48]

b. Legal Explanations. One factor may be the absence of any provision for cash-out mergers—mergers in which some shareholders receive cash or property other than stock. Instead, mergers in Japan may proceed only if the shareholders of the disappearing corporation receive stock in the surviving corporation. As a result, Japanese acquirors cannot use the notorious two-tiered bids (a tender offer followed by a cash-out merger) so popular in the United States in the early 1980s.[49]

The other relevant Japanese rules on corporate control transactions roughly parallel their American counterparts. To structure an acquisition as a merger (the quintessential "friendly" deal—i.e., an acquisition to which incumbent managers have agreed), the directors first draft a merger agreement (Commercial Code, §408(a)). They then call a shareholders' meeting (Commercial Code, §231). If two-thirds of the shares of both firms approve, the merger takes effect (Commercial Code, §408(c)), and dissenting shareholders acquire appraisal rights (§408-3).

To structure an acquisition as an asset sale, the directors follow the same process. Again, they negotiate an agreement, call a meeting, and obtain a two-thirds vote of the shares of both firms (Commercial Code, §§231, 245). Those who dissent will once more have appraisal rights (Commercial Code, §245-2).

Even tender offers follow rules similar to those in the United States. Upon announcing an offer, for example, the offeror files elaborate disclosure documents with the government. It must keep the offer open for at least twenty days.[50] And it faces a variety of other regulations that, again, track their American counterparts.

c. Cross-Shareholdings. Because the legal differences are minor, many commentators turn to the cross-shareholding arrangements to explain the dearth of tender offers in Japan. In essence, they argue that corporations place large quantities of their stock in the hands of friendly investors. Those investors then refuse to tender in hostile acquisitions.

Unfortunately commentators often exaggerate the extent of the cross-shareholdings. Generally they cite figures close to 75 percent. Yet 75 percent is not the amount of cross-shareholding among business partners. It is the percentage of all shares held by corporations. Real cross-shareholding among business partners instead probably runs only 10 to 30 percent among most firms with such arrangements.[51] In the end, those cross-shareholdings may explain some of the dearth of hostile acquisitions, but hardly all. They may explain some, since an acquiror will now need to pay a price high enough to obtain two-thirds of the float rather than one-half. They certainly do not explain all, since freezing 25 percent of a firm's stock seldom makes an acquisition impossible.

d. Substitutability. Perhaps, however, much of the reason for the near-total absence of hostile bids goes to the interchangeability of friendly and hostile bids. Suppose a potential acquiror finds the absence of cash-out mergers or the presence of cross-shareholdings a cost. He need not simply choose between (1) pushing the hostile bid anyway and (2) dropping the acquisition. He can also try to make the bid a friendly one. As a result, for legal rules and cross-shareholding arrangements to eliminate hostile bids, they need not make such bids impossible. They need only make them less profitable than a friendly bid.

To transform a hostile bid into a friendly one, an acquiror need only bribe the target's senior executives. Granted, if disclosed, the payoffs might be a fiduciary duty breach. Yet neither in Japan nor in the United States need anyone disclose them. Rather, an acquiror can pay the bribes as early retirement bonuses, consulting contracts, or high-paying honorific positions. In short, if an acquiror finds that law or cross-shareholdings make a tender offer inconvenient, he can simply negotiate the deal as a merger. To induce the target board to agree, he can use the premium he would otherwise have paid target shareholders in the tender offer to bribe the target directors instead.

Although we have no data on disguised bribes, note that mergers and asset sales are not rare in Japan.[52] Japanese entrepreneurs *do* negotiate corporate control transactions. They just negotiate friendly, rather than hostile, ones.

F. Inefficiencies

For all its basic good sense, Japanese corporate law contains an unusual number (to lawyers used to Delaware rules) of senseless restrictions. It is hard to know what to make of these rules except, to paraphrase an old book review, that perhaps they fill a much-needed gap. The Commercial Code, for example, has long banned a firm from buying or redeeming its own stock unless it retires it. While it now includes several exceptions, the basic ban remains (Commercial Code, §§210 to 211-2).

Likewise, although the Commercial Code allows stock transfer restrictions, it allows only one size and color: arrangements where a potential seller who finds a buyer must obtain the consent of the board and where a board that refuses must find the seller an appropriate buyer (§§204 to 204-5). The restriction will work in some firms, certainly. Others will want a nearly universal ban on transfers. Still others will want to let a shareholder force the firm to buy the stock, even when he cannot himself find a potential buyer.

The Commercial Code requires all corporations to hire an auditor to monitor the directors (§§273–280). As one might expect, most observers claim the scheme completely fails. The Commercial Code also gives directors no ability to operate by unanimous consent without a meeting.[53]

Until 1991, the Commercial Code required all firms to have seven incorporators (now reduced to one) and required those firms formed by private subscription to apply to the court for an inspection by a court-appointed auditor (an expensive process). Even today, it requires firms to apply for a court-appointed inspector if the incorporators contribute any property other than cash (Commercial Code, §§173, 181). And while some of the worst rules have disappeared, bad new ones appear regularly. Effective in 1982, for example, the Diet raised the minimum price of new stock to ¥50,000 (Commercial Code, §166). Effective in 1991, it imposed on all corporations a minimum capitalization of ¥10 million (Commercial Code, §168-4).

II. The Mob
A. Corporate Governance

Of all aspects of Japanese corporate practice, the *sōkaiya* remain the most bizarre. If paid appropriately, they silence all other shareholders at the general meeting. If not, they harass, intimidate, and blackmail the board. As Mark West put it:

> For a fee, these *sōkaiya* . . . contract to keep order at shareholder
> meetings. If management and [the *sōkaiya*] cannot reach an agree-
> ment on the "fee" arrangements, [the *sōkaiya*] then disrupt the
> next meeting or print scandalous stories in one of the monthly
> *sōkaiya* newspapers.[54]

To spread *sōkaiya* resources as thinly as possible, most firms now coordinate with other firms and hold their shareholders' meetings at exactly the
same time.

The many accounts to the contrary notwithstanding, the most important point about these *sōkaiya* involves what they do not do: they do not
affect corporate governance. General meetings of public companies are not
fora for deliberation and discussion in Japan, to be sure. They are not fora
for deliberation and discussion here either, and we have no reason to think
they would become such fora absent the *sōkaiya*.

Whether in the United States or in Japan, the general meetings of public companies are rigged affairs. They are not rigged because of *sōkaiya*.
They are rigged because of proxies—as well they should be. Virtually
everywhere the board collects the necessary proxies before the meeting. Because it then holds the votes it needs to obtain the result it wants, the meeting itself is a formality. Mob or no mob, no deliberation will occur.

No one deliberates at the shareholders' meeting because deliberation
would benefit no one. Shareholders seldom know how to run the firm.
Given their collective action problems, they seldom have any incentive to
learn. Consequently shareholder deliberation would seldom improve the
quality of decision making at large corporations. Sensibly enough, in neither the United States nor Japan do firms encourage that deliberation.

By contrast, the corporate control market can indeed improve corporate performance—but only if a majority shareholder can ultimately control the general meeting. Toward that end, Japanese courts hold general
meetings to strict rules. When *sōkaiya* break them, the courts declare the
meetings void.

Consider the example of Chisso. The firm was a longtime chemical
manufacturer and a dominating presence in the small coastal town of
Minamata.[55] For decades, it had dumped its effluents in the local bay. By
the 1950s, residents began to notice a bizarre disease, both among animals
and among themselves:

> Birds seemed to be losing their sense of coordination, often falling
> from their perches or flying into buildings and trees. Cats, too,

were acting oddly. They walked with a strange rolling gait, frequently stumbling over their own legs. Many suddenly went mad, running in circles and foaming at the mouth until they fell—or were thrown—into the sea and drowned. Local fishermen called the derangement "the disease of the dancing cats," and watched nervously as the animals' madness progressed.[56]

It did indeed progress and had the same effects among the residents themselves: it numbed, crippled, turned incoherent, and ultimately often killed. Upon doing autopsies, doctors discovered that it had eaten away large parts of the victims' brains.

Chisso was causing the disease, and by 1959, Chisso knew it. That year its scientists confirmed that the disease resulted from the mercury it dumped into the bay. From the sludge at the bottom of the bay, the mercury worked its way up the food chain into fish and eventually humans. Once there, it destroyed the central nervous system. Chisso promptly buried the report and continued dumping mercury for another six years.

Some victims sued and won damages in court.[57] Some victims lobbied and obtained new legislation.[58] The government itself prosecuted Chisso's president and local factory manager and obtained negligent homicide convictions.[59] But some of the victims protested more directly, and one of the ways they protested was to buy Chisso stock and obtain the right to attend the firm's general meeting.

Faced with the prospect of protestors at the meetings, Chisso turned to *sōkaiya*. For the November 1970 general meeting, the majority of the protestors entitled to enter found their way blocked, and those who entered found their questions and motions ignored. Within five minutes, the meeting was over. Claiming that all this violated proper corporate procedure, the protestors sued. By 1974, they won in the district court, and on appeal, both the high court (in 1979) and the Supreme Court (in 1983) affirmed: the contested meeting was void.[60]

B. Payments to *Sōkaiya*

The hardest question about the *sōkaiya* is the most basic: Why do some firms pay? A clue to the answer lies in the way a modest recent change in the law has apparently cut *sōkaiya* payments dramatically. We begin by outlining the service (subsection 1), annoyance (subsection 2), and blackmail (subsection 3) theories to *sōkaiya* payments and conclude by examining the implications of the recent changes in the law (subsection 4).

1. A Service

Why would most ordinary firms want *sōkaiya* to keep order at a meeting? Chisso may have wanted to keep the protesters out, but its brutality makes it an outlier everywhere. After all, most companies do not knowingly kill their neighbors in large numbers. Why, to rephrase the question, would a more quotidian board care what shareholders asked? They may ask embarrassing questions, but silencing them at the meeting will not stop the disclosure. Instead, it will merely induce them to talk to reporters. Given the competitive magazine market in Japan, a board that muzzles its shareholders merely moves the forum for its embarrassment from the meeting to the newsstand.

2. Annoyance

Sometimes the *sōkaiya* have no real information about the firm. Absent information, they cannot blackmail. Instead, like the Kōnos, they can only annoy. Although the truly obnoxious can annoy indeed, most firms will pay them only modest amounts, if they pay them at all. Newspapers revealed in 1997 that several large firms had been paying *sōkaiya* extremely large amounts. It would be odd indeed if business executives had paid them that much money merely to ask them to behave more politely at the meetings. All the stereotypes about shame and face-saving in Japanese culture notwithstanding, if a *sōkaiya* demanded $1 million just to be polite, most Japanese executives we know would tell him to go ahead and make their day.

3. Extortion

Sometimes, however, the *sōkaiya* have damning information about either the firm or its senior executives. Sometimes they know about tax fraud, for instance, or securities violations, or other white-collar crime. They know about mistresses and assorted personal infidelities. In exchange for keeping quiet, they will demand large sums.

When *sōkaiya* have this information, why firms pay them is no puzzle. Firms everywhere pay mobsters with information. The only puzzle is the connection to the annual meeting. Suppose the Commercial Code let firms cancel the annual meeting. Would the blackmail end? Consider in this regard the implications of a recent legal change.

4. The Law

a. Old Law. Paying *sōkaiya* to silence shareholders has long been a crime in Japan. Take Tōyō denki seizō, K.K. Tōyō now specializes in industrial-grade electrical equipment, but in the early 1960s, it had hoped to enter the consumer television market. Toward that end, it hired an "inventor," who then announced a new, better, brighter TV. Alas, all he did was buy a Toshiba TV set and crank up the voltage. When news of the debacle began to leak, Tōyō managers feared for their careers. Lest they face embarrassing questions at the general meeting, they hired two well-known *sōkaiya*.

In paying the *sōkaiya*, the Tōyō managers broke the law. Under section 494 of the Commercial Code, anyone who makes an "improper solicitation" with respect to the exercise of shareholder rights violates the criminal provisions of that code. According to the court, in paying the *sōkaiya* to prevent others from "fairly speaking or fairly exercising their vote" at the general meeting, the Tōyō managers did just that.[61]

b. New Law. In order allegedly to reduce *sōkaiya* payments, in the early 1980s the Diet eliminated the need to prove a solicitation (Commercial Code, §§294-2, 497). Instead, prosecutors could now obtain convictions simply by proving that the payments were made in connection with the exercise of a shareholder right.[62] If the change seems trivial, that is the point. Although it received much press, it changed very little in the law. Nor did the legal change much alter enforcement practices. According to attorney Hideaki Kubori, of recent prosecutions of officers at twenty-four firms on *sōkaiya*-related charges, all prison sentences were suspended, and no fine exceeded ¥200,000.

Notwithstanding the modesty of the legal changes, most evidence (tentative to be sure) suggests that payments to *sōkaiya* in connection with the annual meetings have fallen radically. Take the surveys by legal-commercial publisher Shōji hōmu. It regularly surveys a couple thousand firms about their general meetings. Obviously its respondents may lie, and obviously (given newspaper accounts) some firms still pay *sōkaiya* large amounts. Yet, at least according to those Shōji hōmu surveys, *sōkaiya* are a nonissue. Over three-quarters of the firms explicitly claimed that no shareholders had contacted them before the meeting at all.[63]

c. Implications.. If a minor change in the law could eliminate shareholder-meeting payoffs, the reason is simple. The small increase in legal risk to *sōkaiya* payoffs did not stop payments to the mob. It merely induced the mob to shift the forum of its blackmail from the shareholders' meeting to other contexts.[64] Some, like the Kōno family, demand inflated payments for potted plants or sue for access to shareholder lists. Others file strike suits as derivative actions and then demand settlements. Still others locate evidence of corporate misbehavior and then pass it on to their affiliated crime syndicates. Like Vito Corleone, those affiliates then make the offers that no corporate executive would reasonably refuse.

Interesting enough as it is to speculate on why corporate extortion in Japan, but not in the United States, took the form of *sōkaiya* payoffs for so long, that speculation hides an essential commonality between the two countries: as long as wealthy executives cheat on the law, their taxes, and their wives, others will blackmail them. For decades, blackmail in Japan may have taken the form of shareholders' meeting payments. Apparently as a result of a minor legal change, however, it has now shifted to other means. That such a trivial change could induce that shift suggests simply that the earlier tie to the meetings was primarily happenstance.

III. Stock Prices
A. Orthodox Accounts

At least as prevalent as accounts of *sōkaiya* are stories about the allegedly longer-term perspective of Japanese firms or about the willingness of Japanese managers to ignore stock market cues.[65] Michael E. Porter captured the gist of many of these accounts. American institutional investors, he wrote, impose goals that "are purely financial and are focused on quarterly or annual appreciation of their investment portfolio." Those stock market measures, he implied, often miss a firm's long-term prospects. By contrast, Japanese owners look to the "long-term." As a result, for senior Japanese executives "current earnings or share prices play only a modest role in promotion or compensation." For them, stock prices "have virtually no direct or indirect influence."[66]

Porter did not invent this tale. It is a staple of the popular press and comes with a long academic pedigree. Already in the 1970s, sociologist Rodney Clark was concluding that for Japanese firms "high profitability, a large return on assets or capital employed, is unlikely to be a very important goal." Instead, they pursue "aims which are given rather lower priority in the West, such as the provision of welfare to employees."[67] Because of the greater job security, echoed business consultants James C. Abegglen and George Stalk, Jr., a "Japanese manager is able to look further into the future and is freer to do what is necessary to ensure a successful future." Ultimately Japanese managers "are freed from the tyranny of accountants, and from the terrible pressures throughout the U.S. organizations for steady improvement in earnings per share."[68] "Even in practical terms," claimed sociologist Ronald Dore, "Japanese managers do not have to be too worried about their share price."[69]

And yet these accounts miss something essential about economic performance. Unless a firm produces good products cheaply, few consumers will buy its goods. Unless it makes a market return on its investments, few will lend it money or buy its stock. Unless shareholders price stock by considering the firm's long-term prospects, they throw money away. According to economic theory, these several factors should drive managers to maximize long-term prospects and—necessarily and simultaneously—share price. According to economic theory, that phenomenon should be as true in Japan as it is in the United States. As we explain below, it is.

B. Evidence from Japan
1. Introduction

To explore what does drive the way Japanese firms behave, consider three questions: When do outsiders join the board of directors of a Japanese firm? When do senior executives lose their jobs? What determines how much board members make? To answer these questions, we turn to several pioneering empirical studies by Steven N. Kaplan.[70]

The Japanese firms in Kaplan's study had a median of 21 directors (U.S. firms had a median of 15). Unlike U.S. directors, most of the Japanese directors were company officers. Typically they served on the board for about eight years. Each board included a president, who generally functioned as the equivalent of a CEO. In each firm, the top executives (a median of 3 and a mean of 4.2) served as representative directors. We call a director an "outside director" if he ever worked elsewhere.[71]

2. Outside Directors

To determine what induced firms to appoint outside directors, Kaplan considered four possible performance measures:

(a) company stock returns (i.e., dividends plus capital gains)

(b) sales growth (a rough proxy for change in market share)

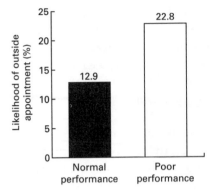

Figure 5.1 Outside Appointments and Stock Returns in Japan (poor versus normal performance is 50% stock return differential)

(c) income change (i.e., change in pretax income as a fraction of total firm assets)

(d) whether income is negative[72]

According to the data, appointments of outside directors increase significantly with (a) and (d), but not with (b) or (c). In short, stock prices matter. When stock prices fall, firms appoint outside directors—both bank and shareholder outsiders. Take figure 5.1: a 50 percent differential or decline in stock returns roughly doubles the odds that an outsider will be appointed to the board (from 12.9 to 22.8 percent). Indeed, outside appointments in Japan are more sensitive to stock prices than in the United States.

Second, an earnings loss matters. If a Japanese firm loses money, figure 5.2 shows that the chance the firm will appoint an outside director either that year or the next doubles—from 12.9 to 26.1 percent.

Third, sales growth has no significant impact on outside appointments. Changes in sales—the proxy for a firm's market share—do not affect the odds that it will appoint outsiders.

3. Internal Change

According to Kaplan's data, an outside appointment also signals that major changes are about to occur internally. Consider three measures of internal change:

(i) the nonstandard turnover of the president (the old president leaves and does not become chairman, something that happens about 30 percent of the time a president loses his or her job)

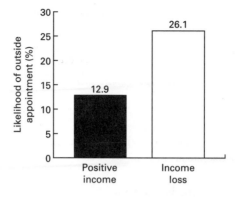

Figure 5.2 Outside Appointments and Earnings Losses in Japan

(ii) the percentage turnover of the representative directors

(iii) the percentage turnover of all of the directors

As table 5.1 shows, when a firm appoints an outsider to its board, the odds of each type of internal change increase substantially.

4. Executive Turnover

Now ask whether the turnover of senior executives is directly sensitive (independent of the outside board appointments) to any of the same performance measures: (a) stock returns, (b) sales growth, (c) income change, and (d) whether income is negative. Turn first to presidents and then to representative directors.

Japanese presidents have a median age of 66 (59 for U.S. CEOs). They have worked in their firms for a median of 39 years (28 years for U.S. CEOs) and serve as president for a mean of 6.7 years (9.7 years for U.S. CEOs). When a president leaves his or her job, 68.5 percent of the time he or she becomes chair of the board. Our interest, of course, is in those cases when the president does not become chair.

The turnover of the president (not becoming the chair of the board) is significantly related to (a), (c), and (d), but not to (b). In other words, Kaplan finds that the turnover is significantly related to share price, to income change, and to whether a firm is profitable. Suppose a firm's stock price underperforms the market by 50 percent. The odds that its president will lose his or her job and not become chair increase from 3.5 to 8.5 percent. Or suppose the firm has a loss. The odds jump by about 9 percent,

Table 5.1 Likelihood of Major Internal Changes with Outside Board
Appointments (in Percent)

	Years without Outside Appointment	Years with Outside Appointment
Nonstandard presidential turnover	3.9	11.1
Representative director turnover	14.4	24.5
All director turnover	12.1	16.3

Source: Steven N. Kaplan and J. Mark Ramseyer, "Those Japanese Firms with Their Disdain for Shareholders: Another Myth for the Academy," 74 *Wash. U. L.Q.* 403 (1996).

from 3.5 to 12.5 percent. For presidential tenure as for outside appointments, stock price and profits matter.

Kaplan also finds that the turnover of representative directors is significantly related to all four performance measures. Again, suppose a firm's stock price underperforms the market by 50 percent. The statistical analysis implies that the turnover of its representative directors will increase from 14.3 to 18.9 percent. Or suppose the firm reports a loss. Turnover jumps from 14.3 to 25.3 percent.

Readers may ask whether those increases in turnover are meaningful. After all, even in very bad years the majority of representative directors keep their jobs. Perhaps the best way to consider this is to compare what happens to representative directors in Japan with what happens to executive directors in the United States. Figures 5.3 and 5.4 indicate that the effects are qualitatively identical. Turnover in the United States increases

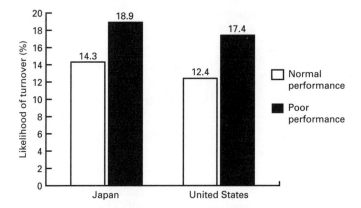

Figure 5.3 Top Executive Turnover and Stock Return (poor versus normal performance is 50% stock return differential)

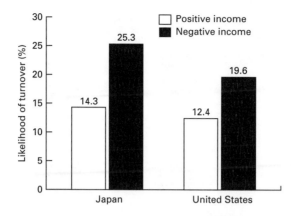

Figure 5.4 Top Executive Turnover and Negative Income

with poor performance by roughly the same amount as in Japan. In other words, poor stock and earnings performance has roughly the same impact (or lack of impact) on top executives in Japan as it does on top executives in the United States.

5. Management Compensation

Consider now the determinants of executive compensation. More particularly, ask whether—as orthodox observers claim—compensation practices in Japan give senior personnel an incentive to govern the firm in ways that emphasize market share, while deemphasizing profitability and stock price. Consistent with the previous discussion, the answer is no. Kaplan again uses the four performance measures and traces their effect on the cash compensation of Japanese directors (generally the most senior executives).

The compensation of Japanese directors is significantly related to all four performance variables. The performance measure that explains the most variation in the data is whether the firm made a profit. The measure that explains the least variation is sales growth. A director of a firm that reports a loss can expect to see his pay cut 13 percent (over the following two years). A director of a firm with a 50 percent increase in stock value can expect pay raises of more than 9 percent.

Again, what happens in Japan is not aberrational. In fact, it closely resembles the experience in the United States. Figures 5.5 and 5.6 illustrate this by comparing the effects of stock returns, sales growth, and earnings losses on the cash compensation of Japanese directors and American CEOs.

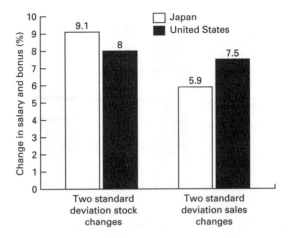

Figure 5.5 Top Executive Compensation and Performance

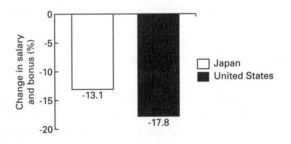

Figure 5.6 Top Executive Compensation after Earnings Loss

Conclusions

Efficient economic growth requires that people organize some activities in groups, and corporate law provides the rules by which they can govern their groups. Given Japanese economic success, it should come as no surprise that most Japanese corporate rules make reasonably good sense. Only on relatively minor issues are the rules sometimes inefficient. That inefficiency, in turn, probably results from the lack of competitive pressure among incorporating government entities.

Given the occasional role of the *sōkaiya*, Japanese shareholders' meetings seem odd affairs. Yet the oddness is largely cosmetic. Shareholders' meetings are not important fora for deliberation in large firms anywhere anyway. When *sōkaiya* do collect large amounts, they probably do not do so for policing the meetings. They do so through the universal phenomenon of blackmail.

Although observers argue that Japanese firms ignore stock market cues, the observers are wrong. The competitive pressures of stock and product markets should apply as strongly in Japan as anywhere else. According to recent empirical evidence, they do: Japanese firms respond—and respond closely—to stock price signals.

6   CIVIL PROCEDURE

Things seen around the capital:
    night muggings, burglaries, fake royal orders,
Servants, horses, senseless riots,
    shaved heads who left the order, new men who joined,
Men named to lordships, men without a clue,
    title guarantees, royal commissions, pointless fights,
Litigants from the provinces,
    files stuffed with documents,
Flatterers, slanderers, Zen and Ritsu priests,
    back-stabbing low life.
And the court house—
    swamped by the shrewd and the witless both but,
    when all is said and done, with nothing to show. . . .

And on it goes, a piece of graffiti scribbled in the capital in 1334.[1] Litigants (along with muggers, thieves, slanderers, and priests) clogged the streets of Kyoto to sue over commissions, tax assessments, and real estate titles. Civil litigation in Japan enjoys a long tradition.

If fourteenth-century scribblers thought litigants then brought moronic claims, they could learn a trick or two from the 1990s. Witness the plaintiffs who sued Prime Minister Hashimoto for smoking cigarettes. By chain-smoking, claimed they, he violated their constitutional right to "wholesome and cultured living." Bravely they would go, it seems, where no litigant had gone before. Not just litigation, but public idiocy, too, enjoys a long tradition.[2]

Modern Japanese civil procedure bears almost no resemblance to fourteenth-century process, just as modern American procedure bears almost none to fourteenth-century English procedure. But where much of modern Japanese substantive law (e.g., torts, contract) parallels its U.S. counterpart, procedure differs radically. Largely, those procedural differences reflect two constitutional differences: the use exclusively of a single national court system in Japan, but of parallel state and federal systems in the United States; and the use exclusively of bench trials in Japan, but of jury and bench trials in the United States.[3]

We begin in section I by tracking the procedural implications of a unitary court system (subsection A). We then explore the differences that follow from an absence of juries (subsection B) and summarize some of the

136

other principal procedural differences (subsection C). Finally, we study the enforcement powers of the Japanese courts (section II).

I. The Law
A. Federalism
1. Implications

In the United States, the state courts exercise general subject-matter jurisdiction, but the national courts exercise only limited jurisdiction. In the United States, both the state and the national courts exercise personal jurisdiction bounded largely by state territorial lines. In the United States, both the state and the national courts make law. In contrast to all this, in Japan (as in most advanced capitalist countries) *all* courts are national—and the procedural consequences are profound.

Indeed, the use of a single court system in Japan vitiates fully half of what U.S. Civil Procedure professors teach. In many U.S. law schools, instructors spend an entire year on the course. Of that year, most devote half (and, one might add, the half most students think the more interesting) to issues peculiar to the dual court system.

2. Subject-Matter Jurisdiction

Take subject-matter jurisdiction. Most U.S. professors spend several weeks on the arcane mysteries of federal-question and diversity jurisdiction. Must a plaintiff raise the federal issue in the complaint, for example, or can he rely on the defendant's raising it in the answer? Can the plaintiff aggregate claims against multiple defendants to meet the jurisdictional minimum? If he raises a federal claim in the complaint, can he add other state claims? If he brings a federal claim, can the defendant counterclaim on a state law issue?

In Japan, all these issues and more disappear. Over nearly all major disputes, the district courts have original subject-matter jurisdiction. The only exceptions are minor. Claims of under ¥900,000 must begin in summary court, for instance.[4] Electoral law claims must often begin at the high court level.[5] Antitrust claims must often begin at the Tokyo High Court.[6] Yet for most disputes, the law of subject-matter jurisdiction is marvelously dull: the district courts have it.

3. Personal Jurisdiction

a. Jurisdiction and Venue. Or take personal jurisdiction. Could Oregon lawyer Mitchell sue California client Neff in Oregon and satisfy

137

the judgment by seizing the local real estate that Senator Pennoyer had the bad judgment eventually to buy? Could the state of Washington sue the International Shoe Company in local court over its tax liability when the company had no local office? Could Heitner sue Greyhound directors in Delaware by sequestering their Greyhound stock? With only one national court system, the Japanese personal jurisdiction rule is again dull: the national courts have it.[7]

Questions of venue remain, but largely for litigating convenience. Over individual defendants, venue generally lies at their residence (Code of Civil Procedure (CCvP), §4(b)).[8] Over corporate defendants, it lies at their principal place of business (CCvP, §4(d)). Alternative venues do exist. In tort disputes, for example, the plaintiff may also sue where the tort occurred (CCvP, §5(i)). As one plaintiff once showed, in a defamation case against a newspaper, this means venue will lie anywhere it sells its papers.[9] In contract disputes, the plaintiff may sue where the defendant was to perform (CCvP, §5(a)). As one lawyer once showed, when a client promises to pay his lawyer with real estate, this means venue for the fee dispute will lie wherever that property is.[10] And in land disputes, the plaintiff may sue wherever the land sits (CCvP, §5(l)).

Based as American jurisdictional rules are on notions of sovereignty, if a plaintiff sues in the wrong place, the court (subject to some exceptions) must dismiss the case. The Japanese venue rules are based on convenience. Accordingly if a plaintiff sues in the wrong place, the court merely transfers it to the right place (CCvP, §16).

b. Absent Defendants. When a plaintiff cannot find a defendant within Japan, he can serve process by publication (CCvP, §110(a)). Although doing so will raise issues of notice, it will not raise those of jurisdiction. For process is not (as in the *Pennoyer* tradition) a prerequisite to jurisdiction. It is simply the presumptive mode of notice. Jurisdiction depends on whether the defendant is present, is domiciled, or has committed various acts in Japan.[11] If he meets one of those tests, the court has power over the plaintiff's claims against him—personal service or no, adequate notice or no.

The dispute between businessman Aubrey Newland and a construction firm in 1954 illustrates the ramifications. A few months after Newland left Japan, the firm sued him. Following the rules that apply when a plaintiff cannot serve process internationally,[12] it published the service. It then obtained a default judgment, which it likewise published. Only when it attached his car, though, did Newland learn of its suit. He promptly appealed the judgment (an appellant can introduce new evidence and contest factual claims on appeal; see subsection B.7). Although he was beyond the statutory time for appeal the court let him proceed. Given his ties to Japan, he had no grounds for contesting jurisdiction. Because he was not responsible for the delay, the court let him appeal the judgment.[13]

c. In Rem and Quasi in Rem. Japanese courts recognize neither in rem nor quasi in rem jurisdiction. Given any country's need to quiet title, the absence of in rem jurisdiction is a puzzle. That Japan makes do without it probably testifies to the general effectiveness of its real estate registry system (see subsection 2.I.F).

The only analogue to quasi in rem jurisdiction lies in a modified venue rule: If a defendant has no known Japanese domicile, plaintiffs may sue him wherever they can locate his assets (CCvP, §5(d)). For example, Nakako Yasutomi's husband drowned when a Dutch freighter sank his yacht in Tokyo Bay. Yasutomi claimed gross negligence, but could not serve routine process, since the Dutch firm kept no office in Japan. To serve process, she instead attached another of the company's freighters when it sailed into town. Much as in U.S. quasi in rem cases, she could now proceed with her claim.[14] Note, however, a distinction: although, if she won, she could use the ship to satisfy her judgment, that judgment was in personam. If the ship brought less than the judgment (unlikely to be sure) and she found other corporate assets, she could apply the unsatisfied portion of the judgment against those other assets.

4. Choice of Law

And take choice of law. When a swinging train door on the Erie Railroad hit Tompkins while he walked the tracks, American courts had to decide whether national or local common law governed.[15] Japanese courts would not have faced the issue, for no local courts exist to make local law. Instead, all case law is national, and so is almost all statutory and regulatory law that matters. In the domestic context, choice of law is simply not an issue.

B. Juries
1. Discontinuous Trials

If the lack of a parallel local court system in Japan eliminates half of most U.S. Civil Procedure syllabi, the absence of juries kills much of the rest. Granted, even U.S. bench trials differ significantly from Japanese trials. That difference, however, largely results from the way even U.S.

Table 6.1A Length of Time to Judgment:
Contested Cases in Japanese District Courts (1994)

Time	n	Percentage
Less than 1 year	20,554	53.2
1–2 years	9,939	25.7
2–3 years	4,372	11.3
Over 3 years	3,775	9.8
Total	38,640	100.0

Source: Saikō saiban sho, ed., *Shihō tōkei nempō, 1994*
[Annual Report of Judicial Statistics, 1994] (Tokyo: Hōsō kai,
1995), vol. 1, 118 (contested *hanketsu* judgments only).

bench trials follow basic procedural formulae established in the jury trial context.

Consider first what the absence of juries in Japan (and most other advanced capitalist countries) does to trial timing.[16] Freed from any need to impanel a group of six to twelve rookies for the job, courts need not hold trials in a single block of time. Instead, they can hold them as series of discontinuous hearings separated by several weeks each.[17]

This creates an obvious implication for measuring delay: in comparing trial speed across countries, the relevant measure is months from filing to judgment. From time to time, U.S. critics bemoan how long trials take in Japan. In doing so, they ignore the straightforward implications of discontinuous trials. In the United States, parties wait months or years before going to trial, but once there finish the trial quickly. In Japan, parties proceed quickly to trial (to the first meetings with the judge), but wait months or years before it finishes.

By the metric that matters—total time to judgment—Japan is neither speed demon nor laggard. Although a few cases take many years, over half finish within a year of filing (table 6.1A). Compare statistics from the U.S. federal courts (table 6.1B). The U.S. data measure how long existing cases have been pending. Paired with table 6.1A, they suggest a simple point: Japan seems quicker than some U.S. jurisdictions and slower than others.

2. Pretrial

A discontinuous trial necessarily blends pretrial and trial procedure. Under discontinuous trials, the parties do not start with a discrete pretrial phase and then (and only then) proceed to trial. Rather, they first meet with a judge and identify the most critical and contested issues. They choose one, recess to gather evidence and marshal arguments on the issue,

Table 6.1B Length of Time Pending: Cases Pending in U.S. District Courts, 1994

Time	All Circuits		Second Circuit	
	n	Percentage	*n*	Percentage
Less than 1 year	145,807	64.4	14,589	49.5
1–2 years	47,754	21.1	7,081	24.0
2–3 years	18,424	8.1	3,760	12.7
Over 3 years	14,086	6.2	4,065	13.8
Total	226,071	100.0	29,495	100.0

Source: Administrative Office of the United States Courts, ed., *Judicial Business of the United States Courts* (Washington, D.C.: Administrative Office of the United States Courts, 1994), table C-6.

and reconvene. If the plaintiff loses on a critical issue, the trial ends. If he wins, they move to the next issue. Again, they recess to gather data and prepare arguments and then reconvene. Steadily, but discontinuously, they proceed through the issues until the plaintiff either loses or proves all the constituent elements of his claim. In the process, the gate-keeping rules between pretrial and trial (like Rule 12(b)(6) and summary judgment motions) inevitably disappear.

3. Discovery

Although American critics frequently point to the absence of discovery in Japan, the point is a red herring. For its absence follows straightforwardly from the use of discontinuous trials. In the United States, the need to try facts before a specially impaneled jury forces lawyers to concentrate preparation into a discrete pretrial phase. Discovery is merely its name. In Japan, the trial itself blends the American trial equivalent with the American discovery equivalent.

Granted, even between court hearings Japanese lawyers cannot conduct the indiscriminate and largely unsupervised fishing expeditions that characterize some American discovery. Instead, to obtain evidence they generally must convince the judge to order others to testify or to produce documents (though recent changes in the Japanese Civil Procedure Code allow parties a bit more independence than before). The requirement that the judge generally intervene changes the potential for abuse. Because U.S. judges often leave the process unmonitored, plaintiffs can sometimes extort settlements on fake claims by threatening massive discovery. Because Japanese judges more actively police the process, they make such strike suits that much harder.

Crucially Japanese judges do have the power they need to make the disclosure process work. If a judge finds a request for information valid, he can order the opposing party to comply. Should the party refuse, depending on the issue he can fine him, throw him in jail, or find the disputed fact in the other party's favor. Should a third party refuse to comply with an order to testify or produce documents, he can, again, fine him or throw him in jail (see section II).

4. Settlements

All this has at least two implications for settlements. First, it pushes postfiling settlements closer to the expected litigated outcome. Not only can a Japanese judge repeatedly and self-consciously urge the parties to settle,[18] but also because he regularly discusses the case with them, he almost inevitably conveys information about how he plans to decide the case. At that point, they lose much reason to stay in court. Instead, they can both gain by settling the case by reference to that expected judgment (see section 4.II).

Second, the disputes that do go to judgment will tend to be ones where the parties disagree about the expected outcome *on appeal*. Because they are likely to agree about how their trial judge will rule, the cases that do not settle will disproportionately be ones where the parties agree about the trial decision, but not the appealed outcome. Consistent with this, a significant fraction of parties do appeal. During 1994, 38,640 cases proceeded to a contested district court judgment. During the same year, they pursued 14,570 to the high courts, suggesting an appeal rate of perhaps 40 percent.[19]

5. Judicial Involvement

Judges generally take a more active role in Japan than in the United States.[20] Not forced to save factual issues for the jury, if they so choose they can aggressively control the case. Judges who want to do so, for example, can demand documents, pester witnesses, name experts, and open new lines of questions (e.g., CCvP, §§149, 151). Indeed, they have even transformed the prerogative into something of a duty. Under modern Japanese common law, a judge who fails aggressively to pursue this "clarifying function" may commit reversible error.[21] As the Supreme Court explained in a dispute over title to farm land:

> Suppose a party makes a legally untenable argument that one
> could transform into a proper claim by rationally reinterpreting

the asserted facts. If the record contains evidence to back such a reformulated claim, . . . a judge who nonetheless denies recovery violates his duty of clarification.[22]

It is, at first blush, a bizarre rule. By forcing judges to save tightwad clients from the mediocre lawyers they hire (or, with pro se parties, to save them from themselves), it violates most of what we know about efficient incentives. Because of the public subsidy to the courts, litigants will not have the right incentive to invest in legal help unless they have reason to do it right the first time. The simplest way to give them that incentive, of course, is to make them pay if they do it wrong. By contrast, a rule that lets a party appeal on the grounds that the judge did not fix his lawyer's bad job gives him precisely the wrong incentive. In effect, it gives him the incentive to try twice: (1) once with low-budget lawyers and (2) again with better lawyers if his first attempt fails.

In a world without juries, the Japanese rule is less perverse than it seems. First, recall that the trial proceeds in fits and starts, with the parties talking regularly with the judge. It does not radically raise a judge's burden to tell him he must—in the course of these discussions—stop a lawyer from doing obviously stupid things. Second, note that on appeal or retrial in Japan (see subsection B.7), the second judge just pulls the file, rereads it, and hears whatever extra evidence seems necessary. In such a world, appeals and retrials cost the public far less than where a judge must impanel a new jury and start from scratch.

All that said, the Japanese rule in practice probably differs less from American practice than this account suggests. In the United States, we do have a rule that requires parties who hire cheap lawyers to live with what they buy. And we apply it religiously to the facts. But we apply it less scrupulously to the law. The reason is simple: the statement of the facts is a private good, while the summary of the law is in part a public good. Put more colloquially, if a plaintiff hires a low-budget lawyer whose bad work results in wrong facts in the F. Supp., no one else will care. Indeed, because no one but the parties cares about the facts, American courts let parties stipulate to facts that are brazenly untrue. Courts in Japan do the same (CCvP, §§159, 179).

The law is different, for on the law the courts do care. If a cut-rate lawyer bungles the law and that wrong summary appears in the F. Supp., everyone using the reporter suffers. Precisely because courts have an independent interest in getting the law right, American judges faced with bad

143

counsel often table caveat emptor. Rather than rely on a bad lawyer, they tell their clerks to do the research the cut-rate lawyer should have done. Japanese courts have the same independent interest in the accuracy of the law, and the "duty of clarification" sometimes simply restates that point: judges should get the law right even when lawyers are harried, lazy, or dumb.

6. Preclusion

a. The Rules. Again because they do not use juries, Japanese courts apply narrower preclusion rules than U.S. courts. First, they straight-forwardly reject issue preclusion (collateral estoppel). Although lower court judges and academics sometimes explore the concept, the rule remains that which the Supreme Court reiterated in 1969: no preclusion.[23]

Second, Japanese courts apply claim preclusion (res judicata) more nar-rowly than in U.S. courts. By section 114 of the Code of Civil Procedure, the order in a final judgment binds the parties (and those in privity; see CCvP, §115).[24] Because the courts limit that preclusive effect to the claims the parties actually made rather than (as in much modern American law) to all claims they might have made about the matter at stake,[25] the rule cov-ers relatively little.

For example, in 1956 Niichi Maekawa entrusted property to a ware-house that then wrongly transferred it to a third party. Through the mistake, Maekawa lost ¥300,000. He first sued in summary court for ¥100,000 (apparently then the jurisdictional limit for the summary courts). He lost and appealed to the district court. That court decided that he (1) had lost ¥300,000, but (2) had himself been negligent and (3) was, therefore, entitled only to ¥80,000. Having first asked for ¥100,000 in summary court, Maekawa now filed a second suit in district court for the remaining ¥200,000. Held the Supreme Court on appeal: Claim preclusion did not bar the suit.[26]

b. The Logic. The logic to these narrow preclusion rules again flows from the lack of juries. Modern U.S. courts apply issue preclusion and broader notions of claim preclusion because of the expense involved in impaneling juries.[27] Given that cost, they give parties but one chance. Hav-ing had that chance, not only may parties not try the same claims again, but also they may not try related claims either.

A narrow claim preclusion rule costs much less in Japan. Suppose a plaintiff raises claim *A* in case 1. He and the defendant introduce a wide variety of evidence, but the defendant wins. Now suppose the same plaintiff files case 2. In it, he raises a different legal claim (claim *B*) that involves many of the same facts as claim *A*. Nominally, under Japanese law case 2 is distinct from case 1, and the parties will need to re-prove all issues. In fact, however, because parties in Japan present most evidence in documentary form, the parties to case 2 need only refile the papers they submitted in case 1.

Moreover, in deciding the facts in case 2, the judge will know that a colleague already heard the evidence and decided the facts once. Although not bound by the earlier findings, by basic norms of collegiality and professional respect (not to mention the efforts of most mortals to economize on effort), most judges will probably defer to the earlier judge anyway. As a result, the principal expense in case 2 will be the (relatively minor) cost of applying a new legal theory to predetermined facts. And if all this is so, then the economies to a broader claim preclusion rule are quite modest.

The absence of issue preclusion involves the same logic. Although litigants can nominally retry facts in Japanese cases, in practice most judges will defer to the earlier adjudication. As with claim preclusion, any economies to a broad issue preclusion rule would be small.

7. Appeals

Because they do not reserve factual issues for the jury, Japanese judges on appeal review questions of fact as well as those of law.[28] Indeed, they run the first appeal largely as a continuation of the trial hearings themselves.[29] They first review the evidence presented below. They then take new evidence and hear new witnesses as necessary. Subject to some limits, they even accept arguments the parties missed below.[30] Only on further appeal to the Supreme Court do they limit themselves to questions of law.[31]

Most other appellate rules resemble those in the United States. Only the party who loses may appeal: the winning party may expand his claims on appeal only if part of a cross-appeal in reply to the appellant.[32] Subject to several exceptions, neither party may appeal anything other than a final judgment (CCvP, §§281, 283), and neither may appeal errors that do not affect the outcome (§302).[33]

8. Evidence

The effect of the lack of juries goes further, for it eliminates nearly the entire field of evidence. Granted, Japanese courts do maintain evidentiary rules, and some scholars even write books in the field.[34] Largely, though, it is a field to which people pay much less attention than in the United States.

And for good reason. Where a jury decides the facts, what a judge lets it hear affects the result. Where the judge himself decides both what evidence to admit and what that evidence proves, elaborate evidentiary rules can become a silly mind-game. In effect, they require him to ignore evidence he himself has heard. Given psychological realities, the field understandably becomes one to which fewer people devote resources.

C. Other Differences
1. Joinder

If several parties either have similar legal interests or have legal interests that are based on similar facts, a judge may let them join as plaintiffs or be joined as defendants (CCvP, §38). Ultimately the issue will depend on the savings involved. If permissive joinder threatens to generate large diseconomies, the judge can later sever the cases for trial.[35]

If a court cannot partition a judgment among several parties, at least in theory they *must* join. For example, two people who jointly bought land from Hatsugorō Kuge drafted the purchase agreement as though they had bought it from his son. To confirm their title, they later sued the son. Midstream in the litigation, one of them withdrew. Held the Supreme Court: (1) Compulsory joinder applied; (2) therefore, the suit could not proceed without both; and (3) therefore, once they had joined, neither could independently withdraw.[36] If a party subject to the compulsory joinder rule does not initially join the suit, the other may not sue without him. When one community sued to establish its right to the common, the court required that it join all its members. Their rights—if they were rights at all— were rights in common. Compulsory joinder applied, and if anyone refused to join, the suit could not proceed.[37]

2. Class Actions

Japanese courts do not recognize class actions. Although parties to a large suit can sometimes choose representative litigants (CCvP, §30), the judgment will bind only the parties named. The mandatory joinder rules, moreover, will prevent some victims of collective harms from obtaining even injunctive relief. Take the citizens of the city of Buzen. For environmental reasons, seven of them sued to enjoin a new power plant. Because they demanded relief whose effects extended beyond themselves, they could not proceed. The law provided for no class actions, and unless all citizens joined, no one had standing to sue.[38]

3. Counterclaims

Defendants may raise counterclaims at any time during a trial, but the counterclaim must relate to the plaintiff's initial claim.[39] For example, when defendant Fukuji Nara fell behind in his debt to Saiichirō Kobayashi, Kobayashi assigned the note to plaintiff Takeshi Kurosawa. Kurosawa then began threatening criminal prosecution and demanding usurious interest. Although defendants generally pay their own attorney's fees (see chapter 1), when plaintiffs make exceptionally abusive claims, defendants can demand their fees.[40] Faced with Kurosawa's extortionate threats, Nara could properly counterclaim for his attorney's fees.[41]

II. Judicial Power
A. Remedies
1. The Issue

In a provocative series of writings, John Haley claims that Japanese judges lack sufficient power to enforce the law they make. "Few means of coercion to enforce compliance with judicial orders exist" in Japan, he argues.[42] Instead, the "lack of judicial contempt powers or any analogous coercive sanctions . . . preclude effective formal enforcement."[43] This is an important and profound claim. Necessarily it asserts that courts have little power. Necessarily it also implies that law plays but a trivial role in Japanese society.

2. Seizure

Unfortunately Haley overplays his hand. Japanese judges do indeed have contempt powers and do indeed control ways to force parties to comply with their orders—in fact, a wide variety of powerful ways. Begin with the most obvious. Suppose a plaintiff sues for damages. If he can locate the defendant's assets, then (as Haley rightly notes) he can have those assets seized and sold.[44] Granted, if the defendant has no assets, the plaintiff has little recourse. If a defendant has no assets, however, few sensible plaintiffs anywhere will bother suing him for damages, formal enforcement or no.

3. Per Diem Penalties

Japanese courts can also force obstinate defendants to comply through per diem penalties. Suppose a plaintiff demands an injunction or a defendant fails to perform as ordered. Under section 172 of the Civil Enforcement Act,[45] a court can order the defendant to pay a large penalty for every day he refuses to perform.

Take the Daia construction firm. It claimed that the neighbors of one of its construction projects were deliberately blocking access to the site. It sued, and the court enjoined its neighbors. By court order, if they continued to block access, Daia could clear any obstructions, charge them for the cost, and collect ¥500,000 for every day they kept its employees from working.[46]

Similarly take the residents of one condominium complex who found the mob using a unit as its business office (see chapter 2). They sued, and the court enjoined the mob from using the unit. For every day it ignored the injunction, it owed the residents ¥1,000,000.[47]

Or take family law disputes. One mother with legal custody over her four-year-old daughter could not induce her ex-husband to give up the girl. Rather than kidnap her daughter, she sued. The court gave her ex-husband two weeks. If he did not return the girl by then, he owed his ex-wife ¥30,000 (this from a man with a monthly take-home pay of about ¥400,000) for each day he stalled.[48]

4. Prior Law

None of this is new. Although the Civil Enforcement Act itself took effect in 1980, it did not introduce these rules. Instead, it merely recodified what had been the practice for decades under what was then section 734 of the Code of Civil Procedure.[49] Again, consider child custody disputes. For decades, parents who refuse to surrender a child have potentially faced daily penalties. Yoshiko Iwata was born in 1941. Because her mother died the next year, she spent much of her life in her maternal grandfather's home. In 1955, however, the court awarded custody to her father. When her grandfather refused to surrender custody, the court gave him 70 days. Unless he gave up his granddaughter by then, he owed ¥300 a day.[50]

Courts have imposed these per diem penalties in a variety of disputes, but intellectual property cases illustrate their usual approach. Chūbu kankō, K.K., ran coffee shops and cabarets, from the Silver Slipper to the Swing Swing Star. Although it provided live music, it did not pay royalties. In 1959, it found itself sued, and a court soon enjoined it from playing the music without paying the required royalties. When Chūbu ignored the injunction, the court ordered it to pay ¥70,000 a day as long as it continued to violate the injunction.[51]

Trademark violations raised similar issues. Take the 1964 court that ordered a firm to change its infringing trademark to a noninfringing one. Unless it complied, the court warned, it could order penalties.[52]

The per diem penalty cases reached even labor disputes. In 1972, Nittsū shōji, K.K.—an affiliate of a large Japanese moving company—was locked in a battle with its union. The union sued, and the court ordered Nittsū to start bargaining in good faith within three days. Should it stall, it would owe the union ¥50,000 a day.[53] Two years later the Ashiwara firm found itself in a similar dispute. Again, the union sued, and again, the court ordered the firm to bargain in good faith. Should it stall, it would owe the union ¥50,000 a day.[54]

B. Judicial Control

In gathering evidence, too, Japanese judges control flexible, wide-ranging powers. Once more, Haley argues the contrary: "[N]o coercive mechanism exists to compel witnesses to respond truthfully or to release documents." [55] In fact, the most coercive mechanism is the simplest: as under Rule 37(b) of the U.S. Federal Rules of Civil Procedure, if a party refuses to produce or destroys a document, a Japanese judge can find the disputed question in favor of the other party (CCvP, §224).

Yet Japanese judges also wield a variety of other mechanisms. If anyone refuses to testify when subpoenaed, a judge (on his own initiative) can order the police to bring him to court (CCvP, §194). If the person still will not testify, the judge can (again, on his own initiative) fine him (CCvP, §§192–193). And if he still refuses, then (so long as a prosecutor cooperates) the judge can throw him in jail.[56] Take the witness who sulked and refused to talk: "I've got a hangover," he explained. "And I get in a lousy mood when someone makes me get up in the morning." The judge promptly held him in contempt.[57]

Japanese judges lack contempt powers, writes Haley. "Japanese courts do not enjoy the broad equitable powers of common law courts to fashion remedies, nor do they exercise contempt powers." [58] Just as the flexible per diem penalties illustrate the broad powers Japanese courts have to fashion remedies, the hungover witness illustrates the way they explicitly exercise contempt power. On all issues affecting order in the courtroom (though only those issues), a judge forthrightly and explicitly controls contempt powers. When one judge read the judgment in a labor case, Masaoto Iwai yelled out, "Capitalist dog!" The judge threw him in jail for seven days.[59] When demonstrators outside a courthouse shouted, "Impeach Judge Wada," Judge Wada gave them several days, too.[60]

In contrast to the "sanctionless law" he found in Japan, Haley ascribes to U.S. judges a panoply of powers: "By failing to obey a court order . . . , the defendant faces the possibility that he will be fined whatever amount the judge believes will provide sufficient compulsion, or that he will be jailed until he complies."[61] Japanese judges control similar—even if not identical—sanctions and have for decades. Japanese law is not sanctionless, and Japanese courts are not powerless: imperfectly to be sure (and what court system can claim perfection?), Japanese judges control the tools they need to make the people they face obey the rules they articulate.

Conclusions

Civil procedure is different. In many areas of the law, Japan and the United States track each other closely. In much of civil procedure, they diverge radically. In the United States, courts maintain elaborate rules of subject-matter jurisdiction, personal jurisdiction, and choice of law; they carefully segment trial and pretrial, maintain broad preclusion rules, constrain fact-finding on appeal, and impose complex rules of evidence. In Japan, none of that holds.

These differences between Japanese and U.S. civil procedure follow logically from two fundamental differences: the United States maintains parallel national and state courts, but Japan does not; and the United States guarantees jury trials, but Japan does not. Given these basic choices, most of the procedural rules in the two countries are reasonable corollaries. The two systems are different, but not haphazardly. Given the initial choices about federalism and juries, the principal procedural differences follow predictably and sensibly.

7 CRIMINAL LAW AND PROCEDURE

Shoeless Joe Jackson, Eddie Cicotte, all those other Black Sox fiends: for throwing the 1919 World Series, they found themselves banned forever from the sport they loved. They are dead now, but only sort of—marooned in that liminal world of baseball purgatory. If only someone would plow under a corn field, if only someone would build a diamond, they would come. Happily, but quietly, we are told, they would come back to play one last game in their field of dreams.

If ever there was a crime against nature, throwing baseball games is surely it. But like baseball, crimes against nature transcend cultural boundaries. In mid-1969, while investigating the mob's role in off-track betting on professional baseball, the Japanese police happened across the name of Nishitetsu pitcher Ratsuyuki Nagayasu. One lead led to another, and within a few months, they had uncovered evidence that at least nine ballplayers (maybe more) had been throwing games. In connection with at least twenty games during the last two seasons, they had taken some ¥8 million from the mob. The baseball organization expelled several players, including Nagayasu, and the police initiated prosecutions. By the middle of 1970, five pitchers stood convicted.[1]

Producers in the sports industry would like to invest in popular entertainment; consumers would willingly pay high prices for tickets to good entertainment. But because consumers will pay those high prices only if they think the games honest, industry producers need some way credibly to promise them an unrigged game. To that end, criminal penalties for rigging games can help—though the baseball industry itself probably has adequate incentives to police itself against rigged games, wholly aside from state enforcement.

Given the economies of scale to law enforcement, a governmentally enforced criminal law can in many areas form an important part of an efficient legal system.[2] Without stability and security to their property and person, most citizens will not invest in economic activities (whether building factories or buying baseball tickets) at anywhere close to efficient levels. Although they can (and will) individually take some precautions against crime, other precautions will sometimes (not always) be cheaper when provided in bulk. Along with property, contract, and tort law, criminal law will sometimes (not always) help give that security in bulk.

Moreover, because the goals people hope to achieve through criminal law enforcement—security of person and property—cross national and cultural lines, the ways successful legal regimes implement criminal law will tend to converge. Notwithstanding the different ancestry of Japanese criminal law (the substantive Criminal Code is a prewar German-inspired statute) the Japanese regime closely resembles the regime in place in the United States. As with so many other areas of the law, the differences exist, but the similarities overwhelm.

We start by outlining the gist of substantive Japanese criminal law (subsection I.A). Here we discuss issues of intent (subsection 1), mistake (subsection 2), capacity (subsection 3), duress and necessity (subsection 4), consent (subsection 5), accomplice liability (subsection 6), and impossibility (subsection 7). For expositional simplicity (though at the cost of considerable gore), we focus primarily on homicides and omit the details to most other crimes (like throwing baseball games). We then turn to several basic questions of procedure (subsection I.B). Finally, we examine the low rates of violent crime (subsection II.A), the high conviction rates (subsection II.B), and the role of the organized crime syndicates (subsection II.C).

I. The Law
A. Substantive Law
1. Intent

a. Introduction. The intent requirement in Japanese criminal law follows from section 38(a) of the Criminal Code:

> Actions taken without the intent to commit a crime shall not be punishable; provided, however, that this rule shall not apply when the law otherwise specifies.[3]

Section 38(a) thus automatically incorporates an intent requirement into crimes like murder (Criminal Code, §199):

> Any person who kills another shall be punishable by death, by hard labor for life, or by hard labor for a term of not less than three years.

Although the Criminal Code does not specify separate degrees of murder or distinguish between murder and manslaughter, it does (through the proviso in section 38(a)) define several negligent homicides:

> §210: Any person who, through negligence, causes the death of another shall be punishable by a fine of not more than ¥500,000.

§211: Any person who, by failing to exercise the care required in the performance of his regular activities, causes the death of another, shall be punishable by no more than five years of imprisonment or hard labor, or by a fine of not more than ¥500,000.

Anyone who causes the death of another through gross negligence shall be punishable by the same.

For courts, the hard questions have concerned those statutory provisions (particularly vicarious liability) that seem intended to apply regardless of a defendant's state of mind. Critics argue that they violate the Constitution, usually on the ground that strict liability violates the bans on double jeopardy, on ex post facto laws, or on cruel and unusual punisments (Const. arts. 36, 39). Faced with such challenges, the Japanese Supreme Court holds that vicarious liability offenses merely presume negligence. To the court, such statutes "should be understood as presuming the negligence of the employer in selecting or supervising the employees, or in otherwise failing to take the care necessary to prevent their illegal action." [4] Accordingly, a defendant can defend by showing that he acted with due care. [5]

b. Intentional Crimes. To convict someone of a crime requiring intent, prosecutors must show that he knew the results that would probably result from the actions he took and took them anyway. Consider a man who had worked at the Akada clinic as a driver since 1967. He was getting married and needed a raise. He asked for one, but when he received a smaller raise than he wanted, he decided to torch the clinic. Given that many of the patients on the second floor were crippled, he urged them to go outside. "The moon is lovely tonight," he assured them. "It's refreshing out there. Go on outside." When most of the patients did not budge, he proceeded with his plan. He went downstairs, dumped nine gallons of gasoline, and lit it. Ever the conscientious employee, he then chased back upstairs. He rescued some of the patients and injured himself severely in the process.

Because two patients died in the fire, prosecutors tried the driver for murder. Due to his heroics, the trial court held that he lacked an intent to kill and acquitted him. The appellate court reversed. That he preferred not to kill the patients did not obviate intent. He knew some of them might die, but lit the fire anyway. For intent, that sufficed. [6]

To be liable for murder, one need not even know about the person who dies. Instead, one need only intend to kill *some*one and take actions that do kill someone, whether the person intended or someone else. Masatate Chiba, for example, wanted a gun. He believed in the coming communist millennium, but also believed that only armed revolution would bring it.

153

To acquire the gun he needed for that revolution, he decided to rob a police officer. On the evening of February 15, 1972, he approached officer Shizuo Tanaka from behind and blasted him with a homemade contraption that shot three-inch construction nails. The nail blew a hole through Tanaka, traveled another 100 feet, and gouged through a young banker besides. Surprisingly neither died.

In his defense, Chiba announced that every citizen retained the natural right to armed revolution; that in a society like Japan, which outlawed guns, that right necessarily included the right to steal guns; that in shooting Tanaka he merely exercised his natural right to revolution. Maybe he was lucky: people have been hanged for more modest speeches, and Chiba only got eight years. To the court, that Chiba was guilty of Tanaka's attempted murder (Criminal Code, §203) was straightforward. The only hard question was whether he was also guilty of the attempted murder of the banker 100 feet away. He was indeed, said the court. His intent to murder Tanaka was sufficient to convict him of the attempted murder of both.[7]

c. Negligent Crimes. People took it hard when they lost *kabuki* grandmaster Masaru Morita to a blowfish (subsection 4.III.C). They took it hard enough that prosecutors soon filed negligent homicide charges (Criminal Code, §211) against the chef who carved the fatal filet. The chef replied that he had prepared the liver by time-honored methods, elaborately leaching the poison by soaking and washing the meat. He had served blowfish livers to 4,000 customers over the past nine years with no mishap. Morita died because he was old and sick anyway. He (the chef) could not have foreseen that Morita would die from the liver and, absent that foresight, could not have been negligent.

The court convicted the chef. Effectively it held that a chef who serves blowfish livers is necessarily negligent because one can always foresee the potential for death. The Osaka High Court had held to the contrary earlier,[8] but—said the court—medical knowledge had changed. Whatever the case then, everyone in the trade now knew that soaking and washing blowfish meat would not completely remove the poison. Indeed, for that very reason, by regulation the Kyoto government had banned blowfish liver sales. The chef knew the risks. In taking them anyway, he committed negligent homicide.[9]

2. Mistake

In general, ignorance of the law is no excuse, but mistake of fact may be. By section 38(c) of the Criminal Code:

Ignorance of the law is not evidence of lack of intent to commit the crime; provided, however, that depending on the circumstances it may justify a reduced penalty.

In truth, of course, the distinction between mistakes of fact and law are anything but clear. In 1924, the Supreme Court faced a defendant prosecuted for hunting flying squirrels out of season. The regulations covered *musasabi,* but the defendant thought *musasabi* were different animals from the flying squirrels he called *moma.* They were in fact the same, and the court declared his mistake one of law and affirmed his conviction.[10] The next year it faced a defendant prosecuted for hunting badgers out of season. The regulations covered *tanuki,* but in the defendant's community *tanuki* were different animals from the badgers they called *mujina.* Without a hint of its 1924 opinion, the court declared his mistake one of fact and acquitted him.[11]

3. Capacity

a. Introduction. Japanese law recognizes lack of capacity as a defense. Specifically section 39 of the Criminal Code provides:

(a) Actions by one lacking mental capacity shall not be punishable.
(b) Actions by one with reduced mental capacity, [if otherwise punishable,] shall be punished with a reduced penalty.

According to the Supreme Court:

Both mental incapacity and reduced mental capacity concern mental damage. They differ, however, in degree. The former [Criminal Code, §39(a)] refers to a condition where the person either lacks the ability to distinguish good from evil, or lacks the ability to structure his actions according to that distinction. The latter [Criminal Code, §39(b)] refers to a condition where he possesses such abilities, but—because of the mental damage—possesses them only at a greatly reduced level.[12]

Those who lack the ability either to distinguish good from evil or to live accordingly bear no criminal penalties; those who have that ability, but only at a low level, are subject to lower penalties.

b. Insanity: Okamura; Abe. Sadao Okamura joined the naval Self Defense Force in 1962. Schizophrenic, he eventually had to check into a hospital for six months. He continued out-patient treatments for nine more months after that. While still in the military, he fell madly in love with

155

Seiko Tajiro, sister to his high-school friend Matsuyuki Tajiro. The love was neither requited by Seiko nor welcomed by her family. Instead, the Tajiros seem primarily to have wished Okamura would just go away. Whatever other reasons they may have had (mental instability does come to mind), as good leftists they also had no use for the Self Defense Force and told him as much.

Incensed by their aloofness and outraged by their politics, on the night of January 3, 1969, Okamura went to the Tajiro home. It was two months after he had stopped his out-patient treatment. "Communists like Matsuyuki Tajiro are a cancer on society," he later declared. "The world would be better off if they disappeared." Toward that end, he did the best he could. As his friend Matsuyuki was not home, he talked to Seiko's older sister, who convinced him to leave. He then called a "friend" who drove a cab, but part way home changed his mind. He ordered his friend back to the Tajiro home and told him to come inside with him. Once there, he pulled out a 2½-foot steel bar and smashed his friend on the head. With similar ferocity, he beat Seiko's sister, her three sleeping daughters (ages seven, five, and one), and two neighbors who rushed to help. All except his friend and the youngest girl died.

Okamura's mental capacity depended on his medical and personal history, the Supreme Court explained, and on the circumstances of the crime as well as the reports of the examining doctors. Here one doctor had found him a schizophrenic with a "defective personality," but concluded that he could still function in society at a reduced level. The other found the disease so extreme that Okamura could not have controlled his actions during the crime. Because Okamura had prepared for the crime (bringing a steel bar, cutting the telephone line to the house) and had protected himself afterward (hiding the bar and the coat he wore), the court did not find mental incapacity (§39(a)). Instead, it cited the bizarreness of the crime and the content of the medical reports and held mitigation in order (§39(b)).[13]

More macabre still was the tale of Sada Abe.[14] By the time the police caught up with her in 1936, it had been nearly three days: three days since she had left her lover Kichizō Ishida, three days since she had strangled him in bed, lain for hours at his side—then carved her name in his thigh, dipped her finger in his blood, written "Sada, Kichi, alone, together," and sliced off his sex organs. For three days, she had worn his loin cloth and carried his organs between her breasts. What with her body heat and the passage of time, they were starting to rot. The stench bothered the police, but not

Abe. As the detectives interrogated her about the crime, she begged them to let her hold them again. "I loved Ishida," she explained. "I loved him and couldn't help it. I didn't want any other woman to touch him. I wanted him to be mine, positively mine." "So I killed him," she added—and burst out laughing.

For over a decade, Abe (now age 31) had worked as a beautiful, highly paid geisha and prostitute. Determined to learn the restaurant trade, at the instigation of an older patron she had signed on as a maid at Ishida's (age 42) restaurant. Quickly they fell madly in love and began a flamboyantly passionate affair. When his wife discovered them, Abe left. Ishida soon left as well, and they rendezvoused at a hotel where they closeted themselves in their room for what the newspapers later assumed had been marathon lust. And there they stayed, until she strangled him in his sleep (or so the court officially found).

Prosecutors charged Abe with murder and the desecration of a corpse. The court expected a crowd. It set trial dates for November 25 and December 8 and announced it would admit only 300 spectators. A crowd it was, easily the most spectacular media event in Japanese court history. Newspapers called her the "heroine of mad passion." Never mind the cold winter night. Would-be spectators ("Osada fans," the papers called them) camped out in front of the courthouse the night before to obtain the tickets. By 5 A.M., the crowd had grown so large that the court admitted the first 300 and sent the rest home.

The court found Abe guilty as charged and sentenced her to six years in prison. It was a light sentence, for courts could—and did—sentence people to death for murder. From 1927 to 1936, the state hanged an average of nineteen people each year.[15]

In Abe's case, her lawyer (to Abe's visible distress in the courtroom) had argued insanity and diminished capacity. The judge found the latter, but not the former. Propelled by "a drunken impatience driven by a monopolizing lust," Abe had experienced only diminished mental capacity. Because during the months since the crime she had shown remorse and come to realize her licentious ways, she also seemed likely to rehabilitate herself. For both of those reasons, it imposed the mild penalty.

  c. Intoxication. Defendants can sometimes cite their own drug abuse to mitigate or excuse their crimes. Apparently high on some form of speed, one mobster in 1980 concluded that his girlfriend was cheating on him with another member of the mob. Turning paranoid, he decided he had to find her. He grabbed his girlfriend's sister as a hostage and threw

157

her in his car. When he stopped for gas, he fired his shotgun to scare the attendant. When the police chased him, he turned and shot the squad car. And when, stopped at a roadblock, he noticed the detective who was talking to him break into a smile, he shot the detective dead.

To the court, section 39(b) of the Criminal Code applied, but not section 39(a). The speed had not so totally overwhelmed the defendant that he could not distinguish good from evil or control his actions. It did, though, cause hallucinations, and it did otherwise reduce his ability to think. That, accordingly, warranted a diminished capacity defense.[16]

4. Duress, Necessity, and Self-Defense

a. Introduction. For generations of American law students, criminal law has begun with the dark and stormy night of *The Queen v. Dudley and Stephens:*[17] if sailors find themselves adrift on the high seas, miles from land, with water, water everywhere and not a drop to drink, may they draw lots and eat the loser? Because the sailors in fact did not draw lots, but merely killed the weakest among them, the case replaces questions of consent with those of necessity: can the imminent starvation of all justify the murder of the few?

On its facts, *Dudley and Stephens* resembles nothing so much as the accounts told by the Japanese soldiers who survived their trek through the Philippine jungle in the last months of World War II. Ill-trained, underarmed, facing a powerful Allied offensive, and abandoned by their own command, in early 1945 the Japanese draftees in the Philippines began an aimless, but desperate, trip across the plains and through the jungle— walking, climbing, crawling until they simply dropped dead of starvation or disease. For the Japanese army, the Philippines were a graveyard. As recounted in *Fires on the Plain,* a few responded to the imminent death by killing and eating their colleagues.[18] Yet it was not an issue domestic Japanese courts faced. In the chaos of the war's end, offenders were more likely to have been tried, if tried at all, in one of the thousands of war crimes trials.

To domestic Japanese courts, issues of duress, necessity, and self-defense involve two sections of the Criminal Code:

> Duress or necessity (§37(a)): Actions taken to avoid a present and sudden threat to the life, health, liberty, or property of oneself or others, if unavoidable, shall not be punishable if the harm inflicted through the action does not exceed the harm prevented through it; provided, however, that depending on the circumstances

action that inflicts a harm greater than the harm prevented may also be excused or subject to a reduced penalty.

Self-defense (§36): (a) Actions taken to defend the rights of oneself or others from sudden unfair infringement, if unavoidable, shall not be punishable.

(b) Depending on the circumstances, action that exceeds a defensive level may also be excused or subject to a reduced penalty.

Consider first cases of duress and necessity, then cases of self-defense.

b. Duress and Necessity. In 1988, the defendant joined the Aum cult—the very cult of 1995 subway nerve-gas attack fame. He convinced his elderly mother with Parkinson's disease to join, too, and she then gave the group some ¥45 million. Kōtarō Ochida joined in 1990 and worked as a pharmacist in the cult clinic, where the defendant's mother stayed.

The defendant left the cult in 1992. Ochida left in early 1994, but continued to worry about the defendant's mother. As "treatment" for her Parkinson's, the cult was giving her scalding (117° F) baths, and she was not showing progress. When Ochida asked the defendant to help him rescue her from the cult, the defendant first thought it a bother. Eventually he agreed, and on the night of January 29, 1994, he, his father, and Ochida drove to the cult compound.

While his father stayed in the car, the defendant and Ochida broke into the clinic. They found the defendant's mother, but as they carried her out, cult members spotted them. The defendant and Ochida sprayed tear gas at the attacking cultists and tried to escape, but to no effect. The members caught them, handcuffed them, and took them to the "Priest's Room."

There, as the defendant later recalled it, one of the cult leaders announced an ultimatum: "You're going to hell for sure. You can pick one of two paths. You can kill Ochida and go home. Or if you can't kill Ochida we'll kill you right here." The defendant hesitated, but the leader promised again that he would release him if only he killed Ochida. The defendant then agreed. He stuck a plastic bag over Ochida's head and sprayed it full of tear gas. While Ochida flailed about, the cult members held him down, and the defendant wrapped a rope around his neck and strangled him. The defendant went home, and the cult members took Ochida to their special basement microwave oven and incinerated him.

The court convicted the defendant of murder. Although one of the cult leaders had threatened him, the threat was not so imminent as to excuse him under section 37. Instead, because the defendant had taken such drastic steps while not under threat of imminent harm (so the court found—though one might wonder), the threat served only as a mitigating circumstance.[19]

  c. Self-Defense. Courts seem to recognize self-defense more readily than necessity or duress. The former, after all, generally arises when a defendant injures or kills the very person who attacked him; necessity and duress arise when he injures or kills a third party. Given this difference, section 37 of the Criminal Code excuses conduct for duress or necessity only when a defendant inflicts injury no greater than the injury avoided. Section 36 imposes no such limit on defense.

  As a plain-vanilla self-defense case, take a March 1996 Tokyo District Court opinion. A and B were members of the same mob. While at a *karaoke* bar, A grabbed the mike and started to sing. "Quit it," shouted B. "You're a lousy shit." A kept singing, and after several minutes, the argument turned into a brawl. Eventually others separated the two, and A went home. As B had a reputation for escalating fights, A worried that B would soon come for him. Calculating that he could not safely stay home, he jammed a kitchen knife in his belt and left again about 1:30 A.M. that night. Sure enough, before he had gotten very far, B appeared at the end of the street. "Bastard," B shouted and lunged at him with a knife. A ducked, but B slashed him on the neck. A pulled his knife and stabbed him. B died, but to the court, it was excusable self-defense.[20]

  Other cases are less clear. Take two political gangs that resembled nothing so much as Marxist Hatfields and McCoys, or even Huck's Grangerfords and Shepherdsons. As New Left groups formed and re-formed, allied and reallied throughout the 1960s, the hostilities between two of the larger camps—the Japanese Marxist Student Alliance Central Faction (the Central Faction, Chūkaku-ha) and the Japanese Marxist Student Alliance Revolutionary Marxist Faction (the Revolutionary Faction, Kakumaru-ha)—hardened into permanent war. For the students and ex-students in these groups, principled opposition to the Vietnam War, nuclear arms, colonialism, imperialism, and university tuition hikes increasingly took a back seat to beating and occasionally killing each other.

  By the early 1970s, the clashes between fringe-left groups were frequent and bloody. According to police records:[21]

	1969	1970	1971	1972	1973	1974	1975
Clashes	308	175	272	183	238	286	229
Injuries	1,145	527	420	338	573	607	543
Deaths	2	2	2	2	2	11	20

Of these clashes, the battles between the Central and the Revolutionary Factions were generally the most common. Of all clashes involving left-wing groups in 1975, 70 percent were battles between the Central and the Revolutionary Factions. Of the twenty deaths, sixteen were from those battles.

Occasionally these brawls raised questions of self-defense. In late 1971, for example, the Central Faction held a meeting at a large hall in Fukuoka. At one point, a Central Faction member spotted a rival. "The Revolutionary Faction's here!" she yelled. Central Faction members chased after the Revolutionary Faction members and beat them with steel bars.

At their trial, the Central Faction members pleaded self-defense. The court noted that the Revolutionary Faction members had themselves come armed with steel bars, but that the Central Faction members had obviously brought their own (and wooden poles and hockey sticks) as well. This was not a case where Central Faction members responded to the exigencies as best they could, said the court. It was one where they had foreseen the violence and welcomed it. As such, it was one to which section 36 of the Criminal Code did not apply.[22]

5. Consent

a. Introduction. Whether a victim's consent excuses a crime depends on the crime involved. Sometimes consent will transform the character of the act itself. If *A* freely consents to *B*'s taking *A*'s money, for example, the transaction is a gift rather than theft. Yet if *A* freely consents to *B*'s taking *A*'s life, the act remains a crime (Criminal Code, §202):

> Any person who offers encouragement or assistance in the commission of a suicide shall be punishable by 6 months to 7 years of imprisonment or hard labor. Anyone who kills someone upon his request or encouragement shall be punishable by the same.

b. S–M. The Abe-Ishida affair gave rise to several theatrical productions and movies. Upon her release from prison, Abe herself made money playing herself. Recalls movie critic Donald Richie, she regularly made dramatic—if also "faithless" in the way she exploited her own passion—entrances at a Tokyo pub in the years after the war. Wearing a bright kimono, she would flamboyantly descend a staircase into the drinking throng.[23] But in 1972, director Nagisa Ōshima received a proposition from the French film company Argos. A star film maker and a darling of the intellectual circuit, Ōshima had international visibility that within Japan only Akira Kurosawa could top. The French government had just shut down its censorship offices. Said Argos, would he collaborate on a pornographic movie?

To Argos, Ōshima suggested the Abe-Ishida affair. Argos agreed. Ōshima called it *Ai no koriida* [In the Realm of the Senses] and filmed it in the Daiei studios in Kyoto. To avoid (he thought) Japanese censors, he shipped all the film undeveloped to Argos in France. There they processed and he edited the film. Crucially, where Abe testified that she had strangled her lover in his sleep, Ōshima had her strangling him in the middle of sex.

Released in 1976, the film was the smash hit at Cannes—and proved, as the ever-irreverent critic Edward Seidensticker inimitably put it, "that the Japanese can still turn out fine pornography."[24] Demand was so high that festival organizers scheduled an unprecedented thirteen screenings. Within Japan, perhaps the film gave rise to copycat S–M games, or perhaps Ōshima just played to their preexisting popularity. Whatever the facts, at least two cases of lovers asphyxiated during sex appeared in court shortly after the *Realm* hit the silver screen. The defendant in one was a barmaid having an affair with a regular customer. He liked S–M games and wanted her to choke him during sex. In December 1976, he begged her to choke him again, this time with rope or a belt. She took her belt and wrapped it around his neck. As she tightened her grip, he gasped, "Tighter!" Tighter she tightened it, and soon he died.

One might have guessed the court would invoke section 199 (murder) or section 202 (consented killing), but apparently it thought the intent requirement not met. Instead, it held the barmaid guilty of battery leading to death (Criminal Code, §205):

> Any person who causes the death of another by injuring him shall
> be punishable by hard labor of not less than 2 years.

The risk that he would die was foreseeable. Although he had clearly consented to that risk, the gravity of the harm precluded a finding that consent excused it.[25]

c. Mishima. It is a messy, excruciatingly painful way to go, but for those with the requisite peculiar machismo, that has been its attraction. As Yukio Mishima described it in his 1960 novella *Yūgoku:*

> Like a hawk, the lieutenant stared at his wife. He took his
> knife and brought it to the front. From the angry spread in his uni-
> formed shoulders, she could see him arch up, and throw his torso

against the knife. He had planned to stab it deep into his stomach on the left. A brittle cry sliced the silence in the room.

The lieutenant had done this with his own strength, but his gut felt as if someone had beat him with a steel bar. His mind faded. Momentarily, he forgot what had happened. Yet the five- or six-inch blade stayed buried far within his body, so far that his hand on the paper [wrapped around the handle] touched his stomach.

The lieutenant came to. He was sure the knife had pierced his peritoneum. He tried to breathe. His heart pounded. Somewhere far, far away—not within his own body, but somewhere, the earth split and lava poured with searing pain. . . .

So this is *seppuku*, he thought. Heaven had crashed onto his head, and the earth was tottering wildly. His courage and determination—that courage and determination that had seemed so strong before were now but a thin wire, a fine line chasing desperately the pain that assaulted him. His palms sweated. . . .

With his right hand, the lieutenant tried to pull the knife around, but the blade's tip was tangled in his intestines. At the same time, pressure was forcing the knife out, and he had to push the knife with both hands deep into his stomach as he pulled it around. He pulled. But it would not cut as he wanted. He put all his strength into his right hand, and pulled again. It cut three or four inches.

From deep within his stomach, the pain spread and his belly screamed. Like wildly rung temple bells, it screamed. With each breath he took, with each beat of his heart, the pain rang a thousand bells. He could not smother his cries. He looked, and saw that the knife had reached the point below his navel. . . .

By the time the lieutenant had brought the knife around to the right side of his stomach, the knife was cutting only a shallow path. The blade was visible now, smeared with blood and other fluids. The lieutenant let out a weak cry. He was happy.

To do it, you carve into yourself at the bottom left of your stomach, then bring the knife across, up, and back around in a long circular sweep. If you do it right, your guts will then flop into your lap. Few make it that far, and obviously no one rehearses. Instead, by custom you do the best you can and—once you have made a sufficient mess of yourself—your trusted friend slices off your head from behind.[26]

By 1970, Yukio Mishima was a lunatic intellectual celebrity, an imperialist Japanese cross between Saul Bellow and Hunter Thompson. Born

Kimitake Hiraoka, he had attended the University of Tokyo law department and spent a stint at the Ministry of Finance before turning full-time
to his writing. Now he was forty-five years old, a frequently rumored can-
didate for the Nobel prize, and rivaled within Japan only by his mentor, Ya-
sunari Kawabata.

For Mishima, his art was part of his fringe-right politics. By the late
1960s, those politics had made him desperate, desperate about the rapidly
growing and frequently violent Marxist left. In 1968, he organized his private militia, but for Mishima, Japan's only true hope lay in a revivified respect for the emperor and a more central role for the military. For that, it
needed a constitutional amendment (see subsection 1.I.B.1).

Mishima hoped the left-wing riots would force the government to call
out the army and precipitate a constitutional crisis. But when 800,000 protestors took to the streets on October 21, 1969, the government kept the
peace with just the police. The crisis Mishima had wanted had come—and
gone.

Despondent, Mishima formed a plan. He and his paramilitary colleagues would kidnap a high military official. They would force him to
assemble the troops. Mishima would then lecture them, inspire them, gal-
vanize them into true, loyalist patriotism. Terrorism being beauty in death,
when he had finished his call to arms, he and his paramilitary colleague
Morita would carry out two laboriously choreographed suicides: Mishima
would commit *seppuku,* Morita would behead him, Morita would commit
seppuku, and a junior assistant would behead Morita.

On November 25, 1970, Mishima and his colleagues implemented the
plan. They kidnapped the army chief. They assembled the troops. Mishima
delivered his harangue—but he was not quite Mark Antony, and the soldiers were not at all impressed. Most were just puzzled, perplexed at why
such a brilliant novelist would cavort with the fanatical fringe. Even to the
troops, Mishima seemed a nut out of a time warp. "Fool," they yelled.
"Crazy!" When at the end of his talk he shouted, "*Banzai*" to the emperor,
they shouted back, "Drag 'im down! Shoot 'im down!"

Mishima sat down. He took his knife, thrust it into his stomach, and
disemboweled himself. But if he had the fortitude of his fictional lieutenant,
his colleague Morita did not. Ambition should be made of sterner stuff, for
suicides are easier to choreograph than to implement. Morita was to behead the gutted Mishima, but he could hardly have botched his job worse.
Three swings with his sword, and he still had not completely severed
Mishima's head. Finally, he despaired and handed the sword to his assis-

tant who finished the job. Pursuant to plan, Morita then tried to disembowel himself, too, but he did no better here. He managed only a shallow cut. As planned, the same assistant dutifully beheaded him as well.

The court found the three surviving assistants guilty of violating section 202 of the Criminal Code (consented killing). Given the statute, that Mishima and Morita had consented to their deaths was obviously no defense. With a not-so-subtle sermon for young men who (however honorable they may have been) should have had known better, it rejected their claim that national exigencies justified their action and sentenced them to four years.[27]

6. Accountability for Crimes of Others

Should several people work together to commit a crime, the Criminal Code holds each responsible:

§60: If any person commits a crime in concert with at least one other person, each shall be punishable as if he committed the principal crime.

The code similarly punishes those who encourage others to commit a crime (Criminal Code, §61), as well as aiders and abettors (§§62, 63). In addition, note that a coconspirator who helps plan a crime is liable as a principal, even if he does not participate physically in the crime, and that Japanese law does not recognize felony murder or misdemeanor manslaughter.[28]

One night in the 1940s, Kiyoshi Koseki and Yoriichi Hasegawa broke into the house of Keiji Shibata. Brandishing knives, they demanded money. When Shibata's wife replied that her husband was only a teacher and that the only significant cash they had was the school's money, Koseki refused it. When the only other money she could find was ¥900, Koseki refused that, too.

"I don't want that kind of money," Koseki explained. "I came here because I'm broke. If you're broke too, I don't want it. . . . Go buy your kids some clothes or something. . . . I'm leaving," he announced and walked out the door. About three minutes later, Hasegawa joined him. "Your problem," Hasegawa told him, "is you've got the heart of a Buddha. I took the ¥900."

Had Koseki not left the house early, his accomplice liability would have been straightforward. To the court, however, his liability was straightforward anyway. To avoid liability for what one's collaborators do, one cannot just abandon the criminal project. One must try to stop the project itself. Koseki failed to do that. Once he and Hasegawa decided to rob the Shibatas and broke into their house, he could avoid liability for what Hasegawa did only by taking affirmative steps to stop him.[29]

To be liable as accomplices, those acting in concert must agree to commit their crime. Take the case of the unfortunate young police officer Katsumi Ishihara. Ishihara had the bad luck of being assigned to bust an unlicensed Kobe bar run by a member of the Yamaguchi-gumi, the largest of the Japanese crime syndicates. In response, seven members of the mob began harassing him, and one eventually stabbed him to death. The gangster who stabbed Ishihara was guilty of murder. Absent any agreement to kill, however, the others were guilty only of the lesser crime of battery leading to death (Criminal Code, §205).[30]

At the very least, Mariko Arai had fallen in with the wrong crowd. Born in 1950, by the mid-1970s she was a nursing student in the northern city of Sendai. While in Tokyo, however, she had joined the East Asian Anti-Japanese Armed Front. The aim of the group, as the court later explained, was

> to pursue Japan's responsibility both for the aggression and war it had waged in the past, and for its economic aggression and neocolonialism in the present. Toward that end, the group used bombs to attack the Emperor and various firms involved in overseas activities. By destroying Japan's national and social structure, it would promote the world revolution that would in turn usher in primitive communism.[31]

From 1971 through 1975, the group planted some sixteen bombs. They were not the only group to do so. If not quite the worst of times for someone like Mishima, it was hardly the best of times either. The police estimated the membership in fringe-left groups in 1971 at 47,000 and over the years counted dozens of bombings:[32]

	1971	1972	1973	1974	1975
Bombs planted	62	21	4	15	22
Bombs exploded	37	16	2	6	19

During lunch hour on August 30, 1974, the Armed Front exploded two massive bombs (equivalent, the newspapers said, to 6,700 sticks of dynamite) at the entrance to the downtown Tokyo office of Mitsubishi Heavy Industries. The explosive impact, the flying debris, and the piercing glass (reporters counted 2,500 broken windows) had deadly effect. All told, the Armed Front killed eight and injured, depending on the count, between 150 and 400 people.

The police caught the group the next year. It was set to try them all, but in the nether world of the New Left fringe, the Armed Front had friends in the notorious Japanese Red Army. When the Red Army broke into the U.S. embassy in Kuala Lumpur in 1975 and when it hijacked a JAL airliner in Bombay in 1976, it used the chance to demand the release of several of the arrested members of the Armed Front.

Prosecutors tried the remaining members. Unsuccessfully, the Armed Front members argued lack of intent to kill. Unsuccessfully, to the court, because some of the bombs they used were so powerful that they could reasonably expect massive explosions, because to bomb Mitsubishi they chose a time when the streets were packed, and because they placed their warning call barely three minutes before detonation, far too late to clear the area.

Indeed, testimony and Armed Front documents made it clear that the group found Japanese workers expendable. As the court put it:

> Although other left-wing movements had looked to the Japanese working class for the revolution, [the Armed Front did not believe that] Japanese workers could bring a true revolution. Japanese workers were imperialist workers, after all, and necessarily part of the above colonialism and corporate aggression. A true revolution was instead possible only through the efforts of the workers and peoples of the countries of East Asia—through the efforts of the victims of Japanese colonialism and corporate aggression.[33]

To show murder, the prosecutors did not need to show that the defendants intended or wanted to kill the specific people who died. They did their job if they showed that the defendants intended to bomb Mitsubishi and knew people would probably die in the blast. In the first death penalties imposed on political activists since World War II, the court sentenced the two leaders of the Armed Front to hang.

Prosecutors tried Arai for aiding and abetting. She had contributed money to the group and had bought for it some of the chemicals it needed (an herbicide, $NaClO_3$). Because she lived in Sendai, however, her Tokyo colleagues had kept her in the dark about the specifics of their plans. Because the police caught the Armed Front in 1975, moreover, they had not yet used most of the chemicals she had bought them. The court convicted

Arai anyway. For aider-and-abettor liability on explosives charges, her moral and financial support sufficed.

7. Impossibility

Under Japanese law, a defendant cannot be guilty of attempting a crime where he cannot commit the crime given the means at his disposal (what some U.S. courts call factual impossibility). In late 1916, Nue Takebayashi conspired with one Tokutarō Kanazawa—presumably her lover—to kill her common-law husband, Hisayuemon Nakada.[34] Kanazawa brought her some powdered sulfur, which she mixed into her husband's meal. The sulfur made him sick, but did not kill him. What Kanazawa and Takebayashi did not know is that powdered sulfur will not kill, no matter how large the dose. Faced with a sick, but very much alive, husband, Kanazawa broke into the house and strangled him. To hide the crime, he then torched the house.

The postman always rings twice, of course, and like Barbara Stanwyck, like Nue Takebayashi. The law caught up with the lovers, and for the court, the hard question was whether poisoning Nakada was attempted murder. As death by powdered sulfur was impossible no matter what the quantity (said the court), the poisoning could not constitute attempt. Instead, it was battery.[35]

B. Procedure
1. Arrests

By article 33 of the Japanese Constitution, Japanese police may not arrest a suspect unless they have a judicially issued warrant or are in hot pursuit. The Code of Criminal Procedure (CCrP)[36] (like the constitution but unlike the substantive Criminal Code, a postwar U.S.-mandated creature) largely codifies this principle.[37] It adds, however, two qualifications: it prohibits even many warrant or hot-pursuit arrests for minor crimes (CCrP, §§199(a), 217) and allows warrantless non-hot-pursuit arrests for many of the more serious crimes like murder and arson (§210).[38] Police make about one-third of all murder arrests under this latter exception.[39]

When the police arrest someone, they must produce the warrant (unless the arrest requires none). They must also tell the suspect what the charge is and that he has a right to consult an attorney (Const. art. 34; CCrP, §§201, 203). Should they make an illegal arrest, however, that illegality itself will not necessarily bar any evidence or confession obtained.[40]

2. Interrogation

a. Introduction. Within forty-eight hours of an arrest, the police must transfer a suspect to the prosecutors' office (CCrP, §203(a)).[41] Within another twenty-four hours, the prosecutors must release him, initiate prosecution, or petition the court for a detention order (CCrP, §205(a)). They may ask the court for up to ten days' detention and, when the ten-day period expires, for another ten days. By the end of that detention, they must either release the suspect or prosecute him (CCrP, §208; see table 7.1).

Only exceptionally may prosecutors detain a suspect beyond those twenty-three days. One egregious exception involved an egregious defendant—a cell leader in a terrorist group allied with the Red Army. He had planted several bombs in late 1971 and was arrested early the next year. He survived his twenty days without incriminating himself. Absent the evidence to prosecute, prosecutors reluctantly discharged him. A few weeks later, however, another terrorist confessed and incriminated him. The prosecutors then rearrested the first terrorist and petitioned for redetention. Citing the unusual gravity of the case, the court agreed.[42]

b. Confessions. Prosecutors generally use detention to obtain a confession. After all, they seldom try a case without one. In 1992, they had confessions in 91.8 percent of all trials.[43]

In practice, most interrogation proceeds without an attorney. To be sure, a suspect has the right to consult an attorney as well as the right to remain silent.[44] In fact, though, prosecutors may—and routinely do—limit a suspect's contact with his attorney to fifteen- to twenty-minute sessions.[45] Defendants have tried to exclude confessions they made without their attorneys present, but with noticeably unsympathetic results.[46]

By article 38 of the constitution, a confession must be voluntary and corroborated by other evidence. That prosecutors persistently and aggres-

Table 7.1 Days Detained (1995)*

	$x \leq 5$	$5 < x \leq 10$	$10 < x \leq 20$	$20 < x$	Total
Number	1,012	46,977	38,990	90	87,069
Percentage	1.2	54.0	44.8	0.1	100

Source: Hōmushō, "Heisei 7 nen no kensatsu jimu no gaikyō" [The General Situation of Prosecution Business, 1995], 48 *Hōmu jihō* 33, 46 (1996).

*Number of days that arrested suspects (other than suspects in traffic crimes) were detained before being released or prosecuted.

169

sively question a suspect does not make the confession excludable. Instead, for the most part, the Supreme Court excludes confessions only where a defendant can point to prosecutorial conduct so unusual as to raise serious questions about the confession's reliability: where the prosecutor had promised not to press charges if the suspect confessed (a promise he obviously broke), for example, or where the police kicked and beat the suspect.[47] By contrast, even where the detention was illegal, where prosecutors promised leniency if the defendant confessed, where the police kept the defendant handcuffed during the interrogations, where no one warned the suspect that he could refuse to answer questions, or where prosecutors limited the suspect's contact with his attorney to two- to three-minute sessions, the Supreme Court has admitted the confession.[48]

    c. Pretextual Detentions. Apparently, when investigating a serious crime, Japanese police sometimes arrest a suspect on a more minor crime and use the detention to grill him on the serious crime. Suppose the police are investigating a murder (crime 1). They suspect X, but do not have sufficient evidence to arrest him. If they can tie X to a minor crime (crime 2), they apparently may arrest him on crime 2 and then use the detention to interrogate him on crime 1.

    Critics charge that this practice violates the constitutional ban on warrantless arrests. Although the Supreme Court has agreed in principle, it seldom holds that the principle applies in practice. Take one of the best known cases, a case with enough conspiratorial angles to keep even Oliver Stone happy. Indeed, the case was conspiratorial enough that it did give rise to mystery stories and a movie.

    One afternoon in early 1948, a man with an armband from a Tokyo municipal public health office walked into a small branch of the Imperial Bank. Dysentery had broken out nearby, he announced. He was there at the orders of the American occupation to distribute a dysentery preventive. All sixteen people in the bank were to drink the liquid, he said. They did, and twelve died. It was potassium cyanide. Several months later the police arrested a painter named Sadamichi Hirasawa. Lacking much evidence tying him to the murders, they detained him on an unrelated fraud charge. They then interrogated him about the murders, sixty-two times over the next thirty-five days (the case antedated the current procedural rules). He confessed, and the court sentenced him to hang.

    Two months later Hirasawa retracted his confession, and to this day, many have steadfastly believed him innocent. A layman could not have obtained the poison or used it the way it was used, they argue. The true villain must have been in the Japanese army. Indeed, suggested novelist Seichō Matsumoto, he must have participated in those notorious chemical experiments that the imperial Japanese army conducted on Chinese and Manchurian prisoners of war. As luck would have it, the Korean War broke out in 1950, and to explore using chemical weapons, the Americans took those Japanese chemical war veterans under their wings.

With the "true villains" under U.S. protection, conspiracy freaks had a heyday. On Hirasawa's behalf, they plastered the government with eighteen retrial and five amnesty petitions. Over the rest of his life, Hirasawa spent only eighty-seven days without at least one such petition pending. Given the government's custom of not executing a prisoner while a petition was pending, Hirasawa lived into the 1980s. "In seven more years, I'll be one hundred years old," he told his lawyer in 1985. "Maybe then they'll release me. I'll get myself a young bride between the age of fifteen and twenty. If I live to be 125, then I'll have had twenty-five years together with my new wife." [49] Two years later he died of pneumonia.

Still, if the good is oft interred with a man's bones, the macabre lives after him. When one sympathizer realized Hirasawa had no children, he arranged to have Hirasawa adopt his own son. Under Japanese law, descendents can apparently file petitions on behalf of a convict even after his death. On May 1989, Hirasawa fans duly filed the nineteenth petition.

In examining Hirasawa's detention, the Supreme Court held that the prosecutors had not detained him on the fraud charge solely to grill him on the Imperial Bank murders. Given the absence of a clearly pretextual detention, it did not have to decide what it would have done if the detention had been a pretext. Although the Supreme Court has faced pretextual detention claims several times since, it usually (1) announces that prosecutors should not detain people on pretextual grounds and then (2) finds that they did not do so. Even when they may have, the courts still do not necessarily exclude the confessions obtained. The result is a legal rule that bans pretextual detentions in principle, that seldom applies in fact, and that (even when it does apply) does not exclude confessions obtained. [50]

3. Searches

Article 35 of the constitution bans warrantless searches except incident to an arrest, and the Code of Criminal Procedure largely codifies this rule (CCrP, §§218–222). Crucially, however, the Supreme Court generally does not exclude the fruits of unlawful searches. These rules apply to phone taps as well, though only recently have Japanese courts begun much to issue such warrants.[51]

4. Trials

As in civil cases, Japanese courts do not use juries in criminal cases.[52] At trial, defendants have a right to an attorney, paid for by the state if necessary (Const. art. 37). Of all ordinary criminal trials in district courts in 1994, they retained their own attorneys in 16,207 cases and used nationally provided defense attorneys in 32,932 (they used privately retained attorneys in 262 of the 570 murder trials). As one might expect, those with privately retained attorneys were more than twice as likely to contest their charges as those with nationally provided lawyers.[53]

Defendants also have a right to interrogate witnesses (Const. art. 37) and a right to remain silent (Const. art. 38; CCrP, §311). They are presumed innocent until proven guilty (CCrP, §336). To convict, a judge must believe—as the Supreme Court put it—that a defendant is guilty at a level "that no ordinary man would doubt."[54] Should a defendant not contest the charges, then for the more minor crimes the trial will follow abbreviated procedures (CCrP, §291-2). In 1990, defendants contested charges in only 7.3 percent (3,616) of all criminal trials (49,821).[55]

Whenever a trial involves a serious crime like murder, the court cannot convene unless the defendant's attorney is present (CCrP, §289(a)). In the Mitsubishi bombing case (subsection A.4), the lawyers for the Armed Front apparently tried to use this rule to buy time. By failing to appear, they seem to have hoped to stall as best they could. The court proceeded without them.[56]

Even if convicted, defendants can petition for a new trial—as Hirasawa did with a vengeance. A court may grant such a petition if, among other reasons, it believes the defendant has shown fraud in the initial verdict or "newly discovered evidence mak[es] clear" that he should have been acquitted (CCrP, §435). According to the Supreme Court, this rule requires only that the new evidence raise "reasonable doubts" about the verdict.[57]

Just as civil litigation in Japan is not noticeably slower than its U.S. analogue, so, too, with criminal litigation. If anything, Japanese criminal litigation may be a bit quicker than at least federal criminal litigation. In U.S. federal courts in 1995, the median time from prosecution to final disposition for the total 54,980 cases was 5.7 months. If a defendant pleaded guilty (as he did in the vast majority of cases), it was 5.4 months; if he demanded a jury trial, it was 9.6 months.[58] Japan is a bit quicker. As table 7.2

Table 7.2 Trial Sessions to Judgment and Total Elapsed Time to Judgment (1994)

Number of Court Sessions	Time from Filing to Judgment						
	$1\,mo \geq x$	$2\,mo \geq x > 1$	$3\,mo \geq x > 2$	$6\,mo \geq x > 3$	$12\,mo \geq x > 6$	Over 1 yr	Total
0	268	77	37	16	3	7	408
1	612	4,036	675	119	7	9	5,458
2	478	13,511	8,080	1,124	20	16	23,229
3	19	1,602	5,675	4,911	126	15	12,348
4	0	52	504	2,899	350	9	3,814
5	0	2	36	1,076	511	13	1,638
6 or more	0	0	5	429	1,622	905	2,961
Total	1,377	19,280	15,012	10,574	2,639	974	49,856

Source: Saikō saibansho jimu sōkyoku, ed., Shihō tōkei nempō, Heisei 6 nen [Annual Report of Judicial Statistics, 1994] (Tokyo: Hōsō kai, 1995), vol. 2, table 31-6.

Table 7.3 Sentences Imposed for Murder

A. Japan (Calendar 1994)

	Death Penalty	Life in Prison	Years				Suspended Term
			$x > 5$	$5 \geq x > 3$	$3 \geq x > 1$	$1 \geq x$	
Number	2	13	275	113	49	0	131
Percentage	0.3	2.2	47.2	19.4	8.4	0	22.5

B. U.S. Federal District Courts (Oct. 1994–Sept. 1995)

	Death Penalty	Life in Prison	Years				Probation, Fine, Other
			$x > 5$	$5 \geq x \geq 3$	$3 > x > 1$	$1 \geq x$	
Number	0	21	164	42	13	8	17
Percentage	0	7.9	61.9	15.8	4.9	3.0	6.4

Source: Saikō saibansho jimu sōkyoku, ed., Shihō tōkei nempō, Heisei 6 nen [Annual Report of Judicial Statistics, 1994] (Tokyo: Hōsō kai, 1995), vol. 2, tables 36-1, 36-3; Administrative Office of the United States Courts, Judicial Business of the United States Courts (Washington, D.C.: Administrative Office of the United States Courts, 1995), table D-5.

Note: U.S. figures include first- and second-degree murder.

shows, in 1994 Japanese courts disposed of most of their cases in two to six months, with the median time in the two- to three-month range.

5. Penalties

Should a court impose a penalty of three years' imprisonment or less, it can make the penalty contingent on the defendant's behavior during a probationary period (Criminal Code, §25). When a convict has served a third of his prison time (or ten years, if the term is life), the prison may choose to release him on parole (Criminal Code, §28). As Daniel Foote and John Haley rightly note, Japanese courts do seem to impose milder punishments than U.S. courts (table 7.3).[59]

6. Double Jeopardy

If Ōshima thought he could avoid the censors in Japan, he was wrong. They slashed perhaps a half hour off his movie and airbrushed haze over much of the rest before releasing it. And when he published stills and the screenplay in book form, prosecutors brought charges under the obscenity provisions of Criminal Code §175. It was a mistake. The times were changing, the district court explained. What constitutes pornography depends on community standards, and those standards now warranted a liberalized approach.[60] In the United States, of course, the litigation would have ended there. Ōshima had been tried—and acquitted—of a criminal violation. Anything more would violate the constitutional double-jeopardy protection.

Not in Japan. As the Japanese courts construe it, the double-jeopardy clause (Const. art. 39) protects a defendant from being independently prosecuted twice for the same crime, but does not prevent the state from appealing an acquittal. In 1994, for example, prosecutors brought 87 of all 4,808 appeals to the high courts.[61] Exercising their right to appeal, prosecutors appealed the Ōshima verdict.[62] It was, however, a mistake once again. The high court affirmed. The prosecutors—perhaps finally realizing the publicity they were giving the flamboyant director—decided not to appeal further.

II. Crime and Punishment
A. Murders
1. Race

Japan is safe; the United States is not. Few factoids about Japanese life are as well known as the freedom from violent crime. For the popular observation, there is a statistical basis. In 1993, the murder rate in Japan was 1.6 per 100,000 population. In the United States, it was 10.1 per 100,000. From such comparisons, many observers propose a variety of explanations about what Japanese police and prosecutors are doing "right."

In fact, the usual cross-national comparisons obscure as much as they clarify, for they ignore two phenomena: the economically and racially segmented nature of crime in the United States and the impact of age distribution on crime rates everywhere. We consider economics and race in this subsection and age distribution in the next.

Japan is in large part an economically and ethnically homogeneous society. The United States is not, and violent crime in the United States is an economically and racially segregated phenomenon.[63] Given the general correlation between race and poverty, overwhelmingly it is a "black-on-black" event. In 1993, the U.S. murder victimization rate (we focus on murder because the data are more reliable than for other violent crimes) was indeed 10.1. But for whites, the victimization rate was 5.7 per 100,000 population. For African Americans, it was 40.2 and for African American men, a staggering 69.7.[64]

This is not the place to explore the reasons for the high rates of violent crime in the U.S. inner city. Social scientists have no shortage of theories about the high crime rates, but precious little consensus. Whatever the reason, the segmentation of American crime matters to the U.S.-Japan comparison because it affects our evaluation of how well the two criminal

175

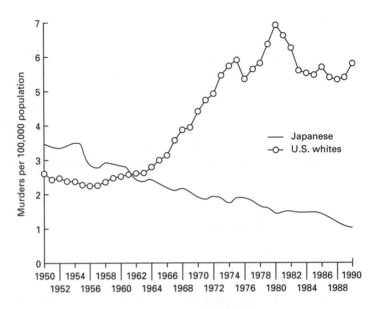

Figure 7.1 Murder Victimization Rates in Japan and among U.S. Whites

Note: For the Japanese data, we use murders reported by the police, a slightly lower figure than that reported by the prosecutorial office. For U.S. data, we use the figures provided by the National Center for Health Statistics, a slightly higher figure than that reported by the FBI.

justice systems perform. Ignoring that segmentation in the United States, most observers of the Japanese criminal justice system have described it as one that works much better than the U.S. system. In the aggregate, it does, of course, but the two systems face very different criminal environments.

Restated, crime control simply presents a far bigger challenge in the multiethnic, socially and economically far more heterogeneous United States than it does in the much more homogeneous and middle-class Japan. Arguably, at 1.6 per 100,000, the murder victimization rate in the largely racially homogeneous and largely economically middle-class Japan more closely resembles the rate among the (similarly largely homogeneous and middle-class) white U.S. communities (5.7 per 100,000) than either resembles the victimization rate among African Americans (40.2). Arguably something is less being done unusually right in the Japanese police departments and prosecutors' offices than something desperately tragic is happening in the U.S. inner cities.

Figure 7.1 illustrates the point. To compare the performance of the two criminal justice systems in more nearly comparable social and economic environments, the figure gives murder victimization rates among U.S. whites and in Japan. Importantly, only since the mid-1960s have Japanese murder rates been lower than the comparable rates among U.S. whites.

2. Demographics

Violent crime also depends on the fraction of the population that is young and male. Blame it on testosterone, or blame it on child-rearing. Whatever the cause, young men commit much of the violent crime in most societies, and crime rates accordingly reflect their density.

In figure 7.1, for example, the lines cross in part because of demographics. Through 1961, U.S. white murder rates were below the Japanese murder rates; after 1961, they have been higher. Not coincidentally the percentage of the general population made up of men in their twenties was also higher in Japan than in the United States through the 1950s and 1960s. Since the mid-1970s, that percentage has been higher in the United States than in Japan.

To illustrate the importance of demographics in violent crime, we regress Japanese and U.S. (white and total) murder victimization rates on the percentage of the society that is male, aged 20–29:

Japan:	Murder rate = 0.49(% Male 20s) − 1.83	R^2: .34
U.S. White:	Murder rate = 1.01(% Male 20s) − 3.12	R^2: .72
U.S. Total:	Murder rate = 1.34(% Male 20s) − 2.40	R^2: .64

Parenthetically, note that U.S. murder rates seem more sensitive to young males than Japanese rates. First, the slope is steeper. For any increase in the young male population, the murder rate increases more quickly in the United States than in Japan. For exactly that reason, of course, the increased youthfulness of American society in the past two decades has had deadly effect. Second, the young male population explains a larger amount of the variation in the data in the United States. The R^2, in other words, is higher in the United States than in Japan. Indeed, among U.S. whites, the percentage of men in their twenties explains nearly three-quarters of the variation in the murder rate.

Figure 7.2 shows the predicted values within reasonable demographic ranges: the expected murder rates (murders per 100,000) given different percentages of twenty- to twenty-nine-year-old men in the general population. For example, if young men constitute 6 percent of the population, the equations predict a murder rate of 1.11 per 100,000 in Japan, 2.94 among whites in the United States, and 5.64 among the U.S. population at large. At 8 percent, the equations predict murder rates of 2.09 (Japan), 4.96 (U.S.

177

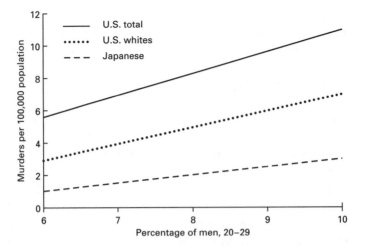

Figure 7.2 Murder Rates as a Function of the Percentage of Men Aged 20–29

white), and 8.32 (U.S. at large). At 10 percent, the equations predict rates of 3.07 (Japan), 6.98 (U.S. white), and 11.0 (U.S. at large).

Figure 7.2 suggests a way to evaluate the performance of Japanese and U.S. criminal justice systems. Typically observers compare the 1.6 murders per 100,000 in Japan with the 10.1 murders in the United States—a ratio of 1 to 6.3. If (as seems apparent) crime depends both on the levels of social and economic diversity and on the shape of the population pyramid, then a better comparison would look to the predictions in figure 7.2 for Japan and the U.S. white population. Over the relevant ranges, this comparison yields figures of 1.1 to 3.1 for Japan and 2.9 to 7.0 for U.S. whites—a ratio of perhaps 1 to 2.4.

B. Conviction Rates
1. Introduction

Japanese courts convict defendants. As most readers have heard, they convict them with a vengeance. In district court criminal cases (excluding those in summary court), they convict 99.9 percent (in 1994, 49,598 out of 49,643) of the defendants. In murder cases, they convict 99.7 percent (587 out of 589). In the United States, federal courts convict only 85.1 percent (for 1995, 46,773 out of 54,980) of the defendants and in murder cases, only 83.3 percent (265 out of 318).[65]

Suspecting that Japanese courts are not giving defendants a fair trial, many observers find these rates troubling. Although not responding directly to the conviction rates, Setsuo Miyazawa is among the more radical:

"forced confessions to false charges" are endemic to Japanese police tactics.[66] Even if less critical, most observers are still bothered by the rates. Constitutional law scholar Lawrence Beer is typical. He quotes a former judge, for instance, to suggest that Japanese judges face improper psychological pressures to convict:

> [W]hen a judge issues an acquittal, the faces of his superiors and the displeased faces of prosecutors with whom he's become friendly will appear in his mind. Those sorts of psychological pressures exist at the subconscious level, and there's a psychological brake at work that leads judges to issue as few acquittals as possible.[67]

2. Plea Bargains

a. Introduction. These differences in conviction rates hide two distinct phenomena: that defendants and prosecutors more commonly negotiate plea bargains in Japan than they do in the United States (a guilty plea will, of course, appear in the data as a conviction) and that Japanese prosecutors ditch more weak cases than do their U.S. colleagues. Take each in turn.

Preliminarily note that although Japanese law formally recognizes neither guilty pleas nor plea bargains, in effect Japanese defendants regularly plead guilty. Impossibility in form emphatically does not cause an absence in fact. Japanese defendants can indeed decide not to contest prosecution, and if they so decide, they effectively plead guilty.[68] Because no defendants anywhere have much incentive to plead guilty unless doing so lowers their penalty, that they regularly so plead suggests they and police or prosecutors regularly strike implicit bargains.

Granted, some people confess for reasons having nothing to do with the expected value of their punishment. Dostoevsky would not be the literary saint that he is if they did not. In one famous 1910 Japanese crime, passersby found the corpse of a beautiful young woman in what is today downtown Tokyo, but was then called Mitsubishi meadow. Police identified her as Otsuya Kinoshita. Only ten years later while in custody on other crimes did her killer confess. He had been her lover, he said, and had killed her when he learned she was already married to someone else. By some accounts, he confessed after a detective saw him mumble a prayer to Amitabha as they walked across Mitsubishi meadow. By others, he confessed because she haunted him every night in his dreams. By either account, he confessed for reasons having nothing to do with any plea bargain.[69]

Yet many defendants do decide to confess out of self-interest, and a confession in anticipation of a reduced sentence is nothing but an implicit plea

179

bargain. Because the courts formally ban plea bargains, cases that would settle in the United States proceed to abbreviated trials in Japan. Yet the substance remains a bargain: the defendant confesses and pleads remorse, and the court shows leniency. No one explicitly cuts a deal. But the defendant knows, the court knows, and the defendant knows the court knows (1) that if the court threw the book at the defendant, fewer defendants would confess, and (2) that if defendants routinely contested guilt, they could quickly swamp the courts.[70]

b. The Data. Defendants more often plead guilty (i.e., more often negotiate explicit or implicit plea bargains) in Japan than in the United States. In Japan, of the 49,856 cases in ordinary district courts in 1994, the defendants contested their guilt in only 3,648 cases (7.3 percent). If most uncontested trials are functionally equivalent to plea bargains, then over 90 percent of all ordinary criminal cases are plea-bargained in Japan. In the United States, of the 54,980 cases in federal district courts in 1995, defendants contested their guilt in 11,877 cases (21.6 percent). Effectively they plea-bargained less than 80 percent of the time.[71]

c. The Logic. The reason Japanese defendants and prosecutors more commonly reach negotiated outcomes probably tracks the logic to out-of-court civil settlements (section 4.II). Recall the dynamic: settlement costs less than litigation. Consequently, if a plaintiff and a defendant can agree about the expected value of the litigated outcome, they have no reason to litigate. Instead, they both gain if they settle out of court by that expected value. Given the greater predictability of Japanese courts (a function in part of the absence of juries), Japanese civil disputants are more likely to agree about the litigated outcome than are their U.S. peers. Necessarily they are more likely to settle.

This logic applies directly to criminal cases. If a prosecutor and a defendant can agree on the defendant's odds at trial, then the defendant has little reason to contest his guilt. Rather, he can discuss the issue with the prosecutor and then confess. Although judges formally determine sentences, "[p]rosecutors file sentence requests," as Foote notes, and those requests "are usually accorded considerable weight."[72] The prosecutor will signal to the court that it should punish the defendant by the expected (risk-adjusted) value of a contested judgment. Should the prosecutor and the defendant so signal, both will receive a verdict that tracks that risk-adjusted value of the contested verdict. Both then save the resources they would otherwise have spent at litigation.[73]

Because of the ban on plea bargains in Japan, police, prosecutors, and defendants cannot do this formally, of course. But inability in form is not incapacity in fact. In exchange for a confession, a prosecutor can control the sentence a defendant receives in a wide variety of ways: he can prosecute on reduced charges, he can recommend a lighter sentence, or he can ignore aggravating circumstances. Every time he cuts such an implicit bargain, the deal will appear in the judicial statistics as a conviction.

3. Prosecutorial Resources

Plea bargains do not explain all of the difference in conviction rates between the United States and Japan, however, for even among contested cases, the conviction rate is higher in Japan. Defendants contested their guilt in 3,648 cases in 1994, but were acquitted in only 45. As a result, the conviction rate in Japanese contested cases was 98.8 percent. In the U.S. federal courts in 1995, defendants contested their guilt in 11,877 cases and were acquitted (or had charges dismissed) in 8,207 cases—yielding a conviction rate of 30.9 percent.[74] Arguably this higher Japanese conviction rate follows from the more severe resource shortage among Japanese prosecutors.

Basic figures outline the contours of the shortage. To handle their civil and criminal affairs, the federal and state governments in the United States employ 66,227 lawyers (27,985 at the federal level, 38,242 at the state). Japan, by contrast, employs about 2,000. Those Japanese prosecutors handle the 2 million cases (1 million, if one excludes traffic offenses) forwarded to them from the police each year. Even given that Japan has only half the U.S. population, that the Japanese crime rate is lower (subsection II.A), and that the Japanese government hires legally trained nonlawyers (analogous to the private-sector employees detailed in subsection 1.II.C), at 1,000 criminal cases per prosecutor per year, it is hard to see the Japanese government as anything but understaffed.[75]

The consequences of the relative Japanese personnel shortage bear directly on conviction rates.[76] Should a defendant contest liability, an overworked prosecutor evaluated on the basis of the convictions he obtains will focus his efforts on those defendants against whom he has the strongest evidence (whether this is socially desirable is, of course, a separate issue). After all, doing so generally lets him maximize his demonstrable output (defendants convicted) subject to his resource constraint (his time). All else equal, in other words, one would expect prosecutors facing some cases with strong evidence and some with weak to start with the former and move to the latter only as time permits.

In so many words, this is what Japanese prosecutors themselves admit. Of the 919,000 people arrested for Criminal Code crimes in 1995 (the figure primarily excludes traffic violations), prosecutors brought charges against only 161,000 (17.5 percent). Even of the 1,822 people arrested for murder, they tried only 781 (42.9 percent).[77] By their own terms, they dropped half their murder cases not because of any "official lenience"—not because the defendant, as one American scholar suggested, "acknowledge[d his] guilt, express[ed] remorse, and compensate[d his] victims."[78] Rather, they dropped them because they could not prove their cases. In about two-thirds of the dropped murder cases, they simply lacked adequate suspicion against the person arrested.[79]

If all this is true, then Japanese conviction rates are high not because courts are railroading innocent defendants. Rather, they are high because prosecutors are freeing guilty defendants—because they have too few resources to prosecute any but the strongest cases.[80] Potentially, in other words, as a society devotes increasing resources to prosecution, the observed conviction rate (conviction/cases prosecuted) will *fall*. As prosecutors obtain more resources, they will increasingly prosecute their weaker cases.[81] As they do, the observed conviction rate will drop. To put it all most bluntly, Japan may have a high conviction rate simply because its prosecutors are too busy to try any but the most brutally and flagrantly guilty defendants.

C. The Mob
1. Stability and Crime

Ironically, the lower rates of violent crime in Japan may also result from the way the police have generally failed to imprison the leaders of the organized crime syndicates (loosely known as the *yakuza*). For in failing to do so, they have brought an organizational stability to the underworld. That stability, in turn, has kept turf battles far more modest than among the urban street gangs in the United States. The logic again follows the simple rationale to litigation and repeated deals (see sections 3.II, 4.II).

First, gangs will fight only if they cannot agree about the outcome of a fight. Like litigation, fights are expensive. Because they are expensive, rival gangs both gain if they can find ways to solve their disputes without fighting. They can devise those cheaper solutions, though, only if they can roughly agree about their prospects under war. Provided they agree about those prospects, neither gains by initiating war. Instead, both gain by staying peacefully within the confines of the expected contested outcome.

Second, because mobs (like business executives everywhere) earn gains from trade, they benefit from an environment where they can credibly commit to each other. Unlike executives in the legal sector, however, mob members cannot use the courts to give their promises credibility—A cannot assure B that B can collect damages in court from A should A renege. As a result, they have little choice but to trust to the profitable prospects of future trades. Yet for trades to be self-enforcing, the mob members involved must be able to expect that their trades will continue indefinitely into the future. For self-enforcing promises, in short, they need peace, not war.

Both factors suggest that the police reduce violence by reducing the aggressiveness with which they attack senior mob leaders. After all, the greater the stability within the mob hierarchy is,

(1) the more predictable the future is, and the fewer the occasions are when mutually optimistic gangs will decide that war is more profitable than peace; and

(2) the better able gangs will be to rely on the prospects of future dealings to make their promises credible, and the more profits they will be able to anticipate through keeping the peace.

Criminal syndicates usually will start shooting each other only when they find the present unstable and the future uncertain. Fiction to be sure, recall that the bloodbaths in the *Godfather* series occurred after a don died. With the don gone and the future a wild guess, the rival mobs were more likely both (1) to entertain mutually optimistic estimates of their gains from violence (hence to be unable to agree on the terms of a truce) and (2) to see smaller future gains from adhering to their past patterns of repeat dealings (hence to be unable to structure profitable self-enforcing promises).

Like the Corleones, like the Crips, the Bloods, and the Gangster Disciples. The more often the police regularly incarcerate senior gang members, the more territories in south central Los Angeles and south Chicago will remain up for grabs, and the gains from trade will stay low. With uncertain territories and low future gains from trade, violence ensues.

That U.S. urban street gangs kill so often results directly from their instability. That instability, in turn, results in part (if only in part) from the aggressiveness with which police have attacked gang leaders. Crucially for Japan, Japanese police have treated their mob bosses far more gently.

2. The Syndicates

The modern Japanese organized crime syndicates include several large federations and many smaller groups.[82] As of 1995, the police estimated their total affiliates at 79,300 and formal members at 46,600. Within this world, the largest groups were the Yamaguchi-gumi (as of March 1996, with 18,300 members), the Inagawa-kai (5,600 members), and the Sumiyoshi-kai (6,700 members).[83]

Although the Yamaguchi-gumi traces its roots to the prewar years, it is essentially a post-1945 group that owes its size to the organizational strength, brutality, and ruthlessness of one man. In 1943, a small-time thug named Kazuo Taoka walked out of prison onto the streets of Kobe. He had just served eight years for murder. Within three more years, he had taken over the tiny remnant of Noboru Yamaguchi's shipyard gang. Consider him the Lucky Luciano of Kobe, for within a few more years he took over most of the waterfront. From there, he expanded into the other industries on which modern mobs thrive.

Unlike the Yamaguchi-gumi, the Inagawa-kai began in Yokohama and expanded across the greater Tokyo area. Kakuji Inagawa founded the group in the 1940s and ran it for most of the next several decades. As of 1996, he still presided over the organization, but had passed working control to his son, Doi Inagawa. Also headquartered in Tokyo, the Sumiyoshi-kai is a more loosely run federation than either of these two groups.

The syndicates earn most of their revenues from drugs (primarily speed), gambling (including baseball), and the protection rackets. As of 1989, the police estimated their revenues from illegal operations at ¥1,046 billion and legal revenues at ¥257 billion. Of the former, they earned 43 percent from drugs, 21 percent from gambling, and 11 percent from protection.[84]

When the police attack the mob, they primarily use the laws on drugs, battery, and extortion. Of all mob affiliates prosecuted between 1986 and 1995, about 20 percent were prosecuted for drug crimes. About 18 percent were prosecuted for battery-related crimes and 13 percent for extortion. Although the syndicates earned large revenues from gambling, only 4 percent of the prosecutions were brought on gambling charges.[85]

3. Mob Prosecutions

a. Introduction. Despite these prosecutions, Japanese police have not attacked the mob leadership with anything approaching the ferocity with which American police attack inner-city gangs. It is not that Japanese police do not arrest. In 1995, they arrested 33,000 mob affiliates, including 11,700 formal members. Indeed, the Yamaguchi-gumi apparently found about a third of its members (5,120) arrested.[86] Moreover, when prosecutors charge mob defendants, judges typically impose harsh sentences. From mid-1993 through 1995, of the 238 nonmob defendants convicted of firearms violations, 128 received suspended sentences. Of the 308 mob defendants, only 27 did.[87] Of all defendants convicted of murder, only half receive sentences of more that five years (table 7.3). Of all mob defendants, 63.4 percent do.[88] Given these sentencing practices, mob affiliates should constitute a significant block of the prison population. And they do. Of all new inmates in 1981, 48.9 percent (14,848 out of 30,336) had ties to organized crime.[89]

    b. Evidence. Yet perhaps because they seldom participate directly in criminal activities, perhaps because they have powerful friends, the highest leaders in the mobs spend very little time in prison. As of 1978, police estimated that less than 8 percent of the mob leaders (the top-ranking 1 percent of the mob) were in prison.[90] Most obviously, evidence against such leaders is hard to get. Interrogation often fails, for syndicate members tell tales on their superiors at their peril. According to anthropologist Walter Ames (who spent a year with the Okayama police), police raids seldom work much better:

> The police make periodic raids on gangster headquarters throughout Japan, rounding up hundreds of gangsters and seizing drugs, illegal firearms, and swords. However, these raids assume an almost ritual air because most of the gangsters are released in a few days through lack of evidence of criminal acts or because their offenses were minor. It has been remarked by observers, including police officers, that many of the gangs usually receive warning before these massive raids and that most of the weapons and evidence of wrongdoing are concealed and the highest bosses go into hiding.[91]

From the day Taoka took control of the Yamaguchi-gumi in 1946 to the day he died in 1981, he apparently never once went to prison. Inagawa was only slightly less fortunate. From 1945 to the present, he served one three-year term in the 1960s on gambling charges.

    c. Friends. Japanese mob leaders have powerful friends. Japan is not alone in this, of course. Mob leaders everywhere try to buy protection at the top. What is unusual among modern democracies is the degree to which the Japanese mob has succeeded.

The story,[92] reasonably well known, goes back to three class-A (the most notorious) war criminals in Sugamo Prison during the early years of the U.S. occupation: Yoshio Kodama, Ryōichi Sasakawa, and Nobusuke Kishi. Kodama had made his fortune looting East Asia during the war. Upon his release from Sugamo, he used that money to bankroll the emerging conservative political coalition. Partly through those donations and partly because of his close ties with the Tokyo mobs (he used them in his strike-breaking work), he became a powerful political broker. Only when the public learned that he had also worked for years as Lockheed's local bribery agent—funneling vast sums to Prime Minister Kakuei Tanaka and other senior Liberal Democratic Party (LDP) politicians—did his power finally wane.

Kodama's one-time Sugamo cellmate Ryōichi Sasakawa made his fortune running the legalized parimutuel betting empire associated with motorboat racing. Those activities kept him in close touch with the mob, and at one time, he even bragged of being a drinking buddy to Taoka himself. For decades, he remained a powerful and visible conservative.

Kishi had worked in the Manchukuo government during the 1930s as a high-ranking civilian. From there, he eventually became vice munitions minister under Tōjō. By 1955, he was LDP secretary general and, with Kodama's money and support, became prime minister two years later.

Perhaps it was because of factors like this that few self-respecting intellectuals in the early postwar years admitted to supporting the LDP. But if in 1960 anyone still doubted the party's links to the mob, the events that year ended it. It was the year Japan would renew its security treaty with the United States, and the leftists were adamantly opposed. They organized massive protests in the streets of Tokyo; yet into that mess Eisenhower was scheduled to arrive. Worse, according to plan, he would ride an open limousine with the emperor from the airport into Tokyo.

That someone among the angry, rioting leftists might want to kill Eisenhower or the emperor or both was an easy call, and to "solve" the problem, LDP leaders called Kodama. Would he enlist the support of the mob? Kodama agreed, and soon the head of the "Welcome Ike" committee was meeting with the leaders of the Tokyo syndicates, including both Inagawa and the head of the Sumiyoshi-kai. As one journalist put it:

> Kodama persuaded yakuza leaders of organized gamblers, gangsters, extortionists, street vendors and members of underground

syndicates to organize an "effective counter-force" to ensure Eisenhower's safety. The final plan called for the deployment of 18,000 yakuza. . . . They were supported by government-supplied helicopters, Cessna aircraft, trucks, cars, food, command posts, and first-aid squads, in addition to some 800 million yen in "operational funds." [93]

The left continued to riot, the mob responded, several protestors were injured, and one student died. Faced with the chaos, the government withdrew its invitation to Eisenhower, and Kishi resigned.

These ties between the LDP and the mob leadership remained everywhere to see, but they resurfaced stunningly in 1971. Local Kyūshū boss Takaaki Kusano had been convicted of ordering the murder of two rival syndicate members, and the high court had affirmed the conviction. On appeal to the Supreme Court, he petitioned for interim release. As guarantors for his court appearance, however, he obtained none other than former Prime Minister Kishi, a former minister of justice, and the local Diet representative. Kishi's office denied knowing anything about the matter, and to its credit, the court denied the release petition. Yet the political damage—identifying the LDP once again as the party of the mob—was already done.[94]

4. Turf Battles

The relative scarcity of prosecutions against senior mob leaders has contributed to the stability among the mobs, and that stability has contributed to lower levels of violence. Table 7.4 shows the results. Most obviously, mob turf wars have caused very few deaths. The table unfortunately misses the "Osaka wars" of 1975–1978 between the Yamaguchi-gumi and the Matsuda-gumi. It does, however, capture the more violent succession dispute within the Yamaguchi-gumi after Taoka's death (1981–1989).[95] Even during the height of the dispute in 1985, only thirty-two people died from the battles. By police estimates, from 1979 to 1995, only 0.4–5.4 percent of the organized crime killings were related to turf wars. Indeed, during the entire period, only 240–640 killings per year were related to organized crime at all. By contrast, turf war in the United States (with its 26,000 homicides a year) leads to enormous loss of life. According to noted criminologist and economist John Lott, "In larger urban areas, where most murders occur, the majority of murders are gang related turf wars over drugs." [96]

Table 7.4 Murder and the Mob

	Murder Arrests			Mob Turf Wars			Mob Gunfights		
	A. Total	B. Mob Affiliated	Col. B/ Col. A (Percentage)	Fights	C. Deaths	Col. C/ Col. B (Percentage)	Fights	D. Deaths	Col. D/ Col. B (Percentage)
1972	2,188	524	23.9						
1973	2,113	538	25.5						
1974	1,870	480	25.7						
1975	2,179	640	29.4						
1976	2,113	641	30.3						
1977	1,988	554	27.9				108	10	1.8
1978	1,843	495	26.7				71	15	3.0
1979	1,841	493	26.8	29	7	1.4	69	11	2.2
1980	1,560	412	26.4	63	12	2.9	94	16	3.9
1981	1,712	509	29.7	56	7	1.4	116	15	2.9
1982	1,768			84	2		125	10	
1983	1,789			198	12		230	19	
1984	1,788			109	6		139	18	
1985	1,833	598	32.6	293	32	5.4	326	44	7.4
1986	1,692	564	33.3	218	18	3.2	317	59	10.5
1987	1,651	493	29.9	187	18	3.7	286	39	7.9
1988	1,408	356	25.3	128	3	0.8	249	28	7.9
1989	1,323	345	26.1	156	4	1.2	268	19	5.5
1990	1,238	349	28.2	146	16	4.6	255	35	10.0
1991	1,159	265	22.9	47	5	1.9	182	23	8.7
1992	1,175	255	21.7	39	5	2.0	174	17	6.7
1993	1,218	241	19.8	77	4	1.7	178	16	6.6
1994	1,275	270	21.2	44	4	1.5	210	29	10.7
1995	1,295	252	19.5	28	1	0.4	128	21	8.3

Sources: Keisatsu chō, ed., Keisatsu hakusho [Police White Paper] (Tokyo: Ōkura shō, various years); Hōmushō, ed., Hanzai hakusho [Crime White Paper] (Tokyo: Ōkura shō, various years), 419; Nihon bengoshi rengō kai, ed., Bōryokudan no fuhōkōi sekinin [The Tort Liability of Violent Groups] (Tokyo: Yūhikaku, 1994).

Conclusions

Mother's corpse was hard. And all stretched out. I spread her legs, and leaned her right side against the wall. Then, I took the knife I had put next to the wooden slatted floor of the bathroom, and bent down. I lifted her right ankle with my left hand. With the knife in my right hand I started to slice through her skin. It was about 4 inches below the knee. The skin gave way, and the meat fell off the bone. But the bone itself was too hard. I pushed and pulled the knife against it but couldn't cut through. . . .

I decided to try a saw. I remembered there was one in the tool cabinet at the north end of the veranda, one from a store in Sumiyoshi. I went and got it, and cut through the bone. I took the foot I had cut off, wrapped it in cloth, and stuck it in a nylon bag. . . .[97]

And on it goes—the confessions of a matricidal thirty-six-year-old. He had earlier done some prison time. Released on probation, he had returned to his mother's house and married a young divorcee. Unable to hold a job and chronically in debt, he felt pestered by his wife and harassed by his mother.

I couldn't drink the liquor I wanted. I didn't have money for pachinko [see section 9.I]. Once I did pawn the bicycle that I commuted to work on, and made money with the cash at pachinko. But then I bought liquor. Pachinko. It's the only thing I like. I don't lose often. Actually, when I try I can make as much money at pachinko as I can working. So in early May 1960, I stopped working.[98]

A dead mother would, he reasoned, buy him time from his creditors. When on June 8, 1960, he found her sleeping, he strangled her and stuffed her in the closet. Three days later he dragged her out, carved her into small bits, packed them in a wicker basket, placed it on the back of his bicycle, and dumped it all in the woods. Caught, he confessed and was hanged in 1968.[99]

There is crime in Japan, even brutal crime, and the government recognizes the gains to responding. The police investigate, the prosecutors prosecute, and the hangmen and wardens punish. Given the economies of scale to basic law enforcement, most economically successful societies provide governmentally funded protection against harm to one's person or property. Japan is no exception. With an assortment of modest differences to be

189

sure, through criminal law and police protection it creates a world much like the one in which most Americans (if middle class and white) live.

The cruelty, the ruthlessness, the gore—all those aspects of criminal pathology that we associate with the United States apply to Japan, too. But with the gore also comes the pathos, those tales we would instinctively find touching if only we could be sure we were not being manipulated toward early parole or a pardon. If Alcatraz had its birdman, Japan has had its death-row poets:

> Knowing not that I sit on death row,
>   the sparrow comes to my window.
> I love it, and daily give it bread.
> I yearn for things to love, and stand
>   looking out my window,
>   looking at the wild flowers that bloom wet with rain.
> Lacking any more even the will to kill a snake,
>   I stare at my hands,
>   I who once killed a man.

If it was manipulation, it did not work. The poet was hanged in 1975.[100]

8 ADMINISTRATIVE LAW

Shōichi Taira and his wife, Kimiko Iizuka, wanted to open a public bath "with private rooms attached." Culturally eclectic if nothing else, they called their place Turkish Hawaii. It was what Japanese in the 1960s called a "Turkish bath." It was what we would call a brothel. Turkish baths did eventually disappear from Japan, but only after a Turkish diplomat hopped in a cab at Narita Airport and asked for "the Turkish embassy." When the cabby dropped him off in front of a brothel of that name, he complained to the Japanese government. To head off a row, the ever-resourceful brothel trade association decided its members should rename themselves "soaplands." Soaplands they remain today.

But in the 1960s, soaplands were still Turkish baths. And to open a Turkish bath, Taira and Iizuka needed a permit. They bought a piece of land not subject to any restrictions against Turkish baths and then applied for that permit. Unfortunately for them, their new neighbors fumed. They wanted no brothel, at least not in their backyard. They begged the city and prefectural government officials to deny Taira's application. When the prefectural officials instead suggested they have a nearby lot declared an official playground, the neighbors agreed. They submitted their application on June 4, 1968, and by June 10, the playground was official.

Turkish Hawaii opened its doors in July, only to find itself closed within a few months. It was now 134.5 meters from a playground, and the relevant statute prohibited such bathhouses within 200 meters of official playgrounds. What were Taira and Iizuka to do? They had searched for land where they could legally open a bath "with private rooms attached." They had followed proper regulatory procedures. They had invested large sums in buying the land and in building and decorating the establishment. At the last minute, local residents had manipulated the regulatory apparatus to run them out of business.

Taira and Iizuka sued.[1] The story of this chapter is the story of the rules that govern suits such as theirs. So table for the moment the actual outcome of their complaint, and consider those rules instead. Under the rules, the Japanese Constitution sets basic (if loose) constraints on how broadly the legislature can delegate rule-making. Together the constitution and various regulatory statutes guarantee most regulated parties a right to a hearing on issues directly affecting their welfare. If an agency decides such an issue against them, usually they can petition for reconsideration within the agency.

Japanese law also gives courts the power to review administrative rulings. It limits that review to statutorily defined "administrative dispositions," however, and gives the right to demand review only to those who can show a "legal interest." Together these rules take many (not all) disputes involving basic policy issues and large numbers of parties out of the ambit of judicial review and keep in the courts only the more routine cases. When courts do review administrative actions, they usually do so under an abuse-of-discretion standard.

We begin by outlining the basics of administrative law (section I). We start with the constitutional constraints on delegation (subsection A) and turn successively to administrative review (subsection B), judicial review (subsection C), the prime ministerial veto (subsection D), and the 1993 Administrative Procedure Act (subsection E). We then explore what is easily the best known phenomenon in Japanese administrative law: administrative guidance (section II). We conclude by integrating Japanese administrative practice into a broader framework of political economy (section III).

Observant readers will notice that we ignore rule-making procedures. Given the lack of any overarching rule-making process, the procedures vary from issue to issue. Because of the enormous resulting variation, we omit the subject from this chapter.

I. The Law
A. Constitutional Constraints

Constitutional limits on statutory delegation set the outer contours of Japanese administrative law. Although the constitution gives the cabinet authority to "enact cabinet orders to execute the provisions of this Constitution and of the law" (art. 73), it declares the Diet "the sole law-making organ" (art. 41). It adds that a cabinet order may not "include penal provisions . . . unless authorized by such law" (art. 73), that "no person shall be deprived of life or liberty . . . except according to procedure established by law" (art. 31), and that local governments shall only have the power to "enact their own regulations within law" (art. 94). Because of all this, agencies can regulate—but only if they stay within statutorily authorized constraints.

That agencies regulate within statutory bounds is easy to state, but hard to detail. In section II, we illustrate what can happen when agencies step beyond those bounds. More typically, courts find that they have properly remained within their statutory constraints. During the first years after the war, for example, the Allied occupation continued the elaborate wartime controls in the food market. The statute at stake authorized the government to stabilize supply and imposed criminal penalties on those who violated it. The details it left to regulation.

The scheme had been a disaster during the war, and it continued a disaster under the occupation. Shortages on the legal market were so bad that one judge who refused to patronize the black market simply starved to death.[2] Eisaburō Sugioka was a more ordinary fellow, if at least as unfortunate. Caught in Nagasaki at the end of the war, he had lost his wife to the bomb, and his oldest son had been left crippled. Hoping to make do, he left the bombed remains of the city and returned with his children to his home village. There he started a flour and noodle factory. Too bad for him, he violated the food market controls, and the police induced him to confess. In his defense, he argued that the regulations exceeded their statutory bounds.[3] He lost, for as a high court explained in a similar case, the constitution did allow limited delegation, and the food control regulations fell within those limits:

> Article 73(f) of the Constitution presupposes both that statutes may delegate matters, and that those delegated matters may be decided by regulation. In other words, when the Constitution states that regulations may not impose penalties unless authorized by statute, it necessarily implies the converse—namely, that a statutorily authorized regulation may validly restrict the rights of citizens and punish those who violate it.[4]

Much the same issue arose in the sexual services industry. Prostitution had been legal before the war and stayed legal nationally until 1957. Soon after the war, however, several cities banned it on their own. When arrested, prostitutes and pimps challenged these local bans as an improper exercise of delegated authority (because Japan lacks a federal structure, the law in many ways treats local governments as bureaucratic agencies). Not so, declared the Supreme Court. The Regional Self-Government Act authorized local governments to regulate adult entertainment for the sake of the public health and welfare, and it further authorized criminal penalties. Given those broad statutory contours, local governments could properly ban people from selling or brokering sexual services.[5]

Finally, consider Fumihiro Nishioka, a lawyer with a passion for the Spanish Civil War. In 1981, Nishioka went to Granada and bought two sabers worn by officers in the war. One dated from 1905, the other from 1834. Upon his return to Narita Airport, the police confiscated his swords under the 1958 arms control statute.[6] Although the statute bans most guns and swords, it does let owners keep swords with artistic or cultural value. Accordingly, Nishioka petitioned to register his new sabers. Alas, the Ministry of Education had drafted regulations that allowed people to register only Japanese swords. Nishioka's swords had artistic and cultural value, but (being Spanish) fell outside that range.

In court, Nishioka argued that the regulations exceeded the bounds of the statute. The statute let the government register swords with artistic and cultural value, he reminded the court. Hence, a regulation that limited registration to Japanese swords violated the statutory design. The court disagreed. Shortly after the war, the Allied occupation had tried to confiscate all weapons. The Japanese government had pleaded that it exempt heirloom Japanese swords, and the current regulatory system continued that arrangement. Although the government was willing to let national heirlooms survive, it also wanted Japan disarmed. The mob and fringe-right groups were already acquiring registered antique foreign guns.[7] Even if it made sense to preserve national heirlooms, it made less sense to let Japanese import dangerous foreign heirlooms besides.

To the Supreme Court, all this was reason enough.[8] The Ministry of Education's regulation was a "rational" interpretation of the statute, and the regulation excluded Nishioka's sabers. However rational the regulation, the denouement would have left even Yossarian of *Catch-22* fame proud: the "two historic sabers," one Tokyo newspaper blandly reported, will now "be destroyed."[9]

B. Administrative Review
1. *The Right to a Hearing*

If government agency *A* faces a major question involving the rights of petitioner *P*, *P* will often have a right to a hearing. Whatever the constitutional constraints, a statute often gives *P* that right explicitly (and sometimes courts require hearings even when statutes do not mandate them).[10] Should the police want to revoke *P*'s driver's license, for example, they must give him a hearing. Should the government want to revoke a realtor's license or even a nightclub or bar owner's permit, it must offer a hearing. Even should it only want to revoke a gun permit, it must offer a hearing.[11]

2. The Balancing Test

The general right to a hearing is not absolute. Instead, absent a statute to the contrary, whether an applicant can demand one depends on an obviously muddy comparison between his own interests and the procedural costs to the agency. By way of example, take K.K. Guynox, a firm that produced a computer program called Electronic Brain Academy—Scenario II. Ostensibly it was educational—it quizzed the user about current events. But Guynox claimed an innovative (well, maybe not so innovative) way to motivate high school boys. Think of it as floppy-disk strip poker. If the user answered a question correctly, a high school girl appeared on screen and stripped off a piece of clothing. Most other details the court left discreetly unexplained, but the developer insisted that users could not bypass the questions. The only way they could undress the girl was to learn the material quizzed.

Unfortunately for Guynox, the Miyazaki prefectural governor decided the program was unhealthy and banned retailers from selling it to minors (those under age eighteen). Guynox sued. After all, few people over age eighteen were likely to want its program. Although the governor had relied on a review committee to classify the program as unhealthy, he had not notified Guynox or given it a chance to make its case. That failure, it argued, was grounds to void the classification.

In rejecting Guynox's claim, the court reasoned that the rights to notice and a hearing were not absolutes. How much process was due instead depended on "a balance between the costs to the petitioner and the interests promoted through the administrative disposition." On the one hand, Guynox's loss was minor—a ban "only" on sales to minors. On the other, speed was of the essence in the classificatory process (for reasons the court did not detail), and providing notices and hearings for the developers of all the products the committee evaluated would have been overwhelmingly cumbersome. Given that balance, the governor could properly skip notice and hearings.[12]

3. Agency Review

Now suppose agency A has denied petitioner P's claim.[13] P will often want to ask A to reconsider. He could sue A in court, but litigation is expensive, and courts generally review agency actions only for illegality or abuse of discretion (see subsection C.4). Besides, sometimes courts will refuse to hear *P*'s claim unless he has exhausted his administrative remedies anyway (see subsection C.5).

When *P* petitions *A* for reconsideration, his claim will generally go to the same agency that made the initial determination.[14] In demanding administrative review, he can ask for review of a broad range of dispositions (Administrative Complaints Inquiries Act (ACIA), §§4–6),[15] including agency *in*action (§§2(b), 7).[16] If successful, he can have the reviewing forum cancel or modify the initial disposition or (in an agency inaction claim) tell the initial forum what to do (ACIA, §§40, 47, 51). Unless he can show irreparable harm, he does not stay the initial disposition simply by filing his petition (ACIA, §34).

For this administrative review, *P* can appear in person (ACIA, §25).[17] He can introduce evidence (ACIA, §26), and he can present witnesses (§27). When necessary, he can obtain discovery against the government of (1) the documents on which the agency initially based its factual findings or (2) the documents forwarded to the reviewing officer from those involved in the initial disposition (ACIA, §§28, 33).[18]

C. Judicial Review
1. Introduction

Suppose petitioner *P* dislikes the action agency *A* took on his claim. He has sought administrative review and lost. May he ask a court to review what the agency did (or did not do)? If he does, what must he show? To explore these issues, consider five aspects of judicial review in Japan: the requirement that an agency have made an administrative disposition (subsection 2), the rules on standing (subsection 3), the standards by which courts review a claim (subsection 4), whether a petitioner must exhaust his administrative remedies first (subsection 5), and the discovery available against the government (subsection 6).[19]

2. Administrative Disposition

a. The Basic Rules. A court will review an agency determination under the general administrative litigation rules only if it involved an "administrative disposition"—a test that can parallel the U.S. doctrine of "ripeness".[20] The test is important because the arcane taxonomy of suits against the government resembles nothing so much as our own well-interred writs. If agency action involved an administrative disposition, then review lies under the administrative litigation rules. If it did not, then review lies (if it lies at all) under ordinary civil procedure rules. As the Supreme Court articulated the distinction:

> The term phrase disposition by an administrative agency does not refer (as argued) to all action that an agency takes based on law. Rather, it refers to those actions based on law that a national or public organization (the subject of the public powers) takes that directly structure or determine the rights and duties of citizens.[21]

Granted, this reads a bit like the caller who reported "I'm in a phone booth at the corner of Walk and Don't Walk"—but in fact the routine cases are clear. If an agency rejects a permit application, it exercises its public powers. It determines the rights of the applicant and thus subjects itself to judicial review under the administrative litigation rules. If an agency closes a grocery store for selling spoiled fish, it does the same.[22]

By contrast, if an agency buys a fleet of cars on the open market or builds for them a large garage, it exercises only private powers. Necessarily it does not determine the rights and duties of citizens (as Japanese courts construe the concept) and makes no administrative determination. The agency must follow the usual rules of property and contract, of course. Courts will review its actions under the usual rules of civil procedure.

Whether a suit proceeds as an administrative or a civil suit can have important implications, though they do not necessarily cut one way or the other. On the one hand, if the suit lies under the administrative litigation rules, then the review will include issues that a civil court would generally ignore (like the procedural course of the agency's determination). On the other, if the suit lies under the civil procedure rules, then sometimes large advantages follow. Most prominently, if the administrative rules apply, a petitioner may not obtain a preliminary injunction (Administrative Case Litigation Act (ACLA), §44).[23] If ordinary civil rules apply, a petitioner who can show irreparable harm may indeed sue for that remedy.[24]

 b. Public Power. Consider some examples. If a public school expels a student, it exercises its public power and thus makes an administrative disposition. Tarō Kōno was a high school student at Ansei, a Hiroshima public school. During class in November 1980, he slugged his music teacher. The class had gone bad, he later explained, and he had simply tried to help restore order. It was not help the music teacher appreciated. He checked with the principal and then called Kōno's mother. "Make him sit at home and think about what he did," he told her. A few days later Kōno's homeroom teacher talked with her, too. "He won't be able to study at Ansei High," he explained. "Let's talk about what he should do." The principal was willing to help him find a job or night school program, but Kōno himself wanted to return to Ansei. When the principal refused to have him back, Kōno sued for a preliminary injunction. Because the case involved an administrative disposition, the court rejected the claim straightforwardly—no preliminary injunction.[25]

c. Private Conduct. If a local government tries to build a sewage treatment plant, under Japanese law it exercises only civil powers: it buys land, hires an engineering firm, and deals with contractors. In none of these roles does it exercise what the courts consider public power. Given this private character, neighbors who want to stop a sewage plant can sometimes preliminarily enjoin it.

The plaintiffs in one 1972 case, for example, farmed. When the local sewage association (organized by several municipal governments) decided to double the capacity of its nearby plant, they thought it a threat to their property—not to mention their noses—and sued. Although the court found too little evidence of harm to warrant a preliminary injunction, the administrative disposition requirement did not block their claim. Courts in other cases have indeed enjoined sewage plants. On the ACLA's section 44 ban on preliminary injunctions, the 1972 court explained:

> Given the character of sewage disposal, [constructing a sewage treatment plant] does not involve the exercise of public power by the local agency. Neither can one predict that it will obviously restrict the rights of individuals or impose duties on them. Accordingly, it does not involve the "disposition by an administrative agency, or other action constituting the exercise of public power" within the scope of section 44 of the Administrative Case Litigation Act.[26]

d. Internal Matters. When an agency takes action that directly affects only its internal affairs, that, too, is not an administrative disposition.[27] A typical example involved the use of circulars (*tsūtatsu*)—formal instructions from high-level bureaucrats to their subordinates—in the burial industry. Traditionally, Japanese temples interred the cremated remains of their parishioners. Given the associated public health issues, this sometimes placed them under the regulatory arm of the Ministry of Health and Welfare (MHW). The question that arose in the 1950s and 1960s concerned the remains of the heterodox.

The relevant statute required temples to inter remains as requested unless they could point to a "proper reason" to refuse. Throughout the 1950s, the MHW interpreted this to allow temples to refuse to inter members of rival sects. That arrangement broke down, though, when the rapidly growing Sōkagakkai started competing people away from the mainstream denominations. As the faithful deserted the mainstream temples for the Sōkagakkai, the temples responded by refusing to inter them when they died. To the MHW, this presented a Japanese night-of-the-living-dead nightmare: bodies without a home. To forestall the disaster, it changed its position in 1960 by internal circular: a decedent's religious loyalties would no longer constitute a "proper reason" to refuse to inter. In response, the mainstream temples sued.

The Supreme Court rejected their challenge. A circular, it explained, is purely an intra-agency affair. "It does not directly bind the general citizenry," it noted. "And it certainly does not bind the courts." As it involved no more than an internal agency instruction, it was not subject to judicial review. A temple that wanted to contest the MHW's new interpretation could simply ignore it and turn the bodies away. It could then wait for the MHW to try to enforce its new interpretation. Then—but only then—would the courts resolve the issue.[28]

3. Standing

For petitioner P to challenge agency A, he must also have standing to sue. To have that standing, by ACLA §9 he must have a "legal interest" in the case. Again, the routine cases are clear: agency A refuses P a permit for his Turkish bath—P has standing; agency B closes P's pawn shop—P has standing. It is the odd cases that are obscure and that sometimes (but only sometimes) seem to track the "zone of interest" inquiry in the United States.

To explore the obscure, consider, in turn, disputes over nuclear reactors, zoos, and bathhouses. Although Japan relies heavily on nuclear power, the reactors have their share of opponents, both opponents of nuclear power generally and opponents of nuclear power in their backyards. When these opponents challenge the reactors' permits, they generally lose on the grounds that the government followed proper procedures and took reasonable safety precautions. Crucial for our purposes here, they do not lose on standing. Consistently the courts instead hold that the industry regulatory statute emphasizes safety, that the reactors potentially threaten the safety of nearby residents, and that those residents thus have standing to challenge the safety of the reactors.[29]

199

Zoos are legally different, it seems. K.K. Koizumi African Lion Safari planned a largely cageless 180-acre zoo on the foothills of Mt. Fuji. To the neighbors who challenged its permit, it both jeopardized their water and threatened their lives. With obvious distress, they told the court about the 4,100 pounds of excrement and 2,500 pounds of urine the animals would produce each day. Much of it, they claimed, would flow directly into their water supply untreated. They also told it the zoo was on a fault line. If and when the next quake hit, many of the animals would escape. Yet within a dozen miles were four cities. Picture, they told the court, those angry, hungry lions roaming the streets.

If the court was sympathetic, it did not let it show. Although the reactor courts routinely grant neighbors standing, the zoo court refused. The difference apparently derived from the regulatory statutes involved. Where the nuclear regulatory statute stressed (however indirectly) the interests of the neighbors, the municipal planning statute at issue in the zoo permit did not. Instead, it emphasized sensible overall municipal design. Given the stress on general city welfare rather than more local concerns, the neighbors lacked standing.[30]

Mind you, one should not think this indifference to human welfare unusual in the modern regulatory state. Patrick Hoctor lived outside Terra Haute and kept three lions, two tigers, seven ligers, six cougars, and two leopards. To tell him to build an eight-foot fence, the Department of Agriculture had to argue (as Richard Posner observed, bemused) "that if one of those Cats mauled or threatened a human being, the Cat might get into serious trouble and thus it is necessary to protect human beings from Big Cats in order to protect the Cats from human beings, which is the important thing under the [Animal Welfare] Act."[31]

But just as traffic signals in New York are just rough guidelines—or so we are told—standing rules can take odd turns. Public (non-Turkish) bathhouses fall under a regulatory statute that articulates public health concerns, but only vaguely. In the 1950s, Kyoto baths further fell under a city regulation that imposed a minimum 250 meters between them. When the city licensed a new bath 208 meters from an existing bathhouse, the incumbent bathhouse owner sued. As generalized as the statutory focus on public health was, the Supreme Court granted the incumbent owner standing. To reach that conclusion, it read into the statute exactly the political bargain most modern social scientists would have suspected: that the Diet had designed the statute to cut competition and transfer monopoly rents from consumers to incumbent bathhouse owners. The statute, as the court more politely put it, prevented the "managerial chaos brought about by needless competition." Given this statutory focus on incumbent economic advantage, standing followed as a matter of course. Crucially, however, it followed only because the court read into the vague statute a specific and highly parochial intent.[32]

4. Standard of Review

Courts review most agency decisions under a standard that leaves the agency considerable flexibility. In the usual civil case, of course, a plaintiff must prove his case more likely than not. In administrative cases, too, the petitioner bears the burden of persuasion. What he must generally prove, though, is illegality or an abuse of discretion. By the terms of section 30 of the ACLA, he must show that the agency acted illegally, "exceeded the scope of its discretion, or abused its discretion."

A 1988 case involving a medical association illustrates the rule. Several renegade doctors had left their local association and petitioned the government to recognize their new group. Claiming that two official local associations would confuse consumers, the government refused. The renegade doctors sued, and the Supreme Court rejected their claim. Whether to recognize a new medical association was, it explained, "entrusted to the broad discretion" of the agency. The doctors could challenge its decision only if they could show that the decision "lacked a basis in fact, for example, or was egregiously inappropriate (in light of prevailing social norms)—and [the agency] thus either exceeded or abused its permissible discretion."[33]

The standards have enormous play in them, and they also vary by context. For reasons of length, we do not pretend to cover the issue fully. In cases involving government jobs, the courts do seem to give agencies relatively broad discretion to demote employees. They give less discretion to fire them.[34] In cases involving nuclear reactors, they forthrightly place the burden of proof on safety on the government. Given the enormous advantage that the government has in expertise and access to data, the Supreme Court explained, it must both (1) bear the burdens of production and persuasion and (2) show that its decision was not irrational.[35]

5. Exhaustion of Remedies

Because of the costs of litigation and the restrictive review standards courts apply, petitioners will often find it pays to petition the agency before they sue. Courts, to most petitioners, will be a last resort. According to the ACLA, however, if for some reason a petitioner prefers to sue immediately, he may do so. He need not exhaust his administrative remedies first (ACLA, §8). There are exceptions, but they vary by field. Petitioners in a foreign exchange dispute, for example, traditionally need to demand administrative review first. So, too, do those in a tax dispute.[36]

6. Discovery

In administrative cases, petitioners may invoke the standard discovery provisions of the Civil Procedure Code (§220). Through those provisions, the judge can demand access to all documents that relate to the legal relationship between the petitioners and the government. Courts construe the rule broadly enough to reach a variety of documents: for instance, taxpayers can obtain the evidence by which the tax bureau calculated their income, those victims of Minamata disease (see section 5.II) who sued the government for its role in the disaster could obtain the medical reports the government held, neighbors of nuclear power plants can obtain safety-related documents, and professors challenging the Ministry of Education's textbook certification procedure can obtain the minutes of certification committee meetings.[37]

D. The Prime Ministerial Veto
1. The Veto

One of the odder features of Japanese administrative law is the veto it gives the prime minister. Although an administrative suit does not ordinarily stay an agency's contested disposition (ACLA, §25(a)), a petitioner who can show irreparable harm can demand such a stay (§25(b)). Curiously, but crucially, if a court grants him the stay but the prime minister decides it threatens the public welfare, the prime minister can veto the stay (ACLA, §27).[38]

In April 1971, the emperor and empress were to visit the atomic-bomb memorial in Hiroshima. For several groups, it was a chance to make news. For those on the fringe left tied to the Central Faction (the Chūkaku-ha; see subsection 7.I.A.4), it was a chance to snub the throne. They enlisted anti-imperial A-bomb victims and Japan's outcast (*burakumin*) community. Together they planned a march. For those in the fringe-right Patriotic Front (the Aikoku sensen dōmei), it was a chance to celebrate the imperial institution. They, too, planned a march. And for those in several paramilitary groups from out of town, it was a chance to knock some leftist heads.

Facing the risk of bloodshed and the certainty of embarrassment, the

Hiroshima Public Safety Commission (HPSC) banned the demonstrations. Both the left and the right sued, and in both cases, on the day before the visit the Hiroshima District Court ordered the HPSC to permit limited marches. Prime Minister Eisaku Satō would have none of it. Early the next day he exercised his section 27 right and vetoed the order.[39]

2. The Tokyo Marches

Satō used his veto often, but usually to block antiwar groups from marching past the Diet building and his Tokyo home. A typical dispute occurred in the summer of 1967. A group applied to the Tokyo Public Safety Commission (TPSC) for a march permit, generally a routine matter. The TPSC, however, granted the permit only if it avoided the Diet building.

The protestors sued. The order was illegal, they argued, and the court should stay it. The mandatory rerouting would irreparably harm their constitutional right of self-expression. Quite so, responded a three-judge panel on the Tokyo District Court, and the court granted the stay. Satō now promptly intervened. A march near the Diet building would threaten the public welfare, he explained. The judges dutifully—the ACLA gave them no choice—retracted their order.[40]

The incident was less bizarre than what followed: a virtual war between Satō and the several judges on the Tokyo District Court. A month later another group applied for a march permit. Again, the TPSC granted the permit only if it avoided the Diet. Again, the group sued. Again, the court (the same judges) stayed the order. Again, Satō intervened and vetoed the stay.[41] And again and again, the entire process repeated itself throughout 1968 and 1969.[42]

As if to make the already curious curiouser still, the leader of the first march now sued for damages. He had a constitutional right to march past the Diet, he claimed. In violating that right, the TPSC had caused him emotional distress. For that harm, the city of Tokyo owed him compensation. Dutifully the Tokyo District Court (two of the same judges) awarded him ¥100,000.[43]

And yet the judges never had a chance. As explained in section 1.IV, Japanese judges are career civil servants. They rotate through different jobs every two or three years, and the prime minister effectively (albeit indirectly) controls their assignments. Of the three judges most heavily involved in these skirmishes, the oldest retired. The other two found their careers permanently derailed. The elephant never forgets, and they worked for the elephant. For the rest of their careers, they plodded along on an excruciatingly slow track.[44]

E. The Administrative Procedure Act

What, in light of all this, should we make of the new statute—the 1993 Administrative Procedure Act (APA)?[45] Obviously the Diet did not draft the APA on a clean slate. Japan already had an elaborate statutory and common law of administrative procedure. The puzzle is why the Diet drafted yet another administrative law statute. The old scheme did have some minor problems, and the new act fixed a few of them. The old scheme could also be opaque, and the new act clarified some of it. In part, therefore, perhaps the Diet passed the act because of the thoughtful efforts of prominent scholars in the administrative law community.[46]

But only in part. The problems and obscurities in the law were not of the magnitude that usually induces the Diet to intervene. Certainly no one who has ever studied U.S. administrative law could have thought Japanese administrative law particularly "opaque." Perhaps, therefore, part of the explanation lies elsewhere. One possibility lies in the way U.S. trade negotiators transformed the purported "opaqueness" of Japanese administrative law into a convenient trade issue.[47] In part, to put it most crassly, perhaps the Diet passed the statute as a cheap sop to U.S. negotiators.

Consider the most prominent aspects of the new statute: It encourages agencies to establish time frames within which they will act on an application (APA, §6). It requires agencies to respond promptly to applications rather than to try to solicit revised applications by refusing to accept them (APA, §7). It requires agencies to give affected third parties a hearing if the regulatory statute requires that the agencies weigh those third parties' interests (APA, §10). It requires agencies to hold hearings if the potential harm to an applicant is large relative to the agency's need for speed (APA, §13). It requires agencies to disclose documents on which they base their factual findings (APA, §18). And it requires agencies to limit administrative guidance to requests with which parties voluntarily comply (APA, §32).

As this chapter should make clear, none of this radically changes the law. Instead, it primarily codifies (or recodifies) existing law—which was in many ways already as "transparent" as administrative law anywhere ever gets. The principal effect of the statute apparently was simply to make explicit and systematic that which before was scattered over several statutes and dozens of cases.

The law already required agencies to act promptly. It already required them to accept applications as submitted (see section II). If a regulatory statute looked to the interests of specified third parties, it already forced the agency to hear their complaints. It already mandated a balancing test to determine when to grant a hearing. It already ordered agencies to disclose the documents on which they based their factual determinations. And it already limited administrative guidance to voluntary measures (see section II). The new statute largely makes sense. And little of it was new.

II. Administrative Guidance
A. Introduction

Despite this systematic body of formal administrative law, typically American observers stress how informally Japanese officials govern.[48] Typically, they capture that informality in the Japanese phrase "administrative guidance" (*gyōsei shidō*).[49] Typically, they argue that this administrative guidance precludes effective judicial review. When Michael Young published his exhaustive study of administrative guidance in 1984, he limited himself to claiming only that there were "considerable difficulties for regulated parties seeking to challenge administrative guidance."[50] Others have been less circumspect.

Karel van Wolferen exemplifies the less judicious. By his account, the reluctance of Japanese courts to review administrative action "has had the effect of almost totally insulating bureaucratic activity from judicial review."[51] According to Joseph Saunders, "[I]nformal decisions are not reviewable, because most of what MITI and other agencies do is informal and a matter of 'guidance,' not a legal 'disposition,' and therefore is not reviewable."[52] And according to Chalmers Johnson, "administrative guidance by Japan's powerful state bureaucracy can often result in rampant lawlessness in favor of those enterprises and interests that enjoy privileged access to the bureaucracy." Indeed, "regulation in Japan is not based on any set of laws that an outsider can learn and conform to."[53]

These claims of virtually complete nonreviewability are wrong—and wrong because they both miss the obvious and misstate the law. They miss the obvious because to obtain judicial review of administrative guidance, a firm need simply flout it. The agency will then either roll over and play dead, or it will sue. If it takes the first tack, the firm wins. If it takes the second, the firm obtains its review.

B. Municipal Administrative Guidance
1. *As Envisioned*

The above accounts misstate the law because they miss what courts actually do. To see the real law as applied by real courts, begin exactly where Young begins—with the suburban Tokyo government of Musashino. During the 1970s, local governments began to make a wide variety of demands of developers. In so doing, they justified their schemes by pointing to problems of urban congestion. Lacking explicit statutory authority for these demands, they turned to administrative guidance. The most prominent of all these local governments was Musashino.

Musashino adopted its scheme (it called it outline guidance (*shidō yōkō*)) in 1971. Under this scheme, it demanded that developers of large condominium and apartment complexes do two things: contribute land or money to the city and obtain the consent of the neighbors to their projects. As Young summarized the system:

> This Outline Guidance encouraged developers . . . to take two steps of particular significance. First, in projects over a certain size, the developer was encouraged to provide free land for the construction of one elementary school for every 1000 units or fraction thereof and one junior high school for every 2000 units. . . . Second, developers were to reach an agreement with the surrounding residents regarding the degree to which the planned building might permissibly interfere with the residents' sunlight and ventilation.[54]

If a developer balked, the city refused water and sewage services.

Sometimes developers and local governments reached an impasse. The developer would demand prompt action on its application for the requisite permits. The local government would demand that it give to the city and negotiate with neighbors first. Faced with the deadlock, wrote Young, the courts took an evenhanded approach:

> . . . Japanese courts refuse to determine which claims prevail. Instead, they implement legal standards that favor both plaintiff and defendant. They recognize that the developer has a right to some action on his application for a permit, which the agency may not deny based on considerations unrelated to the safety goals advanced by law. At the same time, courts allow the agencies to withhold action on the permit to advance unrelated goals of sunlight

and ventilation. Still, agencies can withhold the permit only so long as a reasonable expectation exists that the dispute can be resolved by mutual agreement of the parties. The developers cannot, however, take advantage of this limitation on administrative action by refusing from the outset to consider the possibility of a negotiated settlement.[55]

As Young explained it, the municipal governments insisted on the neighbors' consent because insisting on it improved policy. Since local residents knew best the problems that a project would cause, the scheme placed questions of development in the hands of those who understood them best. In Young's words, municipal bureaucrats "may very well [have had] skepticism about the ability of agencies [i.e., themselves] to identify and evaluate the competing interests that must inform governmental determinations."[56]

The courts controlled the developers, Young added, by presuming at the outset that a developer *might* comply. Because a developer might accede to the administrative guidance, the local government could justifiably delay action. If an obnoxious developer did insist from the start that he would not comply, the courts would hold that he abused his rights to develop the property.

2. Comparative Caveats

All this is a bit ingenuous. There is nothing peculiarly Japanese about a local government demanding that landowners contribute to it before developing their property. The Musashino mayor told developers they needed to donate land for a school if they wanted water and sewage. The city of Tigard, Oregon, told Florance Dolan she could double the size of her retail store only if she donated land for a bicycle path.[57] Such schemes, as Justice Scalia put it, are simply "out-and-out plan[s] of extortion."[58] Like adultery, like extortion—some schemes are cross-cultural universals.

There is also nothing evenhanded about telling landowners they need their neighbors' consent before they can develop their property. By doing so, the Musashino government simply gave the neighbors a veto over the project. That veto, in turn, let them extract for themselves much of the gain the developer would otherwise have earned. Rather than "favor both plaintiff and defendant," as Young put it, this straightforwardly transfers cash from developers to local residents. The incentives to the local government should be obvious enough. A government that robs Peter to pay Paul, as G. B. Shaw once noted, can always depend on the support of Paul.

3. As Enforced

a. Introduction. And all this is also a bit irrelevant. It is irrelevant, for shortly after Young published his article, the entire system blew up. Through litigation, those municipal schemes that coupled mandatory bargaining with sanctions like water service refusal, those schemes observers thought so sensible, so balanced, so quintessentially Japanese—the courts gutted them all. Among the institutions that killed the schemes that local governments had crafted so carefully, the Supreme Court played the key role.

b. The Kill. The end began in 1985. That year the Supreme Court announced that a developer could flout a city's administrative guidance and the city could not refuse services.[59] To be sure, it left open the possibility that a developer might act so obstreperously that the city could withhold those services after all. But over the next years, the courts made clear that this was a possibility they would ignore. Obstreperous developers came and went, but the courts refused to let municipalities stall applications. The few cases where the courts did let cities withhold services were ones where the developers violated not administrative guidance, but a statute.[60]

The 1985 case itself involved a Tokyo condominium project. The developer needed a construction permit. He applied, but when the neighbors squawked, the government told him to make peace. After several months of talks, he decided he had wasted enough time. He demanded his permit. Although Tokyo did eventually issue it, by this point it issued it late. Accordingly, he sued for his damages from the delay. Held the Supreme Court, he had "declared his intent not to comply or cooperate with administrative guidance." The city could show no acceptable reason to delay the permit, and that it "needed to delay the issuance to implement its administrative guidance was no defense."[61] For his losses from the time he declared he would not cooperate until the permit issued, Tokyo owed him damages.

c. Yamada. If it was the Supreme Court that killed municipal administrative guidance, more than anyone else it was Kiharu Yamada who gave it the chance. A two-bit businessman with an in-your-face style, Yamada owned and ran Yamaki Construction in Musashino. Shortly after Musashino adopted its outline guidance, he marched into Mayor Kihachirō Gotō's office. Alternatively he complained and he taunted. "You've made something that's not a statute or a regulation," he yelled. "And you're forcing it on us. That violates the separation of powers, it does. You've got a problem? Fight it out in court."[62]

Yamada spent the next several years thumbing his nose at Gotō. He built several condominiums in Musashino. Although he took some modest steps to make peace with neighbors along the way, he seldom conceded anything that mattered. He rarely gave at the office toward the city's educational fund. And he ordered his workers to continue apace, whatever city hall might say.

Blessed with an up-yours litigiousness that matched the best of the American Trial Lawyers Association, Yamada apparently sued whenever suing would pay. When Musashino refused him water and sewage services for flouting the guidance, he sued to enjoin it. He won.[63] When hostile neighbors stopped his crew from working, he sued them, too. Again, he won.[64]

As the melee escalated, the Ministry of Justice sided with Yamada. It sided with a vengeance, for in 1978 it filed *criminal* charges against Mayor Gotō. Gotō had a legal duty to provide water to Yamada's buildings, prosecutors argued. In refusing, he committed a crime. The Tokyo District Court convicted Gotō, the Tokyo High Court affirmed, and by 1989, so did the Supreme Court.[65] The high court explained the general theory:

> The premise behind administrative guidance is that the recipient acts "voluntarily." If there is a chance that a recipient might agree to the administrative guidance, the guidance may be acceptable. If a recipient firmly indicates that he will not comply and allows no possibility that he might change his mind, then . . . any refusal to act on the recipient's application is illegal.[66]

Here, wrote the Supreme Court:

> By the time the defendants denied the water application from condominium builder Yamaki Construction and its buyers, Yamaki had clearly indicated its intent not to comply with Musashino city's outline guidance relating to residential development. . . . Once this point had been reached, . . . it was illegal to refuse to act on application for a water contract.[67]

Make no mistake. For the city to use its power over water to enforce its administrative guidance was not just illegal. To the Supreme Court, it was a crime.

Ever happy to pile insult on injury, Yamada did not let matters lie. When Rome sacked Carthage, it did not just declare victory and go home. It pillaged, it burned, it raped, it killed, and it dedicated the ruins to the infernal gods. Like Rome, like Yamada. Under Japanese law, citizens may sue derivatively on behalf of their community against local officials who misuse government funds.[68] As a citizen of Musashino, Yamada now sued

Gotō. When prosecutors had brought criminal charges against Gotō, the city had paid his attorney's fees. Doing so was illegal, argued Yamada. Gotō should repay the fees to the city. Once again, Yamada won—all the way to the Supreme Court.[69]

With this string of legal victories in hand, Yamada then sued the Musashino government for his own damages. When the city enforced its (now definitively held to be illegal) administrative guidance against him, it caused him economic harm. For that harm, it owed him compensation. The Tokyo District Court agreed and awarded him the cash. This time Musashino did not bother to appeal.[70]

d. The Others. Other firms were already successfully suing by the early 1980s. One developer, for example, applied to the Tokyo government for construction permits on a couple of condominiums. The government cited community opposition and stalled, the developer refused to negotiate, and the court (in 1982) held for the developer.[71] Another developer applied to the Kyoto government for a permit on a hotel. The government told it to negotiate with the neighbors, the developer refused, and the court (in 1984) held for the developer.[72]

By the early 1990s, the feeding frenzy was in full force, and the suits acquired a numbing monotony. One firm applied to the Tochigi prefectural government for a permit on its industrial waste plant. Citing its administrative guidance, the government told it to obtain its neighbors' consent. The firm refused and sued to force the government to accept its application. Consistent with the Musashino cases, the firm (in 1991) won. In stalling, the prefectural government violated the law.[73] Another developer applied to the Yamanashi prefectural government for a construction permit on vacation condominiums. The prefecture withheld action pending compliance with administrative guidance, the developer refused, and the court (in 1992) held for the developer.[74] Yet another developer hoped to build a condominium complex in suburban Fukuoka. The city denied him water unless he reduced the building's size, the developer again refused, and the court (in 1992) found for the developer.[75] And still another developer applied for a golf course permit in Chiba prefecture, the government refused the application, the developer sued, and the court (in 1992) found for the developer.[76]

In one Tokyo suburb (not Musashino), the government had compensated a developer for the damages it had caused by refusing to provide water unless he first settled his quarrels with his neighbors. The citizens then brought a derivative suit, claiming the mayor should never have withheld the water. He was personally liable to the city for the damages the city had had to pay to the developer, they claimed. Yet again, the court sided with the plaintiffs.[77]

e. The End. Eyeing this judicial obliteration of municipal administrative guidance, those developers who had given to a city's educational fund now sensed their chance. Claiming—plausibly enough—that they had contributed under duress, they sued for refunds. Lower courts balked. Although a few ordered the money repaid,[78] several early courts did not.[79] The Supreme Court refused to blink. Faced with a developer who had "donated" some ¥15 million to Musashino, it ordered the city to return the money:

> Outline guidance is not based on law. It is, for the appellee [Musashino city], simply a set of internal standards that cover the administrative guidance to be given entrepreneurs. Through measures like the refusal to provide water service contracts, however, it effectively forces entrepreneurs to comply. . . . [Given that the amounts of the contributions are standardized as well,] it is hard to conclude that the entrepreneurs paid the amounts voluntarily. . . .
>
> Granted, the administrative guidance under the outline guidance was designed to protect the living environment of Musashino citizens from uncontrolled development. Granted, too, the administrative guidance enjoyed broad support from Musashino citizens. Nonetheless, the conduct above went beyond the limits of acceptable administrative guidance—the solicitation of voluntary contributions. Accordingly, it was an illegal exercise of public power.[80]

A rout by any other name would smell as sweet, one Montague once declared. Routs are rare in the law, but if ever there was one, this was it. It was not a rout American observers predicted. All this litigation, after all, concerned those "informal decisions" that most observers had categorically insisted were "not reviewable" in Japan. All this occurred in a country where—according to van Wolferen—"action taken by the private individual against the government [is] virtually unthinkable."[81] And all this involved actions that—to Saunders, as to most other U.S. observers— were simply "informal and a matter of 'guidance,' not a legal 'disposition,' and therefore not reviewable."

III. Political Economy
A. Why Judicial Review
1. *Introduction*

To see the logic behind this pattern of administrative law in Japan, ask first when rational politicians anywhere would want courts to police what bureaucrats do. Politicians are in office because voters elected them, but bureaucrats are in office because politicians (directly or indirectly) hired them and chose to keep them there. If they wanted, politicians could hire their bureaucrats on terms that let them fire or demote the bureaucrats whenever the bureaucrats misbehaved. The puzzle, such as it is, is why they sometimes think they can improve their electoral odds by letting constituents sue the bureaucracy—in effect, by delegating their control over one set of hired hands (bureaucrats) to another (judges).

To explore these issues in more detail, we consider first how politicians can monitor their bureaucrats (subsection A.2) and commit to political bargains (subsection A.3). Then we ask when politicians might choose to delegate monitoring responsibilities to judges (subsection A.4). Finally, we turn to the institutional structure in Japan (subsection B) and to the implications this analysis poses for understanding Japanese administrative law (subsection C).

2. *Monitoring Bureaucrats*

Rational self-interested politicians will try to monitor and control their bureaucrats. Voters elected them (in part) to provide various services, after all, and they hired the bureaucrats (in part) to deliver those services. All else equal, voters will prefer politicians who can induce bureaucrats to deliver those services efficiently over politicians who cannot. Politicians, in turn, might adopt variations on three general schemes to control their bureaucrats.

First, to induce their bureaucrats to perform, politicians could monitor them through their staff. They could assign members of their staff regularly to patrol the bureaucracies for misbehavior, for example. In effect, they could assign those staff to play "police patrol." [82]

Second, politicians could turn to the courts. On several dimensions, politicians will find courts a more efficient monitor than staff who play the cop-on-the-beat role. Generally local constituents are more likely to notice bureaucratic misbehavior than are randomly patrolling staff-members-turned-cops. Through judicial review, politicians can give those constituents an incentive to report that misbehavior to the courts. To ensure that bureaucrats serve their constituents efficiently, promptly, and predictably, in other words, politicians can give their constituents an incentive to sue if bureaucrats do anything else.

Last, politicians can use their staff as private administrative-law-judge equivalents. After all, for a majority politician the choice is not just between randomly patrolling staff and judicial review. Instead, a majority politician can invite dissatisfied constituents to plead their cases directly to his staff. Rather than patrol the bureaucracies themselves, his staff can referee the cases that come in the door. They can then choose the cases that most effectively promote his electoral odds. In those politically attractive cases, they can intervene in the bureaucracy on behalf of the constituents. The administrative law one observes in practice will then depend in part on the relative attractiveness of these three schemes.

3. Credible Commitments

Judicial review can also serve a somewhat different function. Politicians can use judicial review to give their supporters more credible promises. To win elections, they must raise money. To raise money, they must cut deals with interest groups. Absent more, once they take the money, they have an incentive to run—and cheat on any promises they made. Knowing that politicians have that incentive ex post, interest groups will pay less for promises ex ante. Paradoxically, perhaps, politicians can sometimes *increase* the amount they can raise by *decreasing* their ability later to renege.[83]

Strong and independent judicial review can sometimes help politicians limit that ability to renege ex post. Suppose interest group G pays a large sum to majority party M. In exchange, M promises to implement a program advantageous to G. If M passes the statute, but the bureaucracy vitiates the deal by administrative practice (maybe because M told it to do so when it obtained a large payoff from a rival interest group), absent judicial review G can do little except bribe M again. Judicial review mitigates that problem. By making it harder for M to manipulate regulatory practice to renege on its promises, it helps M make its initial promise credible. By helping it make those promises credible, it potentially increases the total cash M can raise.

In itself, however, this concern for credible commitments is not necessarily sufficient to induce self-interested politicians to offer judicial review—for majority politicians have other ways to make their promises credible. Most prominently, they can delegate control over their party to a strong, stable, and well-paid set of leaders. If those leaders earn large (legal or illegal) returns from office and if they have high odds of staying in office, then (given appropriate parameters) any promises they make may be "self-enforcing." So long as they maintain their reputation for keeping their word, they can expect high incomes in the future. Those large expected incomes, in turn, may now make it unprofitable for them to cheat on any promises.[84] The administrative law one observes will thus depend in part on the attractiveness of these various means politicians have to make credible their promises to their donors.

4. The Courts

Yet whether self-interested majority politicians will give courts the power to constrain bureaucrats depends on other things as well. It will depend not just on whether they have other means to control those bureaucrats and other ways to promise credibly. It will depend also on how well they control their judges. Judicial discretion is not free. The more discretion majority politicians give their judges, the higher the risk that a disloyal judge will use that discretion to reduce their electoral odds. In a world where majority politicians have other ways to commit credibly, two obvious propositions follow:

- All else equal, the more efficiently politicians can control bureaucrats through means other than the courts, the less incentive politicians will have to give their judges broad discretion to review administrative disputes.

- All else equal, the more efficiently politicians can control their judges, the more incentive politicians will have to give their judges broad discretion to review administrative disputes.

From this discussion, two polar cases are easy to predict. First, if bureaucrats are loyal, but judges are independent, rational majority politicians will be relatively more likely to give courts little discretion over administrative disputes. Being loyal, bureaucrats will seldom misbehave. Being powerless, judges will seldom reverse them.

Second, if bureaucrats are independent, but judges are loyal, rational politicians will be relatively more likely to delegate to courts enormous discretionary power. Being potentially disloyal, bureaucrats will periodically misbehave. Being loyal and powerful, judges will reverse them when, but only when, they do.

For our purposes, the intriguing question is what politicians will do when they control *both* the bureaucracy and the courts. On the one hand, even tightly constrained bureaucrats sometimes err. Accordingly, even if politicians control bureaucrats closely, if they also control the courts closely, they may choose to give those courts the power to review administrative decisions.

On the other hand, if politicians do control both the bureaucracies and the courts, one will rarely *observe* judges reversing bureaucrats. Although judges will have the power to do so, since loyal bureaucrats will seldom make mistakes, loyal judges will rarely reverse them. In a world where rational politicians closely control both the bureaucracies and the courts, in short, politicians may give judges the discretion to reverse agency action— but judges will almost never exercise it.

B. Japanese Institutional Structure

Given these implications, several aspects of the political and institutional structure of postwar Japan become crucial. First, Japan maintains a parliamentary government. Necessarily this increases the ability of majority politicians to control the bureaucracy. Under a presidential structure, the division of power between the president and the legislature weakens any politician's ability to discipline the bureaucracy. Under a parliamentary structure, majority leaders directly run the bureaucracy. Their greater potential control follows straightforwardly.[85]

Second, during the postwar decades, the Liberal Democratic Party (LDP) won elections—over and over. Obviously it faced odds of less than 1, as its defeat in 1993 showed. Yet it consistently faced high odds, and for nearly four decades, it consistently won.

Because of all this, as majority party from 1955 to 1993 the LDP tightly controlled the bureaucracy.[86] And because it did, college graduates sympathetic to the LDP disproportionately self-selected into bureaucratic careers. One ex-bureaucrat captured the party's control when he reminisced about what happened if legislators asked for information:

> A representative of the Liberal Democratic Party (LDP), for example, who might have sway over office personnel decisions, receives an extraordinary thorough reply, with page after page of extra information that no one is ever likely to read. At the opposite extreme is the Japan Communist Party, which gets no more information than the average person could get with a minimum of effort.[87]

215

Third, the LDP maintained a loyal judiciary (see section 1.IV). By appointing only loyalists to the Supreme Court and by giving those appointees power over the personnel office, the party could indirectly reward and punish judges by the ideological complexion of their performance. By so doing, it could keep its judges largely loyal.

Fourth, if a bureaucrat hurt the LDP's electoral odds, the party encouraged constituents to complain. They did, and the LDP legislators then weighed whether to tell their staff to intervene in the bureaucracy. To accomplish such chores smoothly, most LDP legislators kept multiple staff members at their local offices and regularly dispatched them to the agencies. In short, they made bureaucratic intervention (the use of staff as what we earlier called administrative-law-judge equivalents) a major part of the services they offered their constituents.[88]

Last, a small group of men controlled the LDP. To vie for that control, they first proved two things: that they could win elections consistently and that they could raise money extravagantly. Once they did so, other LDP legislators delegated power to them and implicitly agreed to let them pay themselves handsomely. As a result, throughout this period, the LDP remained under the control of a small group of men with long-term horizons who reasonably expected a large stream of future rents from the party's continued dominance.[89]

C. Implications
1. Introduction

Given this political and institutional structure, our earlier discussion implies that Japanese courts would seldom reverse agencies. Through their tight control over the bureaucracy, LDP leaders minimized agency decisions that threatened party electoral advantage. Through their local corps of staff members, LDP legislators directly reversed agency decisions that did. Through their stable, well-paid, and long-term leaders, LDP legislators made credible promises to their patrons. And through their loyal corps of judges, LDP leaders ensured that courts reversed those rare residual agency actions—but only those actions—disadvantageous to the party.

2. Procedural Limits

And yet the earlier analysis cuts more closely. In choosing when to encourage judges to reverse agencies, rational politicians should differentiate among disputes by political impact. Some disputes they should find more advantageous politically to delegate to judges than others. For example, they will probably delegate minor, everyday problems to the courts. After all, routine cases are ones courts generally handle well.

Many politicians will probably, however, want to keep for themselves those more visible cases with larger political import. Politicians know politics better than judges do. Accordingly, politicians (in regimes like Japan where the majority party can easily intervene in the bureaucracy) will want to remove politically sensitive cases from the courts and deal with them directly.

Japanese administrative law largely reflects this dynamic. The rules governing standing, for instance, do not restrict judicial review in day-to-day cases. Suppose P applies for a permit to open a Turkish bath, a nightclub, or a pawn shop; suppose an agency revokes P's driver's license or gun permit. P has standing to contest the decision in court.

Instead, the standing rules restrict judicial review in large-scale cases involving multiple claimants. Suppose neighbors want to complain about a bar or a zoo. Generally (not always, as the nuclear reactor cases show) the rules prevent them from taking the dispute to court.

This is exactly what rational leaders of a stable parliamentary majority would want. They cannot cheaply intervene in every barber's permit or driver's license revocation and would not earn large political returns from trying. These disputes involve only a few constituents each and seldom concern broader policies. For such small-scale disputes, standard administrative and judicial review works fine.

Majority leaders will, however, want to keep closer control over disputes that concern multiple constituents or broad policy issues. Questions of local environmental policy, of where to run a train line, or of how to plan a city potentially affect many voters. Rather than let constituencies contest these decisions in the courts, politicians (at least those in stable parliamentary governments) do better to decide the questions themselves. Toward that end, Japanese administrative law removes them from the courts. Japanese law delegates disputes with trivial electoral implications to the judges, in short, and shifts the others to the ruling party.

3. Local Governments

Given loyal judges and other means of precommitment, rational self-interested politicians also earn the largest returns from judicial review in those cases that involve officials over whom they have the least control.

The LDP tightly controlled central government bureaucracies like the Ministry of International Trade and Industry (MITI) and the Ministry of Finance. As the theory here predicts, the courts gave those ministries a wide berth.

The LDP did not, however, control local governments. By 1975, it won fewer than 15 percent of the mayoral races.[90] Potentially, therefore, it could earn high electoral returns by cutting local government discretion. As section II illustrates, Japanese courts did just that. If a municipal government tried to regulate informally, courts held its efforts void. If a mayor tried to implement that informal regulation forcefully, courts convicted him on criminal charges.

At this point, it should come as no surprise that Musashino's Mayor Gotō was a Socialist. Neither should it come as a surprise that his patron in the Tokyo government was maverick Governor Ryōkichi Minobe, elected in 1967 with joint Socialist and Communist support. MITI formulated its administrative guidance in the shadow of LDP strategy; Musashino formulated its in the shadow of the leftist opposition. The courts generally rubber-stamped the former; they savaged the latter

Importantly, the difference between MITI and Musashino administrative guidance was not a statutory one. When MITI regulated informally, if often did so with no statutory backing other than its enabling statute authorizing it to regulate in the public interest.[91] That much Musashino could readily match. The Regional Self-Government Act authorizes local governments, for example, to foster education, to promote the welfare of its residents, and to protect the local environment.[92] The difference between MITI and Musashino administrative guidance was not statutory. It was political.

Tentatively to be sure, verdict rates, too, suggest that courts give national governments a wider berth than local governments. Obviously one should be careful. If parties can freely settle their disputes, then the verdict rates among those disputes that do proceed to judgment will disclose very little about any general bias in the law.[93] In Japan, however, some authority (disputed, to be sure) suggests that government litigators may not negotiate settlements.[94] To the extent that the government can settle only sometimes, verdict rates may indeed provide information about the law. Subject to this caveat about selection bias, table 8.1 suggests a bias in favor of national governments: although private parties generally lose against all governments, they lose more overwhelmingly against the national than against the local governments.

Table 8.1 Verdict Rates by Government Sued (1986–1995)

	A. National Government		B. Local Government		Col. B/Col. A
1986	9.16	(251)	6.25	(64)	.68
1987	10.43	(211)	14.00	(50)	1.34
1988	7.20	(250)	19.23	(52)	2.67
1989	9.16	(273)	12.20	(82)	1.33
1990	7.93	(353)	6.10	(82)	.77
1991	9.46	(296)	9.46	(74)	1.00
1992	11.01	(318)	9.68	(93)	.88
1993	7.41	(432)	7.56	(119)	1.02
1994	6.30	(492)	13.08	(130)	2.08
1995	10.30	(369)	14.73	(129)	1.43
Total	8.63 (3,245)		11.09 (875)		1.29

Source: Saikō saibansho jimu sōkyoku, ed., *Shihō tōkei nempō: minji gyōsei hen* [Court Statistics Annual: Civil and Administrative] (Tokyo: Hōsō kai, various years), table 80.

Notes: The percentage of petitioner wins in suits resulting in an opinion (*hanketsu*), followed by the total number of suits in parentheses.

Suits against the local government are those that are listed as *chihō jichi* (regional self-government suits) in the national data; suits against the national government are all other nontax suits.

Conclusions

Taira won. According to the high court, in disingenuously designating the empty lot a playground, the local government violated both his constitutional right to pursue the business of his choice (Const. art. 22) and the constitutional guarantee against uncompensated takings (art. 29). The Supreme Court affirmed, though on the narrower ground that the officials had abused their administrative authority.[95]

Japanese administrative law lets people like Taira protect their property rights and investments in court. When Taira and Iizuka invested in their entertainment facilities, they had done so carefully. They bought a lot where the law allowed such facilities and scrupulously followed the required procedures. When their neighbors manipulated the regulatory apparatus to close them down, they turned to the courts for help. The courts gave them the help they needed. Subject to a straightforward political dynamic, Japanese administrative law protects the property rights people acquire—it protects them not just against rival private claimants, but also against the government itself.

9 INCOME TAX

Quite what his occupation had been the court never said, but maybe the point was moot. By the time it wrote its opinion, Masahisa Miura was doing time in Fuchū prison. By all appearances, he seems to have been a small-scale financier. He lent money, then sued or settled with customers who defaulted. In 1983, however, he tried to go big-time. For an acquaintance, he masterminded an elaborate tax evasion scheme. He used fake debts, fake transfers, fake settlements. For his troubles, he collected ¥150 million.

The deal was Miura's undoing, for the tax office noticed. In the ensuing litigation, his deal raised several tax questions. Most obviously, was his compensation for criminal services taxable? To carry out the scheme, he used his bastard son's help. If the compensation was taxable, could he deduct the ¥300,000 he paid his son? He also paid his longtime lover ¥12.5 million in hush money. Could he deduct that, too?[1]

In this chapter we explore the gist of this tax law—as well as a number of the specifics raised by Miura's plight. We begin in section I by outlining the law's structure (subsection A). We then explain the treatment of gross income (subsection B), business deductions (subsection C), personal deductions (subsection D), and property transactions (subsection E). We include a short discussion of the tax treatment of corporate reorganizations (section II). And we speculate on the effect that the structure of the tax law (rather than just its stability) has had on economic activity (section III).

I. The Law
A. Introduction
1. Global and Schedular Systems

In form, the United States and Japan use radically different income tax systems.[2] The United States maintains a global system, while the Japanese is schedular. More specifically, U.S. law aggregates all income and expenses and then taxes the net. Japanese law distinguishes among a variety of categories of income and taxes each differently.

The logic behind a global system is simple. It is also at least facially compelling: money is money, no matter how earned or how spent. As a result, a sensible tax system would seemingly treat all forms of income and expenses alike. The puzzle is what to make of the schedular systems.

Despite their superficial oddity, schedular systems are less bizarre than they seem. Some observers justify them—dubiously—on the ground that a taxpayer's ability to pay varies with the type of income he earns. Other observers note that a government that taxes some income (e.g., capital gains) at special rates will necessarily need some schedular rules.

In fact, a more general argument goes to enforcement costs. Although the ability to pay may not vary much with the type of income, the ability to cheat does. People in some lines of work and with some kinds of investments can more easily chisel income, pad expenses, and subtly avoid tax than others. By letting people deduct expenses only from associated income items, the schedular system cabins the scope of tax avoidance. By letting people deduct expenses incurred in some activities against income earned in all others, the global system magnifies it.

The point is not lost on U.S. tax administrators. Although Internal Revenue Code (IRC) §61 defines income globally—"all income from whatever source derived"—the code contains a wide variety of schedular facets. Perhaps best known to law students, it lets people deduct gambling losses only from gambling gains (IRC, §165(d)). It does not limit the deduction because gamblers differ from other people in their ability to pay taxes. Whatever other reasons legislators may have had besides, it limits it because gambling so readily lends itself to fraud.

If the U.S. code is a formally global regime with schedular aspects, the Japanese code is a formally schedular regime with an essentially global character. Under the Japanese code, taxpayers separately calculate ten categories of net income: business, compensation, capital gains, interest, dividend, real estate, retirement, timber, occasional, and miscellaneous income. They then total the categories (other than timber and retirement income, on which they pay a separate tax) and calculate their aggregate tax liability.

In two ways, this schedular regime disguises a functionally global scheme. First, it taxes "miscellaneous income." Obvious as the point may be, the regime taxes not just specified types of income, but also most accessions to wealth. Second, it often (not always) lets taxpayers net income and deductions across schedular lines. Should they have losses in business, capital gains, real estate, or timber income, for example, they can generally offset them against other income. The truly schedular characteristics to the system—the limits on cross-category netting—are in fact the exceptions rather than the rule.

2. Rates and Return

Individuals pay tax on their total income at progressive rates. Those rates are high, but hardly confiscatory (Income Tax Act (ITA), §89).[4]

Taxable Income	Marginal Rate (%)
0 to ¥3.3 million	10
¥3.3 to ¥9 million	20
¥9 to ¥18 million	30
¥18 to ¥30 million	40
Over ¥30 million	50

On an aggregate per capita basis, Japanese pay more in tax than do their peers in the United States, but less than do those in other economically advanced capitalist countries. Consider total tax revenues as a fraction of national income for 1989:[5]

	Tax/ National Income	(Tax + Social Security)/ National Income
United States	26.1	36.4
Japan	27.8	38.7
United Kingdom	40.3	50.7
Germany	30.8	52.8
France	33.7	61.8
Sweden	55.8	75.8

Few Japanese file returns. Instead, the law demands that payors withhold taxes on a wide variety of payments, and requires only the very highest paid taxpayers to file returns reporting their income; for the rest, the law lets the withholding satisfy their tax-related obligations. As a result, as of the mid-1990s only about 17 million individuals filed returns.[6] About half of them did so because the law required it, and about half did so to claim deductions they could not otherwise obtain.

B. Gross Income
1. Generally

Japanese courts approach the notion of income much the way U.S. courts do: they look to the net value of the rights and assets individuals receive and to the revenues that businesses earn less expenses. Take a couple of common examples from law school tax classes. A debtor who finds his debt canceled will have taxable income in Japan.[7] So, too, will a criminal who earns money illegally. Two-bit financier Miura (discussed at the outset), for instance, did earn taxable income when paid for orchestrating his fraud.[8]

Japanese tax officers approach the job of finding income with a resourcefulness that would make any Assistant U.S. Attorney proud. Take pachinko parlors. The pinball-like game is wildly and perennially popular. By the mid-1990s, the business was a ¥30 trillion industry, with one machine for every twenty-six Japanese, and in 1995 alone, some thirty children died (most commonly of dehydration while locked in a car) as their parents sat mesmerized by the machines. Icons of excruciatingly bad taste, the parlors every year vie with love hotels and Turkish baths for—would that there were such a prize—the cross-cultural "John Waters Pink Flamingos" award.[9]

Although its charms largely escape foreign observers, pachinko steadfastly remains the single constant in the slippery world of postwar Japan. For decades now, Japanese have traded money for small chrome-plated balls, fed them (a process today automated) through a vertical pinball machine, and watched hypnotized as the balls cascade down the board, the din crowding out everything except the store's intercom playing 1940s-vintage war songs, rock-and-roll, or the seasonal "Rudolph the Red-Nosed Reindeer." Occasionally a ball lands in a slot that triggers an avalanche of additional balls, and the game continues. When an exhausted customer decides to leave, he exchanges his balls for a prize at the door. He then takes it to another store nearby and trades it for cash.

Koreans disproportionately dominate this archetypal Japanese industry. Descended from those who came to Japan before the war to work in Japanese factories, many now keep their citizenship out of ethnic pride. Given the partitioning of the peninsula in 1950s, some are loyal to South Korea, others to North Korea. The discrimination some of them face within Japan has been an intractable domestic political issue. The foreign exchange some of them clandestinely repatriate to North Korea has been an intractable international one.

And the fraud some of the pachinko parlors commit to cheat on their taxes has been an intractable financial issue. According to the National Tax Office, among corporate taxpayers only bars and nightclubs were more likely to cheat than the pachinko parlors. Among unincorporated firms, the pachinko owners placed an unambiguous first. In mean unreported income, the parlors beat out even loan sharks, funeral parlors, and the obstetricians so famous in Japan for doing abortions on a no-receipts cash basis.[10]

Kim was a Korean who ran five pachinko parlors in Kyoto in the 1960s. From 1965 to 1967, he reported taxable income of ¥16.7 million. The tax office claimed ¥120.9 million. He insisted that it had targeted him out of anti-Korean prejudice, but the court said no. Below we shall explore some of the other claims he made. For now, note that he also quarreled with the way the tax office calculated his income.

Kim urged the court to substantiate his claimed income from his bank records and expenses. The tax officers apparently believed that the former were chiseled and the latter padded. Accordingly, they looked until they found partial records of the amount of balls that customers had turned in for prizes. That amount, of course, is something Kim had an incentive not to underreport, since it helped prove his expenses. They also found partial records of the ratio of the balls awarded by the machines to the balls fed into the machines. By dividing the balls exchanged for prizes by that payout ratio, they inferred the revenues collected. By extrapolating that amount onto months for which they had no data at all, they estimated Kim's aggregate income. To the court, all that was fine.[11]

Or take Shigeo Segawa. He ran an empire of brothels euphemistically described (as with the Tairas of chapter 8) as "special public bathing facilities." He ran them indirectly. Having already been convicted of violating the prostitution ban, he was taking fewer chances. Yet through a series of several corporations, he effectively still controlled a chain of these "bathhouses."

In 1986, the Tokyo District Court convicted Segawa of criminal tax evasion. The tax office had not believed his claimed income. Instead, to determine his income, it had first noted that most of the bathhouses had records of the water they used. It then found contemporaneous (and what it thought reliable) records of revenues at one of the bathhouses for part of the period. Using those records, it constructed a revenue per unit of water ratio for the bathhouses and used water records to project real revenues. Where it lacked even water records, it turned to laundry records to find the numbers of towels used and infer revenues from there. All this, too, said the court, was fine.[12]

2. Fringe Benefits

Under Japanese tax law, in principle an employee recognizes as income the fair market value of all rights and assets he receives from his employer (ITA, §36(b)). Should he receive an interest-free loan, for example, he recognizes income on the forgone interest. Should he receive free tuition toward his education, he recognizes income on the tuition.[13]

In fact, the government avoids so theoretically pure an approach. Instead, by administrative practice it treats many low-interest loans to employees as tax-free (ITA Circular, §36-28), and one court even held subsidized vacations to Hong Kong nontaxable.[14] The tax office maintains a generous list of tax-free fringe benefits, and Japanese firms make good use of them: sales of goods or services at submarket prices to employees (ITA Circular, §§36-23, 36-29), meals for working overtime (§36-24), rental housing at submarket prices (§36-40), utilities at subsidized housing units (§36-26), insurance policies (§36-31), and even golf and athletic club memberships (§36-34).

3. Timing

Subject to several exceptions, Japanese law puts businesses and individuals on accrual basis accounting.[15] If parties to a sale negotiate installment payments, for example (again subject to exceptions), the seller will have taxable income on the entire sale at the time title passes. This is so even though, under the terms of the contract, he does not yet have a right to the unpaid installments.[16]

But now consider usurers. If they charge illegally high interest, they do not have a legal right to collect it. Do their illegal receivables constitute taxable income? Jun'ichi Itabashi ran a modest pawn shop and money-lending business in a small city on the southern island of Kyūshū. He charged more than the legal limit on his loans and upon audit faced just that question. To answer it, the Supreme Court sort of (but only sort of) put him on a cash basis. If his customers paid the interest, he had income. If they had not yet paid, then since they also had no legal duty to pay the usurious portion of the interest, he did not yet have taxable income on the excess interest.[17]

4. Imputed Income

Few, if any, tax regimes try to tax imputed income systematically. Japan is no exception. Intriguingly, however, it does tax some of the imputed income a taxpayer earns from the personal use of capital assets (including housing) (ITA, §38(b)(2)).[18]

Most tax systems do not tax the returns someone earns from his investments, provided he directly consumes those returns himself. Take a brutally simple example. Suppose a taxpayer puts $100,000 in a mutual fund and every year uses the return to rent an apartment. Because he triggers tax liability by withdrawing his earnings from the fund, he will buy his housing services with after-tax dollars. Suppose instead he buys a condominium with the $100,000. He will earn a return from that investment in the form of housing services, but will pay no tax on that return. Effectively he will buy his housing services with pretax dollars.

One way to mitigate this problem is simple: reduce an owner's basis in the capital asset by the value of the services consumed, but do not allow him to deduct that amount from current income. When he sells the asset, he will then recognize taxable income equal to the imputed income (housing services, in our example) he consumed.

As a form of rough justice, that is just what the Japanese tax law does. Suppose a taxpayer buys a capital asset with a ten-year useful life for ¥1.5 million. He uses the asset in his household. Under Japanese tax law, he may not depreciate the asset. Notwithstanding, he will be taxed upon resale *as though* he had depreciated it. More specifically, he will reduce his basis as though he had taken depreciation deductions calculated using a fifteen-year useful life (ITA Enforcement Order, §85).[19] Thus, if he sells it in three years for ¥1.6 million, he will have taxable capital gain of ¥1.6 million − (¥1.5 million − ¥100,000 × 3) = ¥400,000. The logic to this scheme (a rough rule of thumb, to be sure) is that an owner realizes imputed income roughly equal to the implicit depreciation allowance. By subtracting that amount from basis, he pays tax on the imputed income upon resale.

5. Income Shifting

Japanese tax law does not allow joint returns. This creates obvious income-shifting problems as high-bracket taxpayers (usually husbands) try to shift their income to their low-bracket spouses (usually wives). Formally, moreover, Japanese courts have no assignment-of-income doctrine with which to shift the income back.

In fact, Japanese courts do try to police income shifting and informally often accomplish much the same result that a U.S. court would accomplish through the assignment-of-income doctrine. Specifically the law includes provisions that (under some conditions) disallow deductions for wages paid to family members.[20] More generally, the courts use substance-over-form principles to reallocate income from the low-bracket taxpayers who formally earned it to the higher-bracket spouses who earned it in fact.

Tarō Kōno was a South Korean entrepreneur who ran three mahjongg parlors in the Tokyo area. Much of the profits from the parlors went directly into his wife's and his daughter's bank accounts. A formalistically inclined court might have found the deposits evidence of his wife's and daughter's respective ownership interests and held them liable for the tax on their shares of the earnings. Not so the Tokyo High Court. Kōno had earned the money, it reasoned, so Kōno owed the tax.[21]

Some courts do more than merely combat strategic income splitting. Granted, most usually do appear to follow economic substance. Sometimes, though, they seem adamantly to insist on what is effectively a joint-return regime. They do so by reallocating all income to a single member of a household, even when economic substance clearly dictates otherwise.

For example, Tei Yoshinaga owned and ran the bar Tei. She lived with one Koga. Koga was married with children elsewhere, but he had apparently abandoned them for her. In 1959, the two decided to open a new bar. To pay for it, Yoshinaga sold her bar Tei and, with the proceeds plus her savings, contributed ¥4.5 million. Koga borrowed ¥5 million from a bank and contributed that.

Yoshinaga and Koga did well with their new bar. They expanded business steadily and within a few years ran four Anglophilic bars—the names changed, but at one time or another they included The Edinburgh, The England, The Windsor, and even The Brontë. In applying for the necessary local permits, they named a different manager for each: Koga for one, Yoshinaga for another, Yoshinaga's daughter for a third, and another woman for the last. Although they reported all income, they filed separate returns for each bar in the name of each registered manager.

Notwithstanding that half the initial capital had come from Yoshinaga, that she worked full-time at one of the bars, that she received no formal wages for doing so, and that she and Koga owned the real estate for the first bar jointly—notwithstanding all this, the court reallocated all profits to Koga. Indeed, not only did it reallocate the profits, but also for splitting the income, it convicted him of criminal tax evasion and sentenced him to an eight-month (suspended) prison term and a ¥2 million fine.[22]

6. Gifts

Much as in the United States, gifts among individuals in Japan are not subject to the income tax (ITA, §9(a)(15)), but are potentially subject instead to a gift tax (part of the Inheritance Tax Act).[23] The tax applies to the total gifts a taxpayer receives, less a basic deduction of ¥600,000 (Inheritance Tax Act, §21-5). By contrast, gifts from corporations (and partnerships) are subject to the income tax rather than the gift tax. The theory presumably is that corporate gifts are more likely to be disguised payments for services than altruistic transfers.[24] As one would expect, gifts of living and educational expenses from a person responsible for the taxpayer's livelihood (basically gifts from parents to their minor children) are subject neither to the income tax nor to the gift tax.

C. Business Deductions
1. Necessary Expenses

In calculating their taxable income, taxpayers may generally deduct their necessary expenses (ITA, §37). Unlike formal U.S. law (IRC, §162), Japanese law imposes no "ordinary" requirement. As Hiroshi Kaneko put it in the leading treatise, deductible business expenses are those "which have a direct relation to the business activity and which are necessary for engaging in that business."[25]

Take Kim, the man who controlled the Kyoto pachinko chain. He claimed a variety of deductions, among them ¥300,000 paid to the All-Japanese-Korean League. Because North Korea had no formal ties with Japan, explained Kim (why he thought this might help his case is anyone's guess), the league functioned as the front organization for North Korea. Kim argued that he should be able to deduct his payment to the league on the ground that the payment helped maintain his status in the Korean community. The court denied the deduction. The payment had no direct relation to Kim's business. Social status was apparently too tenuous a relation, and Kim could not deduct the payment.[26]

Or take, again, bathhouse king Segawa. Among the expenses he deducted was monthly compensation of ¥550,000 to Minako Aoyama. Of this amount, the company denominated ¥250,000 a base salary and ¥300,000 a monthly bonus. Aoyama had worked at the Turkish New Princess, but was also Segawa's lover. Given that relationship, the court decided that the ¥300,000 was a "lover's fee." As such, it was not a necessary expense, and Segawa could deduct only the basic ¥250,000.[27]

2. Employee Business Expenses

Before 1987, employees could deduct only a standard deduction from compensation income. This generated an odd and long-running controversy. Some taxpayers argued that by denying workers a deduction for necessary expenses, the rule violated the equal protection clause of the constitution (art. 14(a)). It placed employees, they explained, in a disadvantageous position relative to the self-employed.

The Supreme Court eventually upheld the rule in 1985,[28] but by 1987, the government had changed it anyway. Since then, employees have been able to deduct specified expenses from compensation income, provided the total of those expenses exceeds the standard deduction (ITA, §57-2). The change is more form than substance, if only because the standard deduction is so generous: for a moderately middle-class taxpayer earning ¥5 million, it is ¥1.54 million (ITA, §28(c)). The expenses he may deduct, moreover, are only ordinary and necessary commuting expenses, moving and educational expenses incurred at the instruction of the employer, professional certification expenses, and travel from his worksite to his family's home where his worksite is far from that home. Notwithstanding the long court battle over the issue, fewer than 100 taxpayers a year itemize these expenses.

3. Capital Recovery

Return once more to Kim and his chain of Kyoto pachinko parlors. During the years at stake, he paid large sums to remodel the parlors. He wanted to deduct the expenses immediately; the tax office wanted him to capitalize the amounts. Perhaps to combat customer boredom, perhaps for a variety of other reasons, pachinko owners once or twice a year install new machines and rotate existing machines among their various stores. The "remodelling" costs Kim incurred were costs associated with moving and installing new machines and redecorating the place in the process. Because Kim incurred the expenses regularly and the improvements often lasted only months, the court let him expense the costs.[29]

When they do depreciate an asset, taxpayers may use either the straight-line or the declining balance method (ITA Enforcement Order, §120). For useful lives, they turn to a table specified by cabinet order.[30] The lives range from sixty-five years for concrete office buildings; to forty-five years for brick movie theaters; to thirty-five years for concrete public baths; to thirty-four years for brick public baths; to twenty-six years for wooden office buildings; to seventeen years for elevators and fifteen years for escalators; to fifteen years for metal desks, chairs, and cabinets; to thirteen years for large steel tankers; to six years for computers; to four to five years for trucks and taxis; to five years for typewriters and *non-*electronic calculators.

The detail is numbing (the table continues for thirty pages), but it does suggest that the government has not systematically tried to use artificially short lives to encourage investment. What attempts it has made to use accelerated depreciation rules have been modest and closely targeted: for example, to prevent environmental pollution, to promote recycling, to spur investments in underdeveloped parts of the country, and to promote the hiring of the handicapped.[31]

4. Fines and Judgments

Taxpayers may not deduct the fines they pay in Japan. Neither may they deduct judgments for intentional or grossly negligent torts (ITA, §45(a)(6)–(7); ITA Enforcement Order, §98). Note that those who receive judgments for personal injury or accidents generally receive them tax-free (ITA, §9(a)(16)).

Curiously, notwithstanding this law, by bureaucratic practice the National Tax Office had been letting firms deduct fines if the government to which they paid them was foreign. Primarily the cases involved Japanese caught fishing off the contested northern islands of Sakhalin and forced to pay fines to the Soviet and then Russian governments. The amounts were modest, and to many voters, the fishermen seemed recklessly heroic. Letting them deduct the fines made good domestic politics.

Enter Daiwa Bank. Fined by the U.S. government in the mid-1990s for its fraud, it, too, deducted the fines on its Japanese return. In doing so, however, it now slashed its Japanese tax liability by ¥1.34 billion. The government promptly announced plans to end the bureaucratic generosity by amending the statute. Henceforth, all fines would be nondeductible, whether domestic or foreign.[32]

5. Illegal Expenses

In theory, taxpayers may deduct necessary expenses, even if illegal. If a seller pays fees to a real estate broker beyond the legal limit, for example, he may still deduct the excess.[33] When Miura (the financier described at the start of this chapter) paid ¥300,000 to his illegitimate son for helping to carry out his tax scam, he could deduct that amount, too.[34]

And yet one senses in some opinions a stinginess that suggests something nontheortical—a "does it stink" test, an understandable reluctance to let disreputable taxpayers deduct the unsavory costs they incur in unpleasant transactions. Miura claimed that he paid his son more, for example. The court simply replied that he had not proven it. He also claimed that he paid his longtime lover ¥12.5 million in hush money. Again, the court claimed insufficient evidence.

This "does it stink" test appears even in regard to less egregious expenses. Japanese brothels, for example, regularly pay protection money to the mob. When they try to deduct the amounts, the courts refuse to let them. It is not that the amounts are not necessary. Judges may sometimes be naive, but to tell a brothel owner he need not pay the goons who appear at his door would give naiveté a bad name. Instead—we read between the lines here—judges dislike the brothel owners, know they flout the prostitution ban, and know they cheat on their taxes. They hate the mob, too, and after all, it is not as though the goons are likely to report the protection money as taxable income. When one entrepreneur ran a couple of "special public bathing facilities" in the early 1980s, he paid ¥5 to ¥7 million a month in protection fees. The court refused to let him deduct the money. "If we allow the deduction," it explained, "the country would effectively be using firms to subsidize the mob." [35]

D. Personal Deductions
1. Interest

Taxpayers in Japan must treat interest expenses according to the rules governing business expenses generally: deductible if, but only if, necessary and directly related to their business. As a result, business interest is deductible. Personal interest, like home mortgage interest, is not.

2. Medical Expenses

Subject to several qualifications, people may deduct unreimbursed medical expenses they or their dependents incur. Because all Japanese are covered by national health insurance, the issue is minor.[36]

3. Charitable Contributions

People may deduct charitable contributions only within various financial limits and only if made to a limited number of government-specified organizations (ITA, §78). Pachinko parlor king Kim, for example, had donated money to the local North-Korean-affiliated schools. The schools did not meet the statutory requirements for approved educational institutions (ITA, §78)—hardly surprising given their decades-long obsession with the Kim Il Sung personality cult. In the 1983 music text for first-graders, for example, fourteen of the twenty-four songs concerned Kim Il Sung. A typical one intoned:

Thank you, Marshal Kim Il Sung,
Who holds all of us in his warm bosom,
Because we are the buds of beautiful flowers.

> Thank you, Marshal Kim Il Sung,
> Who gives all good things first to us,
> Such as the best shoes, decorated with flowers.[37]

For Pachinko king Kim, the lack of official approval was fatal. Given the schools' unrecognized status, he could not deduct his contributions.[38]

Should a taxpayer donate appreciated assets to an approved organization, he does not pay a capital gains tax. He may, however, deduct only his basis in the property (Special Tax Measures Act (STMA), §40).[39]

E. Property Transactions
1. The Basic Rules

Suppose someone sells or exchanges a capital asset. If he has held it for five years or less, he must add the entire gain he realizes upon its sale or exchange to his other income. If he has held the asset for over five years, he includes only half of that gain (ITA, §§22(b)(ii), 33(c)). If he regularly deals in the asset sold (e.g., a real estate broker who sells a building), then he has ordinary business income rather than capital gains income.

To calculate the tax, a taxpayer first divides the assets he transferred into long- and short-term capital assets. He then adds all assets received in each category and subtracts his aggregate adjusted basis from that sum. In effect, therefore, he first deducts his long-term losses from his long-term gains and his short-term losses from his short-term gains (ITA, §33(c)). Should he have a net loss in one category, he may deduct that loss from the income in the other. Should he have an overall net capital loss, he may generally deduct that amount in full from his other income.

These rules may be honored as much in the breach, however, for exceptions and complications abound. Consider the two most important sets of exceptions: those governing securities and those governing real estate.

2. Securities Gains

Before 1989, gains from the sale or exchange of securities were (subject to many further exceptions) exempt from tax. Since then, they have been taxable—but at a flat tax of 20 percent (STMA, §37-10). To figure this tax, an investor calculates his securities gains separately from his other income items. He then pays a 20 percent tax on this amount regardless of whether he is an amateur or a professional.

Investors who entrust their portfolio to a bank or securities firm have a further curious option (STMA, §37-11). Rather than pay the 20 percent capital gains tax directly, they may opt to have it withheld at the time of the transfer and—crucially—to have their gain *deemed* to have been 5 percent of their sales price. Effectively they can choose between a 20 percent tax on their net profits and a 1 percent (20 percent of 5 percent) tax on their gross revenues. Should they pay the 1 percent transfer tax, they have no further tax liability on that transaction.

3. Real Estate

Real estate gains and losses are subject to an enormous array of exceptions and special rules. Most prominently, a taxpayer must first separately total his gains from the sale or exchange of real estate. He must then calculate his tax on his gains without aggregating them with his other income (STMA, §§31–32).

By calculating real estate gains separately, taxpayers avoid the effect of the progressive rate schedule on those gains. Yet the result is not necessarily advantageous. Real estate gains are subject to elaborate rules that sometimes create effective rates significantly higher than those imposed on other income. These rates vary not just by how long a taxpayer held the property, but by the type of property he held and the reasons he held it to boot. The rates depend, for example, on whether he sold land for housing construction, on whether the land lay within specified urban areas, on whether he bought and sold the land as part of a business, on whether he lost the land by eminent domain, and on whether his family occupied the property.[40]

Additionally recall that Japanese landlord-tenant law heavily regulates the rental market (see section 2.II). These rules can cause parties to undertake otherwise bizarre transactions, and the tax code includes special rules to deal with those as well. For instance, where a tenant pays an extremely large up-front fee to a landlord, the tax law sometimes treats it as a partial sale or exchange.[41]

———

As a general review, consider a case that raises not just tax issues, but several contract and tort questions as well. The case involved an organization:

> A philosophy of peace based on the thought of the late Tenzō Nishimura, the philosophy of the "One Family Under the Heavens" [association] affirms the unitary life of the cosmos. . . . The association promotes the spirit of mutual aid and aims for the cultivation of social beings who share a generous spirit of humanity. . . .

And on it went, a charter for the "One Family Under the Heavens" association, founded by one Ken'ichi Uchimura.

233

Born in 1926, Uchimura left school in 1943 to join the navy. He survived his assignment to the *kamikaze* forces, but only to become a door-to-door insurance salesman. Apparently bored and certainly poor, he wanted something extra. To earn that something extra, his wife ran a brothel for several years, but the 1957 prostitution ban then put them out of business. They tried running a hotel and a restaurant, but with lackluster results.

While hospitalized for diabetes in the summer of 1966, Uchimura finally hit on the formula that would save him from Willie-Loman-dom: he would form a series of mutual aid associations to promote Nishimura's philosophy. As he eventually implemented them, in some associations, the members would obtain the right to use various resorts for rest and recuperation. In others, they would acquire automobile insurance policies. In all, they would send money to their immediate recruiter and a more senior member of the association and also pay a substantial enrollment fee to Uchimura.

As pyramid schemes, the associations were wildly successful. Uchimura offered a variety of arrangements, but typically a new member paid ¥40,000 to ¥600,000 and promised to recruit two new members. Of the initial fee, he paid 15 to 25 percent to Uchimura's headquarters and the rest to specified senior members in the chain. Uchimura formed his first association in 1967. By 1980, he had enlisted 1.1 million members and at least one cat, and generated nearly ¥190 billion.

Uchimura tried hard both to seem respectable and to avoid taxes. Toward those ends, he sometimes operated through a church he had formed. Once he even bought a defunct kindergarten and tried to operate through that. He regularly shuttled money around his various organizations.

With his money, Uchimura bought buildings and resorts. He bought luxury cars. He bought at least one helicopter. He bought several planes. He made a movie—*Samurai of the Open Sky*. And through it all, he took care of himself and his family. He put most of the assets in his own name and paid himself and his family handsome salaries besides.

Necessarily, of course, by the late 1970s Uchimura's schemes were reaching the saturation point in many neighborhoods. Most members were receiving little or no return. Indeed, by one court's estimate, somewhere between three-fourths and seven-eighths of the members never recovered their initial investments. One distraught member in Gifu carved his guts out in a classic Japanese suicide. Several others around the country tried to kill themselves as well. To the scheme, courts traced divorces, nervous breakdowns, and family schisms.

The beginning of the end came in 1977. That March the Nagano District Court declared that over 500 dissatisfied members who had sued Uchimura could recover their money.[42] By 1978, things turned worse yet. During the early years, Uchimura had filed no tax returns and for 1970 had claimed taxable income of only ¥360,000. For that tax evasion (the second largest in Japanese history), in 1978 the Kumamoto District Court sentenced him to three years in prison (suspended) and a ¥700 million fine.[43] That year the Diet also banned pyramid schemes outright,[44] but for Uchimura, it hardly mattered. As soon as the March 1977 Nagano verdict hit the press, the game was over:

Revenues Paid to Uchimura's Headquarters (¥)	
Apr. 72–Mar. 73	319 million
Apr. 73–Mar. 74	840 million
Apr. 74–Mar. 75	4,809 million
Apr. 75–Mar. 76	13,100 million
Apr. 76–Mar. 77	14,640 million
Apr. 77–Mar. 78	3,532 million

Even stable revenues will kill a pyramid scheme, and the 1977–1978 revenues were anything but stable. By February 1980, the Kumamoto District Court declared Uchimura bankrupt.

The rise and fall of Ken'ichi Uchimura generated an enormous amount of litigation.[45] Members who sued for their money could argue either unjust enrichment or tort. To show unjust enrichment, they claimed that Uchimura's scheme violated the "public order and good morals" standard of section 90 of the Civil Code (see subsection 3.I.D.4). If so, then the contracts under the scheme were void, and members could sue for a refund.

The courts generally bought the unjust enrichment theory, but with two qualifications. First, because the theory justified only refunds, members could not demand from Uchimura the amounts they had paid other members of the chain. Second, because all contracts under the scheme were void, each member was, in turn, liable to junior members for any amounts he had received from them. As a corollary, however, they could demand from Uchimura and their senior members the full amounts they had paid them, without an offset either for any amounts they, in turn, received from more junior members or for their own idiocy in joining the scheme.[46]

The courts also accepted the tort theory (see section 4.I), but subject to different qualifications. First, because a victim can recover any damages proximately caused by a tort, members could recover from Uchimura not just the initiation fee they paid him, but all amounts they paid to other senior members as well. Second, because courts allow only damages actually incurred, a member could collect only his payment net of any amounts he received from junior members. Third, because Japanese tort law is a comparative negligence regime, a member could receive only damages discounted by his own negligence. The rule was hardest on those members who had joined in the last days of the pyramid. By then, the courts declared, Uchimura was so notorious that anyone who joined was necessarily negligent and entitled to only 50 to 60 percent of his damages.[47]

More relevant here, Uchimura's scams raised a variety of tax questions. First and most basic, did Uchimura have income at all? Given that pyramid schemes violated section 90 of the Civil Code and by 1979 were criminal, the amounts he received were illegal. No matter, said the courts. Illegal income is taxable. The problem was harder than one might think, however, since after the civil verdicts, Uchimura had a legal duty to return all the money he had received. Still no matter, said the courts—it was income.

For Uchimura, these revenues were income that would probably never generate offsetting deductions. If he returned the money as compensation for an intentional tort, then the payment was nondeductible (see subsection C.4). If instead he repaid it in response to an unjust enrichment claim, he did avoid that problem. Yet by the terms of the tax regulations, such amounts were deductible only when paid (ITA Enforcement Order, §141(c)), and Uchimura had not yet paid. Given his insolvency, neither was he likely to pay them any time soon.[48]

Second, did the One Family association owe a gift tax (see subsection B.6) upon Uchimura's transfer of his personally owned assets to it? Because the organization was unincorporated, transfers to it from individuals arguably gave rise to a special gift tax liability.[49]

Third, did Uchimura owe tax on the capital gains he realized when he transferred assets in his various shuffles? If a taxpayer donates appreciated property to a recognized charity, he has no capital gain, but the One Family association was not a recognized charity. If an individual transfers appreciated property to a firm, under U.S. law he can sometimes avoid liability (e.g., IRC, §351), but for individual taxpayers, Japan has no equivalent.

The tax office lost on the second and third issues. It lost for the curious reason that Uchimura completely dominated the One Family association, never incorporated it, and ignored its organizational integrity anyway. Accordingly, said the courts, it lacked the independence to qualify as a separate entity under tax law. Absent entity status, it could not owe a gift tax upon its receipt of assets, and Uchimura could not realize a capital gain when he transferred assets to it.[50]

II. Reorganizations
A. Introduction

Law students in the United States often find the Corporate Tax course a shock. They take the basic Income Tax course thinking (rightly) that they need it. If they have a good instructor, they romp playfully through one brain teaser after another. Delighted, they register for more. Upon arrival in Corporate Tax, they find themselves mired in a swamp of technical and only haphazardly sensible rules. Cursing themselves for missing the drop-add deadline, they swear they will become tort litigators if only they survive.

Japanese corporate tax rules are every bit as arcane as their U.S. equivalents—just differently arcane. We do not systematically introduce those rules here. Too few lawyers and law students have studied the U.S. rules to make the effort worthwhile. Yet some issues are sufficiently critical that we cover them anyway. The tax treatment of corporate mergers and acquisitions is a case in point.

In Japan, corporate reorganizations are formally taxable affairs.[51] In fact, however, by carefully planning their merger, Japanese firms can almost always avoid triggering most tax liability. All this is easiest to see with an example. Readers with no background in corporate tax will still find it arcane, however, and they should unabashedly skip to section III.

Suppose Acquiror K.K. wants to acquire Target K.K. Target supplies intermediate goods that Acquiror incorporates into its own products. Target began several decades ago as a family firm, but has grown rapidly. For the sake of illustration, assume the following numbers:

- Target has a fair market value of ¥1,000 million.

- Target has stated capital of ¥50 million and retained earnings of ¥650 million, giving it a total book value of ¥700 million.

- Target shareholders have an aggregate adjusted basis of ¥200 million in their Target stock.

Note that Japanese law does not use a separate "earnings and profits" account for tax purposes. Instead, it uses standard accounting concepts.

237

Through the reorganization, Target will merge into Acquiror. Target shareholders will receive Acquiror shares worth ¥1,000 million, and Target will disappear. The firms could also negotiate a consolidation, in which they both disappear and a legally distinct firm survives. But because the new firm will not inherit most of the tax attributes (e.g., net operating loss carryforwards) of the constituent firms, firms seldom have reason to choose this tactic. According to merger records, they rarely do.[52]

B. The Nominal Tax
1. Surviving Corporation

Consider now the tax liabilities of the surviving corporation (Acquiror, in our example), the merged corporation (Target), and the shareholders of the two corporations. Acquiror's tax liability will generally depend on

(i)   the net value at which Acquiror enters Target's assets on its books and

(ii) the aggregate par value of the Acquiror stock it distributes to Target shareholders in consideration of the merger (formally—and this is not always the same thing—the increase in stated capital of Acquiror plus any boot paid).

If (i) exceeds (ii), the excess (subject to various exceptions) will be ordinary business income to Acquiror. As such, it will be taxable at the standard corporate rate of 37.5 percent (Corporate Tax Act (CTA), §66).[53] If (ii) exceeds (i), Acquiror will incur no tax liability.[54]

2. Merged Corporation

The tax consequences to Target will depend on

(x) the par value of the Acquiror stock distributed to Target shareholders in consideration of the merger and

(y) Target's capital.

If (x) exceeds (y), the excess (subject, again, to various exceptions) will be liquidation income to Target, taxable at 33 percent (CTA, §99). If (y) exceeds (x), Target will incur no tax liability.[55] In short, if the par value of the stock Acquiror issues to pay for Target is too high, Target would seem to recognize taxable income; if it is too low, Acquiror would seem to recognize taxable income.

3. Shareholders

The tax treatment of Acquiror and Target shareholders is simpler to state. In general, Acquiror shareholders will have no tax liability from the merger. Target shareholders, however, will have tax consequences that, once again, turn on the par value of the Acquiror shares they receive.

First, to the extent the par value of the Acquiror stock distributed exceeds the per share stated capital and capital surplus of Target, Target shareholders will recognize a taxable deemed dividend. Dividends deemed paid to individual shareholders are subject to withholding at 20 percent (or 35 percent in some cases). They are then generally included in the shareholder's gross income and taxed at standard graduated rates (with a credit for the withheld amount).

Second, to the extent Target's per share stated capital and capital surplus exceed a Target shareholder's adjusted basis, the Target shareholder will recognize taxable capital gain. Under current law, individual taxpayers will generally pay a flat 20 percent tax on this amount (STMA, §37-10).[56] Corporate taxpayers will pay a tax on the gain at the business income rate of 37.5 percent.

C. The Actual Tax
1. Introduction

Although by this summary Japanese mergers would appear regularly to be taxable affairs, the appearance is wrong. The devil is in the details, and by manipulating those details, most merging firms can avoid almost all tax liability.

2. Surviving Corporation

Recall initially that Acquiror generally recognizes taxable income on the excess of

(a) the net value at which it enters Target's assets on its books *over*

(b) the aggregate par value of the stock it issues to Target shareholders (again, technically the increase in stated capital of Acquiror plus any boot paid).

This would seem to let it avoid the tax by keeping its par value sufficiently high.

Table 9.1 Stock Price as a Multiple of Par Value

Highest multiple, any firm	105.00
Lowest multiple, any firm	5.90
Mean of highest price as a multiple of par value, all firms	32.04
Mean of lowest price as a multiple of par value, all firms	15.27

Source: Calculated on the basis of data found in Nihon keizai shimbun sha, ed., *Nikkei kaisha jōhō—96 IV* [Nikkei Company Data—Fourth Quarter, 1996] (Tokyo: Nihon keizai shimbun sha, 1996).

Note: Based on stock prices of a random sample of fifty listed firms, 1993 through August 1996.

Not so. Firms do not avoid the tax through high par values. The stock of most listed firms trades at 15 to 30 times par value. Sometimes it trades for as little as 6 times par, but sometimes for as much as 100 times (table 9.1). Because firms will negotiate the merger price by market values, effectively Acquiror would seem to avoid the tax only if Target's assets have a book value 1/15 or 1/30 their real value.

Firms instead avoid the merger tax through the details of the law governing the computation of taxable merger income. Through the merger, Acquiror will recognize taxable income on the difference between book value and par value, but subject to three crucial deductions:

(x) the capital surplus it carriers over from Target,

(y) the retained earnings it carries over, *and*

(z) any amount by which it reduces stated capital in the merger.[57]

In effect, Acquiror can avoid all tax by carrying over Target's capital and retained earnings accounts and not increasing the book value of Target's assets. In most deals, Acquiror will have no reason not to carry over those balance sheet entries and no reason to revalue the assets.

Take a simple example. Target has a market value of ¥1,000 million, a book value of ¥700 million, stated capital of ¥50 million, and retained earnings of ¥650 million. To acquire Target, Acquiror issues stock worth ¥1,000 million, with a par value of ¥40 million, and enters the assets on its books at ¥700 million. To calculate its taxable gain, Acquiror will first subtract the ¥40 million par value from the ¥700 million book value. If it continues Target's retained earnings account, it will also subtract that ¥650 million. Given that it reduced capital by ¥10 million, it will deduct that amount, too. Obviously, excluding ¥650 million + ¥10 million = ¥660 million from ¥700 million − ¥40 million = ¥ 660 million yields a taxable gain of 0. Only if Acquiror either raises the book value of Target's assets or decides not to carry over Target's balance sheet entries will it recognize any taxable gain.

3. Merged Corporation

Target's taxable liquidation income depends on similarly bedeviling rules. Superficially these rules would seem to levy the liquidation tax on the difference between the par value of the Acquiror stock issued and the Target stock retired. In fact, these rules rarely create a tax on the merger either.

Formally (by CTA, §112) Target's liquidation income is the difference between

(a) the aggregate par value of all Acquiror stock issued to former Target shareholders *and*

(b) the capital, capital surplus, and retained earnings of Target.

In a suitably simple world, of course, Target's capital, capital surplus, and retained earnings will equal the net book value of its assets. Given that Acquiror's stock will usually trade at fifteen to thirty times par value (table 9.1), it would be an odd merger indeed where aggregate par exceeded net book value.

Crucially, however, the rules further stipulate that Target may not deduct from its liquidation income the entries for capital surplus and retained earnings that Acquiror carried onto its books (CTA, §112(c)). In other words, either Acquiror may deduct those accounts, or Target may deduct them, but not both. Suppose Acquiror does carry over the accounts to reduce its own liability. Target will avoid liquidation income only if Acquiror issues stock with an aggregate par value no greater than the stated capital of the stock it replaces.

The stock Acquiror issues might indeed have an aggregate par value no greater than Target's stated capital, but not necessarily. Suppose (importantly) that Target's stated capital is equal to the aggregate outstanding par value and that Target is worth ¥1,000 million and has 1 million outstanding ¥50 par shares, each worth ¥1,000. If Acquiror stock also has a ¥50 par value, Acquiror will issue stock with an aggregate par value equal to the par value of the Target stock it replaces only if the market value of Acquiror stock happens to be ¥1,000 as well. If Acquiror stock instead trades for ¥800, Acquiror will need to give Target shareholders 1.25 million shares. In so doing, it will distribute shares with an aggregate par value of

¥62.5 million. If Acquiror needs to carry over Target's balance sheet entries to avoid its own tax, Target will now recognize taxable liquidation income of ¥62.5 million − ¥50 million = ¥12.5 million.

To avoid this tax, firms customarily engineer stock splits (and an accompanying increase in stated capital) before the merger. In the example above, Target could split its stock (Commercial Code, §218).[58] In so doing, it would both lower the per share market price of the stock and raise the aggregate outstanding par value; along the way, it would shift bookkeeping entries from capital surplus to stated capital.

Most straightforwardly, Target would announce a 1-to-1.25 split. It would thereby raise the number of outstanding shares to 1.25 million and reduce the market price of the stock to ¥800. Since Target shareholders would now exchange Target stock with a ¥62.5 million par value (and stated capital of at least that amount) for Acquiror stock with the same par value, Target would incur no liquidation tax.

Note two potential complications. First, should a firm increase its capital account, shareholders could recognize taxable deemed dividend income (ITA, §25(b)(ii); CTA, §24(b)(ii)). Although in splitting its stock a firm does increase the aggregate par value, it can generally also do so by moving the appropriate amount from capital surplus to stated capital. Provided it has the capital surplus necessary to do this, shareholders will recognize no deemed dividend income.

Second, transitional rules in the Commercial Code enable firms to split their stock without running afoul of the minimum par value rules. According to the present Commercial Code, a firm cannot issue par stock unless each share carries a par value of at least ¥50,000 (Commercial Code, §218(b)). As almost all listed firms have ¥50 par value stock, this rule would effectively prevent them from splitting their stock and issuing new shares. In fact, though, transitional rules in the Commercial Code let firms that have outstanding shares with a lower par value issue new shares at the older, lower par value.[59]

Aggregate data confirm this use of stock splits. Consider the capital accounts of the constituent and surviving corporations to mergers (table 9.2). To locate this data, we turned to Fair Trade Commission (FTC) records. Although merging firms regularly report their mergers to the FTC, the FTC has often disclosed only aggregate numbers. Recently it has begun publishing the names of the largest merging firms, but still only with data on firm size. Yet in 1968, it disclosed something very different: the stated capital of the pre- and postmerger firms for the previous five years.

Table 9.2 Effect of Merger on Stated Capital

	Total	Capital		
	Mergers	Increase	Unchanged	Decrease
1963	45	17.78	28.89	53.33
1964	29	13.79	44.83	41.38
1965	14	7.14	28.57	64.29
1966	30	3.33	40.00	56.67
1967	31	9.68	54.84	35.48
Total	149	11.41	39.60	49.99

Source: Calculated from data found in Kōsei torihiki iinkai, ed., *Dokusen kinshi seisaku nijū nenshi* [Twenty Year History of Anti-monopoly Policy] (Tokyo: Ōkura shō, 1968), 604–608.

Notes:

TOTAL MERGERS: All mergers from April 1, 1963, to December 31, 1967, involving stated capital of at least ¥1 billion.

CAPITAL INCREASE: Percentage of firms where the stated capital of the surviving corporation is larger than the total stated capital of the component corporations.

CAPITAL UNCHANGED: Percentage of firms where the stated capital of the surviving corporation equals the total stated capital of the component corporations.

CAPITAL DECREASE: Percentage of firms where the stated capital of the surviving corporation is smaller than the total stated capital of the component corporations.

According to these records, in a tenth of the mergers, the aggregate stated capital of the surviving firm exceeded the sum of the stated capital of the constituent firms; in half of the mergers, aggregate capital decreased; and in 40 percent of the mergers, it stayed exactly the same. If firms merged randomly, this would not happen. If we merged random pairings of firms, stated capital would instead increase about as often as it decreased.

Consider why aggregate stated capital would increase in a merger. In a world without stock splits, it would sometimes increase if the market-price/par-value ratio of Acquiror stock were higher than that of Target stock. There, since the firms would set the merger stock exchange ratio by market prices, the aggregate par value of the Acquiror stock issued would necessarily exceed the aggregate par value of the Target stock retired. If it also exceeded Target's capital account, the surviving firm would have a capital account larger than the sum of the capital accounts of the two constituent firms. Because the par value of the Acquiror stock exceeded Target's capital account, however, Target would necessarily incur the liquidation tax described above.

If firms merged randomly, the market-price/par-value ratio of Acquiror stock should exceed the market-price/par-value ratio of Target stock as often as the latter exceeded the former. Accordingly, the capital of the surviving firm should exceed the capital of the constituent firms as often as it falls below it. The point of table 9.2 is that this does not happen. Instead, because an increase in the capital accounts would signal a liquidation tax to Target, most firms facing that potential tax adjust their market-value/par-value ratios before merging.

4. Shareholders of the Merged Corporation

By using stock splits to equalize the market-value/par-value ratio of the merging firms, the firms also eliminate the potential tax liability of Target shareholders. By equalizing the ratio, the firms ensure that Target shareholders receive Acquiror shares with a par value equal to the par value of the Target shares retired. Necessarily they also ensure that Target shareholders incur no deemed dividend income. The only potential shareholder-level tax will thus be a capital gains tax in those—probably rare—cases where a shareholder has an adjusted basis in Target stock lower than his portion of Target's stated capital and capital surplus.

III. Investment Incentives

Intriguingly, for most of the postwar period, the Japanese tax system avoided the intertemporal bias that usually inheres in income tax regimes. Income taxes, to put it more colloquially, usually encourage people to spend rather than to save. The Japanese income tax did not. Largely it avoided that bias against savings by functioning as a consumption tax rather than an income tax.[60]

A. The Intertemporal Bias
1. The Income Tax

A comprehensive income tax necessarily biases the choice that taxpayers make between consuming now and saving for tomorrow. By taxing the investment income they earn when they save, it encourages them to spend. In the process, it simultaneously distorts the allocation of resources over time and lowers the national savings rate. As the perpetual U.S. concern over the low national savings rate illustrates, this is more than a theoretical issue.

Take a simple example, and as a benchmark, consider first a tax-free world. Suppose the market interest rate is 10 percent. You earn 1,000 this year. You could spend it today, or you could save it and spend it next year. If you save it, by next year you will have $1,000/(1.1) = 1,100$. You will choose, therefore, between spending 1,000 this year and spending 1,100 the next. Because the present value to you of 1,100 a year in the future is 1,100/1.1 = 1,000, all else equal you will be indifferent between spending it now and spending it then.

Posit a 30 percent income tax. You earn 1,000 this year, but must pay 300 in taxes. As a result, you can either spend 700 this year or invest the 700 and spend the proceeds next year. If you invest it, next year you will have 770. On that 70 investment income, however, you will owe a 70(.3) = 21 tax, leaving you with only 749. Because the present value to you of 749 next year is 749/1.1 = 680, you will choose between consumption worth 700 (spend it today) and consumption worth 680 (spend it next year). Ergo, the tax system has reduced your incentive to save.

2. The Consumption Tax

Because of this intertemporal bias to the income tax, many observers urge a consumption tax instead. Under a consumption tax, people pay tax on their resources when they spend them. If each person immediately spends everything he earns, then each will pay the same tax whether he labors under an income tax or a consumption tax. If someone saves his resources for the future, though, he will pay a tax on those resources only when he eventually consumes them. In effect, he will pay tax only on his income net of the amount he saves. Crucially for our purposes here, the consumption tax will not bias his choice between spending today and spending tomorrow.

Suppose, again, that you earn 1,000. To stay consistent with the example above, assume you pay a tax of 300 if you consume your entire net after-tax income this year—yielding a consumption tax rate of 43 percent (700[.43] = 300).[61] If you instead save the amount and consume it next year, you will have 1,000(1.1) = 1,100 at your disposal. Of this amount, you will pay a tax of 330 and spend 770 (after all, 770[.43] = 330, and 330 + 770 = 1,100). Importantly the present value to you of 770 is 770/1.1 = 700. Whether you spend the money this year or the next, you face choices of equal present value.

B. The Japanese Tax System
1. The System

Although the Japanese tax system purports to tax all income comprehensively, for most of postwar history it did not. Instead, it primarily taxed wages and exempted investment income. Although Japan today does tax capital gains (subsection I.E) and interest income, this is largely a recent development.

Things were different immediately after the war. Occupation commander Douglas MacArthur had asked Columbia economist Carl Shoup to come and design a new tax system. Shoup recommended a comprehensive income tax.[62] Given Shoup's logic and MacArthur's troops, the Japanese government enacted what the doctor ordered. Inter alia, it eliminated many of the earlier schedular aspects of the Japanese tax system, taxed capital gains fully (and allowed full deductions for capital losses), and eliminated preferences for interest income.

Come 1952, MacArthur left. The Japanese government then began gutting several of the American reforms in earnest. Quickly it eliminated that most dastardly of American innovations, daylight savings time.[63] Soon it reversed the Shoup changes as well. Investment income was now largely tax exempt: individual taxpayers would no longer owe tax on most capital gains from the sale or exchange of securities (subsection I.E.2) or on interest from bank deposits. And where a comprehensive income tax base would require a deduction for all interest expenses, the Japanese code allowed no personal interest deductions (subsection I.D).

2. Wage Taxes and Consumption Taxes

By exempting investment income, the Japanese income tax closely approximated a consumption tax. A consumption tax taxes income from savings, but defers that tax until the investor consumes the income. The Japanese income tax taxed wages when earned, but permanently exempted any income the taxpayer earned by investing those wages. Because (1) deferring a tax on income is equivalent to (2) taxing the income but exempting any income earned from investing the after-tax proceeds, in important respects the Japanese income tax *was* a consumption tax.

Consider again a simple example. Suppose you earn 1,000 in year 1, but can defer the tax on that income until the following year (as you could under a consumption tax if you decided not to spend the money immediately). During the intervening year, you will earn 10 percent interest—giving you $1,000(1.1) = 1,100$ in year 2. With a 30 percent income tax in year 2, you will pay a tax of $1,100(.3) = 330$, leaving you with 770.

Now suppose you earn 1,000 in year 1, but pay an immediate 30 percent tax. You will keep 700, which you will invest. If you pay no tax on the investment income (as would have happened under the Japanese tax system for most of the postwar period), you will have 700(1.1) = 770 to consume in year 2.

The moral is basic: deferring a tax on income is equivalent to taxing the income immediately and exempting the investment income earned on the after-tax amount. For our purposes, the moral is also more specific: under many circumstances, a consumption tax is equivalent to a tax on wages only. By effectively taxing only wages, the Japanese tax system approximated a consumption tax. In the process, it largely circumvented the intertemporal bias that plagues income taxes and avoided the disincentives to save inherent in the U.S. income tax system.

Conclusions

Before an economy will grow, investors and entrepreneurs need to know that their investments will be safe not just from other individuals, but from the government as well. Like Japanese administrative law, Japanese tax law contributes to that assurance. However imperfectly, it provides a set of clear, stable, and (usually) sensible rules. Those are not always the rules a theorist would choose, granted. The tax rules on corporate reorganizations, for example, raise the transactions costs of corporate acquisitions, distort economic activity—and ultimately raise no revenue. Yet the important point is perhaps more basic: by limiting the scope and scale of government expropriation, the rules help forestall the wide-ranging rent-seeking and rent-avoidance activities that have so often crippled economies in so many places around the globe. In so doing, they have promoted economic growth.

NOTES

Preface

1. Frances Rosenbluth and J. Mark Ramseyer discuss lawmaking during these periods in *Japan's Political Marketplace* (Cambridge: Harvard University Press, 1993) and *The Politics of Oligarchy: Institutional Choice in Imperial Japan* (New York: Cambridge University Press, 1995).

2. For an introduction to this literature, see Mathew D. McCubbins and Terry Sullivan, eds., *Congress: Structure and Policy* (New York: Cambridge University Press, 1987).

3. Readers already have available a book that takes the opposite tack. In *Japanese Law* (London: Butterworth, 1992), Professor Hiroshi Oda has written a book that faithfully captures the way Japanese professors explain the law to themselves and their students.

Chapter 1

1. *Reproduced at* 477 *Hōgaku seminaa* 112 (1994).

2. Douglass North and Robert Paul Thomas, *The Rise of the Western World: A New Economic History* (Cambridge: Cambridge University Press, 1973), 1.

3. R. N. Coase, "The Problem of Social Cost," 3 *J.L. & Econ.* 1 (1960).

4. Robert J. Barro, *Democracy and Growth* (National Bureau of Economic Research Working Paper No. 4909, Oct. 1994); Harold Demsetz, "The Exchange and Enforcement of Property Rights," 7 *J.L. & Econ.* 11 (1964); Douglass C. North, "Institutions, Ideology, and Economic Performance," 11 *Cato J.* 477 (1991); George P. Shultz, "Economics in Action: Ideas, Institutions, Policies," 85 *Am. Econ. Rev. (Papers & Proceedings)* 1 (1995).

5. J. Mark Ramseyer, *Odd Markets in Japanese History: Law and Economic Growth* (Cambridge: Cambridge University Press, 1996).

6. Kikawa v. Hiroshima shi, 1479 Hōritsu shimbun 24, 25 (Hiroshima Ct. App. Oct. 19, 1918). For general discussions of the legal constraints provided by the Imperial constitution, see J. Mark Ramseyer and Frances M. Rosenbluth, *The Politics of Oligarchy: Institutional Choice in Imperial Japan* (Cambridge: Cambridge University Press, 1995), chs. 3, 11.

7. Nihon koku kenpō [Japanese National Constitution], effective May 3, 1947.

8. On the military and legislative districting, see John Owen Haley, *Authority without Power: Law and the Japanese Paradox* (Oxford: Oxford University Press, 1991), 188–190. On freedom of speech, see Lawrence Beer, *Freedom of Expression in Japan* (Tokyo: Kodansha International, 1984).

9. We here ignore (a) the obvious problems involved in positing a single set of preferences for a multimember organization like a legislature and (b) the possibility of logrolls.

10. John Ferejohn, "Law, Legislation, and Positive Political Theory," in *Modern Political Economy: Old Topics, New Directions,* ed. Jeffrey S. Banks and Eric A. Hanushek (Cambridge: Cambridge University Press, 1995), 208–209.

11. "Dō naru shihō shiken kaikaku" [Whether Legal Exam Reform?], 481 *Hōgaku seminaa* 87, 87 (1995).

12. Bengoshi hō [Attorneys Act], Law No. 205 of 1949.

13. "Shihō shiken kaikaku mondai kankei shiryō" [Materials Relating to the Reform of the Legal Examination], 929 *Jurisuto* 160 (1989).

14. *Shihō shiken hikkei* [Judicial Exam Handbook] (Tokyo: Hōgaku shoin, 1996), 77–79.

15. "Beikokuseki kara mo tanjō" [From U.S. Citizens as Well], *Asahi shimbun,* Oct. 30, 1993, at 30.

16. The data in this subsection are taken from a 1990 Japanese bar association study, "Bengoshi gyōmu no keizaiteki kiban ni kansuru jittai hōkoku" [Empirical Report on the Economic Foundation of Lawyers' Work], 42 *Jiyū to seigi* 1 (1991) [hereinafter "1990 Report"]. The study was based on anonymous responses to a questionnaire sent to 4,000 randomly selected attorneys. The response rate was 26 percent.

17. Setsuo Miyazawa, *Hō katei no riariti* [The Reality of the Legal Process] (Tokyo: Shinsan sha, 1994), 299; *see* Nagata v. Yanagisawa, 630 Hanrei jihō 3 (S. Ct. Apr. 20, 1971) (finding illegal litigation-related activity by judicial scrivener).

18. J. Mark Ramseyer, "Lawyers, Foreign Lawyers, and Lawyer-Substitutes: The Market for Regulation in Japan," 27 *Harv. Int'l L.J.* 499, 508–509 (1986).

19. Yasuo Watanabe, Setsuo Miyazawa, Shigeo Kisa, Shōzaburō Yoshino, and Tetsuo Satō, *Gendai shihō* [The Modern Legal System] (Tokyo: Nihon hyōron sha, 1992), 122–124.

20. *See id.* at 127; Michael Young, "Foreign Lawyers in Japan," 21 *Law in Japan* 84, 116 (1988).

21. *E.g.,* Shihō shoshi hō [Judicial Scriveners Act], Law No. 197 of 1950, §2. Ramseyer, *supra* note 18, at 500 n.3(b), is wrong precisely because it misses this point.

22. Araki v. K.K. Shokuhin shizai, 416 Hanrei jihō 67 (Sapporo High Ct. Mar. 4, 1965); Kuni v. [No name given], 601 Hanrei jihō 111 (Ōita D. Ct. Mar. 17, 1970).

23. *As translated in* Tadao Fukuhara, "The Status of Foreign Lawyers in Japan," 17 *Japanese Ann. Int'l L.* 21, 32 n.34 (1973). Fukuhara was involved in drafting the initial statute but, by the 1970s, was said to have some ties to American lawyers trying to enter the Tokyo market.

24. Y.K. Tanaka hōmu kikaku v. Fuji sangyō K.K., 1420 Hanrei jihō 80 (Hiroshima High Ct. Mar. 6, 1992).

25. Nakayama v. Kiyota, 17 Saihan minshū 744 (Sup. Ct. June 13, 1963) (litigation services); Y.K. Tanaka hōmu kikaku v. Fuji sangyō K.K., 1420 Hanrei jihō 80 (Hiroshima High Ct. Mar. 6, 1992) (eviction agents); Kakuta v. Funabashi, 1401 Hanrei jihō 66 (Tokyo D. Ct. Apr. 25, 1991) (same); Furugōri v. Kimura, 553 Hanrei taimuzu 198 (Yokohama D. Ct. Oct. 24, 1984) (real estate work); Araki v. K.K. Shokuhin shizai, 416 Hanrei jihō 67 (Sapporo High Ct. Mar. 4, 1965) (debt collectors); Kimura v. K.K. Miyayama gijutsu kenkyū jo, 683 Hanrei taimuzu 158 (Tokyo D. Ct. July 22, 1988) (document drafters; also discusses the scope of unauthorized practice ban in the act governing administrative scriveners); Kōno v. Otsuyama, 1218 Hanrei jihō 90 (Tokyo D. Ct. Feb. 24, 1986) (divorce work).

26. *See* Watanabe et al., *supra* note 19, at 27. Japan uses the American rule on attorney's fees for most disputes except tort cases—where a winning plaintiff can collect from the defendant (but not vice versa). *See* Saito v. Watanabe, 1092 Hanrei jihō 34 (Sup. Ct., Sept. 6, 1983); Rin v. Uchiyama, 23 Saihan minshū 441, 444–445 (Sup. Ct. Feb. 27, 1969).

27. "1990 Report," *supra* note 16.

28. "The Am Law 100," *The American Lawyer,* July/Aug. 1997.

29. *See* John P. Heinz and Edward O. Laumann, *Chicago Lawyers: The Social Structure of the Bar,* rev. ed. (Evanston, Ill.: Russell Sage Foundation, 1994), 8–11.

30. These figures are from the "1990 Report," *supra* note 16. Note that the bar association's earlier 1980 figures (recapitulated in the "1990 Report") were largely replicated by a Rand Corporation study based on entirely different data and methodologies. *See* Arthur Alexander and Hong Tan, *Case Studies of U.S. Service Trade in Japan* (Rand Note No. N-2169, 1984).

31. There are many accounts of this story. *Compare* Tadao Fukuhara, "The Status of Foreign Lawyers in Japan," 17 *Japanese Ann. Int'l L.* 21 (1973) *with* Takeo Kosugi, "Regulation of Practice by Foreign Lawyers," 27 *Am. J. Comp. L.* 678 (1979).

32. A nice account of this appears in John O. Haley, "Redefining the Scope of Practice under Japan's New Regime for Regulating Lawyers," 21 *Law in Japan* 18, 22–23 (1988).

33. United States–Japan Treaty of Friendship, Commerce, and Navigation, 4 U.S.T. 2063, T.I.A.S. No. 2863 (1953).

34. Gaikoku bengoshi ni yoru hōritsu jimu no toriatsukai ni kansuru tokurei sochi hō [Special Measures Law Regarding the Handling of Legal Business by Foreign Lawyers], Law No. 66 of 1986. For a translation, see 21 *Law in Japan* 193 (1988).

35. *Compare* Haley, *supra* note 32, *with* Glen S. Fukushima, "The Liberalization of Legal Services in Japan: A U.S. Government Negotiator's Perspective," 21 *Law in Japan* 5 (1988).

36. *See generally* J. Mark Ramseyer and Frances McCall Rosenbluth, *Japan's Political Marketplace* (Cambridge: Harvard University Press, 1993), chs. 8–9.

37. The Supreme Court hears routine cases in five-justice panels (comically translated by American scholars as "Petty Benches"). Occasionally it hears important cases en banc (as a "Grand Bench"). High courts hear cases in three-judge panels. District courts hear some cases as a three-judge panel and others (routine criminal cases, for example) with a single judge. Dissenting and concurring opinions are published for Supreme Court decisions, but not for others.

38. J. Mark Ramseyer and Eric B. Rasmusen, "Judicial Independence in a Civil Law Regime: The Evidence from Japan," 13 *J.L. Econ. & Org.* 259 (1997). For the flavor of the debate over this issue, compare John O. Haley, "Judicial Independence in Japan Revisited," 25 *Law in Japan* 1 (1995) with J. Mark Ramseyer, "The Puzzling (In)dependence of Courts: A Comparative Approach," 23 *J. Legal Stud.* 721 (1994).

39. We hold all else equal through multivariate regression analysis—in this case, an ordered probit model. We urge readers familiar with multiple regressions to consult the article itself.

40. Kōshoku senkyo hō [Public Offices Elections Act], Law No. 100 of 1955.

Chapter 2

1. [No names given], 1395 Hanrei jihō 133 (Akita D. Ct. Apr. 18, 1991).

2. Mimpō [Civil Code], Law No. 89 of 1896 and Law No. 9 of 1898.

3. 3 Caines 175 (1895), 2 Am. Dec. 264 (1886)

4. Kuni v. [No name given], 4 Daihan keishū 378 (Sup. Ct. June 9, 1925) (criminal case; holing badger within hunting season obviated criminal sanctions for later killing same badger out of season).

5. Inagaki v. Sone, 11 Daihan minshū 138 (Sup. Ct. Feb. 16, 1932).

6. Ishitsubutsu hō [Act Concerning Lost Objects], Law No. 87 of 1899. Moreover, note that some moveables (e.g., automobiles, ships) are subject to recordation rules.

7. Naigai kōgyō K.K. v. Hondō, 77 Hanrei taimuzu 72 (Tokyo D. Ct. Jan. 31, 1958).

8. The issue in Japan is phrased as one of statute of limitations. As Carol M. Rose put it, "Adverse possession is a common law interpretation of statutes of limitation for actions to recover real property." *Property and Persuasion: Essays on the History, Theory, and Rhetoric of Ownership* (Boulder, Colo.: Westview Press, 1994), 14.

9. Kuni v. Furuyama, 1220 Hanrei jihō 109 (Tokyo D. Ct. Dec. 27, 1985).

10. Morimiya v. Satō, 22 Saihan minshū 3022 (Tokyo D. Ct. May 21, 1965), *aff'd*, 511 Hanrei jihō 46 (Tokyo High Ct. Dec. 19, 1967), *aff'd*, 546 Hanrei jihō 66 (Sup. Ct. Dec. 20, 1968).

11. United States v. Carroll Towing Co., 159 F.2d 169 (2d Cir. 1947). On Japanese nuisance law, see generally J. Mark Ramseyer, *Odd Markets in Japanese History: Law and Economic Growth* (New York: Cambridge University Press, 1996), ch. 3.

12. [No names given], 1395 Hanrei jihō 133 (Akita D. Ct. Apr. 18, 1991).

13. Tatemono no kubun shoyū tō ni kansuru hōritsu [An Act Governing the Divided Ownership, Etc., of Buildings], Law No. 69 of 1962.

14. Mark Schilling, *The Encyclopedia of Japanese Pop Culture* (New York: Weatherhill, 1997), 85–92.

15. Yamashita v. Y.G. Parutii, 1415 Hanrei jihō 113 (Tokyo D. Ct. Jan. 30, 1992).

16. Iwashita v. Masuda, 1178 Hanrei jihō 53 (Yokohama D. Ct. Jan. 29, 1986), *aff'd*, 1213 Hanrei jihō 31 (Tokyo High Ct. Nov. 17, 1986), *aff'd*, 1243 Hanrei jihō 28 (Sup. Ct. July 17, 1987).

17. *E.g.*, Romanesuku noma kanri kumiai v. Y.G. Imagawa ya, 646 Hanrei taimuzu 141 (Fukuoka D. Ct. July 14, 1987) (mob renter evicted); Guriin manshon noma kanri kumiai v. Ahiru, 651 Hanrei taimuzu 221 (Fukuoka D. Ct. May 19, 1987) (mob owner evicted); Majison haitsu kanri sha v. Ishima, 1180 Hanrei jihō 3 (Sapporo D. Ct. Feb. 18, 1986) (auction); Marumi shatō Takatsuji v. Katō, 1251 Hanrei jihō 122 (Nagoya D. Ct. July 27, 1987) (same).

18. Technically these two rights are not easements, but corollaries to the title to one's land.

19. Kōno v. Kōno, 1012 Hanrei jihō 87 (Tokyo D. Ct. Feb. 27, 1981).

20. For a fuller discussion of Japanese water law, see Ramseyer, *supra* note 11, at ch. 2; J. Mark Ramseyer, "Water Law in Imperial Japan: Public Goods, Private Claims, and Legal Convergence," 18 *J. Legal Stud.* 51 (1989).

21. Yoshida v. Kimimori, 2 Daihan minroku 9–19 (Sup. Ct. Oct. 7, 1896).

22. Kinosaki v. Kataoka, 4249 Horitsu shimbun 5 (Kobe D. Ct. Feb. 7, 1938). The plaintiffs appealed, but eventually settled out of court in an agreement that gave the new hotel the right to pipe steam indoors. *See* Takeyoshi Kawashima, Toshitaka Shiomi, and Yōzō Watanabe, *Onsenken kenkyū* [Studies in Hot Springs Rights] (Tokyo: Keisō shobō, 1973), 393.

23. Honda v. Samejima, 3913 Hōritsu shimbun 5 (Tokyo D. Ct. Oct. 28, 1935), *modified*, 4262 Hōritsu shimbun 12 (Tokyo Ct. App. Feb. 24, 1938), *aff'd*, 4301 Hōritsu shimbun 12 (Sup. Ct. June 28, 1938).

24. Toshi keikaku hō [City Planning Act], Law No. 100 of 1968.

25. Kenchiku kijun hō [Construction Standards Act], Law No. 201 of 1950.

26. For a nice introduction to the regulation of sunlight access in Japan, see Frank G. Bennett, Jr., "Legal Protection of Solar Access under Japanese Law," 5 *UCLA Pac. Basin L.J.* 107 (1986).

27. Fūzoku eigyō tō no kisei oyobi gyōmu no tekiseika tō ni kansuru hōritsu [Act Regarding the Improvement, Etc. of the Rules and Business in the Adult Entertainment Industry], Law No. 122 of 1948.

28. At a statutory level, eminent domain law is governed by the Tochi shūyō hō [Land Acquisition Act], Law No. 219 of 1951.

29. *See* Nihon tōkei kyōkai, ed., *Nihon chōki tōkei sōran* [Long-term Japanese Statistics] (Tokyo: Nihon tōkei kyōkai, 1987), 4:332; see also the table before the preface to this book.

30. Tanaka v. Kuni, 7 Saihan minshū 1523 (Sup. Ct. Dec. 23, 1953) (en banc). *See generally* Toshihiko Kawagoe, "Land Reform in Postwar Japan," in *The Japanese Experience of Economic Reforms,* ed. Juro Teranishi and Yutaka Kosai (Houndmills, U.K.: Macmillan, 1993), 178.

31. Nakasako v. Aichi ken kōan iinkai, 320 Hanrei taimuzu 131 (Nagoya D. Ct. Apr. 14, 1975), aff'd, 355 Hanrei taimuzu 207 (Nagoya High Ct. Oct. 20, 1977).

32. *See generally* Sanrizaka shiba yama rengō kūkō hantai dōmei v. Kuni, 1074 Hanrei jihō 45 (Chiba D. Ct. June 30, 1982), aff'd, 37 Gyōsai reishū 424 (Tokyo High Ct. Mar. 25, 1986); Higashiyama v. Kuni, 1182 Hanrei jihō 46 (Chiba D. Ct. Oct. 22, 1985), aff'd in part and rev'd in part, 1371 Hanrei jihō 27 (Tokyo High Ct. Dec. 20, 1990); Sanrizaka shiba yama rengō kūkō hantai dōmei v. Kuni, 32 Sōmu geppō 2538 (Chiba D. Ct. Dec. 26, 1985); Shin Tokyo kokusai kūkō kōdan v. Sanrizaka shiba yama rengō kūkō hantai dōmei, 1356 Hanrei jihō 121 (Chiba D. Ct. Jan. 31, 1990); Sanrizaka shiba yama rengō kūkō hantai dōmei v. Kuni, 758 Hanrei taimuzu 140 (Tokyo D. Ct. Jan. 21, 1991).

33. Civil Code, §177; Fudōsan tōki hō [Real Estate Registration Act], Law No. 24 of 1899, §6.

34. Shakuchi shakuya hō [Land and House Lease Act], Law No. 90 of 1991. This 1991 statute is in fact a consolidation, with only minor changes and liberalization, of three prewar statutes: the Shakuchi hō [Land Lease Act], Law No. 49 of 1921; the Shakuya hō [House Lease Act], Law No. 50 of 1921; and the Tatemono hogo ni kansuru hōritsu [An Act Regarding the Protection of Buildings], Law No. 40 of 1909.

For an excellent analysis of the case law prior to these statutes as well as of the 1991 revisions, see John Owen Haley, "Japan's New Land and House Lease Law," in *Land Issues in Japan: A Policy Failure?* ed. John Owen Haley and Kozo Yamamura (Seattle: Society for Japanese Studies, 1992), 149.

35. Kimura v. Ōtsu, 723 Hanrei jihō 40 (Sup. Ct. Oct. 5, 1973).

36. Nagano v. Takahashi, 15 Saihan minshū 901 (Sup. Ct. Apr. 27, 1961).

37. The only exceptions are new and statutory: certain leases of land for at least fifty years (LHLA, §22), ten- to twenty-year leases (§24), house leases during the temporary absence of the owner (§38), and house leases where the landlord has a firm plan to demolish the building soon (§39). On the history of this regulation, see *supra* note 34.

38. [No names given], 476 Hanrei taimuzu 130 (Osaka D. Ct. Apr. 28, 1982).

39. K.K. Gotō birudingu v. Mandarin shōji K.K., 1356 Hanrei jihō 112 (Tokyo D. Ct. Sept. 29, 1989).

40. Yukio Noguchi, "Land Prices and House Prices in Japan," in *Housing Markets in the United States and Japan,* ed. Yukio Noguchi and James M. Poterba (Chicago: University of Chicago Press, 1994), 11, 12; *see* Takatoshi Ito, "Public Policy and Housing in Japan," in Y. Noguchi and J. Poterba, *id.* at 215, 232 (courts allow rent increases only "at a rate near cost increases or general inflation").

41. For obvious legally induced reasons, condominiums have been popular in Japan as well. Consider home ownership rates: 65 percent—United States, 62 percent—Japan, 51 percent—France, 40 percent—Germany. The Japanese rate, even if lower than that in the United States, is high when one considers that mortgage interest is not tax deductible in Japan, that for regulatory reasons housing loans have been less widely available in Japan than in the United States, and that the price of a house is a higher multiple of household income than in the United States. *See* Yukio Noguchi and James M. Poterba, "Introduction," in Noguchi and Poterba, *supra* note 40, at 1, 3–6.

42. Kensetsu shō, ed., *Kensetsu hakusho* [Construction White Paper] (Tokyo: Kensetsu shō, 1996), 250 (1993 data).

43. Yukio Noguchi, "Land Problems and Policies in Japan: Structural Aspects," in *Land Issues in Japan: A Policy Failure,* ed. John Owen Haley and Kozo Yamamura (Seattle: Society for Japanese Studies, 1992), 11, 17.

44. Noguchi, *supra* note 43, at 15–16.

45. The only exception is the 1991 amendment allowing some fixed-term leases when the landlord has a firm plan to demolish the building. LHLA, §39.

46. Kensetsu shō, *supra* note 42, at Supp. 32.

47. Noguchi, *supra* note 43, at 23; *see also* Tatsuo Hotta and Toru Ohkawara, "Housing and the Journey to Work in the Tokyo Metropolitan Area," in Noguchi and Poterba, *supra* note 40, at 87, 111–112.

48. Nihon jūtaku sōgō sentaa, ed., *Ni dai toshi ni okeru akiya jittai chōsa III* [A Study of the Actual Circumstances of Empty Units in Two Large Cities] (Tokyo: Nihon jūtaku sōgō sentaa, 1991), 6, 13–14, 38–39. Recent changes to the statute allow fixed-term leases where the landlord has firm plans to demolish the building. LHLA, §39.

49. Nobuhisa Segawa, *Nihon no shakuchi* [Rental Land in Japan] (Tokyo: Yūhikaku, 1995), 168 (Tokyo housing market in the 1960s).

50. Noguchi, *supra* note 43, at 12; *see* Ito, *supra* note 40, at 232 ("There is little large-size and/or high quality rental housing in Japan.").

51. Kensetsu shō, *supra* note 42, at 234.

52. Nihon jūtaku setsubi shisutemu kyōkai, ed., *Jūtaku setsubi kiki kankei deeta bukku* [Data Book Relating to Housing Equipment] (Tokyo: Nihon jūtaku setsubi shisutemu kyōkai, 1995), 26 (1993 data).

53. Saitō v. Kuni, 4262 Hōritsu shimbun 10 (Tokyo Ct. App. Feb. 23, 1938).

Chapter 3

1. Hidemasa Maki, *Kinsei Nihon no jinshin baibai no keifu* [The Geneology of the Sale of Humans in Early Modern Japan] (Tokyo: Sōbunsha, 1970), 92. For a discussion of the economics of indentured servitude and child sales contracts in Japan, see J. Mark Ramseyer, *Odd Markets in Japanese History: Law and Economic Growth* (New York: Cambridge University Press, 1996).

2. Maki, *supra* note 1, at 470–471.

3. In addition to the obvious ethical issues, there are economic reasons why one might exclude property rights in other people from this generalization. *See gener-*

ally Yoram Barzel, *Economic Analysis of Property Rights* (New York: Cambridge University Press, 1989), ch. 6.

4. Mimpō [Civil Code], Law No. 89 of 1896 and Law No. 9 of 1898.

5. Kōno v. Otsuyama, 1048 Hanrei jihō 109 (Tokyo High Ct. Apr. 28, 1982). A U.S. court may well reach the same result, but through a different logic. Under U.S. law, a *promise* to give would generally be unenforceable through lack of consideration. If a court let Otsuyama keep the money, it would be either because her intimacy constituted consideration or because the transfer of the card constituted a completed gift of the cash.

6. Alaska Packers' Ass'n v. Domenicoi, 117 F. 99 (9th Cir. 1902).

7. Hori v. Hori, 620 Hanrei jihō 70 (Osaka D. Ct. May 9, 1970).

8. Otsuyama v. Kōno, 819 Hanrei jihō 54 (Tokyo D. Ct. Dec. 25, 1975). *See also, e.g.*, Kōno v. Otsuyama, 1326 Hanrei jihō 139 (Osaka D. Ct. Apr. 20, 1989) (revocation allowed); Katano v. Katano, 664 Hanrei jihō 70 (Niigata D. Ct. Nov. 12, 1971) (same).

9. For complications, see, e.g., Matsuba v. Takahashi, 23 Daihan minshū 387 (Sup. Ct. June 28, 1944) (no contract where parties have different subjective understandings of the contract to which they agreed).

10. Okazaki v. Nankai kōtsū, K.K., 179 Hanrei taimuzu 128 (Osaka D. Ct. June 30, 1965).

11. Itō v. Sehara, 2-2 Daihan minroku 88 (Sup. Ct. Feb. 22, 1896).

12. Yamane v. Maekawa, 2147 Hōritsu shimbun 19 (Sup. Ct. May 7, 1923).

13. Sakabe v. Jushōin, 986 Hōritsu shimbun 25 (Tokyo D. Ct. [n.d., journal issue of Jan. 1, 1915]).

14. Sherwood v. Walker, 66 Mich. 568, 33 N.W. 919 (1887).

15. Hashimoto v. Yoshida, 23 Daihan minroku 284 (Sup. Ct. Feb. 24, 1917).

16. Miyamoto sangyō, K.K. v. K.K. Nakagawa sōgyō, 827 Hanrei taimuzu 183 (Sendai D. Ct. Oct. 30, 1992).

17. For a detailed discussion of the doctrine, see J. Toshio Sawada, *Subsequent Conduct and Supervening Events* (Tokyo: University of Tokyo Press, 1968), 112-161.

18. Iguchi v. Ikegami, 3 Kaminshū 962 (Osaka High Ct. July 14, 1952), *aff'd*, 8 Saihan minshū 448 (Sup. Ct. Feb. 12, 1954).

19. Yamanaka kōkūki K.K. v. Ōizumi, 3 Saihan minshū 226 (Sup. Ct. May 31, 1949).

20. Ōkuma v. Watanabe, 8-2 Daihan minroku 18, 21 (Sup. Ct. Feb. 6, 1902).

21. *E.g.*, Uchiumi v. Takeda, 59 Hōritsu shimbun 9, 10 (Sup. Ct. Oct. 10, 1901); *see generally* Ramseyer, *supra* note 1, ch. 6.

22. *E.g.*, Yanaka v. Nozawa, 21 Daihan minroku 49, 51-52 (Sup. Ct. Jan. 26, 1915) (damages granted for breach of contract to marry); Morooka v. Miyazaki, 8 Hōritsu hyōron min 1034 (Tokyo D. Ct. Oct. 6, 1919) (contract void where one of parties is married).

23. Shimizu v. Nakamura, 430 Hōritsu shimbun 19 (Tokyo D. Ct. May 3, 1907).

24. Tsujiyoshi K.K. v. Sanwa jidōsha unsō, K.K., 65 Hanrei jihō 21 (Osaka D. Ct. June 1, 1955). The point was dictum, since Commercial Code, §578, dictated the no-liability result.

25. *E.g.*, Shimazaki v. Liverpool & London & Grove hoken, K.K., 1011 Hōritsu shimbun 21 (Tokyo Ct. App. Mar. 17, 1915).

26. Namekawa v. Fujita, 262 Hōritsu shimbun 20 (Kobe D. Ct. Jan. 21, 1905).

27. Hōrei [Legal Principles], Law No. 10 of 1898, §7.

28. Dan Fenno Henderson, *Foreign Enterprise in Japan* (Chapel Hill: University of North Carolina Press, 1973) ("Under Japanese law, there is adequate legal support to enforce contracts obligating the parties to arbitrate either in Japan or in the U.S.," p. 333); *see* Komori-Webb U.S.A., Inc. v. K.K. Itō tekkō jo, 1232 Hanrei jihō 138 (Nagoya D. Ct. Ichinomiya Branch Off. Feb. 26, 1987); Texaco Overseas Tankship Ltd. v. Okada kaiun, K.K., 1090 Hanrei jihō 146 (Osaka D. Ct. Apr. 22, 1983); Am. President Lines, Ltd. v. C. Subura, K.K., 10 Kaminshū 2232 (Tokyo D. Ct. Oct. 23, 1959).

29. Legal Principles, §10 (real estate), §11 (tort), §§13–21 (domestic relations); *see* Honeymex Corp., Ltd. v. K.K. Kōka, 835 Hanrei jihō 83 (Tokyo D. Ct. Mar. 29, 1976) (unjust enrichment).

30. *Compare* George v. International Air Service Co., Ltd., 408 Hanrei jihō 14 (Tokyo D. Ct. Apr. 26, 1965) (applying Japanese law), *translated in* Y. Yanagida et al., eds., *Law and Investment in Japan* (Cambridge: East Asian Legal Studies and Harvard University Press, 1994), 244 *with* Singer Sewing Machine Co. v. Bronocks, 568 Hanrei jihō 87 (Tokyo D. Ct. May 14, 1969) (applying U.S. and New York law).

31. Brooks v. Yuzawa, 77 Hanrei taimuzu 32 (Tokyo High Ct. Nov. 28, 1957).

32. Taiheiyō sangyō, K.K. v. K.K. Daimaru, 11 Kōsai minshū 175 (Osaka High Ct. Mar. 3, 1958).

33. Tsukamoto v. Fujiki, 2 Kasai minshū 1330 (Niigata D. Ct. Nagaoka Branch Off. Nov. 19, 1951).

34. "Metsubō" e no kyōfu egaki migoto [Brilliant Evocation of Terror of Descent into "Annihilation"], *Mainichi shimbun,* June 27, 1980 (evening ed.), at 9.

35. Mark Schilling, *The Encyclopedia of Japanese Pop Culture* (New York: Weatherhill, 1997), 82.

36. Otsuyama v. Kōno, 1090 Hanrei jihō 134 (Osaka High Ct. May 25, 1983), *reversing* 1047 Hanrei jihō 137 (Kyoto D. Ct. Nov. 18, 1981) (Apparently Fukasaku is the director's real name; the opinion uses only pseudonyms).

37. Nitō v. Hōya insatsu, K.K., 648 Hanrei jihō 67 (Tokyo High Ct. Oct. 30, 1971); Fukuhara orimono, gōmei gaisha v. Nakatani, 4 Daihan minshū 64 (Sup. Ct. Feb. 19, 1925) (proportional rescission).

38. Itō v. Murai bōeki, K.K., 3 Daihan minshū 362 (Sup. Ct. July 15, 1924).

39. Fujii v. Saiki, 6 Saihan minshū 451 (Sup. Ct. Apr. 25, 1952) (landlord may evict immediately if tenant's sons trash house).

40. Dainichi kagaku sangyō, K.K. v. Y.G. Maruichi shōkai, 304 Hanrei jihō 24 (Osaka High Ct. June 11, 1962).

41. If both parties are at fault, the court will dock the plaintiff's damages by its relative fault. Civil Code, §418.

42. Y.G. Asahikawa kyōryoku sen'i kōgyōsho v. Ōsumi, 18 Hanrei jihō 10 (Sup. Ct. Dec. 18, 1953), *aff'g* 7 Saihan minshū 1452 (Takamatsu High Ct. May 23, 1950), *aff'g* 7 Saihan minshū 1450 (Tokushima D. Ct. n.d.).

43. Seiryō v. Chin, 22 Daihan minroku 1991 (Sup. Ct. Oct. 27, 1916). The Chinese seller rescinded the contract on April 7 and sold the hides on May 4. The buyer argued that the April 7 market price should govern rather than the May 4 price, but effectively the court refused to hold that the buyer was required to resell the goods immediately.

44. 9 Ex. 341, 156 Eng. Rep. 145 (1854). According to *Hadley,* the plaintiff may recover those damages that "may fairly and reasonably be considered [as] arising naturally, i.e., according to the usual course of things, from such breach of con-

tract itself," together with those consequential damages "such as may reasonably be supposed to have been in the contemplation of the parties." *Id.* at 354, 156 Eng. Rep. at 151.

45. Y.G. Asahikawa kyōryoku sen'i kōgyōsho v. Ōsumi, 7 Saihan minshū 1452 (Takamatsu High Ct. May 23, 1950), *aff'd on other grounds,* 18 Hanrei jihō 10 (Sup. Ct. Dec. 18, 1953).

46. For a discussion of the consequences of distinguishing between contracts "to transfer" and "to do," see Steven Shavell, "The Design of Contracts and Remedies for Breach," 99 *Q.J. Econ.* 121 (1984); William Bishop, "The Choice of Remedy for Breach of Contract," 14 *J. Legal Stud.* 299 (1985); Lewis A. Kornhauser, "An Introduction to the Economic Analysis of Contract Remedies," 57 *U. Colo. L. Rev.* 683, 715–716 (1986).

47. Y.G. Hijikata v. Inaba, 508 Hanrei taimuzu 136 (Tokyo D. Ct. June 27, 1983).

48. The lower court opinion is unpublished, though references to it appear in the High Court opinion.

49. *E.g.,* Haneda v. Matsumoto, 2272 Hōritsu shimbun 19 (Sup. Ct. Apr. 1, 1924); Murakami v. Izumi, 1986 Hōritsu shimbun 7 (Miyagi Ct. App. Apr. 22, 1922).

50. Nihon gurando rekōdo, K.K. v. Itō, 21 Kakyū minshū 155 (Nagoya High Ct. Jan. 30, 1970).

51. Banri Asanuma, "Manufacturer-Supplier Relationships in Japan and the Concept of Relation-Specific Skill," 3 *J. Japanese & Int'l Econ.* 1, 3–4 (1989).

52. *Id.* at 4; Yoshiro Miwa, *Firms and Industrial Organization in Japan* (Houndmills, U.K.: Macmillan, 1996), 77, 224–227.

53. Miwa, *supra* note 52, at 15, 72.

54. Neither do manufacturers shift onto their suppliers the risks they face of economic fluctuations. Banri Asanuma, "Risk Absorption in Japanese Subcontracting: A Microeconomic Study of the Automobile Industry," 6 *J. Japanese & Int'l Econ.* 1 (1992).

55. J. Mark Ramseyer, "Legal Rules in Repeated Deals: Banking in the Shadow of Defection in Japan," 20 *J. Legal Stud.* 91, 108 (1992).

56. Ramseyer, *supra* note 55; Tosihiro Matsumura and Marc Ryser, "Revelation of Private Information about Legal Notes in the Trade Credit Bill System in Japan," 24 *J. Legal Stud.* 165 (1995).

57. Stewart Macaulay, "Non-contractual Relations in Business: A Preliminary Study," 28 *Am. Soc. Rev.* 55 (1963).

58. Lisa Bernstein, "Merchant Law in a Merchant Court: Rethinking the Code's Search for Immanent Business Norms," 144 *U. Pa. L. Rev.* 1765 (1996).

59. Robert Ellickson, *Order without Law: How Neighbors Settle Disputes* (Cambridge: Harvard University Press, 1991).

60. Jason Johnston, "The Statute of Frauds and Business Norms: A Testable Game-Theoretic Model," 144 *U. Pa. L. Rev.* 1859, 1866 (1996).

61. Thomas Palay, "Comparative Institutional Economics: The Governance of Freight Contracting," 13 *J. Legal Stud.* 265 (1984).

62. Bernstein, *supra* note 58, at 1790.

63. Paul Joskow, "Vertical Integration and Long-Term Contracts: The Case of Coal-Burning Electric Generating Plants," 1 *J.L. Econ. & Org.* 33 (1985).

64. *E.g.,* Victor P. Goldberg, "Price Adjustments in Long-Term Contracts," 1985 *Wis. L. Rev.* 527, 531–532.

65. Bernstein, *supra* note 58.

66. *See* Richard A. Epstein, *Mortal Peril: Our Inalienable Right to Health Care?* (New York: Addison Wesley, 1997), ch. 19.

67. 146 A. 641 (N.H. 1929).

68. *E.g.,* Mori v. Iwanoiwa, 697 Hanrei jihō 55 (Osaka High Ct. Nov. 29, 1972); Ōnuma v. Kōno, 623 Hanrei jihō 53 (Asahikawa D. Ct. Nov. 25, 1970).

69. Yamamoto v. Isami kōtsū K.K., 485 Hanrei jihō 21, 25–26 (Tokyo D. Ct. June 7, 1967); *see generally* Ikemoto v. Kitakyūshū, 1265 Hanrei jihō 75, 76 (Sup. Ct. Jan. 19, 1988) (Itō, J., concurring).

70. Seizō Shikanai, *Iryō funsō no bōshi to taiō saku* [Strategies for the Prevention of and Reaction to Medical Disputes] (Tokyo: Daiichi hōki, 1994), 191. The survey presents its data as cells. The mean is calculated using the midpoint of each cell.

71. *Id.* at 41.

72. Calculated from data found in Tachiaki Azami and Tomio Nakai, *Iryō kago hō* [Medical Malpractice Law] (Tokyo: Seirin shoin, 1994), 5.

73. A.M. Best Co., *Aggregates and Averages* (Oldwick, N.J.: A.M. Best Co., 1996), 120–121.

74. David J. Nye et al., "The Causes of the Medical Malpractice Crisis: An Analysis of Claims Data and Insurance Company Finances," 76 *Geo. L.J.* 1495, 1501–1502, 1506 (1988).

75. Data for the United States are from A.M. Best Co., *supra* note 73, at 120–121, and Nye et al., *supra* note 74, at 1524.

76. *See, e.g.,* Naoki Ikegami, "Overview: Health Care in Japan," in *Containing Health Care Costs in Japan,* ed. Naoki Ikegami and John Creighton Campbell (Ann Arbor: University of Michigan Press, 1996), 8, 9–10; Naoki Ikegami, "The Economics of Health Care in Japan," 258 *Science* 614 (1992); John K. Iglehart, "Japan's Medical Care System," 319 *New Eng. J. Med.* 807 (1988), 319 *New Eng. J. Med.* 1166 (1988).

77. John Eisenberg and Nancy Foster, "Afterward: Quality and Cost in Japanese and U.S. Medical Care," in N. Ikegami and J. C. Campbell, *supra* note 76, at 143, 149; Ruth Campbell, "The Three-Minute Cure: Doctors and Elderly Patients in Japan," in N. Ikegami and J. C. Campbell, *supra* note 76, at 226.

78. Emiko Ohnuki-Tierney, *Illness and Culture in Contemporary Japan: An Anthropological View* (Cambridge: Cambridge University Press, 1984), 171–172.

79. Yukiko Katsumata, "Comparison of Health Expenditure Estimates between Japan and the U.S.," in N. Ikegami and J. C. Campbell, *supra* note 76, at 19, 27 (the author estimates this as the upper bound on the bribes).

Chapter 4

1. Hasegawa v. Gurūza, 601 Hanrei taimuzu 50 (Yokohama D. Ct. Apr. 9, 1986).

2. Mimpō [Civil Code], Law No. 89 of 1896 and Law No. 9 of 1898.

3. Kōi v. Shinoda, 3191 Hōritsu shimbun 7, 9 (Sup. Ct. Sept. 19, 1930).

4. *E.g.,* Kigura v. Kasaoka, 928 Hanrei jihō 87 (Kyoto D. Ct. Dec. 19, 1978).

5. *See, e.g.,* Matsumoto v. Inoguchi, 4 Daihan minshū 670 (Sup. Ct. Nov. 28, 1925) (invasion of business goodwill actionable), *overturning* Shimaguchi v. Kanda, 20 Daihan keiroku 1360 (Sup. Ct. July 4, 1914) (piracy of traditional Japanese music not actionable as not involving protected right).

6. *E.g.,* [No names given], 573 Hanrei jihō 60 (Sup. Ct. Sept. 26, 1969); Nishimoto v. Okamura, 6 Kasai minshū 2357 (Tokyo High Ct. Nov. 11, 1955).

7. Coquerel v. Clément-Bayard, Req., Aug. 3, 1915, D.P. I1917.1.79.

8. Ishida v. Kanamori, 2648 Hōritsu shimbun 10 (Annotsu D. Ct. Aug. 10, 1926).

9. William Johnston, *The Modern Epidemic: A History of Tuberculosis in Japan* (Cambridge: Council on East Asian Studies, Harvard University, 1995), 4, 109–116, 241.

10. Watanabe v. Mutō, 4536 Hōritsu shimbun 10 (Sup. Ct. Feb. 16, 1940).

11. Nakamura v. Nakamura, 169 Hōsō shimbun 18 (Tokyo D. Ct. Dec. 1, 1961).

12. *E.g.,* Kakihara v. Ide, 19 Daihan minroku 507 (Sup. Ct. June 9, 1913).

13. L.R. 3 H.L. 330 (1868); *see, e.g.,* Abe v. Kuni, 313 Hanrei jihō 4 (Nagoya D. Ct. Oct. 12, 1962); Hakodate ryūan hiryō, gōshi gaisha v. Yamamoto, 23 Daihan minroku 879 (Sup. Ct. May 19, 1917).

14. Morioka dentō, K.K. v. Nakajima, 4172 Hōritsu shimbun 15 (Sup. Ct. July 17, 1937).

15. Akaho v. Kōshin sangyō, K.K., 427 Hanrei jihō 11 (Nagano D. Ct. Matsumoto Branch Off. Nov. 11, 1965).

16. Y.G. Kojima seimenjo v. Koike, 692 Hanrei jihō 44 (Tokyo High Ct. Nov. 29, 1972).

17. Fukuyama v. Nakamura, 17 Daihan minroku 617, 622 (Sup. Ct. Nov. 1, 1911).

18. 159 F.2d 169, 173 (2d Cir. 1947).

19. Kuni v. Shimizu, 25 Daihan minroku 356 (Sup. Ct. Mar. 3, 1919).

20. *See generally, e.g.,* Frank K. Upham, "After *Minamata:* Current Prospects and Problems in Japanese Environmental Litigation," 8 *Ecology L.Q.* 213 (1979); J. Mark Ramseyer, *Odd Markets in Japanese History: Law and Economic Growth* (New York: Cambridge University Press, 1996), ch. 3; Julian Gresser, Koichiro Fujikura and Akio Morishima, eds., *Environmental Law in Japan* (Cambridge: MIT Press, 1981).

21. Kuni v. Hasegawa, 547 Hanrei jihō 38, 39 (Sup. Ct. Feb. 6, 1969).

22. Nakatani v. Matsuda, 12 Daihan keiroku 1315 (Sup. Ct. Dec. 3, 1906); *accord* Tatsuno denki tetsudō, K.K. v. Nishimura, 26 Daihan minroku 1911 (Sup. Ct. Nov. 26, 1920) (railroad crossing accident); Kawamura v. Maeda, 385 Hanrei jihō 51 (Sup. Ct. Sept. 25, 1964) (court has "free discretion" based on facts of case and "principles of fairness").

23. *E.g.,* Kyūshū denki kidō, K.K. v. Nishihiro, 21 Daihan minroku 939, 944 (Sup. Ct. June 15, 1915).

24. Sakamura v. Tsuchiya, 72 Hanrei taimuzu 63 (Sup. Ct. June 20, 1957); Honma v. Ube nama konkuriito kōgyō, K.K., 376 Hanrei jihō 10 (Sup. Ct. June 24, 1964).

25. This is the Supreme Court's rule. Some inconsistency remains in the lower courts: *see, e.g.,* Takahashi v. Ōzaki unsō, K.K., 261 Hanrei taimuzu 248 (Yokohama D. Ct. Kawasaki Branch Off. Mar. 15, 1971) (four-year-old's comparative negligence considered in traffic accident after determining capacity); Sada v. Kuni, 15 Sōmu geppō 769 (Okayama D. Ct. June 30, 1969) (four-year-old's comparative negligence not considered in drowning accident because of lack of capacity); Kiuchi v. K.K. Shinkō shōten, 275 Hanrei taimuzu 242 (Osaka D. Ct. Jan. 27,

1972) (comparative negligence offset proper without inquiry into capacity of four-year-old plaintiff); Yamamoto v. Jitsuyō kōgyō, K.K., 575 Hanrei jihō 58 (Tokyo D. Ct. Oct. 22, 1969) (comparative negligence offset proper even for two-year-old plaintiff).

26. *E.g.,* Kyūshū denki kidō, K.K. v. Nishihiro, 21 Daihan minroku 939, 944–945 (Sup. Ct. June 15, 1915).

27. Miyashita kenzai kōgyō, K.K. v. Yoshii, 490 Hanrei jihō 47, 48 (Sup. Ct. June 27, 1967); Nihō unsō, K.K. v. Hōkawa, 206 Hanrei jihō 14, 14 (Sup. Ct. Nov. 26, 1959). Courts also impute comparative negligence between spouses. *See* Y.G. Hokushū kyūkō v. Wayama, 810 Hanrei jihō 11 (Sup. Ct. Mar. 25, 1976).

28. 248 N.Y. 339, 162 N.E. 99 (1928).

29. Asai v. Miyazaki, 11 Daihan minshū 812 (Sup. Ct. May 3, 1932) (emphasis added).

30. Takada v. Takada, 27 Saihan minshū 681 (Sup. Ct. June 7, 1973). The classic case on point is Osaka shōsen, K.K. v. K.K. Murakane shōten, 5 Daihan minshū 386 (Sup. Ct. May 22, 1926) (where price of lost goods rises dramatically after tort, plaintiff may collect those extraordinarily large lost profits only if price increase was foreseeable).

31. Omuta v. Yoshizawa, 248 Hanrei jihō 15, 18 (Tokyo D. Ct. Feb. 1, 1961).

32. Nakamura v. Fujima, 8 Kakyū minshū 165 (Tokyo D. Ct. Jan. 30, 1957).

33. Itō v. Yamamoto, 721 Hanrei jihō 88 (Matsue D. Ct. Hamada Branch Off. Sept. 28, 1973) (victim also found 40 percent negligent); *see also* Tanida v. Saka, 836 Hanrei jihō 85 (Osaka D. Ct. July 15, 1976) (dog owner liable where young girl, scared by barking dog, steps onto street and is hit by car).

34. Ishizaki v. Ikeda, 4142 Hōritsu shimbun 5 (Tokyo Ct. App. Apr. 28, 1937).

35. Ōmichi v. Okada, 28 Saihan minshū 447 (Sup. Ct. Apr. 25, 1974).

36. *E.g.,* Nishihara v. Fujita, 293 Hanrei jihō 14 (Sup. Ct. Feb. 27, 1962) (no liability where second-grader injures playmate during tag game).

37. Shakai fukushi hōjin Seirei hoyōen v. Yoshinaga, 496 Hanrei jihō 45, 48 (Tokyo High Ct. July 11, 1967).

38. Inomura v. Toyoda, 470 Hanrei jihō 54 (Nagoya D. Ct. Oct. 28, 1966).

39. If *B* himself decides how to do the work, then *A* is not liable. Civil Code, §716. *See* Koike v. Yabunaka, 325 Hanrei jihō 17 (Sup. Ct. Dec. 14, 1962).

40. Hodani v. Kuni, 9 Saihan minshū 2053 (Tokyo D. Ct. Nov. 9, 1953), *aff'd,* 9 Saihan minshū 2061 (Tokyo High Ct. Mar. 14, 1955), *aff'd,* 68 Hanrei jihō 13 (Sup. Ct. Dec. 22, 1955).

41. 9 Kakyū minshū 2061 (Tokyo High Ct. Mar. 14, 1955); *accord* Kihara v. Suzuki, 630 Hanrei jihō 62 (Sup. Ct. Apr. 6, 1971).

42. Kōno v. Otsuyama, 1173 Hanrei jihō 95 (Nagoya D. Ct. Feb. 14, 1985).

43. Hirose v. Miyawaki, 6 Kakyū minshū 240 (Ōsaka D. Ct. Feb. 8, 1955) (twelve-year-old playing catch); Itō v. Anzai, 324 Hanrei jihō 26 (Tokyo D. Ct. Nov. 2, 1962) (fourteen-year-old in bicycle accident).

44. Kitamura v. Yoshida, 27 Daihan minroku 193 (Sup. Ct. Feb. 3, 1921); *see* Yamamoto v. Yamada, 23 Daihan minroku 715 (Sup. Ct. Apr. 30, 1917); Kimura v. Niijima, 116 Hanrei jihō 20 (Tokyo High Ct. Apr. 26, 1957) (eleven-year-old).

45. Kōno v. Otsuyama, 737 Hanrei jihō 39 (Sup. Ct. Mar. 22, 1974), *aff'g* 28 Saihan minshū 362 (Hiroshima High Ct. Matsue Branch Off. July 19, 1972), *aff'g* 28 Saihan minshū 351 (Tottori D. Ct. Yonago Branch Off. Dec. 22, 1970); *see generally, e.g.,* Imada v. Morioka, 241 Hanrei taimuzu 138 (Okayama D. Ct. Kasaoka

Branch Off. Aug. 25, 1969) (parent liable for child's traffic accident); [No names given], 310 Hanrei jihō 37 (Osaka D. Ct. May 26, 1962) (suggesting parental liability for gang rape by sons).

46. The immunity under the Civil Code applies to acts pursuant to the *kōken ryoku* of the state (actions pursuant to its "public powers"). When the government acts in an entrepreneurial capacity (e.g., when it runs a railroad), it is liable directly under the Civil Code.

47. Kokka baishō hō [National Compensation Act], Law No. 125 of 1947.

48. Kōno v. Tokyo, 1378 Hanrei jihō 26 (Tokyo D. Ct. Mar. 27, 1991), *modified,* 1495 Hanrei jihō 42 (Tokyo High Ct. May 20, 1994).

49. Ishioka v. Odagiri, 13 Daihan minshū 1874 (Sup. Ct. Oct. 15, 1934).

50. Yamaki v. Kojima, 295 Hanrei jihō 33 (Tokyo D. Ct. Mar. 1, 1962). Similar dilemmas have plagued American courts for years, of course.

51. *See also, e.g.,* Nojima v. Fukuzawa, 1042 Hanrei jihō 87 (Sup. Ct. Mar. 4, 1982); Katō v. Tokyo to, 455 Hanrei jihō 27, 34 (Tokyo D. Ct. Aug. 9, 1966).

52. Kuni v. Ikenaga, 7 Daihan keiroku 11 (Sup. Ct. Apr. 5, 1901); *see* Tōkyō wan kisen K.K. v. Minakami, 17 Daihan minroku 861 (Sup. Ct. Dec. 20, 1911).

53. Ichirō Katō, *Fuhō kōi* [Torts] 148 (Tokyo: Yūhikaku, 1957) (nominal damages); Zentaro Kitagawa, ed., *Doing Business in Japan* (New York: Matthew Bender, updated), vol. 7, §14:5.02[3] (punitive damages).

54. Nihon kōtsū, K.K. v. Asakawa, 533 Hanrei jihō 37 (Sup. Ct. Aug. 27, 1968) (allowing unusually high recovery for life of promising young man); Ube nama konkuriito kōgyō, K.K. v. Honma, 376 Hanrei jihō 11 (Sup. Ct. June 24, 1964) (valuation possible even for eight-year-old child).

55. Hayakawa v. Nihon kōgyō, K.K., 748 Hanrei jihō 23 (Sup. Ct. July 19, 1974).

56. I. Katō, *supra* note 53, at 229; Daniel Foote, "Resolution of Traffic Accident Disputes and Judicial Activism in Japan," 25 *Law in Japan* 19 (1995).

57. Fukunaga v. Toshikawa seikō, K.K., 683 Hanrei jihō 21, 61 (Nagoya D. Ct. Oct. 19, 1972) (injunction granted under section 709 pollution claim); Komano v. Hanazawa birudingu, K.K., 1243 Hanrei jihō 90 (Chiba D. Ct. Ichinomiya Branch Off. Feb. 7, 1987) (injunction granted under section 709 sunlight rights claim). Note that plaintiffs in sunlight and pollution cases often also claim rights based on real property—where courts have traditionally granted injunctions.

58. Kikuta v. Ueda, 26 Daihan minroku 280 (Sup. Ct. Mar. 10, 1920); Matsuo v. Shirakura, 24 Daihan minroku 498 (Sup. Ct. Mar. 15, 1918).

59. Ishizuka v. Polosovitch, 27 Saihan minshū 1380 (Tokyo D. Ct. Aug. 10, 1966), *rev'd,* 594 Hanrei jihō 68 (Tokyo High Ct. Apr. 8, 1970), *aff'd,* 27 Saihan minshū 1374 (Sup. Ct. Nov. 16, 1973).

60. Adapted from J. Mark Ramseyer and Minoru Nakazato, "The Rational Litigant: Settlement Amounts and Verdict Rates in Japan," 18 *J. Legal Stud.* 263 (1989).

61. Takeyoshi Kawashima, "Dispute Resolution in Contemporary Japan," in *Law in Japan: The Legal Order in a Changing Society,* ed. Arthur Taylor von Mehren (Cambridge: Harvard University Press, 1963), 41.

62. E.g., John Owen Haley, "The Myth of the Reluctant Litigant," 4 *J. Japanese Stud.* 359 (1978).

63. Susan Chira, "If You Insist on Your Day in Court, You May Wait and Wait and Wait," *N.Y. Times,* Sept. 1, 1987, at 4.

64. *See* Foote, *supra* note 56, at 19.

65. Jidōsha songai baishō hoshō hō [Automobile Damage Compensation Insurance Act], Law No. 97 of 1955.

66. Yōji Kanda, *Kōtsū jiko no songai baishō gaku* [Damage Amounts in Traffic Accidents] (Tokyo: Jiyū kokumin, 1994), 289.

67. This 33 percent figure applies only to those cases in which defendants asserted a comparative negligence defense. Because in some fatal traffic accident cases the defendants will not bother asserting the defense, the real figure for comparative negligence reductions is less than one-third. The 33 percent figure is a rough average of a 1969 Japanese Supreme Court survey of 312 district court decisions involving wrongful death. *See* Akio Morishima, "Minji sekinin to kōtsū jiko no yokushi" [Civil Responsibility and the Prevention of Traffic Accidents], 2 *Kōtsū hō kenkyū* 21, 27 table 5 (1972).

68. Because column B includes the amounts paid by insurers in litigated cases, it does not represent only settlements. However, since less than 1 percent of all traffic accident disputes are litigated, we use column B as a proxy for out-of-court settlements.

69. Adapted from J. Mark Ramseyer, "Products Liability through Private Ordering: Notes on a Japanese Experiment," 144 *U. Pa. L. Rev.* 1823 (1996).

70. *See, e.g.,* Patricia M. Danzon, "Tort Reform and the Role of Government in Private Insurance Markets," 13 *J. Legal Stud.* 517 (1984); Richard A. Epstein, "Products Liability as an Insurance Market," 14 *J. Legal Stud.* 645 (1985); George L. Priest, "Can Absolute Manufacturer Liability Be Defended?" 9 *Yale J. on Reg.* 237 (1992).

71. *See, e.g.,* John E. Calfee and Paul H. Rubin, "Some Implications of Damage Payments for Nonpecuniary Losses," 21 *J. Legal Stud.* 371 (1992); Richard A. Epstein, "The Political Economy of Product Liability Reform," 78 *Am. Econ. Rev.* 311 (1988 Papers & Proceedings); George L. Priest, "The Current Insurance Crisis and Modern Tort Law," 96 *Yale L.J.* 1521 (1987); Paul H. Rubin, *Tort Reform by Contract* (Washington, D.C.: AEI Press, 1993); Alan Schwartz, "Proposals for Products Liability Reform: A Theoretical Synthesis," 97 *Yale L.J.* 353 (1988); Alan Schwartz, "The Case against Strict Liability," 60 *Fordham L. Rev.* 819 (1992); W. Kip Viscusi, *Reforming Products Liability* (Cambridge: Harvard University Press, 1991), 75–77.

72. *See, e.g.,* American Law Institute, *Enterprise Responsibility for Personal Injury: The Institutional Framework* (Philadelphia: American Law Institute, 1991), vol. 1, 203–232.

73. *See* William M. Landes and Richard A. Posner, *The Economic Structure of Tort Law* (Cambridge: Harvard University Press, 1987), 280.

74. K.K. Tokiwa shōji v. Yamamoto, 1196 Hanrei jihō 132 (Osaka D. Ct. Feb. 14, 1986) (indemnity action where accident victim had already been compensated).

75. Kigura v. Kasaoka, 928 Hanrei jihō 87 (Kyoto D. Ct. Dec. 19, 1978). Other *fugu* cases include Shimizu v. Kuni, 969 Hanrei jihō 55 (Osaka High Ct. Mar. 14, 1980), and Adachi v. Shōga, 704 Hanrei jihō 80 (Kobe D. Ct. Dec. 21, 1972). On the criminal liability of the chef, see subsection 7.I.A.1.

76. Seizōbutsu sekinin hō [Products Liability Act], Law No. 85 of 1994, effective July 1, 1995. For a "tentative" official translation, see Tsūshō sangyō shō, ed., *Seizō butsu sekinin hō no kaisetsu* [Explanation of the Products Liability Act] (Tokyo: Chūshō sangyō chōsa kai, 1994), 184–188 [hereinafter *1994 MITI Explanation*].

77. *See 1994 MITI Explanation, supra* note 76, at 76 (official commentary).

78. Products Liability Act, §2(b); Keizai kikaku chō, ed., *Chikujō kaisetsu Seizōbutsu sekinin hō* [The Annotated Products Liability Act] (Tokyo: Shōji hōmu kenkyū kai, 1994), 65–66, 69 [hereinafter *1994 EPA Annotation*].

79. Keizai kikakuchō, ed., *Seizō butsu sekinin to baishō rikō kakuho* [Products Liability and the Assurance of Compensation] (Tokyo: Ōkura shō, 1988), 56.

80. The limitation to defectively *manufactured* goods (as opposed to claims over warning or design defects) is only our inference. Because the council's deliberations are not public, we do not know how broadly it interprets the concept of *defect*.

81. Manabu Hayashida, *PL hō shinjidai* [The New Products Liability Act Age] (Tokyo: Chūō kōron sha, 1995), 133.

82. *1994 MITI Explanation, supra* note 76, at Supp. 29, 38; *1994 EPA Annotation, supra* note 77, at 275; Keizai kikakuchō, ed., *Seizōbutsu sekinin seido wo chūshin to shita sōgōteki na shōhisha higai bōshi kyūzai no arikata ni tsute* [Regarding the Proper Comprehensive Measures for the Prevention of and Compensation for Consumer Harms, Centered around a Products Liability System] (Tokyo: Ōkura shō, 1993), 91 [hereinafter *1993 EPA Report*].

83. *1993 EPA Report, supra* note 82, at 13–14, 208; Hayashida, *supra* note 80, at 134; Toshitsugu Matsumoto, ed., *Hayawakari—PL no subete* [Easy to Understand: All about Products Liability] (Tokyo: Nikkan kōgyō shinbunsha, 1992), 111. Like the SG regime, these systems combined safety standards, testing, insurance, and strict liability.

84. *1993 EPA Report, supra* note 82, at 208.

85. *See* W. Kip Viscusi, "The Dimensions of the Product Liability Crisis," 20 *J. Legal Stud.* 147, 151 (1991).

86. *Id.* at 155–157; General Accounting Office, *Product Liability: Extent of "Litigation Explosion" in Federal Courts Questioned* (Washington, D.C.: General Accounting Office, 1988), 23.

87. *See generally* Richard A. Epstein, *Simple Rules for a Complex World* (Cambridge: Harvard University Press, 1995), ch. 12.

88. *1994 MITI Explanation, supra* note 76, at Supp. 28; *1994 EPA Annotation, supra* note 77, at 273–274.

89. *1993 EPA Report, supra* note 81, at 154.

90. *1994 MITI Explanation, supra* note 76, at Supp. 189.

91. Hayashida, *supra* note 81, at 112.

92. On the informational content of warranties, see Howard Beales, Richard Craswell, and Steven C. Salop, "The Efficient Regulation of Consumer Information," 24 *J.L. & Econ.* 491, 509–513 (1981); Alan Schwartz and Louis W. Wilde, "Imperfect Information in Markets for Contract Terms: The Examples of Warranties and Security Interests," 69 *Va. L. Rev.* 1387 (1983).

Furthermore, one suspects (the SG system itself provides no data on point) that the SG firms (like the more reputable American firms) handle the most serious product defects outside of the official claim procedures through straightforward product recalls.

Chapter 5

1. Shōhō [Commercial Code], Law No. 48 of 1899.

2. Kōno v. K.K. Chūō sōgo ginkō, 1279 Hanrei jihō 149 (Nagoya D. Ct. Feb. 25, 1988).

3. *See* Roberta Romano, *The Genius of American Corporate Law* (Washington, D.C.: AEI Press, 1993).

4. *See* Ralph K. Winter, Jr., "State Law, Shareholder Protection, and the Theory of the Corporation," 6 *J. Legal Stud.* 251 (1977); Frank H. Easterbrook, "Antitrust and the Economics of Federalism," 26 *J.L. & Econ.* 23 (1983).

5. William J. Carney nicely discusses the problem in the context of the European Union in "The Political Economy of Competition for Corporate Charters," 26 *J. Legal Stud.* 303 (1997).

6. There are also separate (and less complicated) provisions for partnership arrangements in the Civil Code, §§667 et seq.

7. *See generally* Yūgen gaisha hō [Close Corporation Act], Law No. 74 of 1938; Dennis S. Karjala, "The Closely Held Enterprise under Japanese Law," 7 *B.U. Int'l L.J.* 229 (1989).

8. As of 1986, about 54 percent of all business entities were standard corporations, 43 percent were close corporations, 0.4 percent were general partnerships, and 2 percent were limited partnerships. Nearly all firms with stated capital of more than ¥1 billion were public corporations; of firms with stated capital of less than ¥5 million, only about 40 percent were standard corporations, and 55 percent were close corporations. *See* Yukio Yanagida et al., eds., *Law and Investment in Japan* (Cambridge: East Asian Legal Studies and Harvard University Press, 1994), 273.

9. *See* Thomas L. Blakemore and Makoto Yazawa, "Japanese Commercial Code Revisions Concerning Corporations," 2 *Am. J. Comp. L.* 12, 14–15 (1953).

10. Derivative suits were once uncommon in Japan, for reasons nicely outlined in Mark D. West, "The Pricing of Shareholder Derivative Actions in Japan and the United States," 88 *Nw. U. L. Rev.* 1436 (1994). Because of recent changes reducing the filing fees that apply to such suits, they have become increasingly common. *See* Curtis J. Milhaupt, "A Relational Theory of Japanese Corporate Governance: Contract, Culture, and the Rule of Law," 37 *Harv. Int'l L.J.* 3, 55–57 (1996); Tsūshō sangyō shō, ed., *Kabunushi daihyō soshō no genjō to kadai* [The Present Status of and Issues Raised by Shareholder Derivative Suits] (Tokyo: Shōji hōmu kenkyū kai, 1995).

11. Shōken torihiki hō [Securities Exchange Act], Law No. 25 of 1948, §50, prior to amendment by Law No. 96 of 1991.

12. Ikenaka v. Tabuchi, 1469 Hanrei jihō 25, 30 (Tokyo D. Ct. Sept. 16, 1993). For nice backgrounds to the Nomura dispute, see Curtis J. Milhaupt, "Managing the Market: The Ministry of Finance and Securities Regulation in Japan," 30 *Stan. J. Int'l L.* 423, 460–465 (1994); Milhaupt, *supra* note 10, at 32–34.

13. Under an amendment made since that time, the act does now ban such payments. *See* Securities Exchange Act, §§50-3(a)(iii), 199.

14. Mark Schilling, *The Encyclopedia of Japanese Popular Culture* (New York: Weatherhill, 1997), 264.

15. Daiwa kōgyō, K.K. v. Tezuka, 1005 Hanrei jihō 161, 165 (Tokyo D. Ct. Sept. 30, 1980) (creditor action under Commercial Code §266-3); *see generally* Frederik L. Schodt, *Manga! Manga! The World of Japanese Comics* (Tokyo: Kodansha International, 1983); Schilling, *supra* note 14, at 266–267.

16. In fact, the Nomura compensation scheme did constitute an unfair trade practice under Japanese antitrust law—though the court did not consider the violation grounds for damages. *See* Ikenaka v. Tabuchi, 1469 Hanrei jihō at 31.

17. Matsumaru v. Ōtsuru, 1518 Hanrei jihō 4 (Tokyo D. Ct. Dec. 22, 1994).

18. Mutō v. Izuo kōzai, K.K., 578 Hanrei jihō 3, 4 (Sup. Ct. Nov. 26, 1969)

(citations omitted). The duty of loyalty appears in Commercial Code §254-3, and the duty of care in Commercial Code §254(c) and Civil Code §644. Given the elaborate case law on director fiduciary duties, it seems unlikely that Japanese fiduciary duty rules are significantly more ambiguous than the American counterparts (not known for their clarity). For the argument that fiduciary duty rules are indeed more ambiguous in Japan, however, see West, *supra* note 10, at 1478–1482.

19. Okada v. K.K. Mitsukoshi, 1350 Hanrei jihō 138 (Tokyo D. Ct. Apr. 20, 1990); Kuni v. Okada, 1263 Hanrei jihō 56 (Tokyo D. Ct. June 29, 1987); *see generally* James C. Abegglen and George Stalk, Jr., *Kaisha: The Japanese Corporation* (New York: Basic Books, 1985), 185–186.

20. Takada v. Nihon setsubi, K.K., 835 Kin'yū shōji hanrei 23 (Tokyo High Ct. Oct. 26, 1989).

21. Tsunajima v. Fujimoto, 1079 Hanrei jihō 99 (Nagoya D. Ct. Feb. 18, 1983).

As part of a director's duty of loyalty, the Japanese Commercial Code also includes rules analogous to the American corporate opportunity doctrine. Indeed, in some ways the Japanese rules cut more broadly than their American counterparts. Should a director of firm X wish to take part (in any way) in a firm in the same line of business as X, for example, he or she must disclose his or her plans to the X board in advance and obtain its consent. Should he or she fail to do so, the company may claim his or her profits from it (Commercial Code, §264).

22. Ōkura v. Meisei kōgyō, K.K., 583 Hanrei jihō 76 (Osaka D. Ct. July 24, 1969). In part the case raised the issue of whether the cutting of the check was itself a transaction covered by Commercial Code §265 (as some opinions indicated) or whether it was merely the means of implementing transactions (and not itself subject to section 265), as this court held.

23. *See generally* Shen-Shen Lu, "Japanese Regulation of Insider Trading," 24 *Rev. Sec. & Commodities Reg.* 133 (1991); Tomoko Akashi, "Note: Regulation of Insider Trading in Japan," 89 *Colum. L. Rev.* 1296 (1989).

24. Securities Exchange Act, §157 (formerly §58). There is some limited authority for the proposition that an insider may be liable in tort for his dealings with a shareholder when he fails to disclose material information (and certainly when he actively misrepresents material information). *See* Kōno v. Otsuyama, 1452 Hanrei jihō 54 (Tokyo D. Ct. Mar. 12, 1992).

25. *See* Louis Loss and Joel Seligman, *Securities Regulation* (Boston: Little, Brown, 1991), vol. 7, 3487.

26. Securities Exchange Act, §166 (formerly §190-2).

27. *E.g.,* [No names given], 1438 Hanrei jihō 151 (Tokyo D. Ct. Sept. 25, 1992).

28. Securities Exchange Act, §164 (formerly §189).

29. Securities Exchange Act, §163, (formerly §188); *see, e.g.,* Ōmikenshi, K.K. v. Kōno, K.K., 1444 Hanrei jihō 139 (Tokyo D. Ct. Oct. 1, 1992); K.K. Bando hoteru v. Yōmeishu seizō, K.K., 1428 Hanrei jihō 141 (Tokyo High Ct. May 27, 1992); Y.G. Sanwa entaapuraizu v. Ōkura daijin, 764 Hanrei taimuzu 150 (Tokyo D. Ct. Nov. 2, 1990); Nikkō, K.K. v. Y.G. Sanwa entaapuraizu, 857 Kin'yū shōji hanrei 24 (Kobe D. Ct. July 27, 1990).

30. K.K. Bando hoteru v. Yōmeishu seizō, K.K., 1428 Hanrei jihō 141 (Tokyo High Ct. May 27, 1992).

31. Arita v. Kojima, 596 Hanrei jihō 3, 4–5 (Sup. Ct. June 24, 1970).

32. Kitahara v. Ōhashi, 909 Hanrei jihō 95, 99 (Tokyo D. Ct. Mar. 2, 1978) (Commercial Code §266-3 case).

33. *E.g.,* Tanaka v. Okada, 498 Hanrei jihō 64 (Osaka D. Ct. Apr. 20, 1967) (sales at losses allowed; "long-term decisions often entail temporary losses," and directors "must be given scope for considerable risk"); *see* Milhaupt, *supra* note 10, at 33 n.156.

34. Azuma kōzai, K.K. v. Eda, 771 Hanrei jihō 77 (Tokyo High Ct. Jan. 29, 1975).

35. Masuzawa v. Kuni, 205 Hanrei taimuzu 152 (Tokyo High Ct. Nov. 15, 1966), *aff'd,* 590 Hanrei jihō 75 (Sup. Ct. Mar. 26, 1970).

36. K.K. Yamayoshi shōkai v. Kishi, 551 Hanrei jihō 80, 81 (Sup. Ct. Feb. 27, 1969).

37. *E.g.,* Shigatame, K.K. v. Marushō sangyō, K.K., 663 Hanrei jihō 88 (Sup. Ct. Mar. 9, 1972) (shareholder and director meetings missed).

38. [No name given] v. Kawagishi kōgyō, K.K., 588 Hanrei jihō 38 (Sendai D. Ct. Mar. 26, 1970).

39. Jennifer Robertson, "mon Japon: The Revue Theater as a Technology of Japanese Imperialism," 22 *Am. Ethnologist* 970, 972 (1995).

40. Gotō v. Tsuchida, 598 Hanrei jihō 77 (Osaka D. Ct. May 14, 1969).

41. [Name deleted] shōji Y.G. v. Otsuyama, 694 Hanrei jihō 109 (Ōmura Summary Ct. Sept. 25, 1972).

42. *See generally* Robert W. Dziubla, "Enforcing Corporate Responsibility: Japanese Corporate Directors' Liability to Third Parties for Failure to Supervise," 18 *Law in Japan* 55 (1986).

43. Satō v. Kureyama, 757 Hanrei jihō 113 (Osaka High Ct. Apr. 17, 1974).

44. Mutō v. Izuo kōzai, K.K., 578 Hanrei jihō 3, 4 (Sup. Ct. Nov. 26, 1969). The lower court allowed an offset for the plaintiff's comparative negligence. *See* 348 Hanrei jihō 33 (Osaka D. Ct. Jan. 25, 1963), *aff'd,* 385 Hanrei jihō 64 (Osaka High Ct. July 16, 1964).

45. Commercial Code, §204. This rule applies to K.K.s but not to Y.G.s. Courts do, however, enforce transfer restrictions in the charter. *See* Takagi v. Sumitomo shōji, K.K., 710 Hanrei jihō 97 (Sup. Ct. June 15, 1973) (though transfer still valid as between transacting parties).

46. Furukawa v. Teikoku sankin kōgyō, K.K., 272 Hanrei jihō 30 (Tokyo Summary Ct. Aug. 25, 1961), *aff'd,* 301 Hanrei jihō 30, 31 (Tokyo D. Ct. May 31, 1962).

47. Teikoku sankin kōgyō, K.K. v. Furukawa, 301 Hanrei jihō at 31.

48. On why culture-based explanations do not work in this context, see J. Mark Ramseyer, "Takeovers in Japan: Opportunism, Ideology and Corporate Control," 35 *UCLA L. Rev.* 1 (1987).

49. On mergers in Japan, see *id.* at 31–32. On the importance of two-tiered bids, see Daniel R. Fischel, "Efficient Capital Market Theory, the Market for Corporate Control, and the Regulation of Cash Tender Offers," 57 *Tex. L. Rev.* 1 (1978).

50. Securities Exchange Act, §27-3; Shōken torihiki hō shikō rei [Securities Exchange Act Enforcement Order], Seirei No. 321 of 1965, §8(a).

51. *See* Paul Sheard, "Interlocking Shareholdings and Corporate Governance," in *The Japanese Firm: The Sources of Competitive Strength,* ed. Masahiko Aoki and Ronald Dore (Oxford: Oxford University Press, 1994), 310.

52. Kōsei torihiki iinkai, ed., *Kōsei torihiki iinkai nenji hōkoku* [Fair Trade Commission Annual Report] (Tokyo: Kōsei torihiki iinkai, 1994), 181 (1,917 mergers and 1,153 asset sales in 1994).

53. *See* Karjala, *supra* note 7, at 242.

54. West, *supra* note 10, at 1451.

55. *See generally* Gresser et al., *supra* note 20; David E. Kaplan and Alec Dubro, *Yakuza* (Reading, Pa.: Addison-Wesley, 1986), 174–177; Frank K. Upham, *Law and Social Change in Postwar Japan* (Cambridge: Harvard University Press, 1987), ch. 2.

56. Norie Huddle and Michael Reich, *Island of Dreams: Environmental Crisis in Japan* (Tokyo: Autumn Press, 1975), 106–107.

57. For translations of some of the opinions, see Gresser et al., chapter 4, *supra* note 20.

58. For a discussion of the legislation, see Gresser et al., chapter 4, *supra* note 20, at ch. 6.

59. Kuni v. Yoshioka, 931 Hanrei jihō 6 (Kumamoto D. Ct. Mar. 22, 1979) (two-year suspended sentence), *aff'd,* 1059 Hanrei jihō 17 (Fukuoka High Ct. Sept. 6, 1982), *aff'd,* 1266 Hanrei jihō 3 (Sup. Ct. Feb. 29, 1988).

60. Gotō v. Chisso, K.K., 736 Hanrei jihō 20 (Osaka D. Ct. Mar. 28, 1974), *aff'd,* 945 Hanrei jihō 23 (Osaka High Ct. Sept. 27, 1979), *aff'd,* 1082 Hanrei jihō 9 (Sup. Ct. June 7, 1983). Partial translations appear in Yanagida et al., *supra* note 8, at 499–504.

61. Kuni v. Hobo, 424 Hanrei jihō 19 (Tokyo D. Ct. Aug. 27, 1965), *rev'd,* 501 Hanrei jihō 34 (Tokyo High Ct. Oct. 17, 1967), *aff'd,* 572 Hanrei jihō 3, 4 (Sup. Ct. Oct. 22, 1969). For a partial translation, see Yanagida et al., *supra* note 8, at 498–499.

62. *E.g.,* Kuni v. Yamaguchi, 1103 Shōji hōmu 43 (Nagoya D. Ct. Jan. 28, 1987); Kuni v. [No name given], 553 Hanrei taimuzu 268 (Osaka D. Ct. Feb. 12, 1985). *See* Christopher Lee Heftel, "Survey, Corporate Governance in Japan: The Position of Shareholders in Publicly Held Corporations," 5 *U. Haw. L. Rev.* 135 (1983).

63. "Kabunushi sōkai hakusho" [Shareholder Meeting White Paper], 1408 *Shōji hōmu* 1, 49, 128 (1995). Eighty-seven percent also reported that no share-holders had asked anything at the general meeting—which itself proves nothing, of course: it could show that *sōkaiya* are relatively rare, or that firms massively pay them off, or something in between.

64. Hideaki Kubori, "Bōryokudan sanka de sōkaiya no yakuwari buntan susumu" [The Functional Division of Labor of the *Sōkaiya* Proceeds under the Jurisdiction of the Mob], *Nikkei Business,* May 27, 1996, at 87.

65. The following discussion is based on empirical work by Steven Kaplan and is adapted from Steven N. Kaplan and J. Mark Ramseyer, "Those Japanese Firms with their Disdain for Shareholders: Another Myth for the Academy," 74 *Wash. U. L.Q.* 403 (1996).

66. Michael E. Porter, "Capital Disadvantage: America's Failing Capital Invest-ment System," *Harv. Bus. Rev.,* Sept.–Oct. 1992, at 65, 70–72.

67. Rodney Clark, *The Japanese Company* (New Haven, Conn.: Yale University Press, 1979), 136–137 (emphasis omitted).

68. James C. Abegglen and George Stalk, Jr., *Kaisha: The Japanese Corporation* (New York: Basic Books, 1985), 188; *see* Clark, *supra* note 67, at 103–104.

69. Ronald Dore, *Taking Japan Seriously: A Confucian Perspective on Leading Economic Issues* (Stanford, Calif.: Stanford University Press, 1987), 117.

70. One study was coauthored by Bernadette Minton. *See* Steven N. Kaplan, "Top Executive Rewards and Firm Performance: A Comparison of Japan and the United States," 102 *J. Pol. Econ.* 510 (1994); Steven N. Kaplan and Bernadette A. Minton, "Appointments of Outsiders to Japanese Boards: Determinants and Im-plications for Managers," 36 *J. Finan. Econ.* 225 (1994); Steven N. Kaplan, "Top

Executives, Turnover, and Firm Performance in Germany," 10 *J.L. Econ. & Org.* 142 (1994).

The Japanese companies involved are the 119 publicly held Japanese companies that *Fortune* listed among the 500 largest foreign industrials in 1980. For these firms, Kaplan collected financial, employment, stock price, shareholding, executive, and board data for 1980–1988. As a comparison, we occasionally report below comparable figures from the United States. Those data, too, refer to firms from the 1980 *Fortune* listings.

Kaplan's findings on the importance of stock market performance have been replicated by Jun-Koo Kang and Anil Shivdasani, "Firm Performance, Corporate Governance, and Top Executive Turnover in Japan," 38 *J. Finan. Econ.* 29 (1995); Yukiko Abe, "Chief Executive Turnover and Firm Performance in Japan," 11 *J. Japanese & Int'l Econ.* 2 (1997).

71. Directors with prior appointment in government are excluded on grounds that these "*amakudari* posts" signify very different events. *See generally* J. Mark Ramseyer and Frances McCall Rosenbluth, *Japan's Political Marketplace* (Cambridge: Harvard University Press, 1993), ch. 6.

72. The measure takes the value of 0 if pretax income is positive and 1 if negative. As such, it allows one to test theories suggesting that Japanese firms encounter external monitoring if, but only if, they start to lose money.

Chapter 6

1. Yasaburō Shitanaka, ed., *Nihon shiryō shūsei* [Japanese Historical Materials] (Tokyo: Heibon sha, 1956), 194.

2. "Blowing Smoke," *U.S. News & World Rep.*, Apr. 7, 1997, at 15.

3. Both characteristics are ones Japan largely holds in common with Western European civil law countries, and its procedure predictably tracks much of the procedure there. Much of the inspiration for the discussion below comes from John Langbein, "The German Advantage in Civil Procedure," 52 *U. Chi. L. Rev.* 823 (1985).

Technically Japan has a statute providing for criminal juries, Baishin hō [The Jury Act], Law No. 50 of 1923, but its application remains suspended by Law No. 88 of 1943.

4. Saibansho hō [Courts Act], Law 59 of 1947, §33(a).

5. *E.g.,* Kōshoku senkyo hō [Public Offices Elections Act], Law No. 100 of 1950, §§203-211.

6. *E.g.,* Shiteki dokusen no kinshi oyobi kōsei torihiki no kakuho ni kansuru hōritsu [Act Concerning the Prohibition of Private Monopolization and the Maintenance of Fair Trade], Law No. 54 of 1947, §§85, 86.

7. Obviously issues of personal jurisdiction remain in international suits. The references in the text are to Pennoyer v. Neff, 95 U.S. 714 (1877); International Shoe Co. v. Washington, 326 U.S. 310 (1945); and Shaffer v. Heitner, 433 U.S. 186 (1977).

8. Shin minji soshō hō [New Code of Civil Procedure], Law No. 109 of 1996.

9. Konno v. K.K. Yomiuri shimbun sha, 7 Kakyū minshū 200 (Kōfu D. Ct. Feb. 2, 1956).

10. Koide v. Chin, 1261 Hanrei jihō 48 (Tokyo D. Ct. Oct. 23, 1987).

11. For jurisdiction in international disputes, see, e.g., Malaysian Airlines v. Gotō, 1020 Hanrei jihō 9 (Sup. Ct. Oct. 16, 1981); Koide v. Chin, 1261 Hanrei jihō 48 (Tokyo D. Ct. Oct. 23, 1987).

12. The Code of Civil Procedure (§108) provides for consular service of process on foreign defendants; section 110(c) allows service by publication on foreign defendants when section 108 service is not possible.

13. Oka kensetsu kōgyō, K.K. v. Newland, 262 Hanrei jihō 19 (Sup. Ct. May 26, 1961). The extension of time was authorized by the Code of Civil Procedure, §159 (§97 in the current version of the Code). *See also, e.g.,* Kōno v. Otsuyama, 1052 Hanrei jihō 66 (Sup. Ct. May 27, 1982) (improper use of service by process is not grounds for retrial petition—but is, by implication, grounds for appeal).

14. Yasutomi v. United Netherlands Navigation Co., 199 Hanrei taimuzu 181 (Yokohama D. Ct. Sept. 29, 1966). On jurisdiction in admiralty cases in the United States, see Charles Alan Wright, Arthur R. Miller and Edward H. Cooper, *Federal Practice and Procedure* (St. Paul: West, 1985 & Supp.), vol. 14, §3672.

15. Erie Railroad v. Tompkins, 304 U.S. 64 (1938).

16. For analogous points in the German context, see Langbein, *supra* note 3.

17. Japanese courts do this despite the Minji soshō kisoku [Rules of Civil Procedure], Sup. Ct. Kisoku No. 2 of 1956, Rule 27; Minji soshō kisoku [Rules of Civil Procedure], Sup. Ct. Kisoku No. 5 of 1996, Rule 100; and CCvP, §182, requiring them to hold hearings on a continuous basis as much as possible. Note that even U.S. jury trials are sometimes held in discontinuous hearings.

18. Something explicitly allowed by section 89 of the Code of Civil Procedure.

19. The figure includes all *hanketsu* other than those in default judgments. *See* Saikō saiban sho, ed., *Shihō tōkei nempō, 1994* [Annual Report of Judicial Statistics, 1994] (Tokyo: Hōsō kai, 1995), vol. 1, 118, 160.

20. Japanese courts control litigation more closely than U.S. courts in a variety of other ways. Hostility toward "abusive litigation," for example, is an important part of judicial philosophy in Japan and appears in a wide variety of contexts. *See, e.g.,* Uragami v. Tanaka, 14 Saihan minshū 525 (Sup. Ct. Mar. 22, 1960); Hashiguchi v. Nishikado barubu seizō, K.K., 702 Hanrei jihō 72 (Osaka High Ct. Mar. 20, 1973).

21. This was the prewar rule, which the courts in the immediate postwar years had (temporarily, it seems) abandoned. *See, e.g.,* Okuda v. Hokkaidō denki, K.K., 6 Saihan minshū 1062 (Sup. Ct. Nov. 27, 1952); *see generally* Kohji Tanabe, "The Process of Litigation: An Experiment with the Adversary System," in *Law in Japan: The Legal Order in a Changing Society,* ed. Arthur Taylor von Mehren (Cambridge: Harvard University Press, 1963), 73.

22. Suga v. Kuni, 564 Hanrei jihō 49, 51 (Sup. Ct. June 23, 1969). The cases are legion. Those with similar statements include Hirata v. Katō, 979 Hanrei jihō 52 (Sup. Ct. July 15, 1980); Nihon keirō jūtaku, K.K. v. Shirogane kōgyō, K.K., 1228 Hanrei jihō 80 (Sup. Ct. Feb. 12, 1987).

23. *See* Matsumoto v. Tamadan, 569 Hanrei jihō 48 (Sup. Ct. June 24, 1969).

24. *See* Aoki v. Tsu shi, 983 Hanrei jihō 73 (Sup. Ct. Oct. 23, 1980).

25. *See, e.g.,* Restatement (Second) of Judgments §24.

26. Shiga sōko tochi, K.K. v. Maekawa, 16 Saihan minshū 1720 (Sup. Ct. Aug. 10, 1962). On the application of claim preclusion in the United States to such a dispute, see Bagley v. Hughes A. Bagley, Inc., 465 N.W.2d 551 (Iowa Ct. App. 1990); Donahue v. American Farmers Mutual Casualty Co., 380 N.W.2d 437 (Iowa Ct. App. 1986); Restatement (Second) of Judgments §24 cmt. g, illus. 13.

27. Many U.S. trials are bench trials—but the basic structure of American civil procedure (since the merger of law and equity) has remained one keyed to the demands of jury trials.

28. CCvP, §296; that is, on appeal from a district court trial to the high court or from a summary court trial to the district court. This initial appeal is known as the *kōso* appeal. The second appeal (the appeal from the appellate proceeding) is known as the *jōkoku* appeal. Appeals from rulings other than judgments are known as *kōkoku* appeals and are governed by a separate, but analogous, set of rules (CCvP, §§328 et seq.).

Parties may waive the initial review of fact and appeal immediately to the court two tiers above on the legal questions. CCvP, §311(b).

29. CCvP, §297; *see* Miyazawa v. Aomori ken chiji, 13 Saihan minshū 504 (Sup. Ct. Apr. 9, 1959).

30. *See* Yamamoto v. K.K. Nihon sōgo ginkō, 50 Hanrei jihō 12 (Sup. Ct. Apr. 5, 1955).

31. CCvP, §312; or on appeal to the high court of a case that began in summary court. The line between law and fact is not clear, of course, as the Supreme Court's handling of factual issues sometimes shows. *See, e.g.,* Jinbo v. Nakata, 3 Saihan minshū 383 (Sup. Ct. Sept. 6, 1949).

32. *See* Kōno v. Kōno, 1075 Hanrei jihō 113 (Sup. Ct. Mar. 10, 1983); Tominaga v. Fukoku seimei hoken sōgo kaisha, 134 Hanrei jihō 21 (Sup. Ct. Dec. 13, 1957).

33. *See* Amigake v. Ishikawa, 955 Hanrei jihō 57 (Sup. Ct. Dec. 20, 1979).

34. The law is concentrated in sections 179 to 242 of the Code of Civil Procedure and sections 317 to 328 of the Keiji soshō hō [Code of Criminal Procedure], Law No. 131 of 1948.

35. CCvP, §152; *see* Katō v. Hashimoto, 23 Daihan minroku 1357 (Sup. Ct. Sept. 20, 1917).

36. Magawa v. Magawa, 651 Hanrei jihō 72 (Sup. Ct. Oct. 7, 1971). *But see* Orita v. Yamao, 496 Hanrei jihō 34 (Sup. Ct. Aug. 25, 1967) (eviction suit can proceed without all co-owners).

37. Takamiya v. Kuraishi mura, 468 Hanrei jihō 39 (Sup. Ct. Nov. 25, 1966); *accord* Satō v. Odawara, 667 Hanrei jihō 27 (Sup. Ct. Dec. 9, 1971) (boundary suit cannot proceed without all co-owners); Kōno v. Otsuyama, 1313 Hanrei jihō 129 (Sup. Ct. Mar. 28, 1989) (joint inheritance suit cannot proceed without all co-claimants).

38. Itō v. Kyūshū denryoku, K.K., 1181 Hanrei jihō 77 (Sup. Ct. Dec. 20, 1985).

39. CCvP, §146. Courts sometimes interpret this requirement broadly. In an action asserting forgery in the creation of a note, for example, a counterclaim for the amount remaining due on the note was held to be insufficiently related. Saitō v. Yoshida, 9-13 Tokyo kōsai minshū 258 (Tokyo High Ct. Dec. 26, 1958).

40. *See* Uchida v. Shimada, 519 Hanrei jihō 54 (Tokyo High Ct. Mar. 30, 1968).

41. Kurosawa v. Nara, 653 Hanrei jihō 104 (Maebashi D. Ct. May 28, 1971).

42. John Owen Haley, *Authority without Power: Law and the Japanese Paradox,* rev. paperback ed. (New York: Oxford University Press, 1995), 118. Haley first made the claim in "Sheathing the Sword of Justice in Japan: An Essay on Law without Sanctions," 8 *J. Japanese Stud.* 265 (1982), and then expanded it in *Authority without Power.* As the title to the book implies, the judicial incapacity claim is central to Haley's argument about the role of courts and law in Japan.

43. Haley, *Authority, supra* note 42, at 159.

44. Minji shikkō hō [Civil Enforcement Act], Law No. 4 of 1979, §§43–167.

45. *Id.* §172.

46. Iijima v. Daia kensetsu, K.K., 1397 Hanrei jihō 24 (Tokyo High Ct. May 29, 1991) (annexing the two earlier court opinions detailing these separate remedies).

47. Katō v. Heikawa, 1416 Hanrei jihō 120 (Osaka D. Ct. Dec. 27, 1991). For a detailed examination of the use of Civil Enforcement Act, §172, in injunctive suits against the mob, see Bengoshi jitsumu kenkyū kai, *Minbō monogatari* [Tales of the Mob] (Tokyo: Ōkurashō insatsu kyoku, 1993), 22–24.

48. Maruyama v. Kushima, 41-12 Kazoku saiban geppō 129 (Asahikawa Family Ct. Sept. 25, 1989).

49. Minji soshō hō [Code of Civil Procedure], Law No. 29 of 1890, §734.

50. Iwata v. Matsuoka, 9 kamin reishū 11 (Kobe D. Ct. Jan. 14, 1958); *accord* Itō v. Aoki, 18 Daihan minroku 1087 (Sup. Ct. Dec. 19, 1912). Considerable debate occurred over when custody disputes were subject to such indirect sanctions and when the court could directly order the transfer of the child as though he or she were moveable property.

51. Chūbu kankō, K.K. v. Shadan hōjin Nihon ongaku chosakuken kyōkai, 224 Hanrei jihō 15 (Nagoya High Ct. Apr. 27, 1960); *accord* Tōkai kankō, K.K. v. Shadan hōjin Nihon ongaku chosakuken kyōkai, 232 Hanrei taimuzu 345 (Osaka High Ct. Mar. 14, 1969).

52. K.K. San'ai v. K.K. San'ai, 381 Hanrei jihō 46 (Tokyo High Ct. May 27, 1964), *aff'd,* 485 Hanrei jihō 42 (Sup. Ct. Apr. 11, 1967).

53. Zen Nittsū shōji rōdō kumiai v. Nittsū shōji, K.K., 667 Hanrei jihō 14 (Tokyo D. Ct. May 9, 1972).

54. Zenkoku jidōsha un'yu rōdō kumiai v. Ashihara un'yu kikō, K.K., 762 Hanrei jihō 107 (Osaka D. Ct. Nov. 14, 1974); *see also* Ashiwara un'yu kikō, K.K. v. Zenkoku jidōsha un'yu rōdō kumiai, 293 Rōdō hanrei 25 (Osaka D. Ct. Mar. 3, 1978), *aff'd,* 949 Hanrei jihō 123 (Osaka High Ct. July 20, 1979).

55. Haley, *Authority, supra* note 42, at 159.

56. CCvP, §193. While a fine under section 192 (a ¥100,000 maximum) can be imposed by the judge on his own, the detention under section 193 must be initiated by criminal proceedings through the prosecutors' office. Detention is governed by the Keihō [Criminal Code], Law No. 45 of 1907, §16.

57. In re Ōharu, 20 Kamin reishū 912 (Akita D. Ct. Dec. 12, 1969) (¥5000 fine). The case was under Hōtei tō no chitsujo iji ni kansuru hōritsu [A Law to Maintain Order in the Courtroom], Law No. 286 of 1952, which does not require the involvement of a prosecutor.

58. Haley, *Authority, supra* note 42, at 118. In fairness to Haley, the context of his contempt discussion clearly concerns contempt powers to enforce civil judgments, not contempt powers to maintain courtroom order. Formally the contempt powers of Japanese judges go to the latter; the flexible per diem penalties to enforce civil judgments, though functionally largely equivalent to contempt, formally derive from the Civil Enforcement Act.

59. Iwai v. Kuni, 29 Shōmu geppō 1046 (Tokyo D. Ct. Nov. 17, 1982), *aff'd,* 1159 Hanrei jihō 98 (Tokyo High Ct. May 17, 1985). Iwai claimed, inter alia, that the person next to him had made the statement.

60. Maruyama v. Kuni, 559 Hanrei taimuzu 139 (Tokyo D. Ct. Mar. 29, 1985).

61. Haley, *Authority, supra* note 42, at 267.

Chapter 7

1. *See, e.g., Mainichi shimbun,* Nov. 29, 1969, Mar. 10, 1970, Apr. 11, 1970, July 13, 1970, Aug. 1, 1970, Aug. 24, 1970, Aug. 25, 1970.

2. A point provocatively challenged by David Friedman, *The Machinery of Freedom*, 2d ed. (La Salle, Ill.: Open Court, 1989), 114–126.

3. Keihō [Criminal Code], Law No. 45 of 1907.

4. Kuni v. Uebayashi, 134 Hanrei jihō 12, 12 (Sup. Ct. Nov. 27, 1957).

5. Kuni v. Ōtani, 17 Saihan keishū 15 (Sup. Ct. Feb. 26, 1963). The courts apparently do not consider this to raise burden-of-proof problems—see subsection B.4. Ryuichi Hirano, "The Accused and Society: Some Aspects of Japanese Criminal Law," in *Law in Japan: The Legal Order in a Changing Society,* ed. Arthur Taylor von Mehren (Cambridge: Harvard University Press, 1963), 274, 284, writes that "[a]bsolute liability has thus been extinguished."

6. Kuni v. [No name given], 621 Hanrei jihō 106 (Fukuoka High Ct. May 16, 1970).

7. Kuni v. Chiba, 900 Hanrei jihō 58 (Sup. Ct. July 28, 1978), *aff'g* 865 Hanrei jihō 104 (Tokyo High Ct. Mar. 8, 1977), *modifying* 789 Hanrei jihō 19 (Tokyo D. Ct. June 5, 1975). Because the attempted murders were in connection with the theft of Tanaka's gun, both were attempted robbery-murder, a crime with a higher penalty than attempted murder (Criminal Code, §§240, 243).

On the treatment of attempt under Japanese criminal law, see Hirano, *supra* note 5, at 276–277.

8. Kuni v. Shōga, 613 Hanrei jihō 101 (Osaka High Ct. June 16, 1970).

9. Kuni v. Kasamoto, 966 Hanrei jihō 131 (Sup. Ct. Apr. 18, 1980).

10. Kuni v. [No name given], 3 Daihan keishū 364 (Sup. Ct. Apr. 25, 1924).

11. Kuni v. [No name given], 4 Daihan keishū 378 (Sup. Ct. June 9, 1925).

12. Kuni v. Nishio, 10 Daihan keishū 682, 686 (Sup. Ct. Dec. 3, 1931).

13. Kuni v. Okamura, 32 Saihan keishū 416 (Kōchi D. Ct. Apr. 24, 1970) (imposing death penalty), *aff'd,* 32 Saihan keishū 419 (Takamatsu High Ct. Apr. 30, 1975), *rev'd,* 889 Hanrei jihō 103 (Sup. Ct. Mar. 24, 1978), *on remand,* 38 Saihan keishū 2790 (Takamatsu High Ct. Nov. 2, 1983) (imposing life imprisonment), *aff'd,* 1128 Hanrei jihō 38 (Sup. Ct. July 3, 1984).

On appeal to the Supreme Court from his initial death sentence, Okamura pointed out that the Japanese government had recently released one of the Mitsubishi Heavy Industry bombers to the Red Army in the hijacking incident (see subsection A.6). If such a deadly killer could be released, argued Okamura, how could the court justly execute someone as psychologically impaired as himself?

14. According to literary critic Edward Seidensticker, "the most celebrated criminal of early Shōwa." Edward Seidensticker, *Tokyo Rising: The City since the Great Earthquake* (New York: Alfred A. Knopf, 1990), 125. For some of the accounts of the crime, see *Yomiuri shimbun,* May 19, 1936, May 20, 1936, May 21, 1936; *Tokyo Asahi shimbun,* June 10, 1936, Oct. 1, 1936, Nov. 3, 1936; *Miyako shimbun,* Dec. 10, 1936. Excerpts from the prosecutor's argument appear in *Hōchi shimbun,* Dec. 9, 1936; excerpts from the court opinion appear in *Tokyo Asahi shimbun,* Dec. 22, 1936. The articles are reprinted in *Shimbun shūsei Shōwa hen nenshi, 1936* [Newspaper Compilation—Annual History, Showa Edition, 1936] (Tokyo: Taishō Shōwa shimbun kenkyū kai, 1969).

15. Kaoru Murano, ed., *Nihon no shikei* [The Death Penalty in Japan] (Tokyo: Takushoku shobō, 1990), 222–224. During the 1890s, the mean was 51 executions per year; during the 1980s, the mean was 1.5.

16. Kuni v. [No name given], 1158 Hanrei jihō 249 (Tokyo High Ct. Nov. 27, 1984).

17. L.R. 14 Q.B. 273 (1884).

18. *Nobi* [Fires on the Plain] (Kon Ichikawa, dir., 1959). *See also, e.g.,* Chōichi Ogiwara, *Dokuro no shōgen* [The Testimony of Skulls] (Tokyo: Fumin kyōkai, 1987) (memoirs of a survivor).

19. Kuni v. [No name given], 1578 Hanrei jihō 39 (Tokyo D. Ct. June 26, 1996).

20. Kuni v. [No name given], 1599 Hanrei jihō 149 (Tokyo D. Ct. Mar. 12, 1996).

21. Keisatsu chō, ed., *Keisatsu hakusho* [Police White Paper] (Tokyo: Ōkura shō, various years). By 1996, the annual number of clashes involving leftist groups had fallen to nine.

22. Kuni v. Arikawa, 863 Hanrei jihō 33 (Sup. Ct. July 21, 1977), *aff'g* 31 Saihan keishū 788 (Fukuoka High Ct. Feb. 9, 1976), *modifying* 31 Saihan keishū 765 (Fukuoka D. Ct. Oct. 15, 1974).

23. Donald Richie, *Geisha, Gangster, Neighbor, Nun* (Tokyo: Kodansha International, 1987), 26–28.

24. Seidensticker, *supra* note 14, at 125–126.

25. Kuni v. [No name given], 874 Hanrei jihō 103 (Tokyo D. Ct. June 8, 1977); *see also* Kuni v. [No name given], 893 Hanrei jihō 104 (Osaka D. Ct. Dec. 26, 1977) (husband convicted where wife asphyxiated during S–M sex games).

26. Yukio Mishima, "Yūgoku" [Patriotism], in *Mishima Yukio zenshū* [The Complete Works of Yukio Mishima] (Tokyo: Shinchō sha, 1973), vol. 13, 244–246.

27. Kuni v. Koga, 668 Hanrei jihō 32 (Tokyo D. Ct. Apr. 27, 1972). The literature on Mishima in Japanese is enormous. This account also draws extensively on Henry Scott-Stokes, *The Life and Death of Yukio Mishima* (New York: Farrar, Straus & Giroux, 1974).

28. On coconspirator liability, see Hirano, *supra* note 5, at 288. On felony murder, note that the penalties courts impose on those who commit felonies resulting in deaths are often as high as those they can impose for murder. *Id.* at 284.

29. Kuni v. Koseki, 3 Saihan keishū 2028 (Sup. Ct. Dec. 17, 1949). The case was easier than this suggests, since Koseki also helped consume the money stolen.

30. Kuni v. Shibata, 923 Hanrei jihō 21 (Sup. Ct. Apr. 13, 1979).

31. Kuni v. Daidōji, 973 Hanrei jihō 24 (Tokyo D. Ct. Nov. 12, 1979), *aff'd,* 1062 Hanrei jihō 30 (Tokyo High Ct. Oct. 29, 1982), *aff'd,* 1228 Hanrei jihō 22 (Sup. Ct. Mar. 24, 1987).

32. Keisatsu chō, ed., *Keisatsu hakusho* [Police White Paper] (Tokyo: Ōkura shō, 1976), 268, 271. By 1996, fringe-left activity had so far subsided that the police no longer published membership estimates. In 1995, six bombs were apparently planted by leftist groups (five by the Central Faction), but the *Police White Paper* reported no injuries.

In 1977, the Bureau of Alcohol, Tobacco, and Firearms counted 1,356 explosive bombings in the United States, 1,037 of which resulted in detonations. It counted another 420 fire bombs, of which 339 were ignited. Bureau of Alcohol, Tobacco, and Firearms, *Explosives Incidents, 1978 Annual Report,* (Washington, D.C.: U.S. Department of the Treasury), 2. The most common known reason for the detonations was a labor dispute. *Id.* at 16. By 1994, the numbers had risen to 2,438 explosive bombings (1,916 detonations) and 725 fire bombs (545 ignited), and vandalism had replaced labor disputes as the most common reason for the bombings. Bureau of Alcohol, Tobacco, and Firearms, *Arson and Explosives Incidents Report* (Washington, D.C.: Bureau of Alcohol, Tobacco, and Firearms, 1994), 13, 20.

33. Kuni v. Daidōji, 973 Hanrei jihō at 28.

34. On prewar common-law marriage, see J. Mark Ramseyer, *Odd Markets in Japanese History: Law and Economic Growth* (New York: Cambridge University Press, 1996), ch. 5.

35. Kuni v. Kanazawa, 23 Daihan keiroku 999 (Sup. Ct. Sept. 10, 1917). The question bore on the punishment, since battery was an independent crime, where attempted murder (as a lesser included offense) would have merged with the later murder by strangulation. Hirano, *supra* note 5, at 279, argues that this case is exceptional even under Japanese law.

36. *See generally* B. J. George, "Rights of the Criminally Accused," in *Japanese Constitutional Law,* ed. Percy R. Luney, Jr., and Kazuyuki Takahashi (Tokyo: Tokyo University Press, 1993), 289.

37. Keiji soshō hō [Code of Criminal Procedure], Law No. 131 of 1948. Warrant arrests are at CCrP, §§199–201; hot-pursuit arrests are at sections 212–219. Police may also question people if they suspect a crime may be in progress. They must, however, ask their questions in such a way that the person can freely refuse to answer. In judging the "voluntariness" of an encounter, courts sometimes give the police broad leeway. Kuni v. Sakai, 896 Hanrei jihō 14 (Sup. Ct. June 20, 1978) (police may search a bag without permission during "voluntary" questioning).

38. The latter provision raises obvious constitutional questions, but the Supreme Court has held it constitutional. Kuni v. Tamoto, 67 Hanrei jihō 7 (Sup. Ct. Dec. 14, 1955). Should the police make a warrantless arrest under this provision, they must immediately file for a warrant after the arrest (CCrP, §210(a)).

39. Kōya Matsuo and Masahito Inoue, eds., *Keiji soshō hanrei hyakusen* [One Hundred Criminal Procedure Cases], 6th ed. (Tokyo: Yūhikaku, 1992), 249.

40. Instead, the suspect can use the illegality only to contest his arrest at his custody hearing (e.g., *In re* [No name given], 972 Hanrei jihō 136 (Tokyo D. Ct. Aug. 13, 1980)), or to sue for damages under the Kokka baishō hō [National Compensation Act], Law No. 125 of 1947 (if he can show negligence or intent) or under the Keiji hoshō hō [Criminal Compensation Act], Law No. 1 of 1950 (if he is found innocent).

41. *See generally* Daniel H. Foote, "Confession and the Right to Silence in Japan," 21 *Ga. J. Int'l & Comp. L.* 415 (1991).

42. *In re* [No name given], 665 Hanrei jihō 103 (Tokyo D. Ct. Apr. 4, 1972).

43. Atsushi Fukui, *Keiji soshō hō* [Criminal Procedure], 2d ed. (Tokyo: Yūhikaku, 1994), 258.

44. *See* Const. art. 34 (right to attorney); CCrP, §§30, 204 (right to be informed of right to attorney); Const. art. 38(a) (right to silence); CCrP, §198(b) (right to be informed of right to silence).

Prosecutorial limits on a suspect's contact with his attorney are immediately contestable in court (CCrP, §430). Suspects do not have a right to state-provided attorneys until prosecution has been initiated (CCrP, §36).

45. *See* Nihon bengoshi rengō kai, ed., *Taiho, kōryū, hoshaku to bengo* [Arrest, Detention, Bail, and Defense] (Tokyo: Nihon hyōron sha, 1996), 45.

46. Kuni v. [No name given], 1301 Hanrei jihō 155 (Sup. Ct. Jan. 23, 1989).

47. Kuni v. Abe, 457 Hanrei jihō 63 (Sup. Ct. July 1, 1966); Kuni v. Matsunaga, 153 Hanrei jihō 9 (Sup. Ct. June 13, 1958).

48. Kuni v. Ishikawa, 864 Hanrei jihō 22 (Sup. Ct. Aug. 9, 1977); Kuni v. Ogura, 352 Hanrei jihō 80 (Sup. Ct. Sept. 13, 1963); Kuni v. Hongō, 10 Hanrei

jihō 15 (Sup. Ct. July 10, 1953); Kuni v. Shirogane, 4 Saihan keishū 2359 (Sup. Ct. Nov. 21, 1950); Kuni v. Yamamoto, 4 Saihan keishū 1751 (Sup. Ct. Sept. 21, 1950).

49. *Quoted in* Mark Schreiber, *Shocking Crimes of Postwar Japan* (Tokyo: Yen-books, 1996), 54.

50. Kuni v. Hirasawa, 9 Saihan keishū 718 (Tokyo D. Ct. July 24, 1950), *aff'd,* 9 Saihan keishū 729 (Tokyo High Ct. Sept. 29, 1951), *aff'd,* 47 Hanrei jihō 3 (Sup. Ct. Apr. 6, 1955). The literature on the case is massive. The account here draws on, inter alia, Schreiber, *supra* note 49, at 44–65; Seidensticker, *supra* note 14, at 209–212; Daniel H. Foote, "'The Door That Never Opens'?: Capital Punishment and Post-Conviction Review of Death Sentences in the United States and Japan," 19 *Brooklyn J. Int'l L.* 367, 415–416 (1993); Kōya Matsuo, "Teigin jiken" [The Imperial Bank Case], 900 *Jurisuto* 38 (1988); Takuji Takada, "Teigin jiken no nokoshita mono" [Issues Left by the Imperial Bank Case], 84 *Hōgaku kyōshitsu* 6 (1987).

On pretextual detention, see Kuni v. [No name given], 1092 Hanrei jihō 127 (Sup. Ct. July 12, 1983); Kuni v. Ishikawa, 864 Hanrei jihō 22 (Sup. Ct. Aug. 9, 1977).

51. On the exclusionary rule, see Kuni v. Kuroki, 1291 Hanrei jihō 156 (Sup. Ct. Sept. 16, 1988); Kuni v. Hashimoto, 901 Hanrei jihō 15 (Sup. Ct. Sept. 7, 1978); Kuni v. Sakai, 896 Hanrei jihō 14 (Sup. Ct. June 20, 1978). On phone taps, see Kuni v. [No name given], 1401 Hanrei jihō 127 (Kōfu D. Ct. Sept. 3, 1991).

52. On civil jury trials, see subsection 6.I.B. On criminal juries, see Baishin hō [Jury Act], Law No. 50 of 1923, suspended by Law No. 88 of 1943.

53. Saikō saibansho jimu sōkyoku, ed., *Shihō tōkei nempō, Heisei 6 nen* [Annual Report of Judicial Statistics, 1994] (Tokyo: Hōsō kai, 1995), vol. 2, tables 33-1, 33-3, 33-4. For an ordinary criminal case in district court with three hearings, as of 1996 the government paid the lawyer ¥77,200. Yōichirō Hamabe, *Bengoshi to iu hitobito* [People Called Lawyers] (Tokyo: Sanseidō, 1996), 27.

54. Kuni v. Yusa, 2 Saihan keishū 1123 (Sup. Ct. Aug. 5, 1948).

55. Matsuo and Inoue, *supra* note 39, at 253.

56. Kuni v. Daidōji, 973 Hanrei jihō at 58–62.

57. *In re* Murakami, 776 Hanrei jihō 24 (Sup. Ct. May 20, 1975). *See generally* Foote, *supra* note 50; Daniel H. Foote, "From Japan's Death Row to Freedom," 1 *Pac. Rim L. & Pol'y J.* 11 (1992). From 1986 to 1990, Japanese courts granted eighty-three retrials, and all eighty-three resulted in acquittals. Matsuo and Inoue, *supra* note 39, at 255.

As Foote notes, over the past several decades, Japanese courts have overturned the convictions of several death row inmates upon retrial. Foote, *supra* note 50. Like many observers, Foote concludes that this constitutes a "revelation that . . . innocent men spent the bulk of their adult hours on death row following miscarriages of justice. . . ." *Id.* at 509.

In fact, while the death-row inmates *may* have been innocent, their acquittals upon retrial most emphatically do not show it. It does not take a very skillful lawyer to acquit a client—whether guilty or no—in a trial that takes place several decades (in one case, a half-century) after the crime. Witnesses forget, arresting officers die, evidence disappears—but the state retains the very high burden of proof. It would be a skilled prosecutor indeed who could convict *anyone* fifty years after the crime.

58. Administrative Office of the U.S. Courts, *Judicial Business of the U.S. Courts* (Washington, D.C.: Administrative Office of the U.S. Courts, 1995), table D-6 (1995 is Oct. 1994–Sept. 1995).

59. *See* Daniel H. Foote, "The Benevolent Paternalism of Japanese Criminal Justice," 80 *Cal. L. Rev.* 317, 318 (1992); John O. Haley, *Authority without Power: Law and the Japanese Paradox* (New York: Oxford University Press, 1991), 128–129.

60. Kuni v. Takemura, 945 Hanrei jihō 15 (Tokyo D. Ct. Oct. 19, 1979).

61. Saikō, *supra* note 53, at table 45.

62. Kuni v. Takemura, 1043 Hanrei jihō 3 (Tokyo High Ct. June 8, 1982).

63. Japan is not entirely homogeneous, of course, and some observers argue that Japanese crime is disproportionately concentrated among the various minority groups. Although this may distort the figures for majority Japanese, note that the U.S. census data include several ethnic minority groups (most prominently the Hispanic community) within the category of "white." Some observers also contend that several of these groups suffer from higher crime victimization rates than the majority white population. If so, then the murder rates for the majority white population in the United States are also overstated.

64. U.S. Department of Commerce, ed., *Statistical Abstract of the United States* (Washington, D.C.: U.S. Department of Commerce, 1996), table 316. The range in the United States by state was from Louisiana, with a 15.3 rate, to South Dakota, with 0.6. States with murder rates below the Japanese rate were New Hampshire (1.5), Iowa (1.1), Vermont (0.7), and South Dakota (0.6). *See* John M. Lott, Jr., *More Guns, Less Crime* (Chicago: University of Chicago Press, 1998), table 4.

65. For Japanese figures, see Hōmushō, *Hanzai hakusho* [White Paper on Crime] (Tokyo: Ōkura shō, 1996), 122. For U.S. figures, see Administrative Office, *supra* note 58, at table D-4 (murder includes first and second degree; figures cover October 1994 to September 1995).

66. Setsuo Miyazawa, *Policing in Japan,* trans. F. G. Bennett, Jr. (Albany, N.Y.: SUNY Press, 1992), 3.

67. Lawrence W. Beer, "Introduction," in *The Constitutional Case Law of Japan, 1970 through 1990,* ed. Lawrence W. Beer and Hiroshi Itoh (Seattle: University of Washington Press, 1996), 27 (quoting Dan Foote quoting a former Japanese judge).

68. On the formal absence of guilty pleas, see Haley, *supra* note 59, at ch. 6.

69. *See* Toshiyuki Maesaka, ed., *Satsujin hōtei keesubukku* [Casebook on Murder Trials] (Tokyo: Kōsei sha, 1996), 1–4; Keishichō, ed., *Keishichō shi: Meiji hen* [History of the Police Bureau: Meiji Era] (Tokyo: Keishichō, 1959), 521–522; *see generally* Edward Seidensticker, *Low City, High City* (New York: Alfred A. Knopf, 1983), 76. The murder became the basis for one of the earlier novels by Jun'ichirō Tanizaki, "Otsuya goroshi" [The Killing of Otsuya], in *Tanizaki Jun'ichirō zenshū* [The Complete Works of Jun'ichirō Tanizaki] (1915; reprint, Tokyo: Chūō kōron sha, 1966), vol. 2, 501–570.

70. In a similar quarrel over Germany of the 1970s, John Langbein, "Land without Plea Bargaining: How the Germans Do It," 78 *Mich. L. Rev.* 204, 214–215 (1979), argues that there could not be plea bargains there because confessions do not result in lower sentences. Whatever the case in Germany, in Japan there is ample evidence (anecdotal to be sure) that defendants who confess do receive lighter sentences. *See* Hiroshi Wagatsuma and Arthur Rosett, "The Implications of Apology: Law and Culture in Japan and the United States," 20 *Law & Soc'y Rev.* 461

(1986); John O. Haley, "Comment: The Implications of Apology," 20 *Law & Soc'y Rev.* 499 (1986).

71. *See* Saikō, *supra* note 53, at table 31-4 (excluding traffic crimes); Administrative Office, *supra* note 58, at table D-4.

72. Foote, *supra* note 59, at 352.

73. *See generally* Frank H. Easterbrook, "Criminal Procedure as a Market System," 12 *J. Legal Stud.* 289 (1983).

74. Saikō, *supra* note 53, at tables 31-4, 36-3; Administrative Office, *supra* note 58, at table D-4. If we ignore dismissals, defendants were acquitted in 1,095 of the 4,765 trials in the United States—a conviction rate of 77.0 percent.

75. On the United States, see U.S. Department of Commerce, *supra* note 64, at table 333. On Japan, see Yasuo Watanabe, Setsuo Miyazawa, Shigeo Kisa, Shōsaburō Yoshino and Tetsuo Satō, *Tekisuto bukku gendai shihō* [Textbook: The Modern Judiciary] (Tokyo: Nihon hyōron sha, 1992), 101; Hōmushō, *supra* note 65, at 431. The resource shortage in Japan is rightly noted in Haley, *supra* note 59, at ch. 6.

76. We are indebted to conversations with Frank Easterbrook for this point. *See generally* Richard A. Posner, The Problems of Jurisprudence (Cambridge: Harvard University Press, 1990), 216.

77. Hōmushō, *supra* note 65, at 432.

78. Elmer H. Johnson, *Criminalization and Prisoners in Japan: Six Contrary Cohorts* (Carbondale: Southern Illinois University Press, 1997), 17.

79. Hōmushō, *supra* note 65, at 260 (1995 data).

80. A point at which others have hinted—see the comments by a Japanese prosecutor, Toshihiko Tsubouchi, "Kiso bengi shugi no kōzai" [The Merits and Demerits of Prosecutorial Discretion], in *Keiji soshō hō no sōten (shimpan)* [Issues in Criminal Procedure (New Edition)], ed. Kōya Matsuo and Masahito Inoue (Tokyo: Yūhikaku, 1991), 110 (Jurisuto zōkan); *see also* Foote, *supra* note 50, at 508 ("in Japan the prosecutors have long enjoyed a reputation for only indicting suspects when the evidence of guilt is overwhelming").

81. This is not the inevitable result. Obviously prosecutors could choose to take on additional cases only at a rate that lets them—by devoting increasingly large amounts to each case—keep conviction rates nearly constant.

82. On the history of the mob that follows, see generally David E. Kaplan and Alec Dubro, *Yakuza* (Reading, Mass.: Addison-Wesley, 1986), chs. 3, 5.

83. Keisatsu chō, ed., *Keisatsu hakusho* [Police White Paper] (Tokyo: Ōkura shō, 1996), 194, 206.

84. Hisao Katō, *Soshiki hanzai no kenkyū* [A Study of Organized Crime] (Tokyo: Seibundō, 1992), 124.

85. Hōmushō, ed., *Soshikiteki hanzai to keiji hō* [Criminal Law and Organized Crime] (Tokyo: Yūhikaku, 1997), 112–113.

86. Keisatsu chō (1996 ed.), *supra* note 83, at 203–204. Presumably many lower-level members were arrested several times.

87. Hōmushō, ed., *Hanzai hakusho* [Crime White Paper] (Tokyo: Ōkura shō, 1996), 419.

88. These 1981 data presumably exclude death sentence defendants. Keisatsu chō, ed., *Keisatsu hakusho* [Police White Paper] (Tokyo: Ōkura shō, 1982). If we assume that 25–30 percent of all convicted murderers are mob affiliates (see table 7.4), these figures suggest (roughly) that about 44–45 percent of the nonmob convicts must be receiving sentences of over five years.

89. Keisatsu chō (1982 ed.), *supra* note 88, at table II-38.

90. Norikiyo Hayashi, ed., *Soshiki bōryoku no ichi danmen* [One Aspect of Organized Crime] (Tokyo: Tachibana shobō, 1996), 52. Another 12 percent were likely to be imprisoned soon.

91. Walter L. Ames, *Police and Community in Japan* (Berkeley and Los Angeles: University of California Press, 1981), 127.

92. *Detailed in* Kaplan and Dubro, *supra* note 82, at ch. 3.

93. *Quoted in id.* at 85–86.

94. *Mainichi shinbun,* Oct. 9, 1971, at 23.

95. Schreiber, *supra* note 49, at 237–253. The dispute includes the war between the Yamaguchi-gumi and the split-off Ichiwa-kai.

96. Lott, *supra* note 64, at Preface.

97. Ginsaku Kasa, *Hanzai chōsho* [Criminal Records] (Tokyo: Tokyo hōkei gakuin, 1985), 83–84.

98. *Id.* at 88.

99. *Id.* at ch. 7.

100. *See* Kaoru Murano, ed., *Nihon no shikei* [The Death Penalty in Japan] (Tokyo: Shashoku shobō, 1990), 20.

Chapter 8

1. Y.G. Taira Shōji v. Yamagata ken, 661 Hanrei jihō 25 (Yamagata D. Ct. Feb. 29, 1972), *rev'd,* 756 Hanrei jihō 62 (Sendai High Ct. July 8, 1974), *aff'd,* 889 Hanrei jihō 9 (Sup. Ct. May 26, 1978).

2. Mikiso Hane, *Japan: A Historical Survey* (New York: Charles Scribner's Sons, 1972), 565.

3. Kuni v. Sugioka, 5 Saihan keishū 2463 (Sup. Ct. Dec. 5, 1951). *See, e.g.,* Kuni v. Ubukata, 9 Saihan keishū 109 (Sup. Ct. Feb. 1, 1955); Kuni v. Yanagi, 4 Saihan keishū 73 (Sup. Ct. Feb. 1, 1950); Kuni v. Takeda, 38 Kōsai keishū 39 (Tokyo High Ct. Feb. 17, 1953); Kuni v. Yano, 22 Kōsai keishū 201 (Sendai High Ct. Nov. 26, 1952). For a case to the contrary, see Kuni v. Fujii, 5 Kakyū keishū 799 (Kokura Summary Ct. Aug. 27, 1963), *rev'd,* 375 Hanrei jihō 81 (Fukuoka High Ct. Mar. 7, 1964).

4. Kuni v. Murata, 5 Kōsai keishū 2384 (Sendai High Ct. Nov. 29, 1952).

5. Chihō jichii hō [Regional Self-Government Act], Law No. 67 of 1947. *See, e.g.,* Kuni v. Kobayashi, 12 Saihan keishū 3305 (Sup. Ct. Oct. 15, 1958) (Tokyo ordinance); Kuni v. Matsumoto, 303 Hanrei jihō 2 (Sup. Ct. May 30, 1962) (Osaka ordinance). Prostitution was eventually banned by the Baishun bōshi hō [Prostitution Prevention Act], Law No. 118 of 1956. On the prewar sexual services industry, see J. Mark Ramseyer, *Odd Markets in Japanese History: Law and Economic Growth* (Cambridge: Cambridge University Press, 1996), ch. 6.

6. Jūhō tōken rui shoji tō torishimari hō [Act for the Control of the Possession, Etc., of Firearms and Swords, Etc.], Law No. 6 of 1958.

7. Tokyo to kyōiku iinkai v. Tokyo anteiiku aamuzu, K.K., 34 Gyōsai reishū 1819 (Tokyo High Ct. Oct. 27, 1983), *aff'd,* 34 Sōmu geppō 695 (Sup. Ct. Nov. 20, 1987).

8. Nishioka v. Tokyo to kyōiku iinkai, 1384 Hanrei jihō 38 (Sup. Ct. Feb. 1, 1990), *aff'g* 39 Gyōsai reishū 826 (Tokyo High Ct. Aug. 17, 1988), *aff'g* 1228 Hanrei jihō 55 (Tokyo D. Ct. Apr. 20, 1987). The constitutional dimensions of the argument are only implicit in *Nishioka;* they appear more explicitly in Kuni v. [No name given], 477 Hanrei taimuzu 209 (Tokyo High Ct. June 9, 1982) (criminal prosecution for importation of Colt revolver).

9. "Supreme Court Says Foreign Swords Cannot Be Listed under Control Act," *Japan Times*, Feb. 2, 1990, at 3.

10. *See generally* Gunma chūō basu, K.K. v. Un'yu daijin, 779 Hanrei jihō 21 (Sup. Ct. May 29, 1975); Tokyo rikuun kyoku chō v. Kawakami, 647 Hanrei jihō 22 (Sup. Ct. Oct. 28, 1971).

11. *Driver's license:* Dōro kōtsū hō [Road Traffic Act], Law No. 105 of 1960, §§103 to 104-2; *see* Takisawa v. Saitama ken kōan iinkai, 774 Hanrei jihō 48 (Urawa D. Ct. Dec. 11, 1974). *Realtors:* Takuchi tatemono torihikigyō hō [Act Governing the Residential Building Transaction Industry], Law No. 176 of 1952, §69. *Nightclubs:* Fūzoku eigyō tō no kisei oyobi gyōmu no tekiseika tō ni kansuru hōritsu [Act Regarding the Improvement, Etc. of the Rules and Business in the Adult Entertainment Industry], Law No. 122 of 1948, §41. *Gun permits:* Jūhō tōken rui shoji tō torishimari hō [Act for the Control of the Possession, Etc., of Firearms and Swords, Etc.], Law No. 6 of 1958, §12.

12. K.K. Gainakkusu v. Miyazaki kenchiji, 1495 Hanrei jihō 45, 57, 65 (Miyazaki D. Ct. Jan. 24, 1994), *aff'd*, 883 Hanrei taimuzu 119 (Fukuoka High Ct. Miyazaki Branch Off. Mar. 1, 1995).

13. The outline below follows the procedures given in the Gyōsei fufuku shinsa hō [Administrative Complaints Inquiries Act (ACIA)], Law No. 160 of 1962. Some regulatory statutes exempt their procedures from the ACIA (see section 1(b)). For such exemptions, see, e.g., Kokka kōmuin hō [The National Civil Service Act], Law No. 120 of 1947, §81(a), and Fudōsan tōki hō [Real Estate Registration Act], Law No. 24 of 1899, §157-2.

14. Depending on the statute and institutional structure involved, it may be to a higher level within the agency (*shinsa seikyū*; ACIA, §§3, 5), or to the same level (*igi mōshitate*; §6). In exceptional cases, a petitioner dissatisfied with the first hearing may obtain a second hearing (*sai shinsa seikyū*; ACIA, §8).

15. Gyōsei fufuku shinsa hō [Administrative Complaints Inquiries Act], Law No. 160 of 1962.

16. For example, when the prefectural government did not process compensation claims by Minamata victims (see section 5.II), they sued. The trial court (though not the Supreme Court) found a two-year delay illegal and compensable. *See* Nakamura v. Kuni, 1086 Hanrei jihō 33, 60–61 (Kumamoto D. Ct. July 20, 1983), *aff'd*, 1174 Hanrei jihō 21 (Fukuoka High Ct. Nov. 29, 1985), *rev'd*, 1385 Hanrei jihō 3 (Sup. Ct. Apr. 26, 1991); Matsumoto v. Kumamoto kenchiji, 835 Hanrei jihō 3 (Kumamoto D. Ct. Dec. 15, 1976). Other cases hold that a refusal to accept an application is likewise actionable. *See* K.K. Yōka ichiba kankō kaihatsu v. Chiba kenchiji, 1471 Hanrei jihō 84 (Chiba D. Ct. Oct. 28, 1992).

On what constitutes a disposition (*shobun*), see the discussion of the subject in the context of judicial review, at subsection C.2.

17. Whether the court may deny an oral hearing where the claim is frivolous apparently remains an open issue. *Compare* Satō v. Fukui kenchiji, 1019 Hanrei jihō 63 (Nagoya High Ct. Kanazawa Branch Off. Feb. 4, 1981) (may deny) *with* Kobayashi v. Kōsei daijin, 588 Hanrei jihō 28 (Tokyo D. Ct. Feb. 24, 1970) (may not deny).

18. *E.g.*, Omei v. Nishiyodogawa zeimu shochō, 336 Hanrei taimuzu 274 (Osaka High Ct. Sept. 30, 1975); Naitō v. Osaka kokuzei kyokuchō, 236 Hanrei taimuzu 185 (Osaka D. Ct. June 26, 1969).

19. Note that illegal government action will sometimes lead to tort liability—as was the case, for example, in the Taira case, discussed at the outset of this chapter.

See generally subsection 4.I.E.3; John Henry Merryman, David S. Clark and John O. Haley, eds., *The Civil Law Tradition: Europe, Latin America, and East Asia* (Charlottesville, Va.: Michie, 1994), 745–752.

20. I.e., *shobun*. We follow here the rules for *kōkoku* litigation, the primary category of litigation over unfavorable agency determinations (ACLA, §3). Other, less frequently used categories are detailed in ACLA, §§4-6.

A fuller description of the administrative disposition requirement appears in Robert W. Dziubla, "The Impotent Sword of Japanese Justice: The Doctrine of Shobunsei as a Barrier to Administrative Litigation," 18 *Cornell Int'l L.J.* 37 (1985).

All this is not to say agencies do not play games to try to avoid judicial review. The National Tax Office, for example, will sometimes urge taxpayers to file amended returns "voluntarily" rather than issue a deficiency notice. The former precludes later judicial review; the latter invites it.

21. Machida v. Tokyo to, 395 Hanrei jihō 20, 20 (Sup. Ct. Oct. 29, 1964). For an excellent introduction to these categories, see John O. Haley, "Japanese Administrative Law—Introduction," 14 *Law in Japan* 1, 7–8 (1986).

22. On the damage remedy for torts committed in the course of official agency action, see subsection 4.I.E.3 and Haley's discussion, *supra* note 21, at 11–14. The remedy is in fact broader than torts—for example, the Taira suit challenging the closing of the Turkish bath was brought under this statute as well.

23. Gyōsei jiken soshō hō [Administrative Case Litigation Act], Law No. 139 of 1962.

24. Note that the ACLA, §25, does provide for a close analogue to the preliminary injunction (see subsection D). For a careful analysis of these various legal issues, see Frank K. Upham, "After Minamata: Current Prospects and Problems in Japanese Environmental Litigation," 8 *Ecology L.Q.* 213, 225 n.34 (1979).

25. Kōno v. Okamura, 1003 Hanrei jihō 122 (Hiroshima D. Ct. Jan. 16, 1981).

26. Nakashige v. Kokubunshi Hokasabuchō shi'nyō shori kumiai, 675 Hanrei jihō 26, 30 (Kagoshima D. Ct. May 19, 1972); *see* Fujiwara v. Izumi shi, 663 Hanrei jihō 80 (Osaka D. Ct. Kishiwada Branch Off. Apr. 1, 1972) (building of crematorium not administrative disposition; one-year injunction granted); Kanagawa v. Hiroshima ken Takada gun eisei shisetsu kanri kumiai, 631 Hanrei jihō 24 (Hiroshima D. Ct. May 20, 1971) (preliminary injunction against construction of sewage treatment plant granted), *aff'd*, 693 Hanrei jihō 27 (Hiroshima High Ct. Feb. 14, 1973). *See also* Machida v. Tokyo to, 395 Hanrei jihō 20 (Sup. Ct. Oct. 29, 1964) (construction of trash incinerator not an administrative disposition); Isobe v. Naikaku sōri daijin, 1322 Hanrei jihō 33, 43–44 (Nagoya High Ct. Kanazawa Branch Off. July 19, 1989) (dicta—preliminary injunction against construction of nuclear power plant not foreclosed), *rev'd on other grounds*, 1437 Hanrei jihō 29 (Sup. Ct. Sept. 22, 1992).

27. Put another way, the legality of the internal rule is not ripe until applied to a private party.

28. Tōfukuin v. Kōsei daijin, 548 Hanrei jihō 59, 59 (Sup. Ct. Dec. 24, 1968); *see also* Shūkyō hōjin Keisokuji v. Kōsei daijin, 326 Hanrei jihō 5 (Tokyo D. Ct. Dec. 21, 1962), *aff'd*, 22 Saihan minshū 3186 (Tokyo High Ct. July 31, 1964), *aff'd*, 548 Hanrei jihō 59 (Sup. Ct. Dec. 24, 1968). For an unusual case of judicial review over a circular, see Shioda v. Tsūshō sangyō shō jūkōgyō kyokuchō, 652 Hanrei jihō 17 (Tokyo D. Ct. Nov. 8, 1971).

29. Isobe v. Naikaku sōri daijin, 1437 Hanrei jihō 29 (Sup. Ct. Sept. 22, 1992),

rev'g 1322 Hanrei jihō 33 (Nagoya High Ct. Kanazawa Branch Off. July 19, 1989) (Monju reactor); *see* Inoue v. Tsūshō sangyō daijin, 1441 Hanrei jihō 37 (Sup. Ct. Oct. 29, 1992), *aff'g* 1136 Hanrei jihō 3 (Takamatsu High Ct. Dec. 14, 1984) (Ikata reactor); Onoda v. Tsūshō sangyō daijin, 1441 Hanrei jihō 50 (Sup. Ct. Oct. 29, 1992), *aff'g* 1345 Hanrei jihō 33 (Seidai High Ct. Mar. 20, 1990) (Fukushima 2d reactor).

For a fine study of the Japanese nuclear power industry, see Linda Cohen, Mathew D. McCubbins, and Frances M. Rosenbluth, "The Politics of Nuclear Power in Japan and the United States," in *Structure and Policy in Japan and the United States,* ed. Peter Cowhey and Mathew McCubbins (New York: Cambridge University Press, 1995), 177.

30. Seto v. Shizuoka kenchiji, 1024 Hanrei jihō 43 (Shizuoka D. Ct. May 8, 1981).

31. Hoctor v. U.S. Dept. of Agric., 82 F.3d 165, 168 (7th Cir. 1996) (Posner, C.J.) (emphasis omitted).

32. Hashimoto v. Kuni, 290 Hanrei jihō 6 (Sup. Ct. Jan. 19, 1962), *rev'g* 16 Saihan minshū 72 (Osaka High Ct. Apr. 26, 1958), *aff'g* 16 Saihan minshū 65 (Kyoto D. Ct. June 29, 1957). *See generally* Upham, *supra* note 24, at 239–241.

33. Tokyo tochiji v. Adachi kōhoku ishikai, 1297 Hanrei jihō 29, 30 (Sup. Ct. July 14, 1988). That the burden lies on the petitioner appears more explicitly in Itō v. Iwate kenchiji, 485 Hanrei jihō 35, 36 (Sup. Ct. Apr. 7, 1967).

34. Hiroshimaken kyōiku iinkai v. Imada, 716 Hanrei jihō 27, 28–29 (Sup. Ct. Sept. 14, 1973).

35. Inoue v. Tsūshō sangyō daijin, 1441 Hanrei jihō 37 (Sup. Ct. Oct. 29, 1992).

36. *See* Gaikoku kawase oyobi gaikoku bōeki kanri hō [Foreign Exchange and Foreign Trade Control Act], Law No. 228 of 1949, §57; Hiroshi Kaneko, *Sozei hō* [Tax Law], 6th ed. (Tokyo: Kōbundō, 1997), 631.

37. *E.g.,* Abe v. Higashi Osaka zeimu shochō, 1209 Hanrei jihō 17 (Osaka D. Ct. May 28, 1986) (taxpayer), *aff'd in part and rev'd in part,* 1222 Hanrei jihō 35 (Osaka High Ct. Sept. 10, 1986); Kuni v. Iwamoto, 807 Hanrei taimuzu 258 (Osaka High Ct. June 11, 1992) (Minamata victims); Naikaku sōri daijin v. Kawaguchi, 786 Hanrei jihō 3 (Takamatsu High Ct. July 17, 1975) (nuclear plant); Kuni v. Ienaga, 652 Hanrei jihō 25 (Sup. Ct. Dec. 17, 1971) and 652 Hanrei jihō 28 (Sup. Ct. Dec. 17, 1971), *aff'g* 573 Hanrei jihō 21 (Tokyo High Ct. Oct. 15, 1969) *and* 573 Hanrei jihō 24 (Tokyo High Ct. Oct. 15, 1969) (textbook certification).

38. Early cases illustrating the scheme include In re Zaidan hōjin Chōren gakuen, 23 Gyōsai geppō 393 (Osaka High Ct. Nov. 30, 1949) (closing of school); Tokyo denryoku, K.K. v. Fukushima ken chiji, 3 Gyōsai reishū 1859 (Fukushima D. Ct. Sept. 11, 1952) (dam construction); Hokushō v. Kyoto shi kyōiku iinkai, 5 Gyōsai reishū 1726 (Kyoto D. Ct. July 23, 1954) (firing of teacher); Sakamoto v. Kanazawa ken shūyō iinkai, 6 Gyōsai reishū 2337 (Yokohama D. Ct. Oct. 6, 1955) (provision of land to U.S. base).

39. Tsuchiya v. Hiroshima ken kōan iinkai, 628 Hanrei jihō 36 (Hiroshima D. Ct. Apr. 15, 1971); Petition of Eisaku Satō, 628 Hanrei jihō 37 (Apr. 16, 1971); Tsuchiya v. Hiroshima ken kōan iinkai, 628 Hanrei jihō 36 (Hiroshima D. Ct. Apr. 16, 1971).

40. Hoshino v. Tokyo to kōan iinkai, 483 Hanrei jihō 3 (Tokyo D. Ct. June 9, 1967) (Sugimoto, Nakahira, Senda, JJ.); Petition of Eisaku Satō, 483 Hanrei jihō 11 (Tokyo D. Ct. June 9, 1967).

41. Horii v. Tokyo to kōan iinkai, 487 Hanrei jihō 19 (Tokyo D. Ct. July 10, 1967) (Sugimoto, Nakahira, Senda, JJ.); Petition of Eisaku Satō, 487 Hanrei jihō 19 (Tokyo D. Ct. July 11, 1967); Horii v. Tokyo to kōan iinkai, 487 Hanrei jihō 18 (Tokyo D. Ct. July 11, 1967).

42. *1968:* Anpo haki shoyōkyū kantetsu chūō jikkō iinkai v. Tokyo to kōan iinkai, 19 Gyōsai reishū 141 (Tokyo D. Ct. Feb. 2, 1968) (Sugimoto, Senda, Iwai, JJ.); Petition of Eisaku Satō, 19 Gyōsai reishū 141 (Feb. 2, 1968); Anpo haki shoyōkyū kantetsu chūō jikkō iinkai v. Tokyo to kōan iinkai, 19 Gyōsai reishū 141 (Tokyo D. Ct. Feb. 2, 1968). *1969:* Horii v. Tokyo to kōan iinkai, 553 Hanrei jihō 32 (Tokyo D. Ct. Feb. 26, 1969) (Sugimoto, Nakahira, Iwai, JJ.); Petition of Eisaku Satō, 553 Hanrei jihō 43 (Feb. 26, 1969); Horii v. Tokyo to kōan iinkai, 553 Hanrei jihō 42 (Tokyo D. Ct. Feb. 26, 1969).

43. Hoshino v. Tokyo to, 575 Hanrei jihō 10 (Tokyo D. Ct. Dec. 2, 1969) (Sugimoto, Nakahira, Iwai, JJ.), *aff'd,* 334 Hanrei taimuzu 121 (Tokyo High Ct. Mar. 25, 1976). It awarded these damages three months *after* another panel of the same court had rejected Hoshino's claim against the national government, in part on grounds that the prime ministerial veto was constitutional. Hoshino v. Kuni, 568 Hanrei jihō 14 (Tokyo D. Ct. Sept. 26, 1969).

44. *See* J. Mark Ramseyer and Frances McCall Rosenbluth, *Japan's Political Marketplace* (Cambridge: Harvard University Press, 1993), 172–175; J. Mark Ramseyer, "The Puzzling (In)dependence of Courts: A Comparative Approach," 23 *J. Legal Stud.* 721, 726–727 (1994).

We emphatically do not assert that Satō intervened directly in the judicial personnel office (we simply do not know). Our point—developed at length in section 1.IV—is that the distinction between direct and indirect intervention does not matter. Largely the LDP leadership has been able to obtain the discipline it needs over the courts through indirect means.

45. Gyōsei tetsuzuki hō [Administrative Procedure Act], Law No. 88 of 1993; *see generally* Lorenz Koedderitzsch, "Japan's New Administrative Procedure Law: Reasons for Its Enactment and Likely Implications," 24 *Law in Japan* 105 (1991).

46. On the need for the act, see Katsuya Uga, *Gyōsei tetsuzuki hō no kaisetsu* [Commentary on the Administrative Procedure Act], 2d rev. ed. (Tokyo: Gakuyō shobō, 1996), 22–23.

47. One American observer apparently found Japanese administrative law so opaque that he could complain in 1995 that "Japan is the only major democratic nation without a code of administrative procedure." Chalmers Johnson, *Japan: Who Governs?* (New York: W.W. Norton & Co., 1995), 79.

48. Many of the ideas in this section and section III are also developed in J. Mark Ramseyer, "Rethinking Administrative Guidance," in *Festschrift for Hugh Patrick,* ed. Masahiko Aoki and Gary Saxonhouse (forthcoming).

49. In fact, informal regulation is not peculiarly Japanese, as both Haley and Young rightly observe. *See* John Owen Haley, *Authority without Power: Law and the Japanese Paradox* (New York: Oxford University Press, 1991), 162 (informal regulation is "common to all legal systems"); Michael K. Young, "Judicial Review of Administrative Guidance: Governmentally Encouraged Consensual Dispute Resolution in Japan," 84 *Colum. L. Rev.* 923, 925 n.6 (1984) ("informal activity . . . makes up a large part of the administrative activity in all modern, industrialized countries").

50. Young, *supra* note 49, at 935.

51. Karel van Wolferen, *The Enigma of Japanese Power* (New York: Vantage Books, 1990), 215.

52. Joseph Saunders, "Courts and Law in Japan," in *Courts, Law, and Politics in Comparative Perspective*, ed. Herbert Jacob et al. (New Haven, Conn.: Yale University Press, 1996), 315, 373.

53. Johnson, *supra* note 47, at 79.

54. Young, *supra* note 49, at 931–932.

55. *Id.* at 977.

56. *Id.* at 943.

57. Dolan v. City of Tigard, 114 S. Ct. 2309 (1994); *see generally* Richard A. Epstein, "The Permit Power Meets the Constitution," 81 *Iowa L. Rev.* 407 (1995).

58. Nollan v. California Coastal Commission, 483 U.S. 825, 837 (1987) (Scalia, J.).

59. Tokyo to v. G.G. Nakaya honten, 1168 Hanrei jihō 45 (Sup. Ct. July 16, 1985).

60. *See* Konishi v. Toyonaka shi, 1014 Hanrei jihō 59 (Sup. Ct. July 16, 1981), *aff'g* 915 Hanrei jihō 33 (Osaka High Ct. Sept. 26, 1978); Kawagishi v. Hirakata shi, 1371 Hanrei jihō 122 (Osaka D. Ct. Aug. 29, 1990).

61. Tokyo to v. G.G. Nakaya honten, 1168 Hanrei jihō 45, 47 (Sup. Ct. July 16, 1985) (*partial translation at* Yukio Yanagida et al., eds., *Law and Investment in Japan* (Cambridge: East Asian Legal Studies and Harvard University Press, 1994), 133), *aff'g* 955 Hanrei jihō 73 (Tokyo High Ct. Dec. 24, 1979), *rev'g* 928 Hanrei jihō 79 (Tokyo D. Ct. July 31, 1978).

62. Kuni v. Gotō, 1114 Hanrei jihō at 13.

63. Yamaki kensetsu K.K. v. Musashino shi, 803 Hanrei jihō 18 (Tokyo D. Ct. Hachiōji Branch Off. Dec. 8, 1975). This particular segment of the dispute was eventually settled out of court.

64. Yamaki kensetsu K.K. v. Suzuki, 1151 Hanrei jihō 12 (Tokyo High Court Mar. 26, 1985).

65. Kuni v. Gotō, 1328 Hanrei jihō 16 (Sup. Ct. Nov. 7, 1989), *aff'g* 1166 Hanrei jihō 41 (Tokyo High Ct. Aug. 30, 1985), *aff'g* 1114 Hanrei jihō 10 (Tokyo D. Ct. Hachiōji Branch Off. Feb. 24, 1984).

66. Kuni v. Gotō, 1166 Hanrei jihō at 43.

67. Kuni v. Gotō, 1328 Hanrei jihō at 18.

68. Chihō jiji hō [Local Self-Government Act], Law No. 67 of Apr. 17, 1947, §242-2.

69. Gotō v. Yamada, 1354 Hanrei jihō 62 (Sup. Ct. Mar. 23, 1990), *aff'g* 1186 Hanrei jihō 46 (Tokyo High Ct. Mar. 26, 1986), *aff'g* 1080 Hanrei jihō 40 (Tokyo D. Ct. May 27, 1983).

70. Yamaki kensetsu, K.K. v. Musashino shi, 1465 Hanrei jihō 106 (Tokyo D. Ct. Hachiōji Branch Off. Dec. 9, 1992). The basis for compensation was the National Damage Compensation Act, discussed in more detail in section 4.I.

71. Fujisawa kensetsu, K.K. v. Tokyo to, 1074 Hanrei jihō 80 (Tokyo D. Ct. Nov. 12, 1982).

72. Sankei kankō, Y.G. v. Kyoto fu kenchiku shuji, 1116 Hanrei jihō 56 (Kyoto D. Ct. Jan. 19, 1984).

73. Shiroyama kankyō jōka, Y.G. v. Tochigi ken chiji, 1385 Hanrei jihō 42 (Utsunomiya D. Ct. Feb. 28, 1991).

74. Arakawa kensetsu kōgyō, K.K. v. Yamanashi ken kenchiku shuji, 1457 Hanrei jihō 85 (Kōfu D. Ct. Feb. 24, 1992).

75. Tōhō jūtaku sangyō, K.K. v. Shime machi, 1438 Hanrei jihō 118 (Fukuoka D. Ct. Feb. 13, 1992).

76. K.K. Yōka ichiba kankō kaihatsu v. Chiba ken chiji, 1471 Hanrei jihō 84 (Chiba D. Ct. Oct. 28, 1992).

77. Y.G. Seron nyūsu sha v. Tanashi shichō, 504 Hanrei taimuzu 128 (Tokyo D. Ct. May 11, 1983).

78. *E.g.,* Senboku seikatsu kyōdō kumiai v. Sakai shi, 1239 Hanrei jihō 77 (Osaka D. Ct. Sakai Branch Off. Feb. 25, 1987).

79. Takahashi v. Musashino shi, 1078 Hanrei jihō 95 (Tokyo D. Ct. Hachiōji Branch Off. Feb. 9, 1983), *aff'd,* 1268 Hanrei jihō 39 (Tokyo High Ct. Mar. 29, 1988) (ultimately reversed by the Supreme Court; *see* note 80, *infra*); Hinode jisho, K.K. v. Takaki shi, 1240 Hanrei jihō 92 (Osaka D. Ct. Sept. 26, 1986), *aff'd,* 1343 Hanrei jihō 26 (Osaka High Ct. May 23, 1989); K.K. Kōken v. Ōami shirasato machi, 1333 Hanrei jihō 94 (Chiba D. Ct. Jan. 25, 1989), *aff'd,* 1333 Hanrei jihō 91 (Tokyo High Ct. Oct. 31, 1989); Matsushima v. Itami shi, 1313 Hanrei jihō 145 (Kobe D. Ct. Nov. 18, 1988); *see also* Komae shi v. K.K. Eeru kōsan, 723 Hanrei taimuzu 206 (Tokyo D. Ct. June 12, 1989) (suit by city for unpaid promised donations).

80. Takahashi v. Musashino shi, 1506 Hanrei jihō 106 (Sup. Ct. Feb. 18, 1993).

81. van Wolferen, *supra* note 51, at 215.

82. *See generally* Mathew D. McCubbins and Thomas Schwartz, "Congressional Oversight Overlooked: Police Patrols versus Fire Alarms," 28 *Am. J. Pol. Sci.* 165 (1984).

83. *See generally* William M. Landes and Richard A. Posner, "The Independent Judiciary in an Interest-Group Perspective," 18 *J.L. & Econ.* 875 (1975); Fred S. McChesney, "Rent Extraction and Interest-Group Organization in a Coasian Model of Regulation," 20 *J. Legal Stud.* 73 (1991); Douglass C. North and Barry R. Weingast, "Constitution and Commitment: The Evolution of Institutions Governing Public Choice in Seventeenth-Century England," 49 *J. Econ. Hist.* 803 (1989); Pablo T. Spiller, "Institutions and Commitment," 5 *Indus. & Corp. Change* 421 (1996).

84. *See* David M. Kreps, "Corporate Culture and Economic Theory," in *Perspectives on Positive Political Economy,* ed. James E. Alt and Kenneth A. Shepsle (New York: Cambridge University Press, 1990), 90; Spiller, *supra* note 83.

85. *E.g.,* Spiller, *supra* note 83.

86. *See generally* J. Mark Ramseyer and Frances M. Rosenbluth, *Japan's Political Marketplace* (Cambridge: Harvard University Press, 1993), chs. 6–7.

87. Masao Miyamoto, *Straitjacket Society: An Insider's Irreverent View of Bureaucratic Japan* (Tokyo: Kodansha International, 1994), 29.

88. Ramseyer and Rosenbluth, *supra* note 86, at ch. 6.

89. *Id.* at ch. 5.

90. *Id.* at 48. Instead, many local government officials were now coalition candidates—coalitions that sometimes (but only sometimes) included the LDP.

91. *See* Frank K. Upham, *Law and Social Change in Postwar Japan* (Cambridge: Harvard University Press, 1987), 169.

92. Chihō jiji hō [Regional Self-Government Act], Law No. 67 of 1947, §2.

93. George L. Priest and Benjamin Klein, "The Selection of Disputes for Litigation," 13 *J. Legal Stud.* 1 (1984).

94. *Compare* K.K. Nishizawa v. Nagasaki kenshiji, 12 Gyōsai reishū 2505 (Na-

gasaki D. Ct. Feb. 3, 1961) (may settle) *with* Sasakawa takushoku ringyō, K.K. v. Kuni, 7 Kakyū minshū 1895 (Tokyo D. Ct. July 14, 1956) (may not settle).

95. Y.G. Taira Shōji v. Yamagata ken, 756 Hanrei jihō 62 (Sendai High Ct. July 8, 1974), *aff'd,* 889 Hanrei jihō 9 (Sup. Ct. May 26, 1978).

Chapter 9

1. Miura v. Meguro zeimu shochō, 170 Zeimu soshō shiryō 170 (Tokyo D. Ct. Apr. 26, 1989), *aff'd,* 175 Zeimu soshō shiryō 1252 (Tokyo High Ct. Mar. 19, 1990), *aff'd,* 186 Zeimu soshō shiryō 571 (Sup. Ct. Sept. 13, 1991).

2. Based in part on materials initially prepared as background for Hugh Ault, *Comparative Income Taxation: A Structural Analysis* (The Hague: Kluwer Law International, 1997).

3. *See generally* Eric M. Zolt, "The Uneasy Case for Uniform Taxation," 16 *Va. Tax Rev.* 39, 49–51 (1996).

4. Shotokuzei hō [Income Tax Act], Law No. 33 of 1965.

5. Yukio Noguchi, *Zeisei kaikaku no shinsekkei* [New Designs for Tax Reform] (Tokyo: Nihon keizai shimbunsha, 1994), 240.

6. Japan has a population of 125 million (with 66 million in the labor market). The law does not allow joint returns.

7. *E.g.,* Nōji kumiai hōjin Takeda yōton kumiai v. Takeda zeimu shochō, 169 Zeimu soshō shiryō 571 (Fukuoka High Ct. Mar. 16, 1989), *aff'd,* 173 Zeimu soshō shiryō 770 (Sup. Ct. Sept. 21, 1989).

8. Miura v. Meguro zeimu shochō, 170 Zeimu soshō shiryō 170 (Tokyo D. Ct. Apr. 26, 1989), *aff'd,* 175 Zeimu soshō shiryō 1252 (Tokyo High Ct. Mar. 19, 1990), *aff'd,* 186 Zeimu soshō shiryō 571 (Sup. Ct. Sept. 13, 1991).

9. For estimates about the size of the industry, see Yūgi sangyō keieisha dōyūkai, ed., *Pachinko sangyō keiei hakusho* [White Paper on the Pachinko Industry] (Tokyo: Niki shuppan, 1997), 203. Twenty-eight percent of all Japanese play the game and spend a mean ¥90,000 annually. *Id.* at 207. On the number of machines and stores, see *id.* at 212.

10. *Id.* at 252–254.

11. Kuni v. Nakayama, 179 Zeimu soshō shiryō 4134 (Kyoto D. Ct. Mar. 29, 1985), *aff'd,* 179 Zeimu soshō shiryō 3970 (Osaka High Ct. Oct. 26, 1990). As of the mid-1990s, the standard ball payout ratio was 135–145 percent. The parlors make money because the prizes are converted to cash at about 63 percent of the initial price of the balls. Yūgi sangyō, *supra* note 9, at 243.

12. Kuni v. Eishin kankō, Y.G., 168 Zeimu soshō shiryō 2297 (Tokyo High Ct. Dec. 21, 1988).

13. K.K. Kubota zaimoku ten v. Shimizu zeimu shochō, 9 Shōmu geppō 1025 (Sup. Ct. June 9, 1962) (loan); Daiichi gōkin K.K. v. Kōjimachi zeimu shochō, 610 Hanrei jihō 40 (Tokyo D. Ct. Dec. 25, 1969) (educational fees).

14. *See* Shotoku zei kihon tsūtatsu [Basic Circular on the Income Tax], Choku shin (sho) No. 30 of 1970, §36-28; Susumu kōgyō K.K. v. Shimogyō zeimu shochō, 34 Shōmu geppō 2096 (Osaka High Ct. Mar. 31, 1988).

15. ITA, §36(a); Kuni v. Ōkubo, 425 Hanrei jihō 44 (Sup. Ct. Sept. 8, 1965).

16. Akaboshi v. Kumamoto higashi zeimu shochō, 26 Saihan minshū 2083 (Sup. Ct. Dec. 26, 1972).

17. Itabashi v. Fukuoka kokuzei kyokuchō, 213 Hanrei taimuzu 171 (Fukuoka D. Ct. Mar. 17, 1967, *modified,* 18 Gyōsai reishū 1577 (Fukuoka High Ct.

Nov. 30, 1967), *aff'd*, 649 Hanrei jihō 11 (Sup. Ct. Nov. 9, 1971); *see generally* Minoru Nakazato, "Ihō na shotoku" [Illegal Income], 120 *Bessatsu Jurisuto* 42 (1992).

18. *see generally* Minoru Nakazato and J. Mark Ramseyer, "Shotokuzei ni okeru shakunyūkin rishi no toriatsukai ni kansusu hikaku hō teki kenkyū" [A Comparative Legal Analysis of the Treatment of Interest on Indebtedness under the Income Tax], 17 *Hitotsubashi daigaku kenkyū nempō hōgaku kenkyū* 1 (1987). The Japanese tax office uses the system Richard Epstein proposed at the beginning of his career. *See* Richard A. Epstein, "The Consumption and Loss of Personal Property under the Internal Revenue Code," 23 *Stan. L. Rev.* 454 (1971).

19. Shotoku zei hō sekō rei [Income Tax Act Enforcement Order], Seirei No. 96, 1965.

20. ITA, §56. This is largely ineffective because of various special provisions. Hiroshi Kaneko, *Sozei hō* [Tax Law], 5th ed. (Tokyo: Kōbundō, 1996), 170–171.

21. [No names given], 1361 Hanrei jihō 154 (Tokyo High Ct. Oct. 1, 1990), *aff'd*, 48-6 Saihan keishū 67 (Sup. Ct. Sept. 13, 1994).

22. Kuni v. Koga, 55 Zeimu soshō shiryō 492 (Fukuoka High Ct. Sept. 12, 1968).

23. Sōzoku zei hō [Inheritance Tax Act], Law No. 73 of 1950.

24. Inheritance Tax Act, §21-3(a)(i); ITA Circular, §34-1(e). More precisely, the rule applies to gifts from "juridical persons."

25. Kaneko, *supra* note 20, at 215.

26. Kuni v. Kim, 179 Zeimu soshō shiryō at 4168–4169, 179 Zeimu soshō shiryō at 3992–3994.

27. Kuni v. Eishin kankō, Y.G., 168 Zeimu soshō shiryō 2297 (Tokyo High Ct. Dec. 21, 1988).

28. Ōshima v. Sakyō zeimu shochō, 1149 Hanrei jihō 30 (Sup. Ct. Mar. 27, 1985).

29. Kuni v. Nakayama, 179 Zeimu soshō shiryō 4134 (Kyoto D. Ct. Mar. 29, 1985), *aff'd*, 179 Zeimu soshō shiryō 3970 (Osaka High Ct. Oct. 26, 1990).

30. Genka shōkyaku shisan no taiyō nensūtō ni kansuru shōrei [Cabinet Order Regarding the Useful Lives of Depreciable Assets], Cabinet Order No. 15 of 1965.

31. *Detailed in* Ministry of Finance, *An Outline of Japanese Taxes, 1991* (Tokyo: Ministry of Finance, 1991), 91–95. For a study finding Japanese depreciation rules slightly (but only slightly) less generous than U.S. rules on a variety of capital investments, see American Council for Capital Formation, *Economic Effects of the Corporate Alternative Minimum Tax* (Washington, D.C.: American Council for Capital Formation, 1991), table 10.

32. "Kigyō ni sonkin mitomezu" [Loss to Be Disallowed to Firms], *Yomiuri shimbun*, Aug. 16, 1996.

33. Fukuda v. Takamatsu zeimu shochō, 24 Gyōsai reishū 511 (Takamatsu D. Ct. June 28, 1973), *aff'd*, 26 Gyōsai reishū 594 (Takamatsu High Ct. Apr. 24, 1975).

34. Miura v. Meguro zeimu shochō, 170 Zeimu soshō shiryō 170 (Tokyo D. Ct. Apr. 26, 1989), *aff'd*, 175 Zeimu soshō shiryō 1252 (Tokyo High Ct. Mar. 19, 1990), *aff'd*, 186 Zeimu soshō shiryō 571 (Sup. Ct. Sept. 13, 1991).

35. Kuni v. K.K. Kobayashi Entapuraizu, 1272 Hanrei jihō 159, 161 (Tokyo D. Ct. Dec. 24, 1987), *aff'd*, 177 Zeimu soshō shiryō 96 (Tokyo High Ct. Jan. 17, 1990).

36. *See generally* ITA Circular, §§73-1 through 73-10.

37. Sonia Ryang, *North Koreans in Japan: Language, Ideology, and Identity* (Boulder, Colo.: Westview, 1997), 53.

38. Kuni v. Kim, 179 Zeimu soshō shiryō at 3993–3994.

39. Sozei tokubetsu sochi hō [Special Tax Measures Act], Law No. 26 of 1957.

40. For summaries of these provisions, see Kaneko, *supra* note 20, at 204–207.

41. Tokyo kokuzei kyokuchō v. Okada, 613 Hanrei jihō 16 (Sup. Ct. Oct. 23, 1970); ITA, §32(a); ITA Enforcement Order, §79.

42. Nishi v. Uchimura, 849 Hanrei jihō 33 (Nagano D. Ct. Mar. 30, 1977).

43. Kuni v. Uchimura, 914 Hanrei jihō 23 (Kumamoto D. Ct. Nov. 8, 1978), *aff'd,* 445 Hanrei taimuzu 171 (Fukuoka High Ct. May 27, 1981), *aff'd,* 138 Zeimu soshō shiryō 1035 (Sup. Ct. June 30, 1983).

44. Mugen rensakō no bōshi ni kansuru hōritsu [An Act Regarding the Prevention of Unlimited Chain Associations], Law No. 101 of 1978.

45. In addition to the cases cited elsewhere, see Tenka ikka no kai hasan kanzai nin v. Shūkyō hōjin Daikangū, 528 Hanrei taimuzu 268 (Kumamoto D. Ct. Apr. 27, 1984), *aff'd,* 622 Hanrei taimuzu 229 (Fukuoka High Ct. Sept. 30, 1986); *In re* Uchimura, 431 Hanrei taimuzu 97 (Fukuoka High Ct. July 18, 1980); Tenka ikka no kai hasan kanzai nin v. Zaidan hōjin Higo kōseikai, 1296 Hanrei jihō 55 (Tokyo High Ct. Oct. 31, 1988).

46. Nishi v. Uchimura, 849 Hanrei jihō 33 (Nagano D. Ct. Mar. 30, 1977); Kōno v. Shūkyō hōjin Daikangū, 1218 Hanrei jihō 83 (Hiroshima High Ct. Oct. 23, 1986).

47. Ichikawa v. Uchimura, 934 Hanrei jihō 87 (Shizuoka D. Ct. Dec. 19, 1978); Kōno v. Shūkyō hōjin Daikangū, 1220 Hanrei jihō 97 (Tokyo D. Ct. Sept. 12, 1985); Kōno v. Shūkyō hōjin Daikangū, 1218 Hanrei jihō 83 (Hiroshima High Ct. Oct. 23, 1986); Imaichi v. Tsukioka, 1119 Hanrei jihō 93 (Tokyo D. Ct. Sept. 26, 1983).

48. Uchimura v. Kumamoto nishi zeimu shochō, 135 Zeimu soshō shiryō 200 (Kumamoto D. Ct. Feb. 27, 1984), *aff'd,* 144 Zeimu soshō shiryō 357 (Fukuoka High Ct. Feb. 28, 1985).

49. The liability is imposed by a special provision of the Inheritance Tax Act mandating the tax on gifts to unincorporated associations. *See* Inheritance Tax Act, §66.

50. Tenka ikka no kai v. Kumamoto nishi zeimu shochō, 135 Zeimu soshō shiryō 157 (Kumamoto D. Ct. Feb. 27 1984), *aff'd,* 180 Zeimu soshō shiryō 97 (Fukuoka High Ct. July 18, 1990); Uchimura v. Kumamoto nishi zeimu shochō, 30 Shōmu geppō 1270 (Kumamoto D. Ct. Feb. 27, 1984), *aff'd,* 1395 Hanrei jihō 34 (Fukuoka High Ct. July 18, 1990); *see* Minoru Nakazato, "Case Comment," 852 *Jurisuto* 230 (1986).

51. For an exceptionally clear discussion of the issues involved, see Hideki Kanda, "Kigyō baishū kazei" [The Taxation of Corporate Acquisitions], 1402 *Shōji hōmu* 16 (1995); Tadatsune Mizuno, "Kigyō no gappei, bunkatsu to zeisei" [Taxation and the Merger and Division of Firms], 1104 *Jurisuto* 117 (1997).

52. Of the 2,002 reportable mergers in 1992, only 1 involved a consolidation. *See* Kōsei torihiki iinkai, ed., *Kōsei torihiki iinkai nenji hōkoku* [Annual Report of the Fair Trade Commission] (Tokyo: Kōsei torihiki iinkai, 1993), 145.

53. Hōjin zei hō [Corporate Tax Act], Law No. 34 of 1965. Note that local taxes generally piggyback on the national taxes and raise total rates beyond those given in the text.

54. CTA, §2(s). For details of the calculation, see CTA, §27; Hōjin zei hō sekō rei [CTA Enforcement Order], Sei No. 97 of 1965, §§9, 26.

55. CTA, §§111, 112, 115. *See generally* K.K. Maruki hyakkaten v. Hachiōji zeimu shochō, 221 Hanrei taimuzu 199 (Tokyo D. Ct. Mar. 14, 1968), *aff'd,* 56 Zeimu soshō shiryō 17 (Tokyo High Ct. Jan. 31, 1969), *aff'd,* 75 Zeimu soshō shiryō 704 (Sup. Ct. May 30, 1974).

56. Sozei tokubetsu sochi hō [Special Tax Measures Act], Law No. 26 of 1957.

57. CTA Enforcement Order, §9.

58. Shōhō [Commercial Code], Law No. 48 of 1899.

59. Law No. 74 of 1981, app. §§15, 16.

60. We base our discussion on Minoru Nakazato, "The Impact of the Shoup Report on Japanese Economic Development," in *Retrospectives on Public Finance,* ed. Lorraine Eden (Durham, N.C.: Duke University Press, 1991), 51. The point that the Japanese income tax functioned much like a consumption tax and thereby avoided the intertemporal bias to income taxes is also made in Joseph Isenbergh, "The End of Income Taxation," 45 *Tax L. Rev.* 283 (1990). *See generally* Alvin Warren, "Would a Consumption Tax Be Fairer than an Income Tax," 89 *Yale L.J.* 1081 (1980).

61. Changing the tax rate will not affect the intertemporal neutrality of the consumption tax. If the consumption tax rate were 30 percent, then if the taxpayer consumed the entire amount in year 1, he would pay a tax of 231 and consume 769 (since 769[.3] = 231). If he invested the 1,000 and consumed 1,100 in the following year, he would pay a tax of 254 and consume 846 (846[.3] = 254). The present value of 846 is 846/1.1 = 769. The present value of the consumption is thus the same whether it occurs in year 1 or year 2.

62. He also recommended that national universities appoint tax law professors, a recommendation to which one of us (Nakazato) owes his job.

63. Law No. 84 of Apr. 11, 1952.

SUGGESTIONS FOR
FURTHER READING

On May 21, 1992, death came for the professor. He was 82. With 36 years on the University of Tokyo faculty and with over 90 books and 600 articles to his name, Takeyoshi Kawashima had been an astonishingly productive and influential man. With publications spanning 56 years (based on a 1986 bibliography), this comes to a book every 7½ months and an article every 33 days. (Contrast this with Judge Richard Posner, probably the most prolific American legal scholar of all time. As of January 1993, Posner had 20 books and 221 articles—over a 24-year career, a book every 14½ months and an article every 41 days.)

Easily the preeminent authority on the Civil Code and one of the founders of legal sociology in Japan, Kawashima also powerfully shaped the direction that Western studies of Japanese law would take. Only two pieces of his in English had much impact, but their impact was decisive: "Dispute Resolution in Contemporary Japan," in *Law in Japan: The Legal Order in a Changing Society,* edited by Arthur T. von Mehren (Cambridge: Harvard University Press, 1963), and "The Legal Consciousness of Contract in Japan," 7 *Law in Japan* 1 (C. Stevens, trans., 1974).

Some of Kawashima's books sold exceptionally well. Sales were particularly good for *Nihonjin no hō ishiki* [The Legal Consciousness of the Japanese] (Tokyo: Iwanami shoten, 1974), where he expanded the ideas developed in his 1963 English essay. His students may deny it to the end, but many of those sales surely followed from the way it fit within the read-it-standing-in-the-subway genre of books analyzing why "the Japanese" are different from everyone else. In explaining the alleged Japanese disdain for litigation and contracts, Kawashima ultimately did little more than round up the usual suspects (Japanese society is hierarchical, consensual, and so forth) and parade them as explanations.

For reasons given in chapters 3 and 4, this aspect of Kawashima's work (a minor part of his oeuvre, to be sure) fails. As any survey of Western essays on Japanese law will show, however, it had enormous impact. Serious Western students of Japanese law would thus do well to begin their studies with Kawashima. Psychologists still read their Freud and Jung, anthropologists their Mead and Malinowski. For much the same reason, Western students of Japanese law need their Kawashima.

In this bibliographic essay on Japanese law in English, we do not try to be exhaustive. Neither do we try to include all of the best essays (though we do try to ignore the worst). That we omit an essay thus says little about its merit. Instead, we simply try to offer a sample of works that, read conscientiously, will give readers a reasonably representative sense of the English-language scholarship on Japanese law. Those who need a comprehensive bibliography should consult Hiroshi Oda and Sian Stickings, eds., *Basic Japanese Laws* (Oxford: Oxford University Press, 1997); Matthias K. Scheer, *Japanese Law in Western Languages, 1974–1989: A*

Bibliography (Hamburg: German-Japanese Lawyers Association, 1992); or the lists compiled periodically under the aegis of *Law in Japan*.

General Works

Readers have several single-volume introductions to which to turn: John Owen Haley, *The Spirit of Japanese Law* (Atlanta: University of Georgia Press, 1998); Hiroshi Oda, *Japanese Law* (London: Butterworth, 1992); and Dan Fenno Henderson, *Foreign Enterprise in Japan: Laws and Policies* (Chapel Hill: University of North Carolina Press, 1973). Although different from our book in many ways, each provides a concise and reliable introduction to the field.

Readers wanting more detailed discussions can examine two multivolume loose-leaf services: Zentaro Kitagawa, ed., *Doing Business in Japan* (New York: Matthew Bender, updated), and Mitsuo Matsushita, ed., *Japanese Business Law Guide* (North Ryde, Australia: CCH International, updated). Because both services draw on many authors, careful readers will quickly notice large quality variations. Readers should also check the back issues of *Law in Japan: An Annual,* painstakingly edited during much of the past two decades by John Haley and Daniel Foote.

Casebooks

Several scholars have lately published casebooks on Japanese law. Kenneth Port recently issued his *Comparative Law: Law and the Legal Process in Japan* (Durham, N.C.: Carolina Academic Press, 1996). John Henry Merryman, David S. Clark, and John O. Haley, eds., *The Civil Law Tradition: Europe, Latin America, and East Asia* (Charlottesville, Va.: Michie, 1994), surveys civil law systems more generally. By including extensive material on Japan within this broader project, the editors let readers explore Japanese law within a multinationally comparative framework (something we in this book, for example, do not do). Yukio Yanagida, Daniel Foote, Edward Johnson, Mark Ramseyer, and Hugh Scogin, eds., *Law and Investment in Japan* (Cambridge: East Asian Legal Studies and Harvard University Press, 1994), focuses on the legal issues that arise in cross-border investments. Koichiro Fujikura, ed., *Japanese Law and Legal Theory* (London: Dartmouth, 1995), offers an intriguing selection of articles on Japan.

Three older casebooks also survive. Two cover the entire field of Japanese law: Hideo Tanaka and Malcolm Smith, eds., *The Japanese Legal System* (Tokyo: University of Tokyo Press, 1976), and John O. Haley, Daniel H. Foote, and Dan Fenno Henderson, eds., *Law and the Legal Process in Japan* (Seattle: University of Washington School of Law, updated). Julian Gresser, Koichiro Fujikura, and Akio Morishima, eds., *Environmental Law in Japan* (Cambridge: MIT Press, 1981), deals, as the name implies, with environmental law.

Legal History

Unfortunately readers still lack a suitable introduction to modern Japanese legal history. Although in many ways comprehensive, Carl Steenstrup, *A History of Law in Japan until 1868* (Leiden: E.J. Brill, 1991), looks only at the earlier periods and in any case is more a historian's book than a lawyer's. Dan Henderson,

290

Conciliation and Japanese Law, 2 vols. (Tokyo: University of Tokyo Press, 1965), deals primarily with the earlier period as well and concentrates on the history of settlement.

The best discussions of the formative period of modern Japanese law probably appear in John O. Haley, *Authority without Power: Law and the Japanese Paradox* (New York: Oxford University Press, 1991), and the various essays collected in Arthur von Mehren, ed., *Law in Japan: The Legal Order in a Changing Society.* Other discussions of the period, albeit with more haphazard coverage, can be found in Mark Ramseyer, *Odd Markets in Japanese History* (New York: Cambridge University Press, 1996), and Mark Ramseyer and Frances Rosenbluth, *The Politics of Oligarchy* (New York: Cambridge University Press, 1995).

Law and Society

For U.S. scholars, Kawashima's happiest legacy is the vast scholarship on Japanese law and society that he, by example, encouraged. Indeed, there are probably more (and more interesting) essays about Japanese law and society than about law and society in any European country—this despite the fact that U.S. scholars have studied European law more extensively than Japanese. For an excellent annotated bibliography as of the late 1980s, see Eric Feldman, "Annotated Bibliography: Japanese Law and Society," 21 *Law in Japan* 19 (1988).

These studies in law and society point in many directions. One early work was Yoshiyuki Noda, *Introduction to Japanese Law,* translated by A. Angelo (Tokyo: University of Tokyo Press, 1976). Noda makes many points that track Kawashima's. Unfortunately, although he based the book on lectures he gave in 1962–1963, its publication in the 1970s will suggest to many that he merely took Kawashima as given and embroidered the legend. By contrast, one of John Haley's first articles—and certainly his first widely read article—was a full-scale attack on Kawashima's 1963 essay: "The Myth of the Reluctant Litigant," 4 *Journal of Japanese Studies* 359 (1978).

Modern legal sociology on Japan has continued to grow, and two award-winning books now anchor the field: Frank K. Upham, *Law and Social Change in Postwar Japan* (Cambridge: Harvard University Press, 1987), and Haley's *Authority without Power.* Through a fascinating series of case studies—pollution, sex discrimination, the outcast community, and industrial policy—Upham explores "the way in which elites use legal rules and institutions to manage and direct conflict and control change at a social level" in Japan (p. 1). Although legal rules influence the direction of change, Upham argues that those rules are themselves manipulable affairs. By manipulating them appropriately, the elites can channel conflict away from formal rules and institutions into more informal fora. Because Japanese "bureaucratic leadership is exercised through informal processes" (p. 21), hypothesizes Upham, by channeling conflicts into informal fora, the elites help ensure their own power and control.

Haley proposes a different, but equally original and provocative, thesis, one captured by the title *Authority without Power.* He meticulously surveys several centuries of Japanese legal history and a wealth of data about modern Japanese legal practice. Through this, he focuses on what he sees as the "relative weakness of most

291

forms of law enforcement in Japan" (p. 14). With this weakness, he argues, has come a "separation of authority from power" (p. 13). Although "the jurisdictional mandate [of the] government or state seems pervasive," he explains, "its capacity to coerce and compel is remarkably weak" (p. 14). The result, to Haley, is Japanese "consensual governance" (p. 193)—a "dependence on extralegal, informal mechanisms of social control" (p. 14).

Of works dealing with the role the government plays in the Japanese economy, readers face a particularly wide variety. In "Privating Regulation: The Implementation of the Large-Scale Retail Stores Law," in *Political Dynamics in Contemporary Japan,* edited by Gary D. Allison and Yasunori Sone (Ithaca, N.Y.: Cornell University Press, 1993), Upham studies the interest-group pressures the government faces; in "The Man Who Would Import: A Cautionary Tale about Bucking the System in Japan," 17 *Journal of Japanese Studies* 323 (1991), he traces the way the government informally enforces those interest-group preferences. By contrast, Michael Young argues that the government more impartially mediates conflicts. It does so, according to Young, by encouraging interested parties to negotiate with each other: "Administrative Guidance and Industrial Policy: Participatory Policy Formation and Execution in Japan," in *Eibeihō ronshū* [Studies in Anglo-American Law], edited by Kōichirō Fujikura (Tokyo: Tokyo daigaku shuppankai, 1987), and "Judicial Review of Administrative Guidance: Governmentally Encouraged Consensual Dispute Resolution in Japan," 84 *Columbia Law Review* 923 (1984). For a rational-choice approach to these issues, see Mark Ramseyer and Frances Rosenbluth, *Japan's Political Marketplace* (Cambridge: Harvard University Press, 1993).

Traffic accidents are perhaps the quintessential source of tort litigation in modern society. For a fascinating interchange on how Japanese courts handle such disputes, compare Daniel Foote, "Resolution of Traffic Accident Disputes and Judicial Activism in Japan," 25 *Law in Japan* 19 (1995), and Takao Tanase, "The Management of Disputes: Automobile Accident Compensation in Japan," 24 *Law and Society Review* 651 (1990).

Medicine generates highly charged legal controversies within the United States, of course, and it does so within Japan as well. For several careful studies, see Robert B. Leflar, "Informed Consent and Patients' Rights in Japan," 33 *Houston Law Review* 1 (1996); Robert B. Leflar, "Personal Injury Compensation Systems in Japan: Values Advanced and Values Undermined," 15 *University of Hawaii Law Review* 743 (1993); Eric Feldman, "Defining Death: Organ Transplants, Tradition, and High Technology in Japan," 27 *Social Science and Medicine* 339 (1988); Stephan M. Salzberg, "Japan's New Mental Health Law: More Light Shed on Dark Places?," 14 *International Journal of Law and Psychiatry* 137 (1991); and Naoki Ikegami and John Creighton Campbell, eds., *Containing Health Care Costs in Japan* (Ann Arbor: University of Michigan Press, 1996).

Even all this, however, disguises the wide variety within the law and society research. Just within the last dozen years, for instance, we have seen studies ranging from on-site investigations of pollution victims, Robert Kidder and Setsuo Miyazawa, "Long-Term Strategies in Japanese Environmental Litigation," 18 *Law and Social Inquiry* 605 (1993); to surveys on attitudes toward law and litigation,

V. Lee Hamilton and Joseph Sanders, *Everyday Justice: Responsibility and the Individual in Japan and the United States* (New Haven, Conn.: Yale University Press, 1992); to an analysis of the role apology plays in the legal system, Hiroshi Wagatsuma and Arthur Rosett, "The Implications of Apology: Law and Culture in Japan and the United States," 20 *Law and Society Review* 461 (1986); to studies of the right to privacy, Dan Rosen, "Private Lives and Public Eyes: Privacy in the United States and Japan," 6 *Florida Journal of International Law* 141 (1990).

Constitutional Law

Through recent publications, readers can consult both Japanese scholarship on constitutional law and Japanese court cases: Percy Luney and Kazuyuki Takahashi, eds., *Japanese Constitutional Law* (Tokyo: University of Tokyo Press, 1993); John M. Maki, ed., *Court and Constitution of Japan: Selected Supreme Court Decisions, 1948–1960* (Seattle: University of Washington Press, 1964); Hiroshi Itoh and Lawrence Beer, eds., *The Constitutional Case Law of Japan: Selected Supreme Court Decisions, 1961–1970* (Seattle: University of Washington Press, 1978); and Hiroshi Itoh and Lawrence Beer, eds., *The Constitutional Case Law of Japan: 1970–1990* (Seattle: University of Washington Press, 1996).

Family Law

Over the past several years, Taimie Bryant has clarified an important series of questions on Japanese family law: "'Responsible' Husbands, 'Recalcitrant' Wives, Retributive Judges: Judicial Management of Contested Divorce in Japan," 18 *Journal of Japanese Studies* 407 (1992); "Sons and Lovers: Adoption in Japan," 38 *American Journal of Comparative Law* 299 (1990); and "Marital Dissolution in Japan: Legal Obstacles and Their Impact," 17 *Law in Japan* 73 (1984). Another intriguing article is Veronica Taylor, "Prostitution Law and the Family: Japan and Victoria," 6 *Law in Context* 99 (1988). For Japanese family law before World War II, see Ramseyer, *Odd Markets in Japanese History,* ch. 5.

Criminal Law

For criminal law, readers are fortunate to be able to turn to a large collection of thoughtful work. Much of the best is by Daniel Foote: "'The Door That Never Opens?': Capital Punishment and Post-Conviction Review of Death Sentences in the United States and Japan," 19 *Brooklyn Journal of International Law* 367 (1993); "The Benevolent Paternalism of Japanese Criminal Justice," 80 *California Law Review* 317 (1992); and "Confessions and the Right to Silence in Japan," 21 *Georgia Journal of International and Comparative Law* 415 (1991). For two classics, see Shigemitsu Dando, *Japanese Law of Criminal Procedure,* translated by B. J. George (Littleton, Colo.: Rothman, 1965), and Shigemitsu Dando, *The Criminal Law of Japan: The General Part,* translated by B. J. George (Littleton, Colo.: Rothman, 1997).

Readers also have available several fascinating empirical criminological studies: Setsuo Miyazawa, *Policing in Japan: A Study on Making Crime,* translated by F. Bennett (Albany, N.Y.: SUNY Press, 1992); Walter L. Ames, *Police and Com-*

munity in Japan (Berkeley and Los Angeles: University of California Press, 1981); and David H. Bayley, *Forces of Order: Police Behavior in Japan and the United States* (Berkeley and Los Angeles: University of California Press, 1976).

Antitrust

The most prominent and prolific Japanese scholar in antitrust is Mitsuo Matsushita. His recent treatise in English appears as Mitsuo Matsushita and John Davies, *Introduction to Japanese Antimonopoly Law* (Tokyo: Yūhikaku, 1990). Other studies of Japanese antitrust enforcement include Harry First, "Antitrust Enforcement in Japan," 64 *Antitrust Law Journal* 137 (1996), and John O. Haley, "Antitrust Sanctions and Remedies: A Comparative Study of German and Japanese Law," 59 *Washington Law Review* 471 (1984).

Property

There have been relatively few works on Japanese real estate law. Several exceptionally fine studies, however, are Frank G. Bennett, Jr., "Building Ownership in Modern Japanese Law: Origins of the Immobile Home," 27 *Law in Japan* (forthcoming); Frank G. Bennett, Jr., "Clash of Titles: Japan's Secured Lenders Meet Civil Code Section 395," 38 *Netherlands International Law Review* 281 (1991); and John O. Haley, "Japan's New Land and House Lease Law," in *Land Issues in Japan: A Policy Failure?*, edited by John O. Haley and Kozo Yamamura (Seattle: Society for Japanese Studies, 1992).

Intellectual Property

To date, Teruo Doi has largely monopolized the field of Japanese intellectual property law in English: Teruo Doi, *The Intellectual Property Law of Japan* (Alphen aan den Rijn, The Netherlands: Noordhoff, 1980), and Teruo Doi and Warren L. Shattuck, *Patent and Know-How Licensing in Japan and the United States* (Seattle: University of Washington Press, 1977).

Labor Law

Readers have a choice of two full-length labor law books—one a translated treatise and one based on a visit by an American scholar to Japan: Kazuo Sugeno, *Japanese Labor Law,* translated by Leo Kanowitz (Seattle: University of Washington Press, 1992), and William Gould, *Japan's Reshaping of American Labor Law* (Cambridge: MIT Press, 1984). For the amusing story of how the Sugeno treatise came to be translated, see Leo Kanowitz, "Translating a Japanese Labor Law Treatise," 39 *American Journal of Comparative Law* 417 (1991).

Law and Economics

As recently as the mid-1980s, few scholars took a law and economics approach to Japanese law. Two pioneering economists in the field were Koichi Hamada and Yoshirō Miwa. Among Hamada's early work is the fine "Liability Rules and Income Distribution in Product Liability," 66 *American Economic Review* (1976). For a more recent study, see Koichi Hamada, "Product Liability Rules: A Consideration of Law and Economics in Japan," 46 *Japan Economic Review* 1 (1995). Most of Miwa's early work was published in Japanese, as in his excellent *Dokkinho no keizai gaku [The Economics of Antitrust Law]* (Tokyo: Nihon keizai shimbun sha, 1982). More recently, he has begun to publish in English as well. See, e.g., the influential *Firms and Industrial Organization in Japan* (Houndmills, U.K.: Macmillan, 1996).

Over the last decade, several additional scholars have begun to publish innovative work, particularly in corporate law: Hideki Kanda, "Taxes and Structure of Japanese Firms: Hidden Aspects of Income Taxation," 74 *Washington University Law Quarterly* 393 (1996); Curtis Milhaupt, "A Relational Theory of Japanese Corporate Governance: Contract, Culture, and the Rule of Law," 37 *Harvard International Law Journal* 3 (1996); Curtis Milhaupt, "The Market for Innovation in the United States and Japan: Venture Capital and the Comparative Corporate Governance Debate," 91 *Northwestern University Law Review* 865 (1997); and Mark West, "The Pricing of Shareholder Derivative Actions in Japan and the United States," 88 *Northwestern University Law Review* 1436 (1994).

Treatises

On several other subjects, readers will find careful practitioner-oriented treatises: Takaaki Hattori and Dan Fenno Henderson, *Civil Procedure in Japan* (New York: Matthew Bender, 1983); John Huston, Toshio Miyatake, Griffith Way, and Vicki L. Beyer, *Japanese International Taxation* (New York: Transnational Juris Publications, updated); and Louis Loss, Makoto Yazawa, and Barbara Ann Banoff, *Japanese Securities Regulation* (Tokyo and Boston: University of Tokyo Press and Little, Brown, 1983).

Those few readers determined and conscientious enough to slog their way through a bibliographic essay deserve a break. For that, they should pick up what is surely the most marvelously offbeat law review article on Japan to appear in years: Mark D. West, "Legal Rules and Social Norms in Japan's Secret World of Sumo," 26 *Journal of Legal Studies* 165 (1997).

STATUTES

References are to page numbers.

§283	145
§296	270n. 28
§297	270n. 29
§302	145
§311	270n. 28
§312	270n. 31
§§328 et seq.	270n. 28
§734 (old)	148, 271n. 49

Code of Criminal Procedure

§30	274n. 44
§36	274n. 44
§198	274n. 44
§199	168
§§199–201	274n. 37
§201	168
§203	168
§204	274n. 44
§210	168, 274n. 37
§§212–219	274n. 37
§217	168
§§218–222	171
§289	172
§291-2	172
§311	172
§§317–328	270n. 34
§336	172
§430	274n. 44
§435	172

Commercial Code

§68	110
§69	110
§70	110
§71	110
§73	110
§76	110
§80	110
§146	111
§154	111
§156	111
§157	111
§166	123
§168-4	123
§173	123

§181	123
§200	111
§204	266n. 45
§§204 to 204-5	111, 123
§§210 to 211-2	123
§218	242
§222	111
§231	121
§234	111
§237	111
§241	111
§242	111
§245	121
§245-2	121
§254	265n. 18
§254-3	265n. 18
§255	111
§256	111
§256-2	111
§256-3	111
§260-2	111
§261	111
§263	108
§264	265n. 21
§265	265n. 22
§266-3	119–120, 265n. 32
§§273–280	123
§294-2	127
§406-2	111
§408	121
§408-3	121
§494	127
§497	127

Condominium Act

| generally | 28–30, 252n. 13 |

Constitution (1889)

| generally | 4 |

Constitution (1947)

art. 1	4
art. 4	4
art. 9	4
art. 14	4, 228

INDEX